Story and Art by Arina Tanemura

SAKURA HIME
The Legend of Princess Sakura

Characters

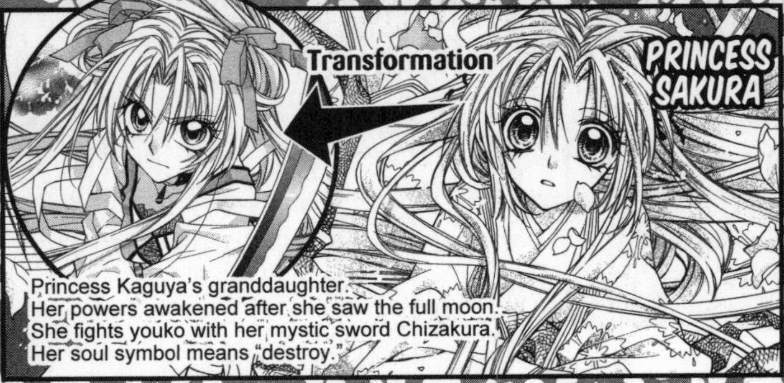
PRINCESS SAKURA
Transformation
Princess Kaguya's granddaughter.
Her powers awakened after she saw the full moon.
She fights youko with her mystic sword Chizakura.
Her soul symbol means "destroy."

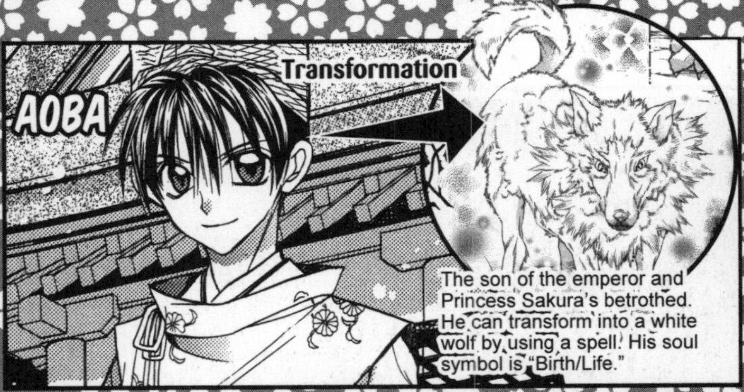
AOBA
Transformation
The son of the emperor and Princess Sakura's betrothed. He can transform into a white wolf by using a spell. His soul symbol is "Birth/Life."

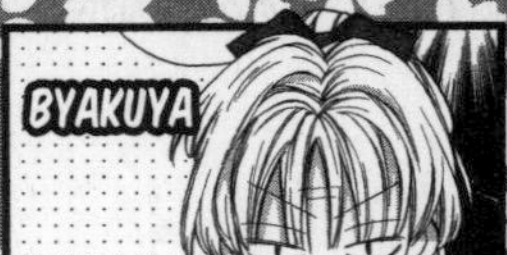
BYAKUYA
A priestess who knows Princess Sakura's secret.

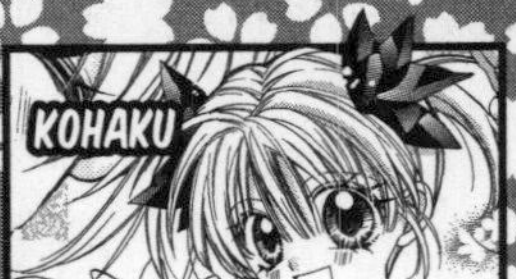
KOHAKU
A ninja. Klutz.

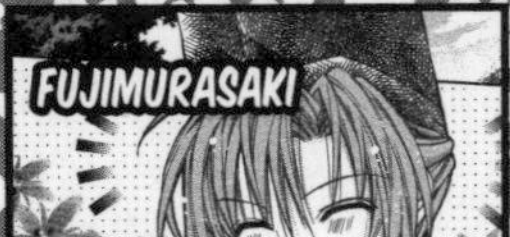
FUJIMURASAKI
Aoba's uncle and the Togu (next emperor).

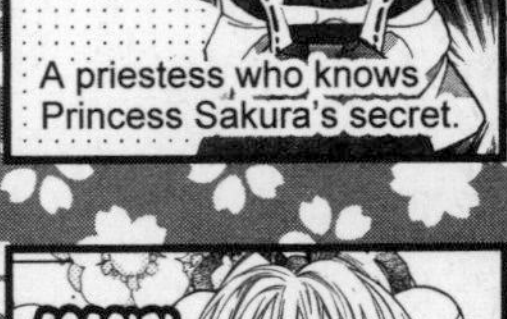
ASAGIRI
A mononoke. Princess Sakura's companion.

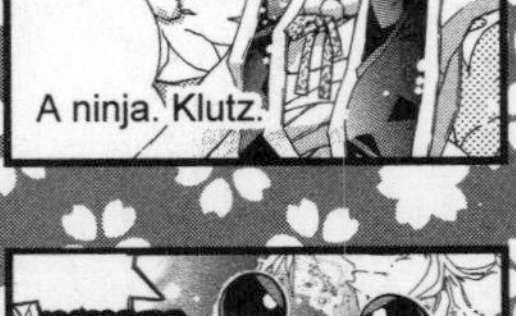
HAYATE
GEK
Kohaku's childhood friend. He can return to human form when there's a full moon.

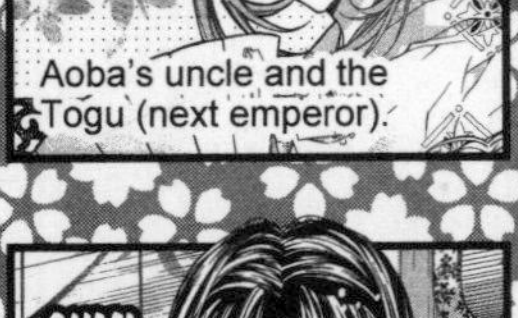
OUMI
Princess Sakura's lady-in-waiting. She was turned into a youko by Enju.

RURIJO

MAIMAI

ENJU

SHURI

UKYO

Princess Sakura's older brother. He used to be kind, but he has a deep hatred of humans now.

SAKURA HIME
The Legend of Princess Sakura

Story Thus Far

Heian era. Princess Sakura is 14 years old and learns from Byakuya that she is the grand-daughter of Princess Kaguya, a princess from the moon. She is the only person able to wield the mystic sword Chizakura that can kill the demon youko. And at the same time, she finds out that her fated soul symbol is "destroy"...

Aoba discovers this and captures Sakura, intending to kill her. Fujimurasaki arrives and Sakura is given orders from the emperor to officially hunt down a youko.

Sakura travels to Uji where she is told by her lady-in-waiting, Oumi, that the councilor is a traitor. But then Oumi turns into a youko and attacks Sakura...!

The person behind the treachery is a mysterious man named Enju, who is Sakura's brother Kai whom she believed to be dead... He had been tricked by the emperor and held captive in a water chamber. The experience gave him a strong hatred of humans. He stole Sakura away and brought her to Shura Yugenden.

After finding out where Sakura is, Aoba and the others succeed in entering Enju's hideout, but they have no choice but to defeat his followers to save her.

Byakuya defeats Maimai, Kohaku defeats Shuri, and Asagiri now faces Ukyo. Asagiri and Ukyo were once lovers, but their fate took an abrupt turn when Asagiri was chosen to be the next sacrifice to their god. Now Ukyo hates Asagiri for destroying their village...

SAKURA HIME
The Legend of Princess Sakura

CONTENTS

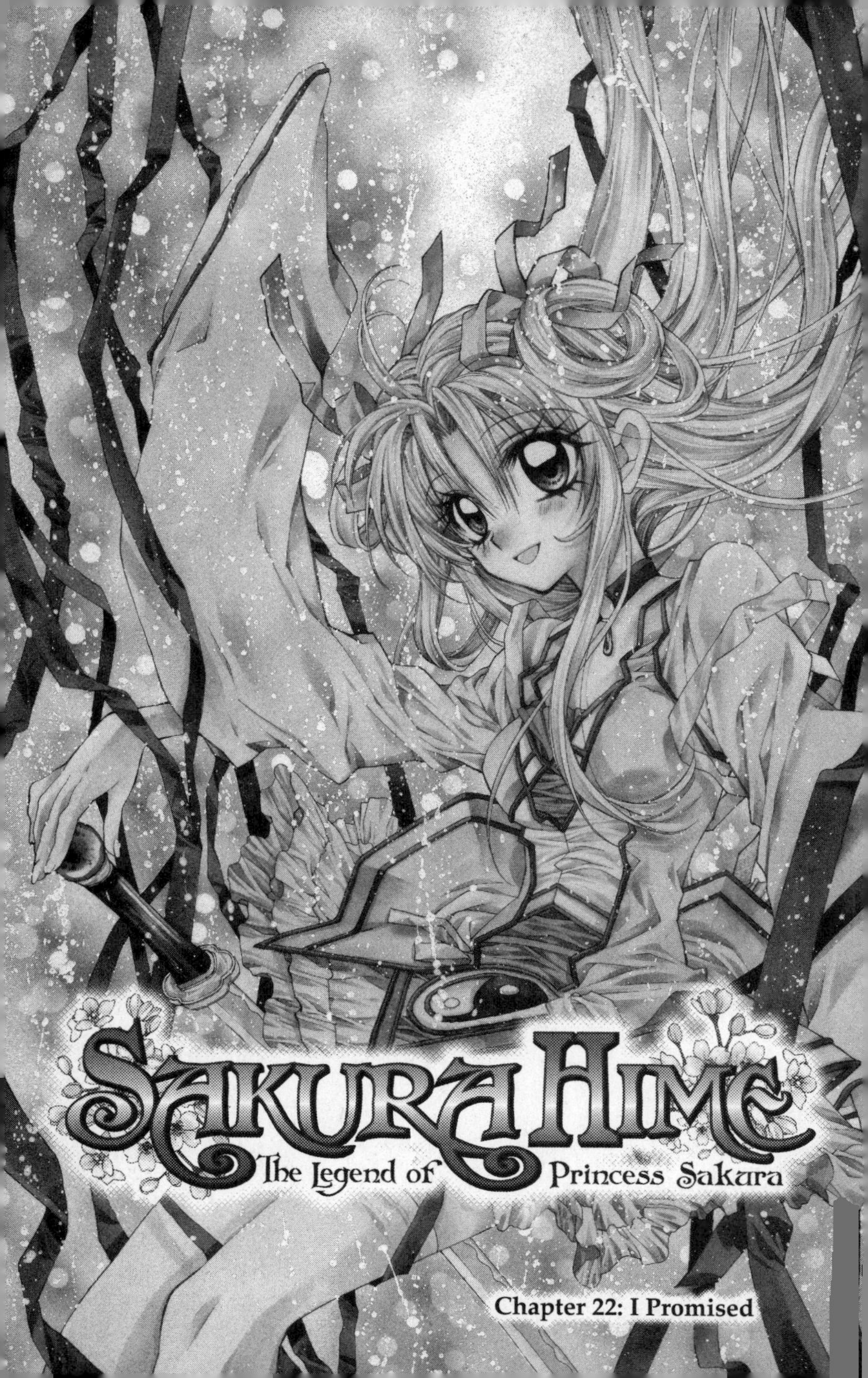
Sakura Hime
The Legend of Princess Sakura
Chapter 22: I Promised

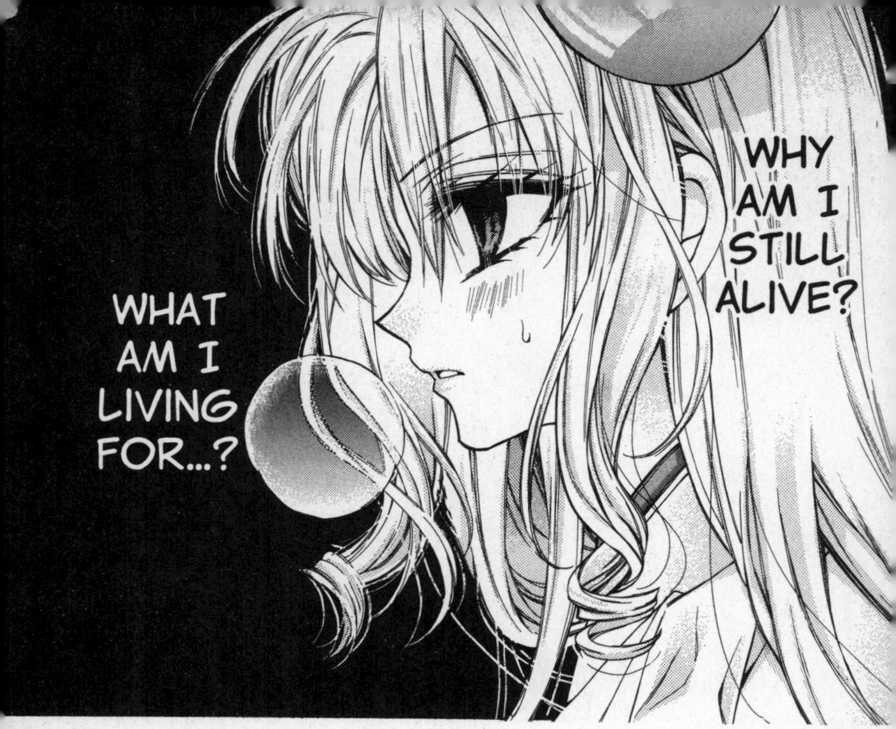
WHY AM I STILL ALIVE?
WHAT AM I LIVING FOR...?

Chapter 22: I Promised ※I'm giving away the story.

My editor bluntly said, "Tanemura-san, you've got no love for Ukyo, have you?" D-Do you think so?

This chapter made me think that Asagiri's ennui may be due to the secret she's hiding. These two are on the cover of this volume, and they remind me of snow. There's something ephemeral about them.

Asagiri's "What am I living for...?" is the theme of this manga series, I think. I don't know when the answer to that question will become clear, but the almighty creator of this series—me—(laugh) figured out the answer while working on this, so if a character were to die, they'd probably die as the answer comes clear.
(That makes it sound like someone is going to die, but I really mean "if someone were to die.")

At any rate, Asagiri is easy to draw. The main reason is because she's small. On the other hand, it's a pain for me to color Ukyo's hair.

(Is that the reason my editor said that?)

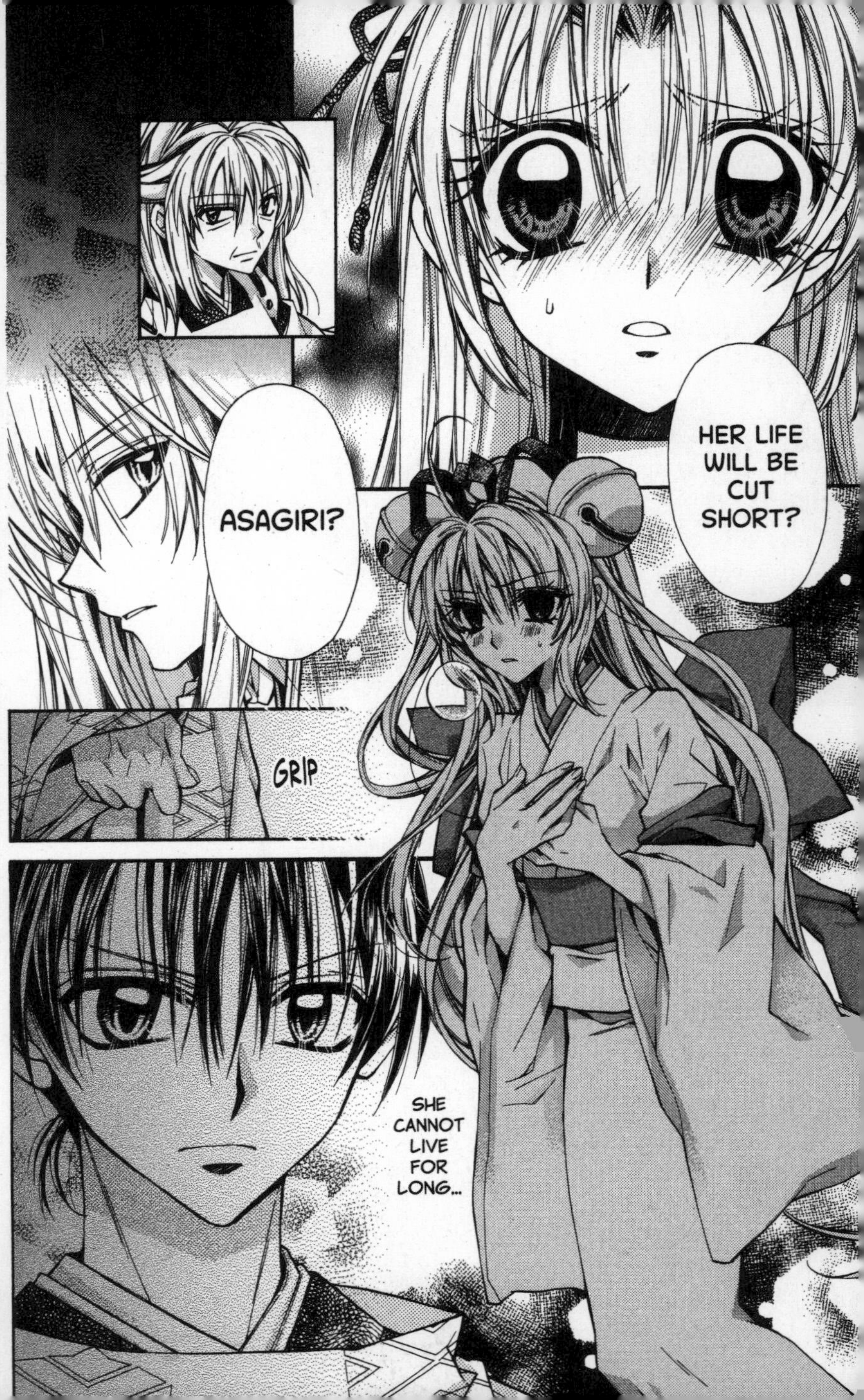
HER LIFE WILL BE CUT SHORT?
ASAGIRI?
GRIP
SHE CANNOT LIVE FOR LONG...

GREETINGS

Hello, it's Arina Tanemura.
I bring to you volume 7 of *Sakura Hime: The Legend of Princess Sakura*.

It's already volume 7... Wow. *Sakura Hime* will definitely become the longest series I've ever worked on.

The January issue of the magazine is holding the second popularity vote right now, so if you are reading this in real time, send in a vote. ♪

Last time Sakura was in first place, Asagiri in second, and Rurijo had third.

I wonder who will get first place this time?

The long Shura Yugenden arc will end with volume 7. I'll continue to do my best to make this work exciting, so please support me.

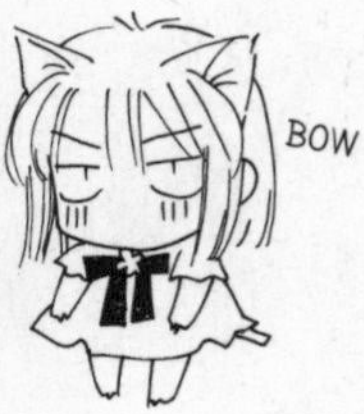
BOW

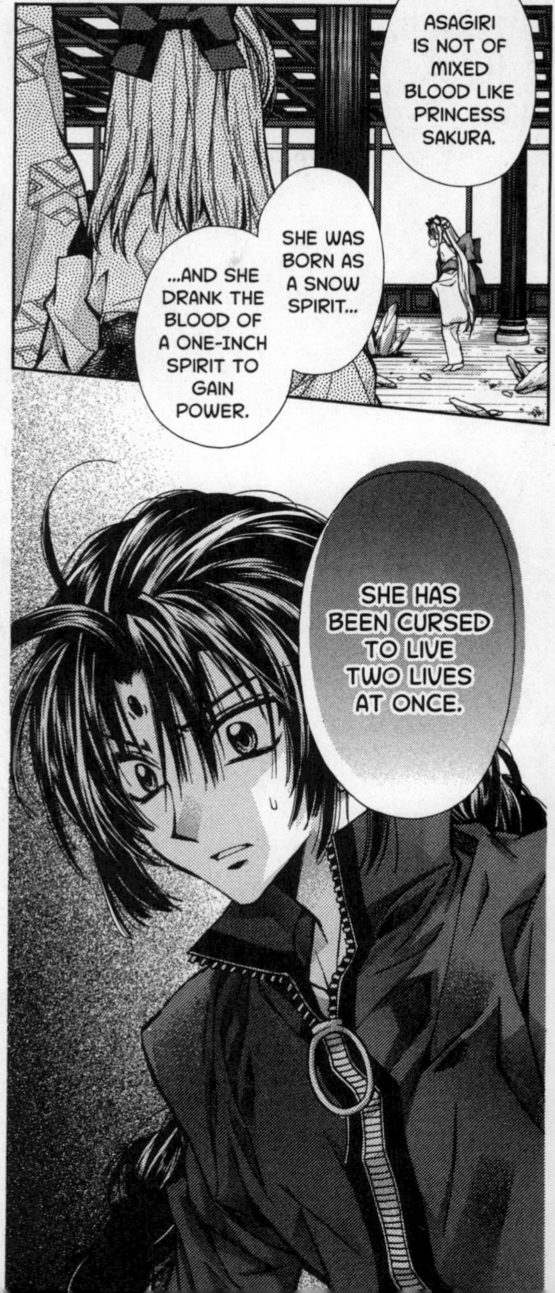
ASAGIRI IS NOT OF MIXED BLOOD LIKE PRINCESS SAKURA.
SHE WAS BORN AS A SNOW SPIRIT...
...AND SHE DRANK THE BLOOD OF A ONE-INCH SPIRIT TO GAIN POWER.
SHE HAS BEEN CURSED TO LIVE TWO LIVES AT ONCE.

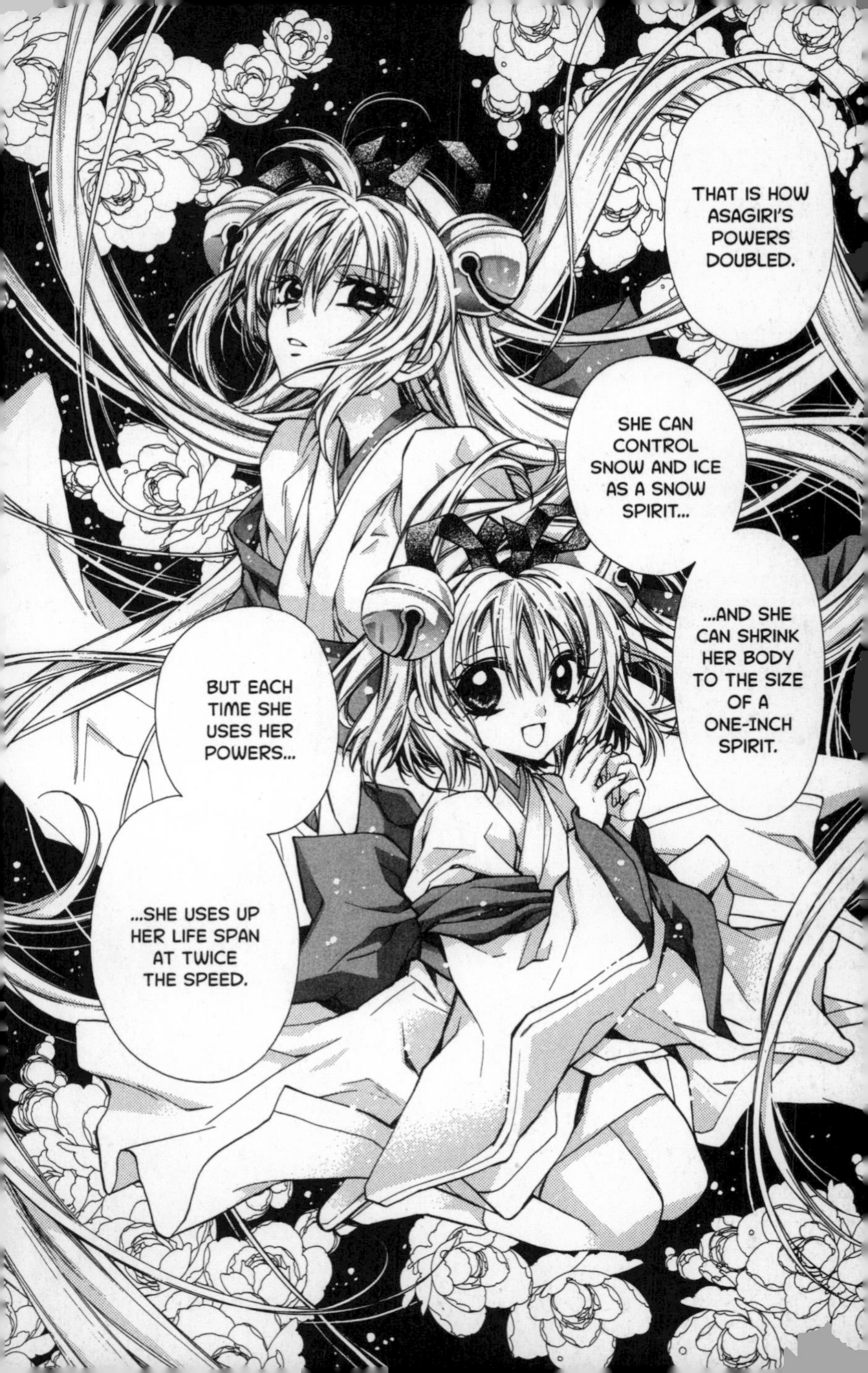
THAT IS HOW ASAGIRI'S POWERS DOUBLED.
SHE CAN CONTROL SNOW AND ICE AS A SNOW SPIRIT...
...AND SHE CAN SHRINK HER BODY TO THE SIZE OF A ONE-INCH SPIRIT.
BUT EACH TIME SHE USES HER POWERS...
...SHE USES UP HER LIFE SPAN AT TWICE THE SPEED.

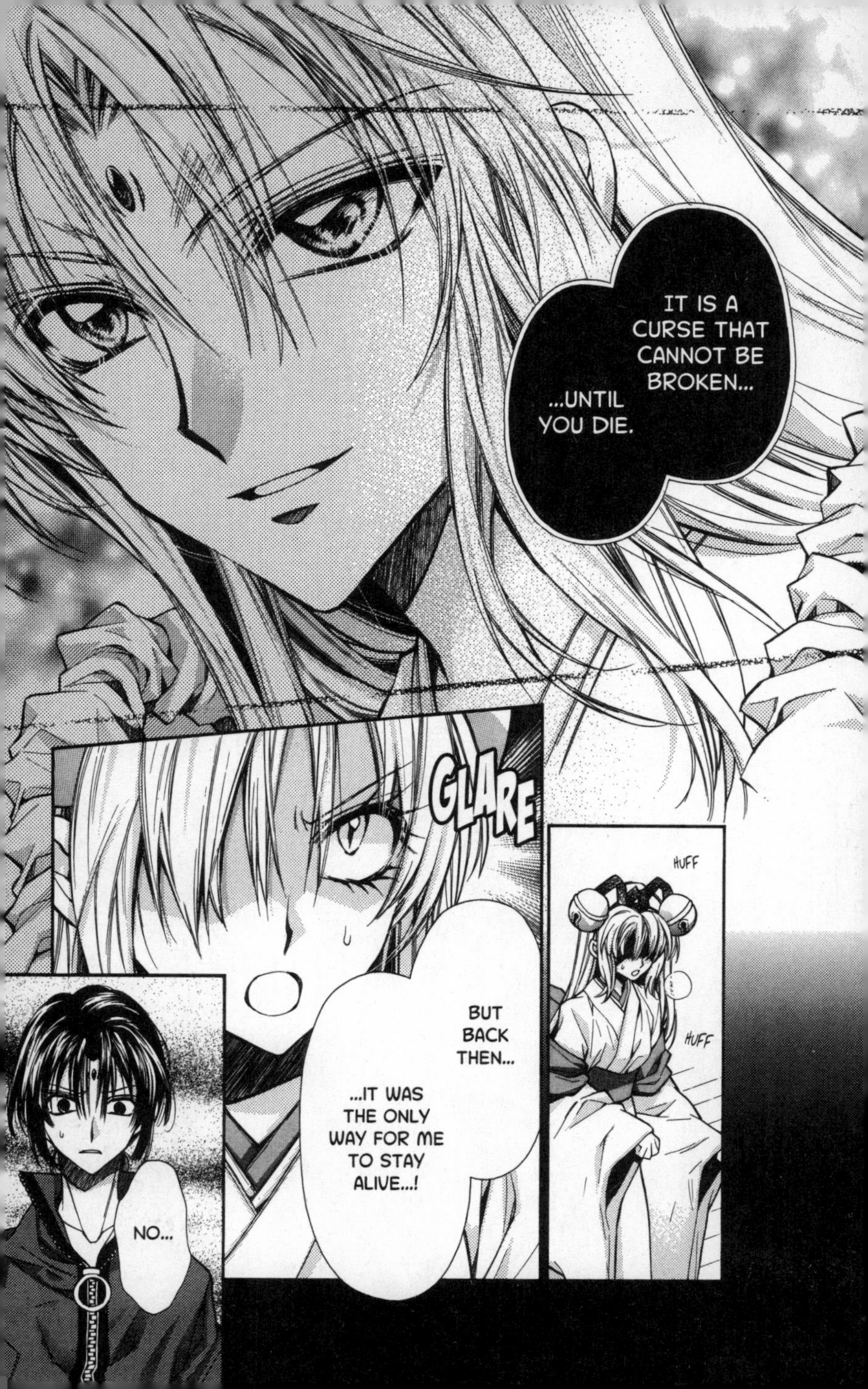
IT IS A CURSE THAT CANNOT BE BROKEN...
...UNTIL YOU DIE.
HUFF
HUFF
GLARE
BUT BACK THEN...
...IT WAS THE ONLY WAY FOR ME TO STAY ALIVE...!
NO...

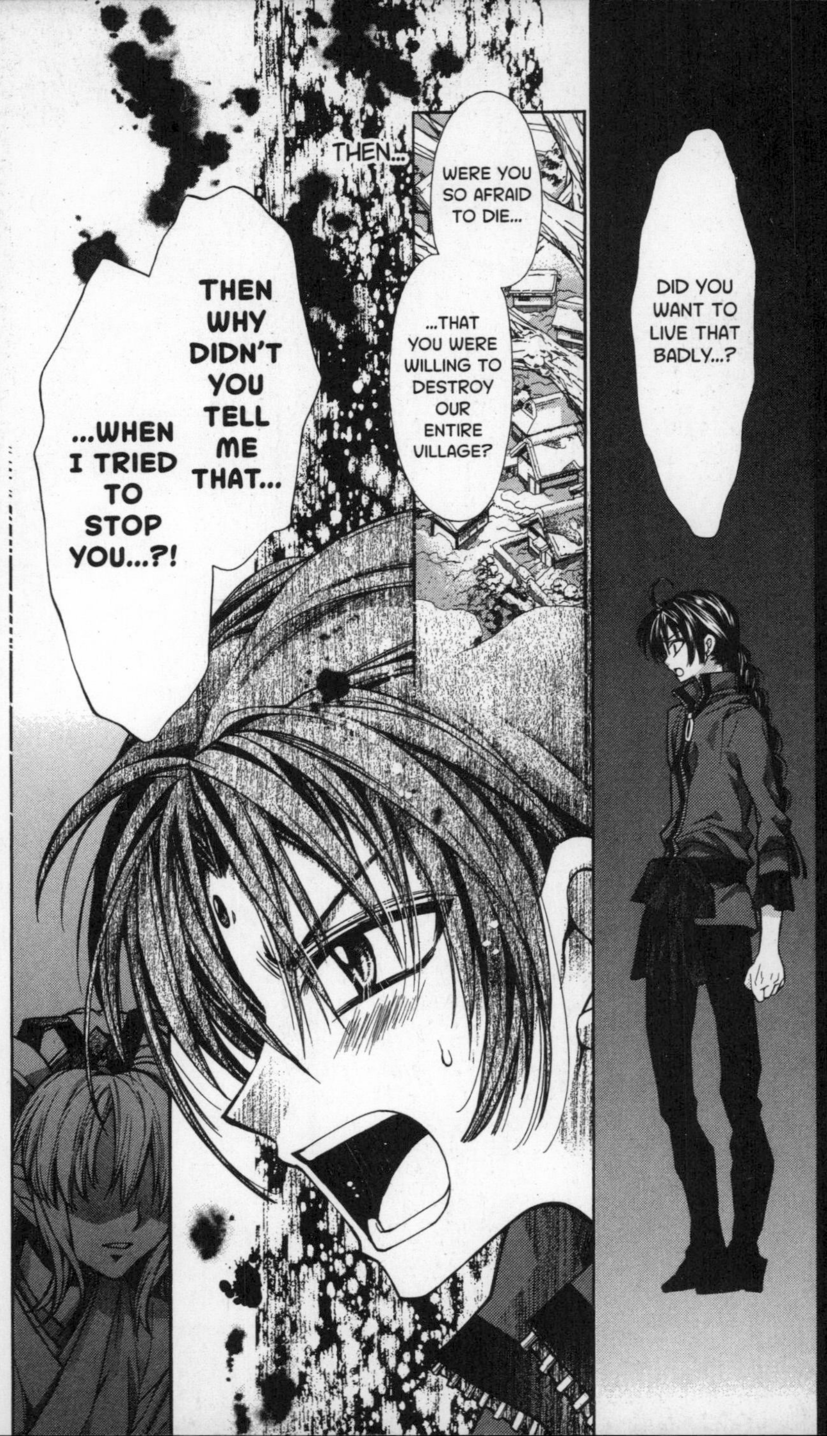
DID YOU WANT TO LIVE THAT BADLY...?
THEN...
WERE YOU SO AFRAID TO DIE...
...THAT YOU WERE WILLING TO DESTROY OUR ENTIRE VILLAGE?
THEN WHY DIDN'T YOU TELL ME THAT...
...WHEN I TRIED TO STOP YOU...?!

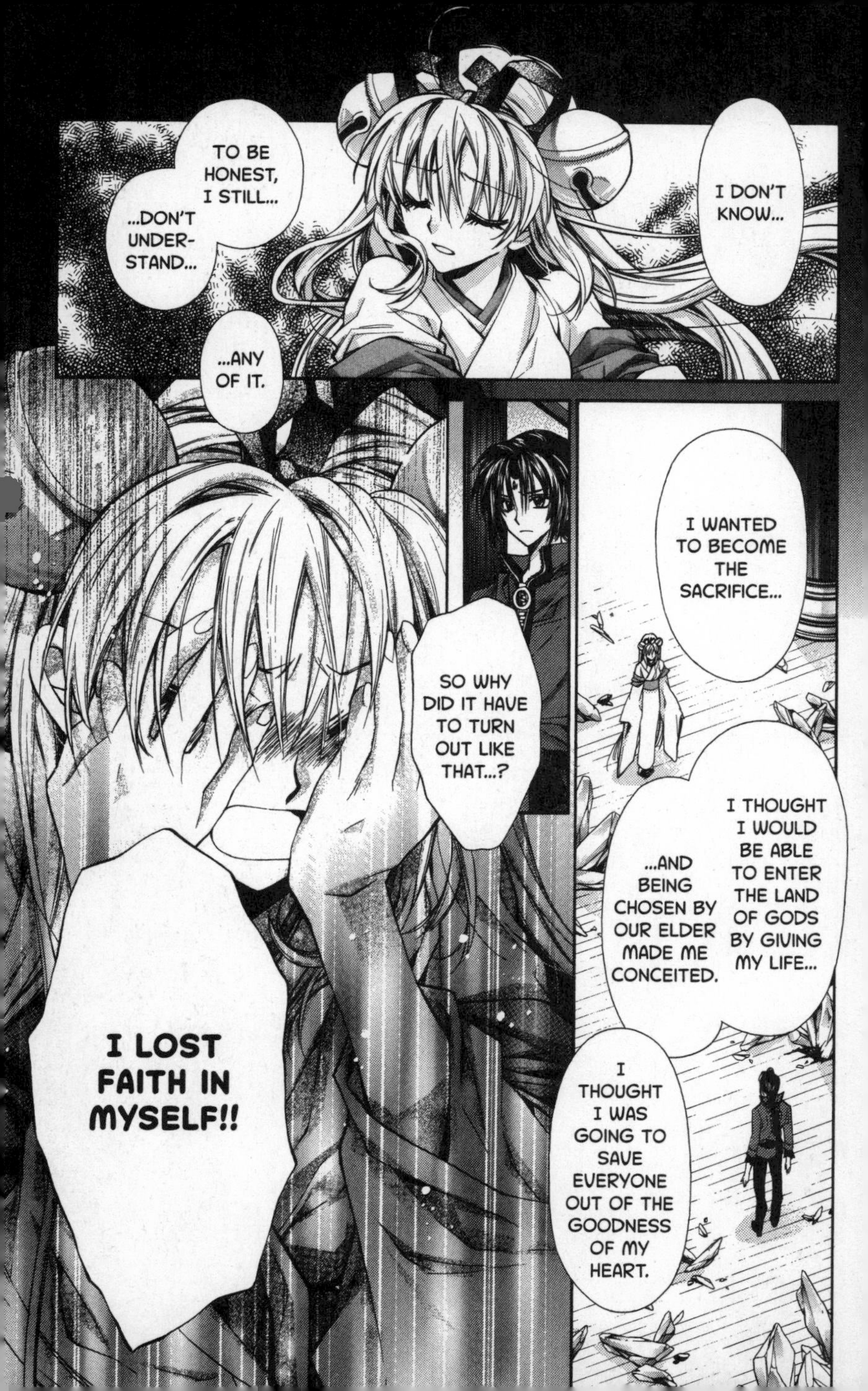
I DON'T KNOW...
TO BE HONEST, I STILL...
...DON'T UNDERSTAND...
...ANY OF IT.
I WANTED TO BECOME THE SACRIFICE...
I THOUGHT I WOULD BE ABLE TO ENTER THE LAND OF GODS BY GIVING MY LIFE...
...AND BEING CHOSEN BY OUR ELDER MADE ME CONCEITED.
I THOUGHT I WAS GOING TO SAVE EVERYONE OUT OF THE GOODNESS OF MY HEART.
SO WHY DID IT HAVE TO TURN OUT LIKE THAT...?
I LOST FAITH IN MYSELF!!

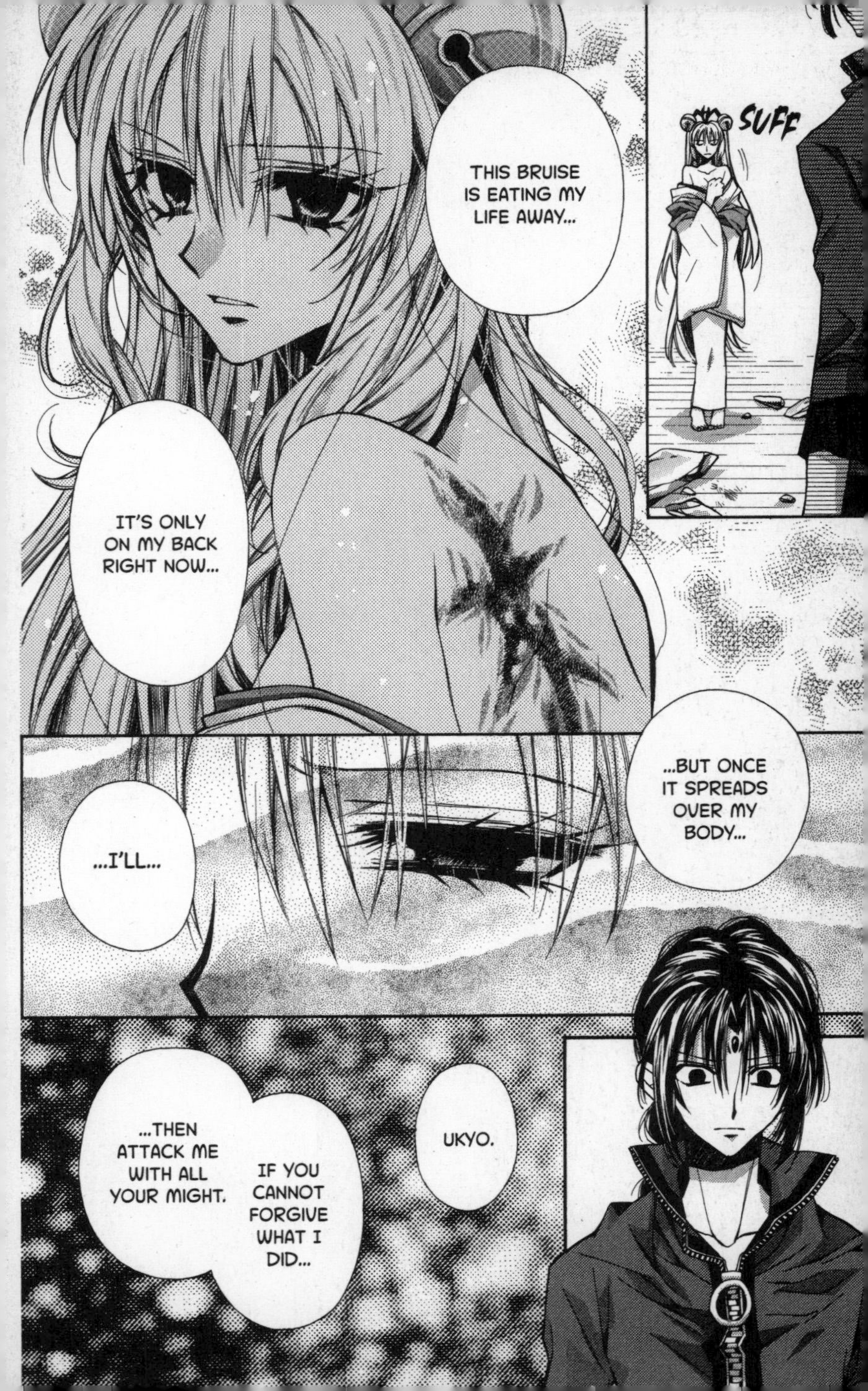
SUFF
THIS BRUISE IS EATING MY LIFE AWAY...
IT'S ONLY ON MY BACK RIGHT NOW...
...BUT ONCE IT SPREADS OVER MY BODY...
...I'LL...
UKYO.
IF YOU CANNOT FORGIVE WHAT I DID...
...THEN ATTACK ME WITH ALL YOUR MIGHT.

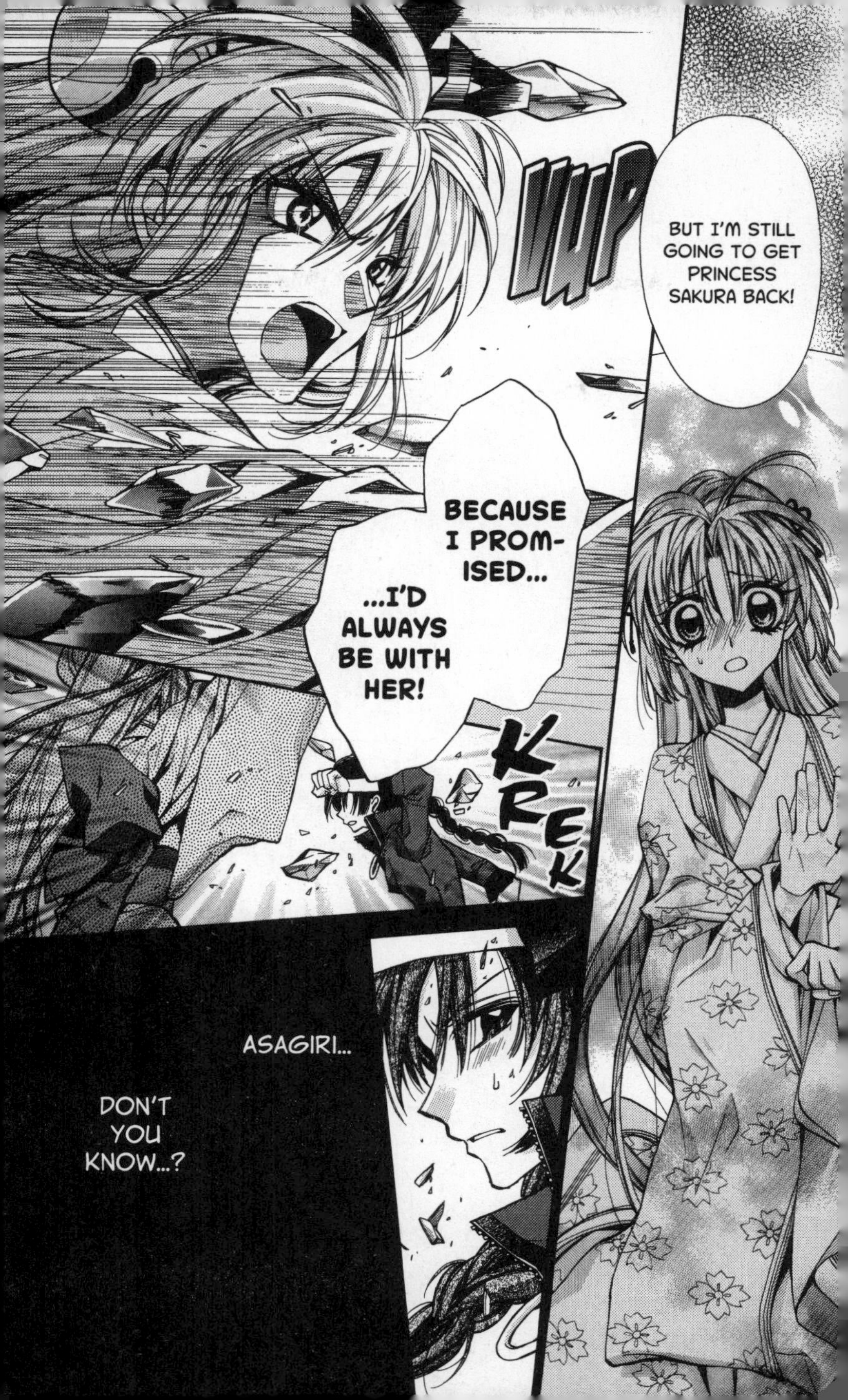
BUT I'M STILL GOING TO GET PRINCESS SAKURA BACK!
WHIP
BECAUSE I PROMISED...
...I'D ALWAYS BE WITH HER!
KREK
ASAGIRI...
DON'T YOU KNOW...?

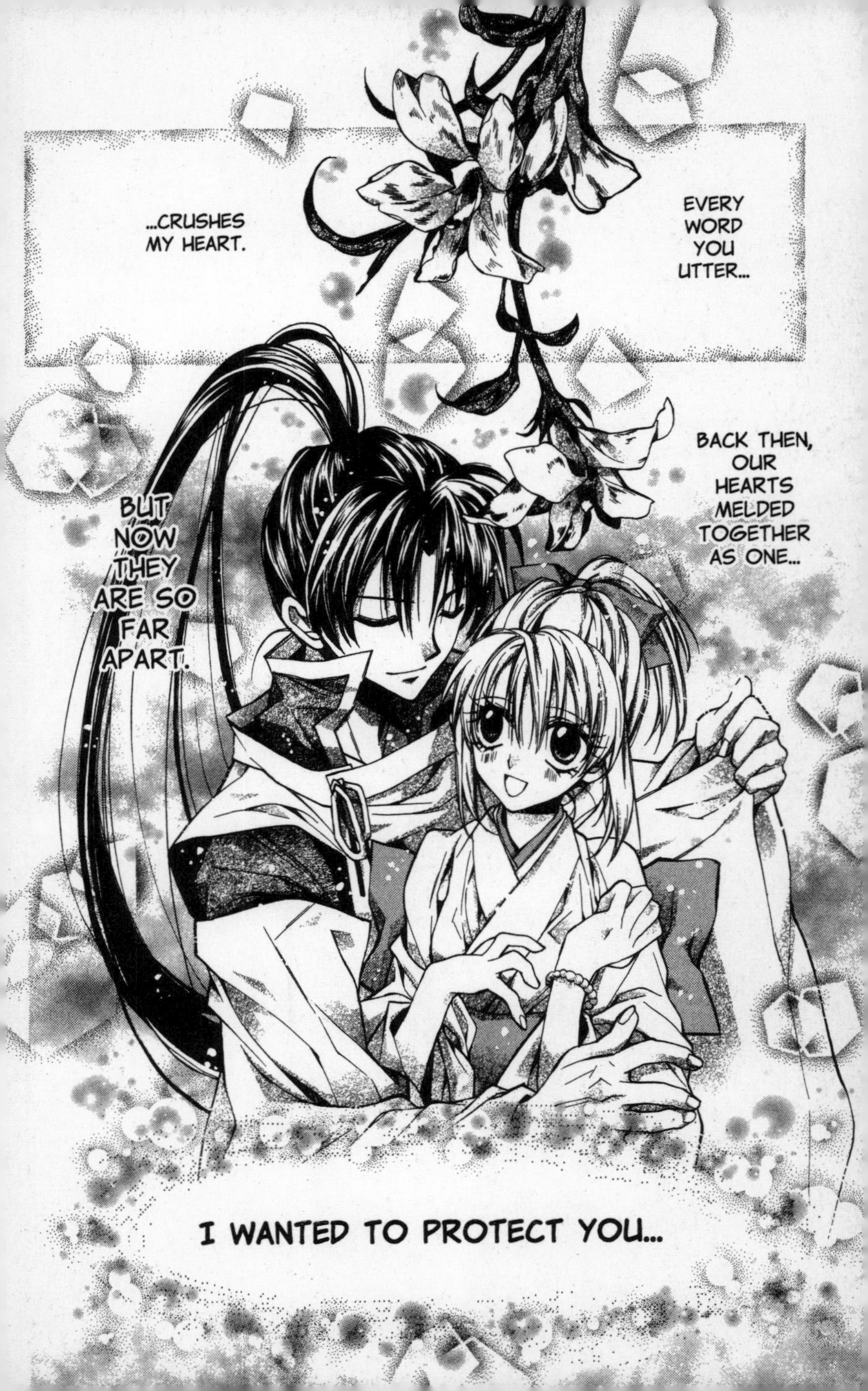
EVERY WORD YOU UTTER...
...CRUSHES MY HEART.
BACK THEN, OUR HEARTS MELDED TOGETHER AS ONE...
BUT NOW THEY ARE SO FAR APART.
I WANTED TO PROTECT YOU...

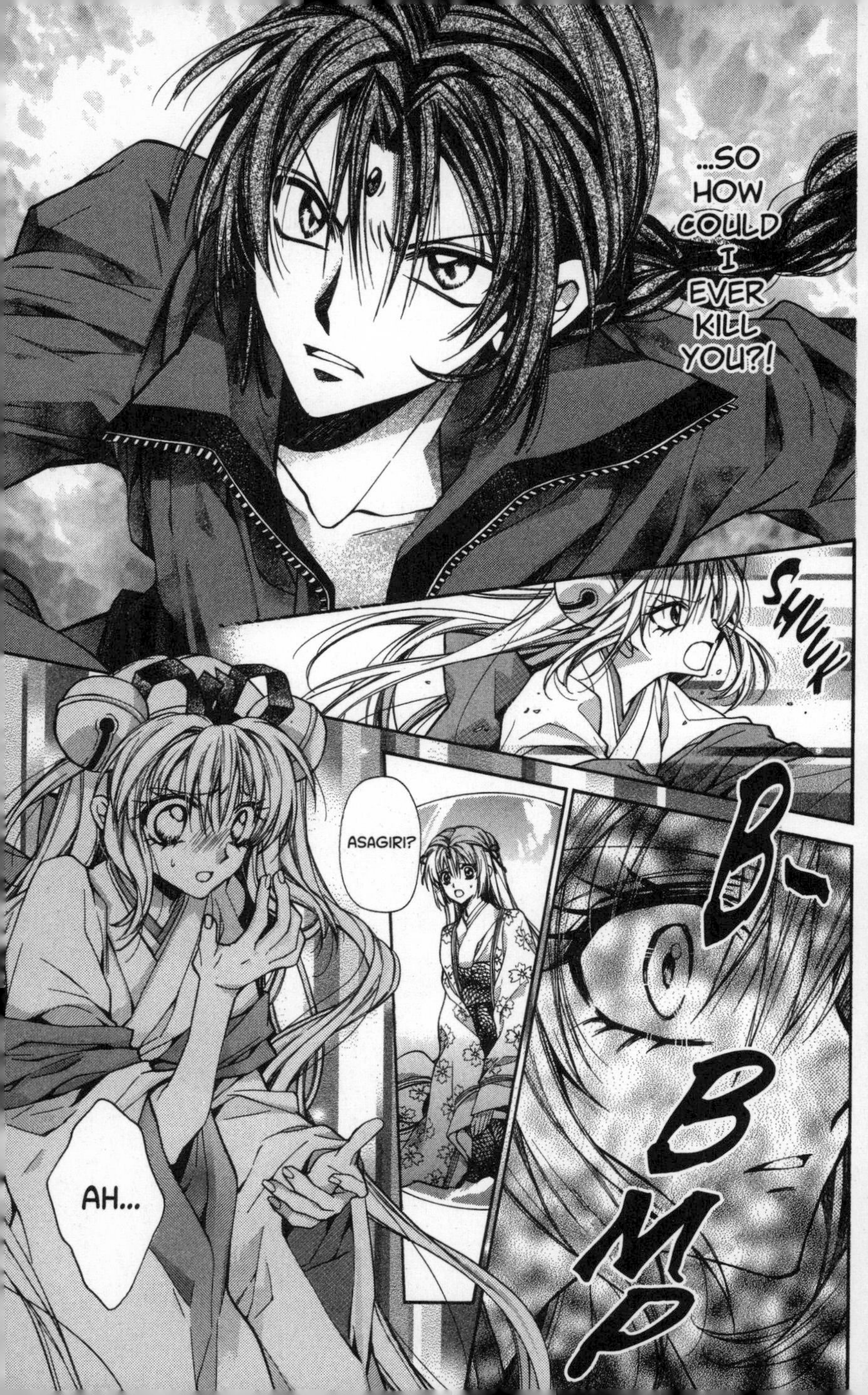
...SO HOW COULD I EVER KILL YOU?!
SHUUK
B-BMP
ASAGIRI?
AH...

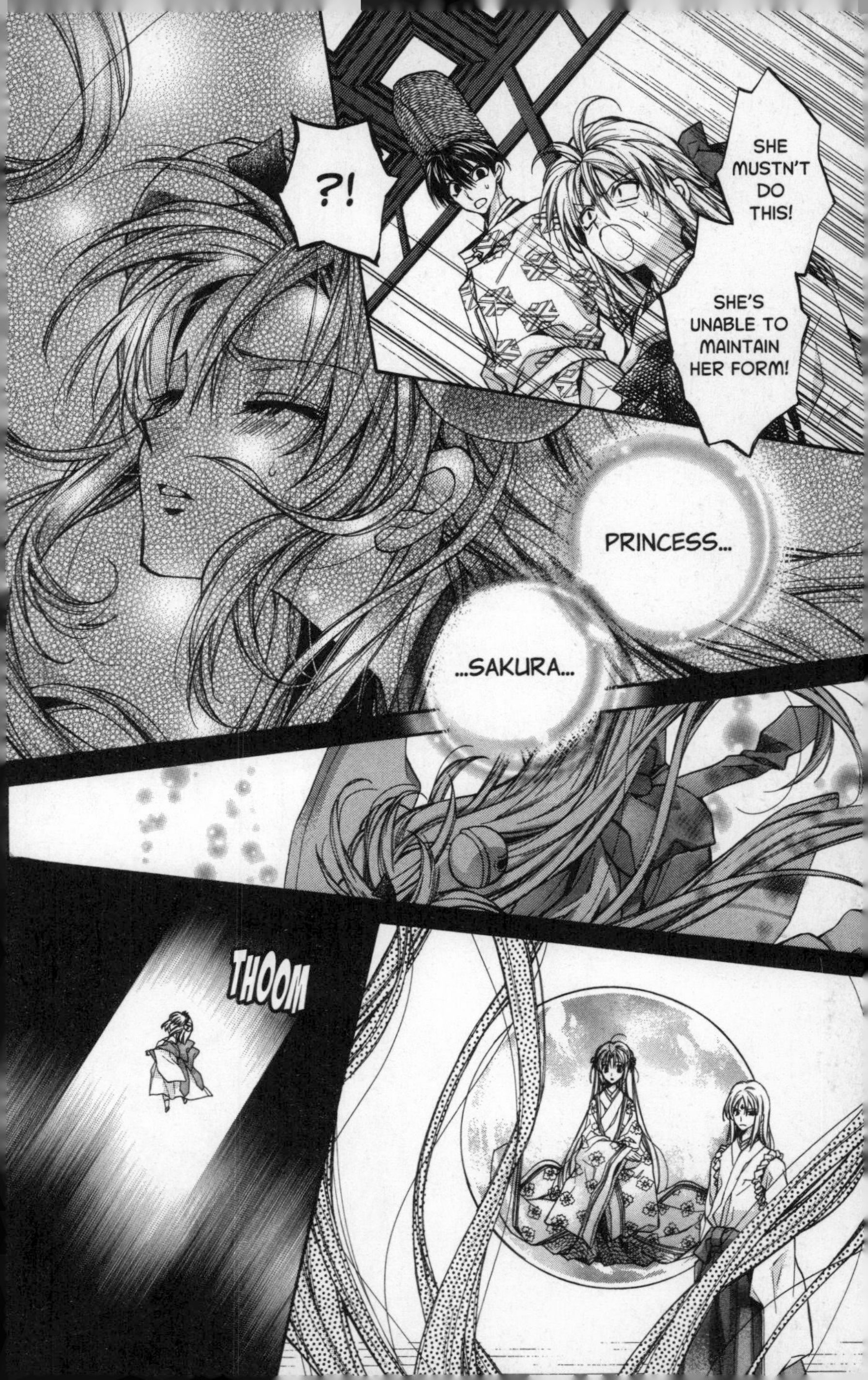
SHE MUSTN'T DO THIS!
SHE'S UNABLE TO MAINTAIN HER FORM!
?!
PRINCESS...
...SAKURA...
THOOM

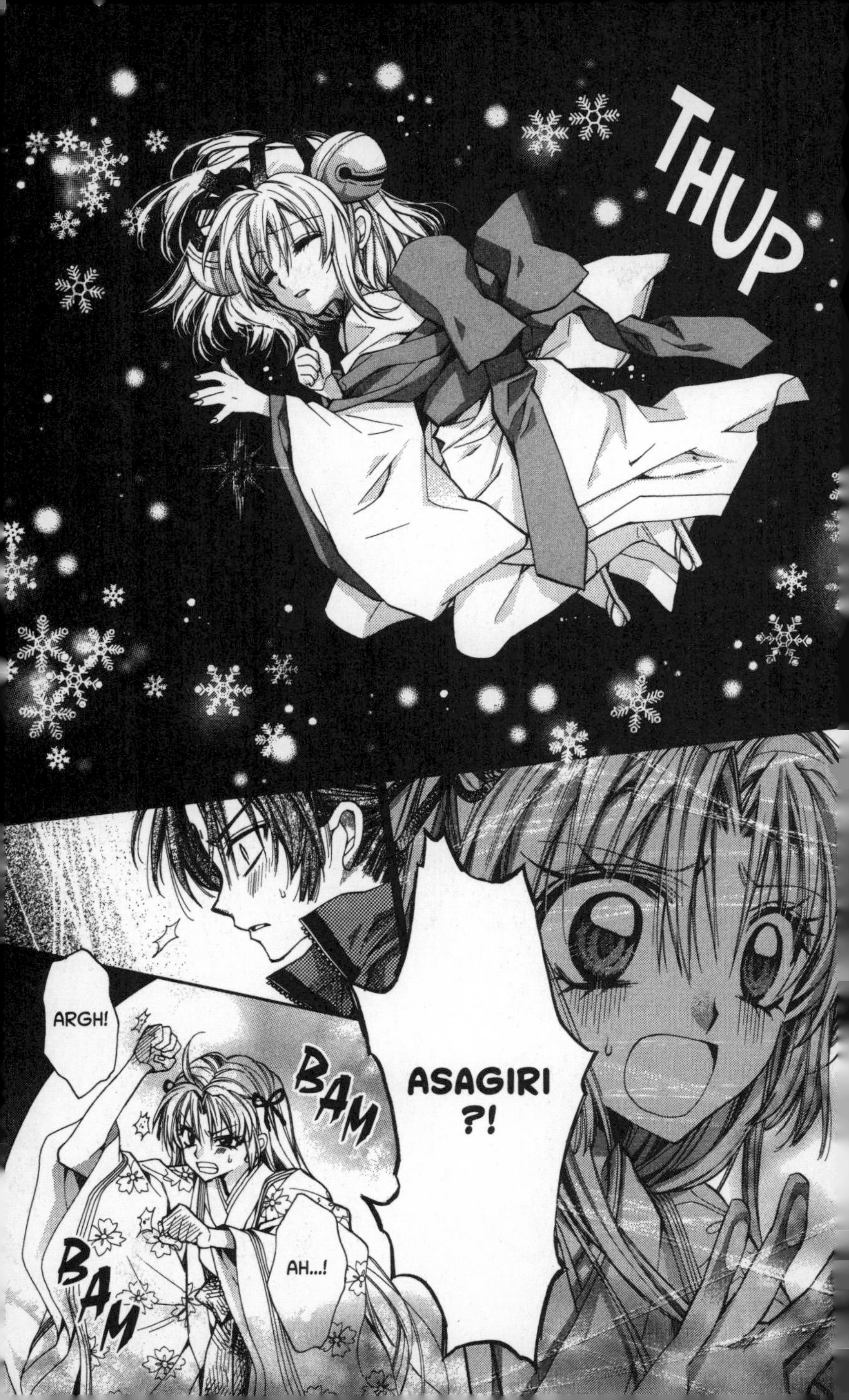
THUP
ASAGIRI ?!
ARGH!
BAM
AH...!
BAM

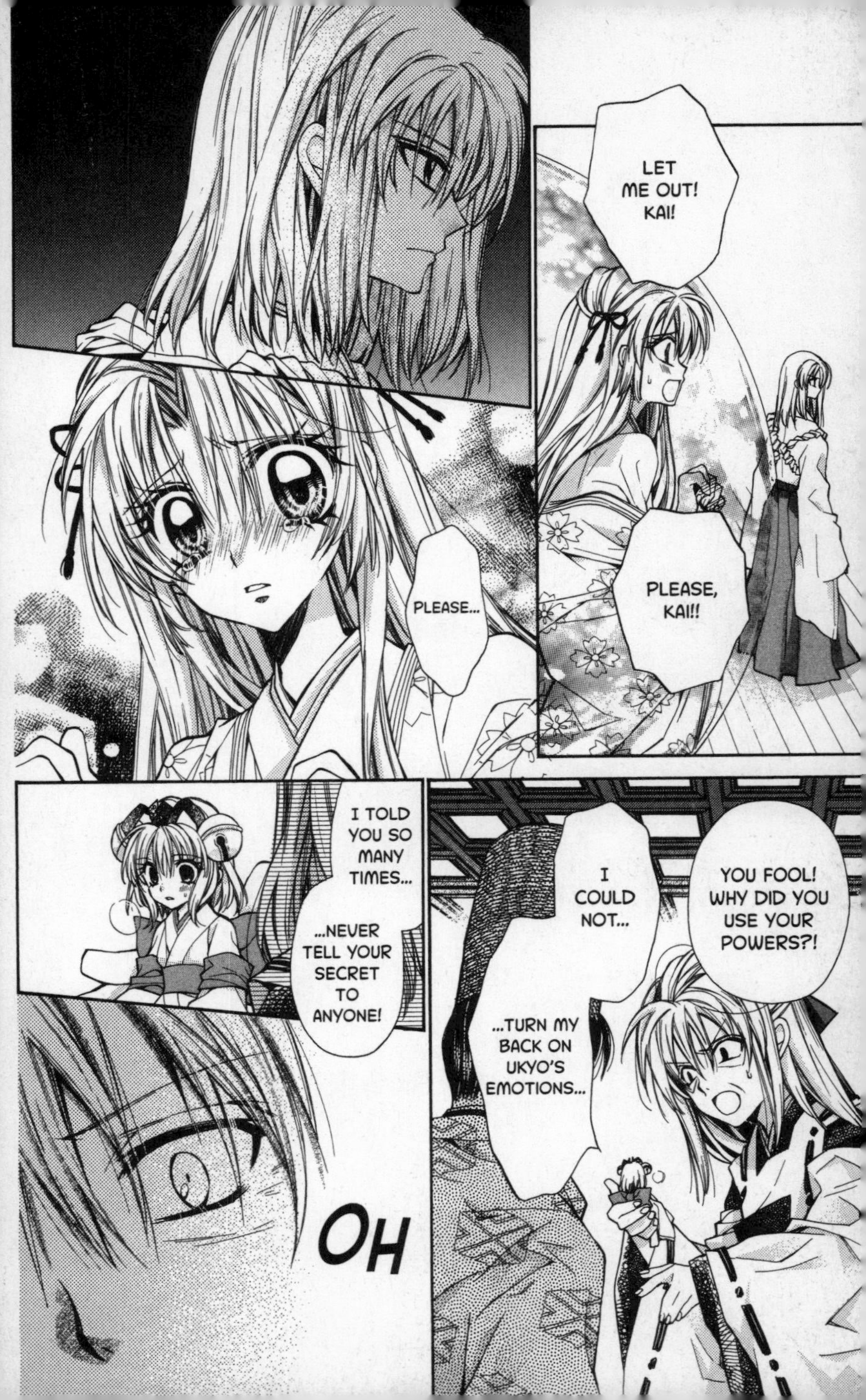
LET ME OUT! KAI!
PLEASE, KAI!!
PLEASE...
YOU FOOL! WHY DID YOU USE YOUR POWERS?!
I COULD NOT...
...TURN MY BACK ON UKYO'S EMOTIONS...
I TOLD YOU SO MANY TIMES...
...NEVER TELL YOUR SECRET TO ANYONE!
OH

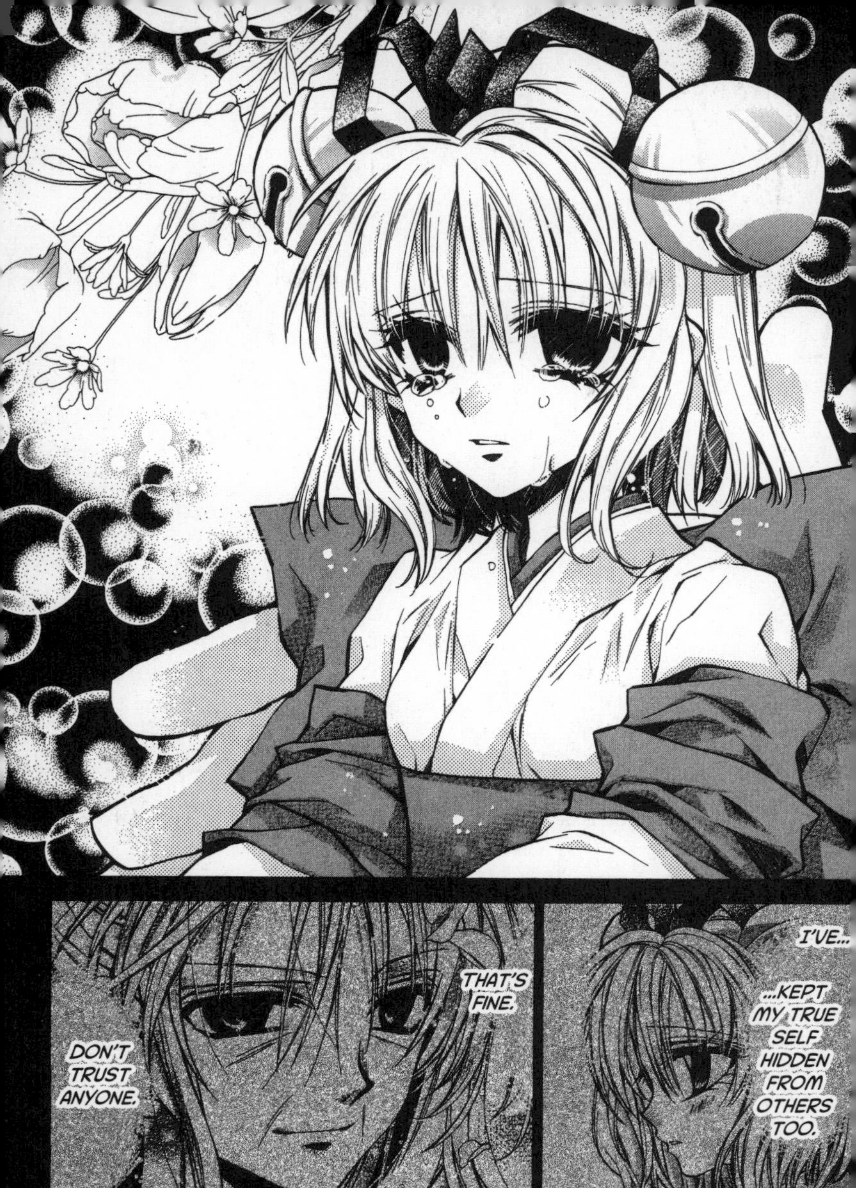
I'VE...
...KEPT MY TRUE SELF HIDDEN FROM OTHERS TOO.
THAT'S FINE.
DON'T TRUST ANYONE.

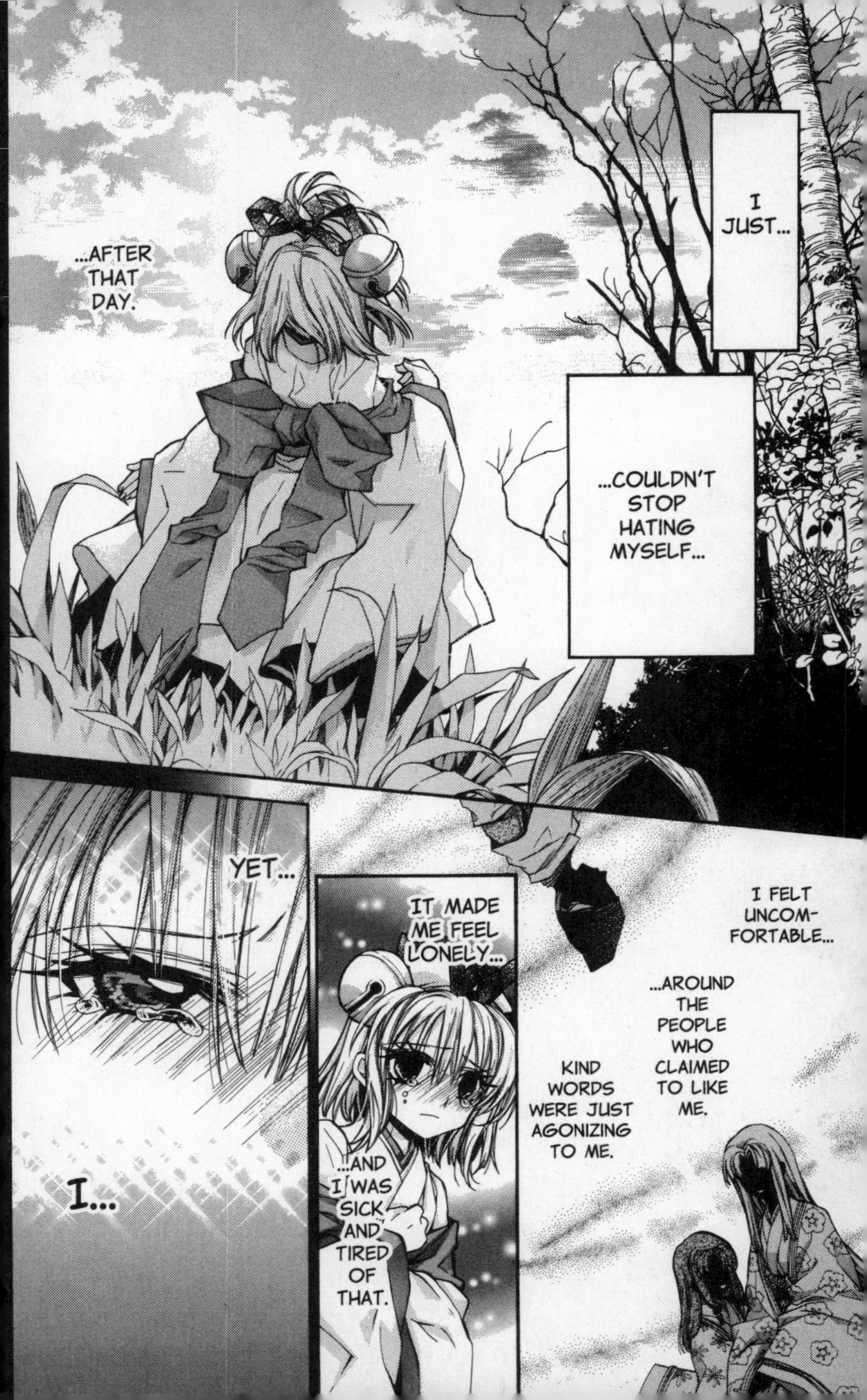
I JUST...
...COULDN'T STOP HATING MYSELF...
...AFTER THAT DAY.
I FELT UNCOM-FORTABLE...
...AROUND THE PEOPLE WHO CLAIMED TO LIKE ME.
KIND WORDS WERE JUST AGONIZING TO ME.
IT MADE ME FEEL LONELY...
...AND I WAS SICK AND TIRED OF THAT.
YET...
I...

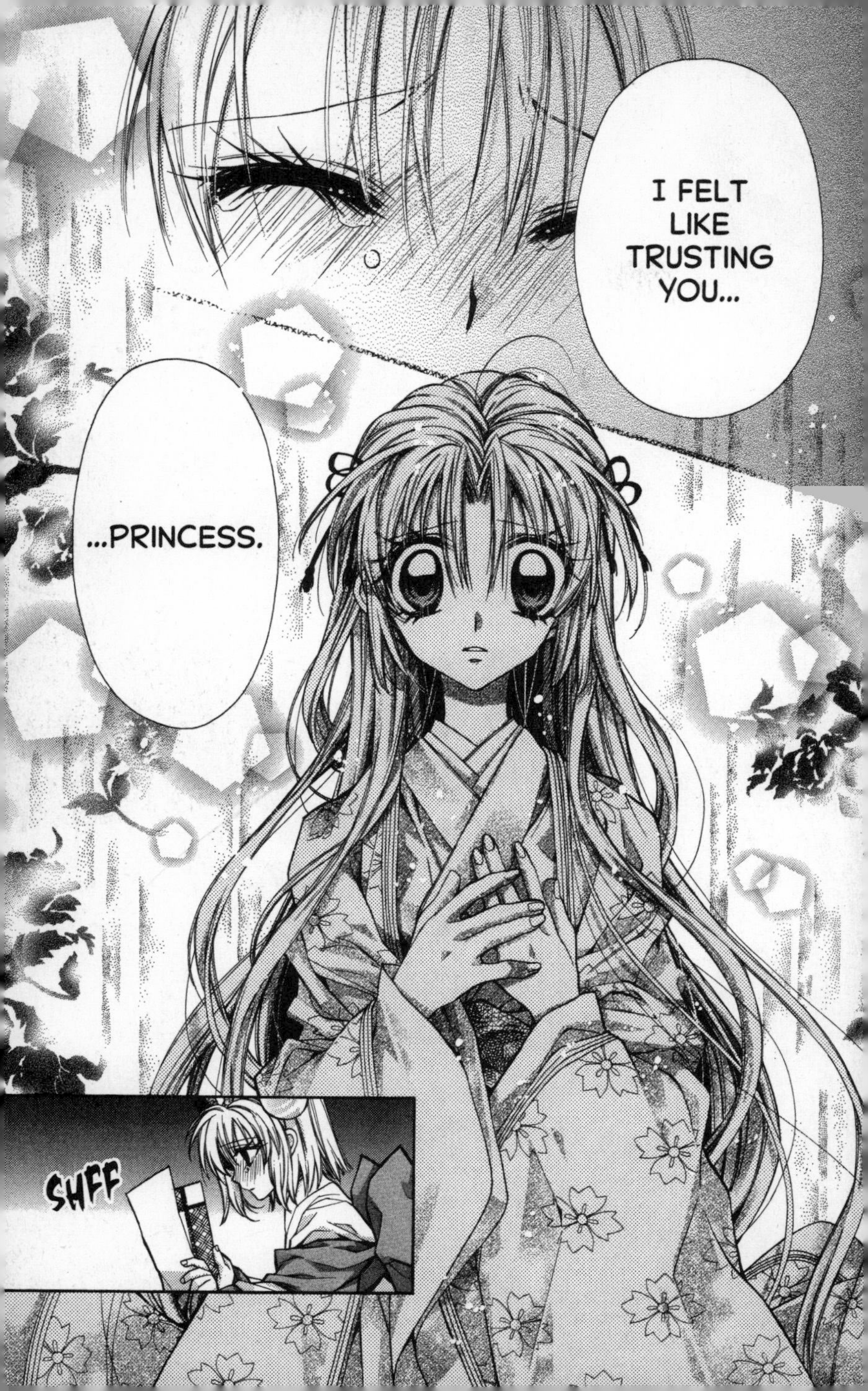
I FELT LIKE TRUSTING YOU...
...PRINCESS.
SHFF

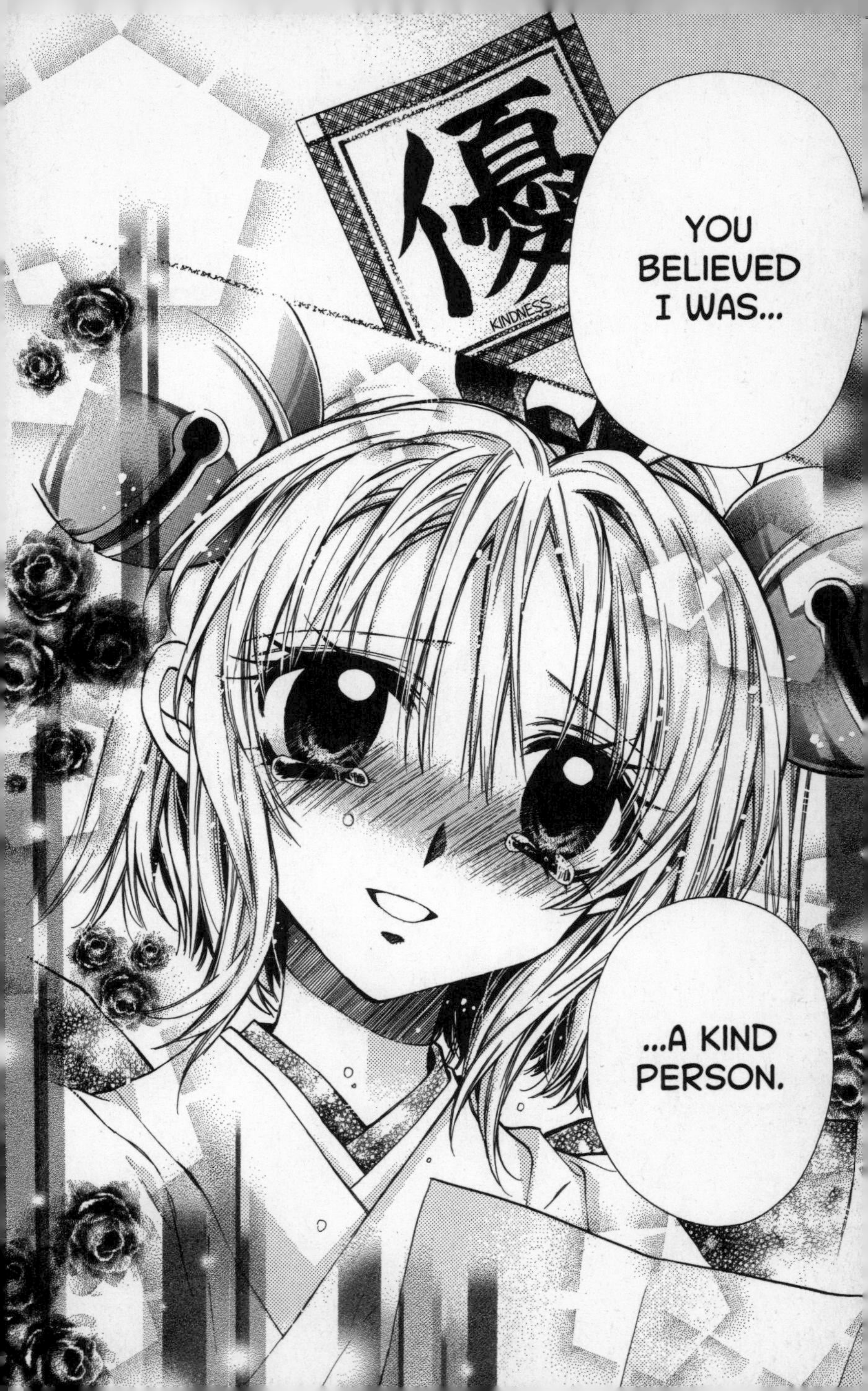
KINDNESS
YOU BELIEVED I WAS...
...A KIND PERSON.

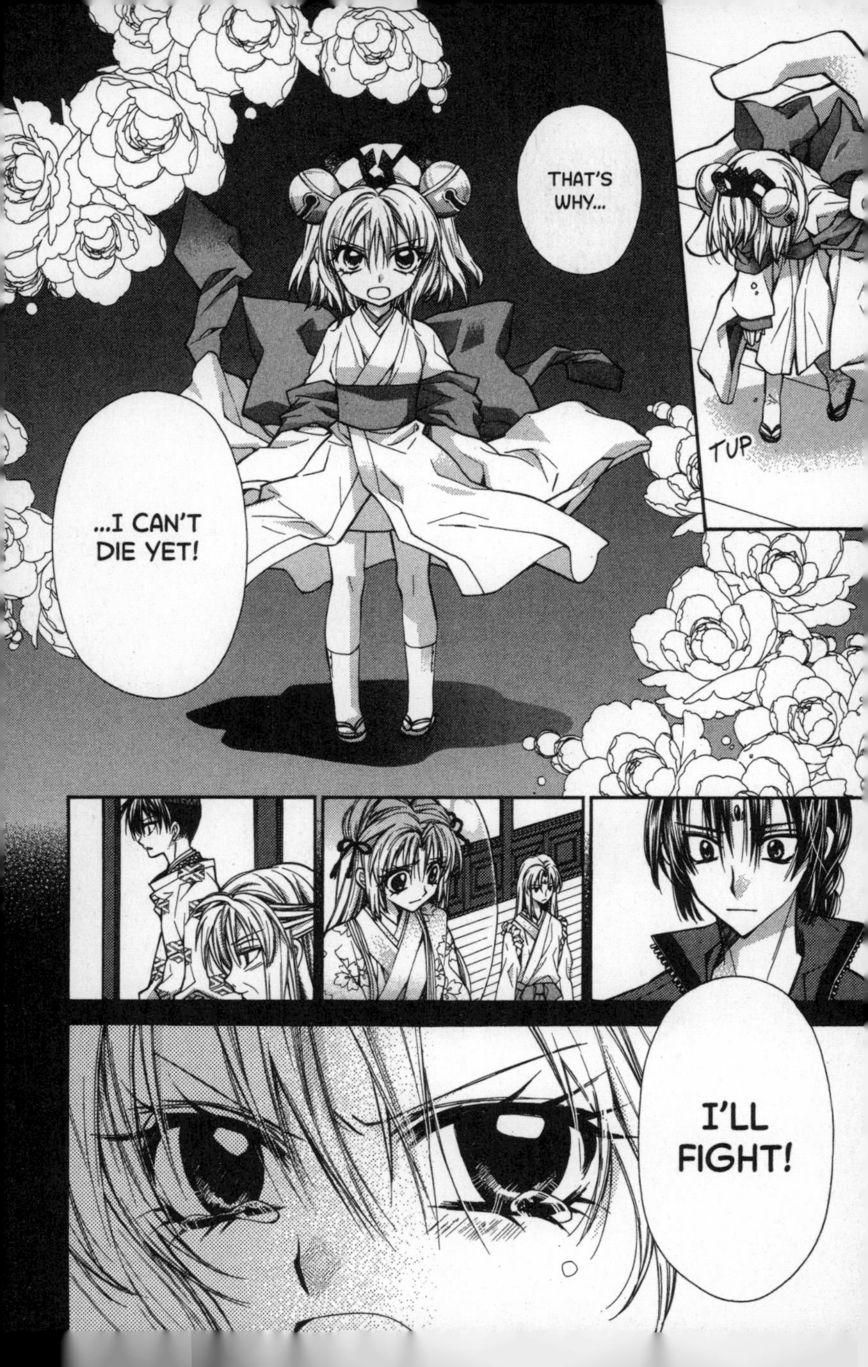
TUP
THAT'S WHY...
...I CAN'T DIE YET!
I'LL FIGHT!

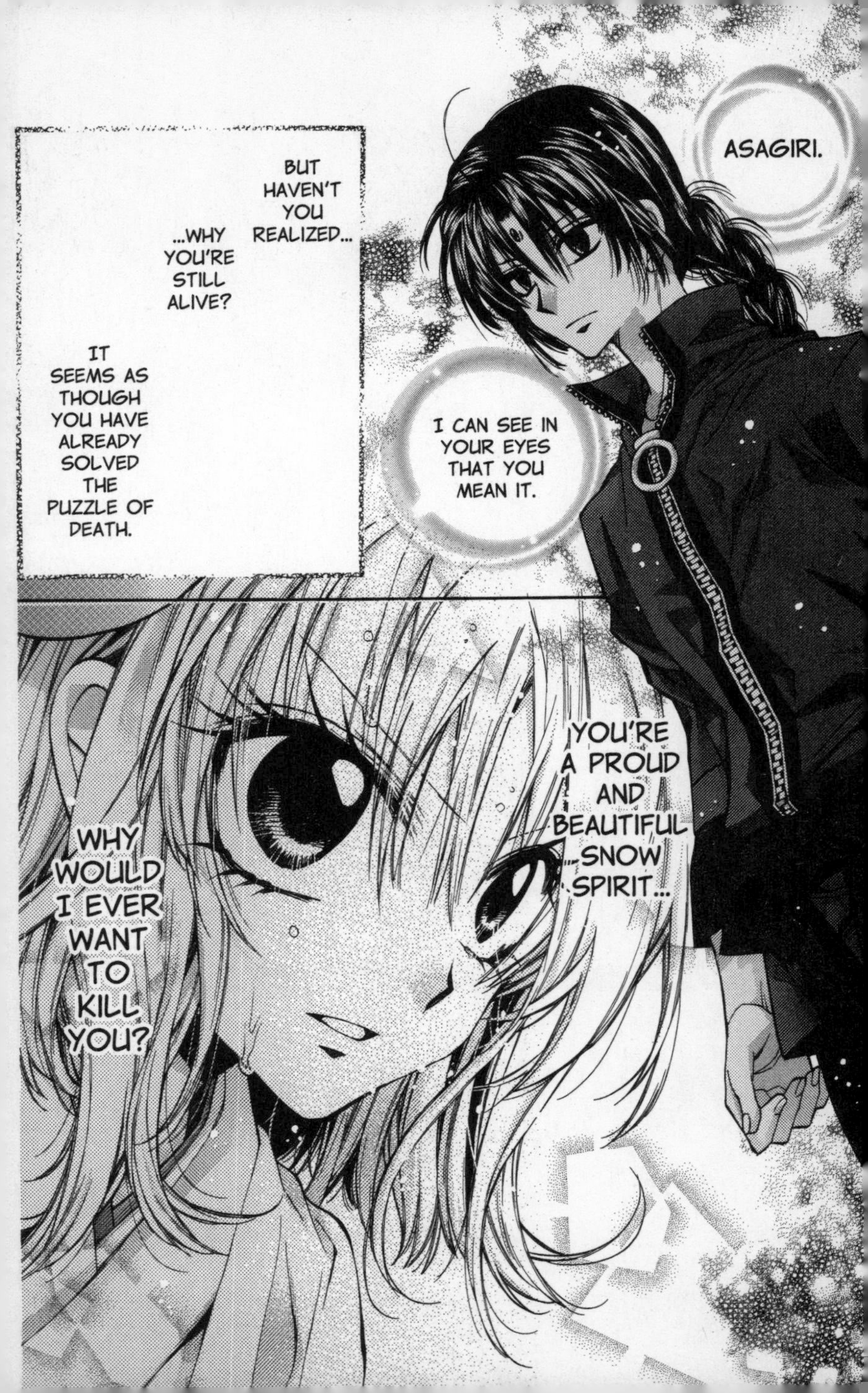
ASAGIRI.
I CAN SEE IN YOUR EYES THAT YOU MEAN IT.
BUT HAVEN'T YOU REALIZED...
...WHY YOU'RE STILL ALIVE?
IT SEEMS AS THOUGH YOU HAVE ALREADY SOLVED THE PUZZLE OF DEATH.
YOU'RE A PROUD AND BEAUTIFUL ...SNOW SPIRIT...
WHY WOULD I EVER WANT TO KILL YOU?

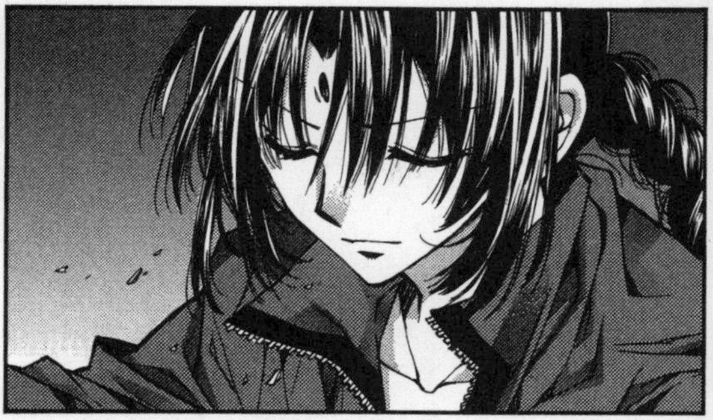

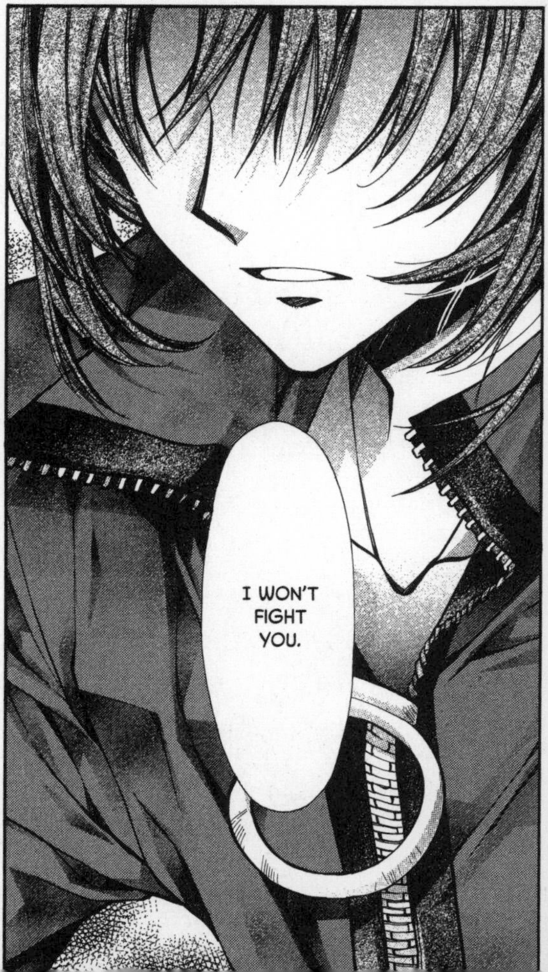
I WON'T FIGHT YOU.

On the Radio with myco

Currently I have a radio program on Nippon Broadcasting System's cell phone radio station "All Night Mobile" with myco-chan. She voiced Mitsuki in *Full Moon.*

We've talked about how we want to do something together, and hopefully we'll be able to get that project moving on the radio show. We're asking for messages for us over twitter, so if you have a twitter account, please hashtag #arimy to send us a message! ᵛ (Send messages about what you want us to do on the radio show and events you'd like to see!)

Don't forget the hashtag. It's #arimy. ᵛ

The name of the show is "In Love with Full Moon." Please listen to it. (It costs 100 yen to listen to each file if you don't mind that.)

myco and I have great chemistry together, but I probably would never have met her if it hadn't been for the *Full Moon* anime. Fate is a very interesting thing, isn't it...? I would love to have Yakkun come on the show as a guest too.

If you are interested, please listen here:

http://mobile.1242.com/lf_mobile

It's "In Love with Full Moon." Please remember the address. ᵛ

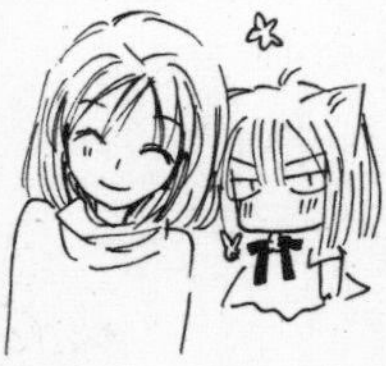

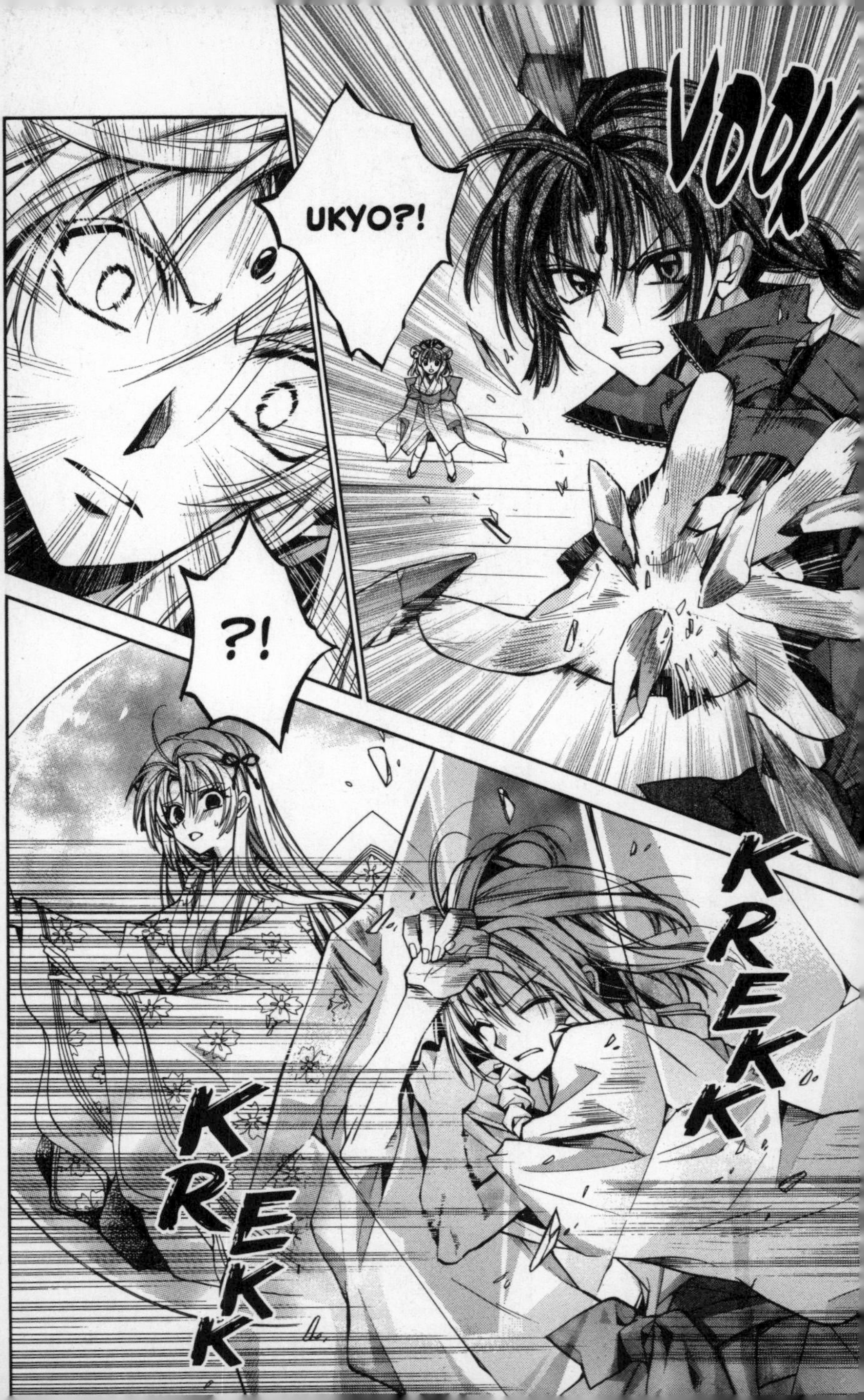
UKYO?!
?!
KREKK
KREKK

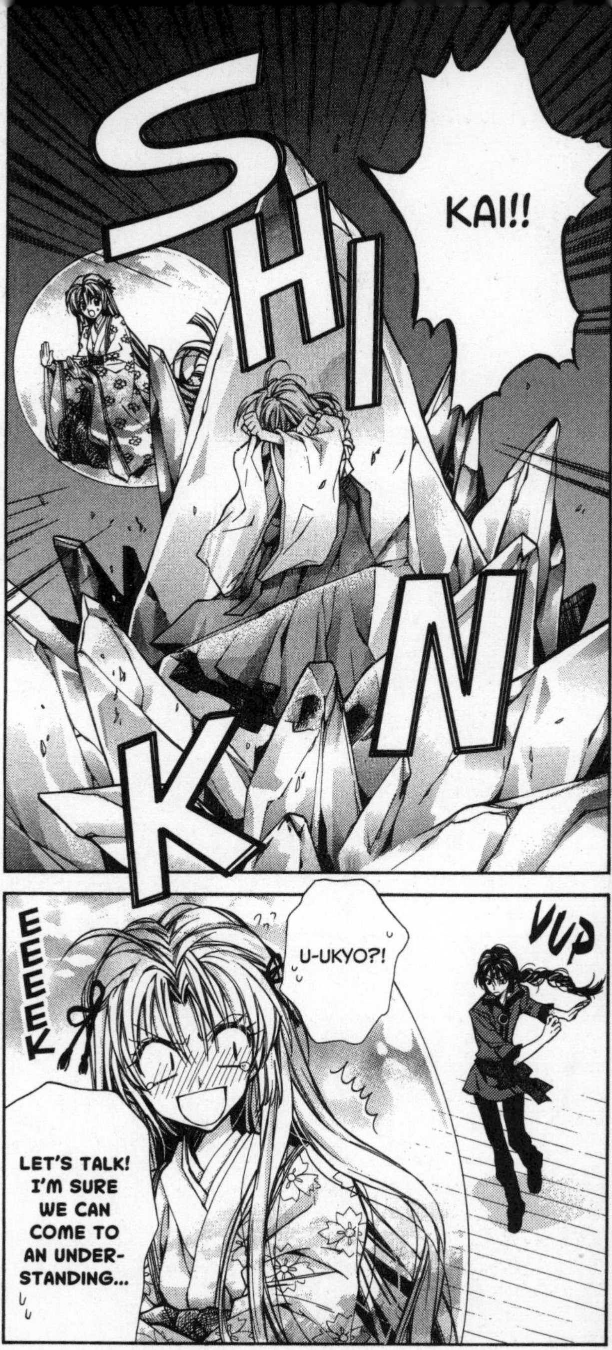
KAI!!
SHINK
VUP
U-UKYO?!
EEEEK
LET'S TALK! I'M SURE WE CAN COME TO AN UNDER-STANDING...

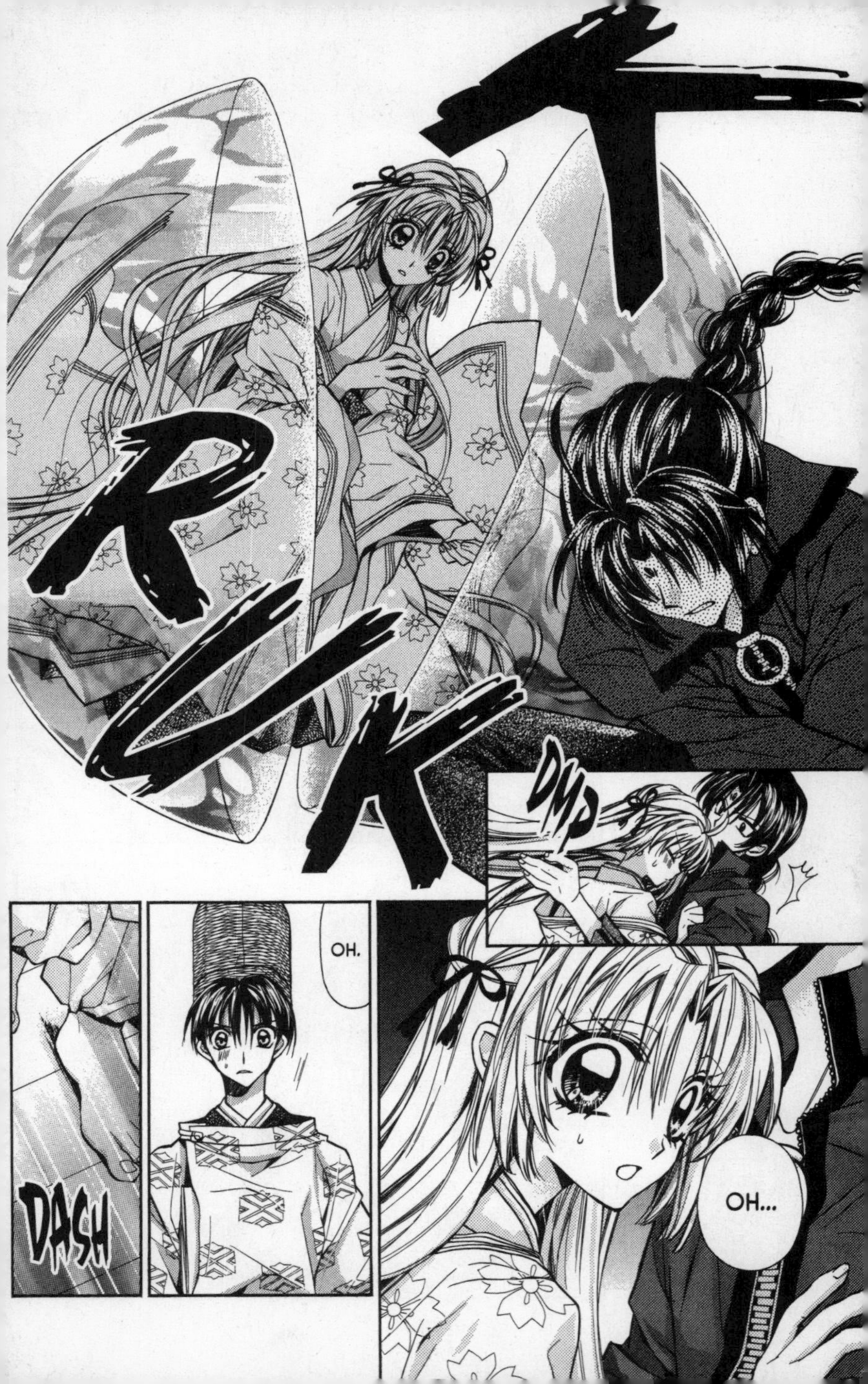
TRUK
DMP
OH...
OH.
DASH

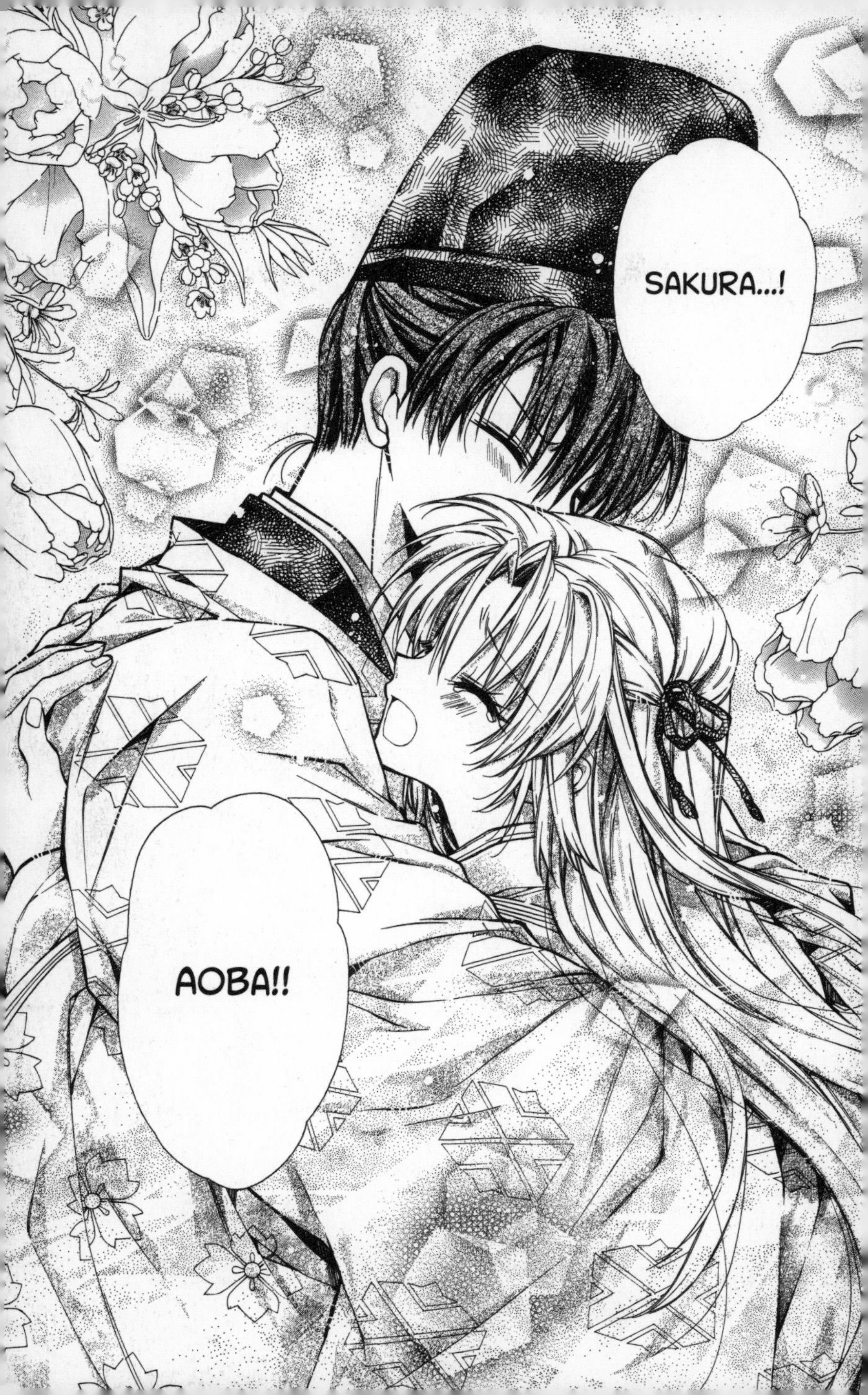
SAKURA...!
AOBA!!

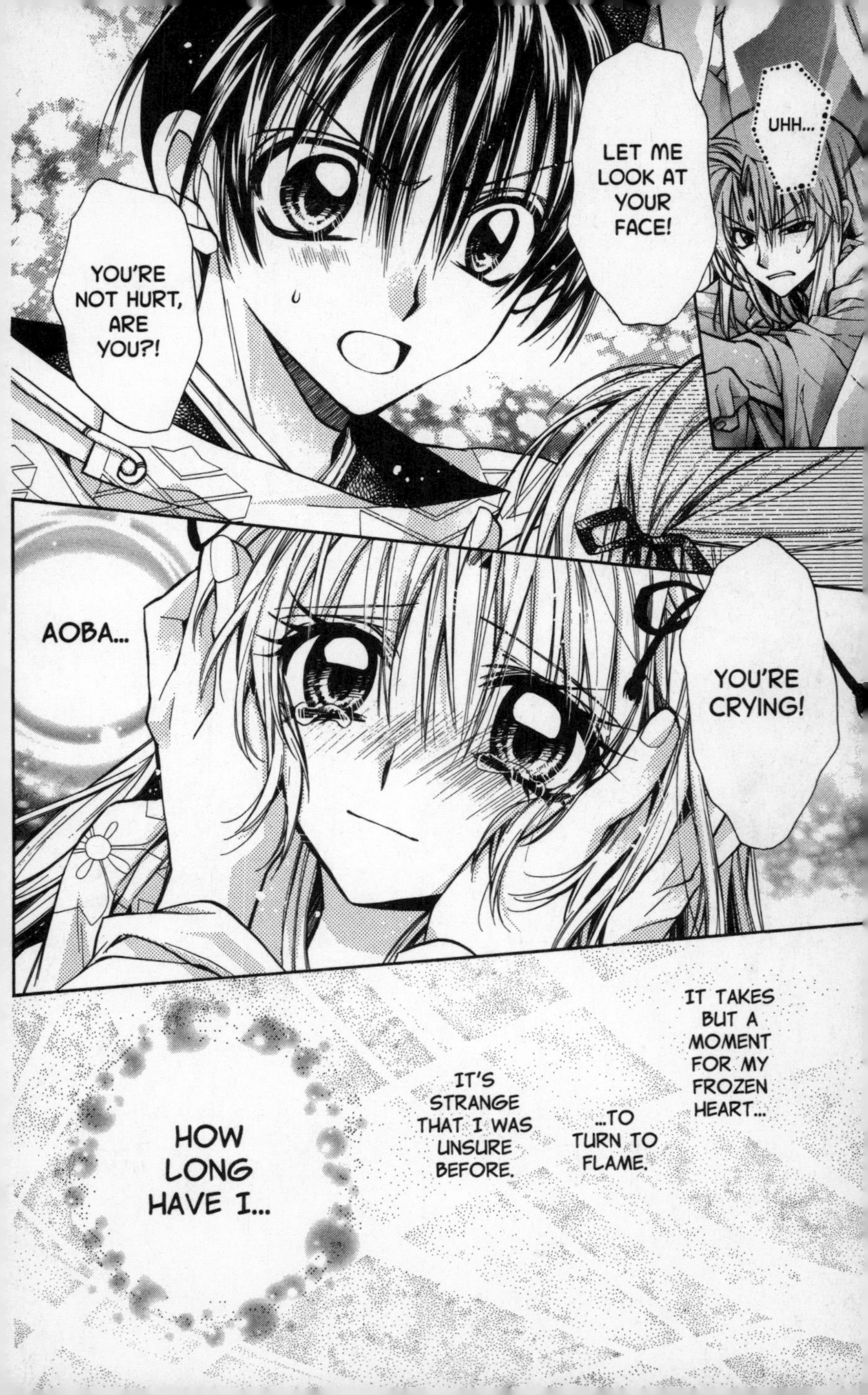
LET ME LOOK AT YOUR FACE!
YOU'RE NOT HURT, ARE YOU?!
UHH...
YOU'RE CRYING!
AOBA...
IT TAKES BUT A MOMENT FOR MY FROZEN HEART...
...TO TURN TO FLAME.
IT'S STRANGE THAT I WAS UNSURE BEFORE.
HOW LONG HAVE I...

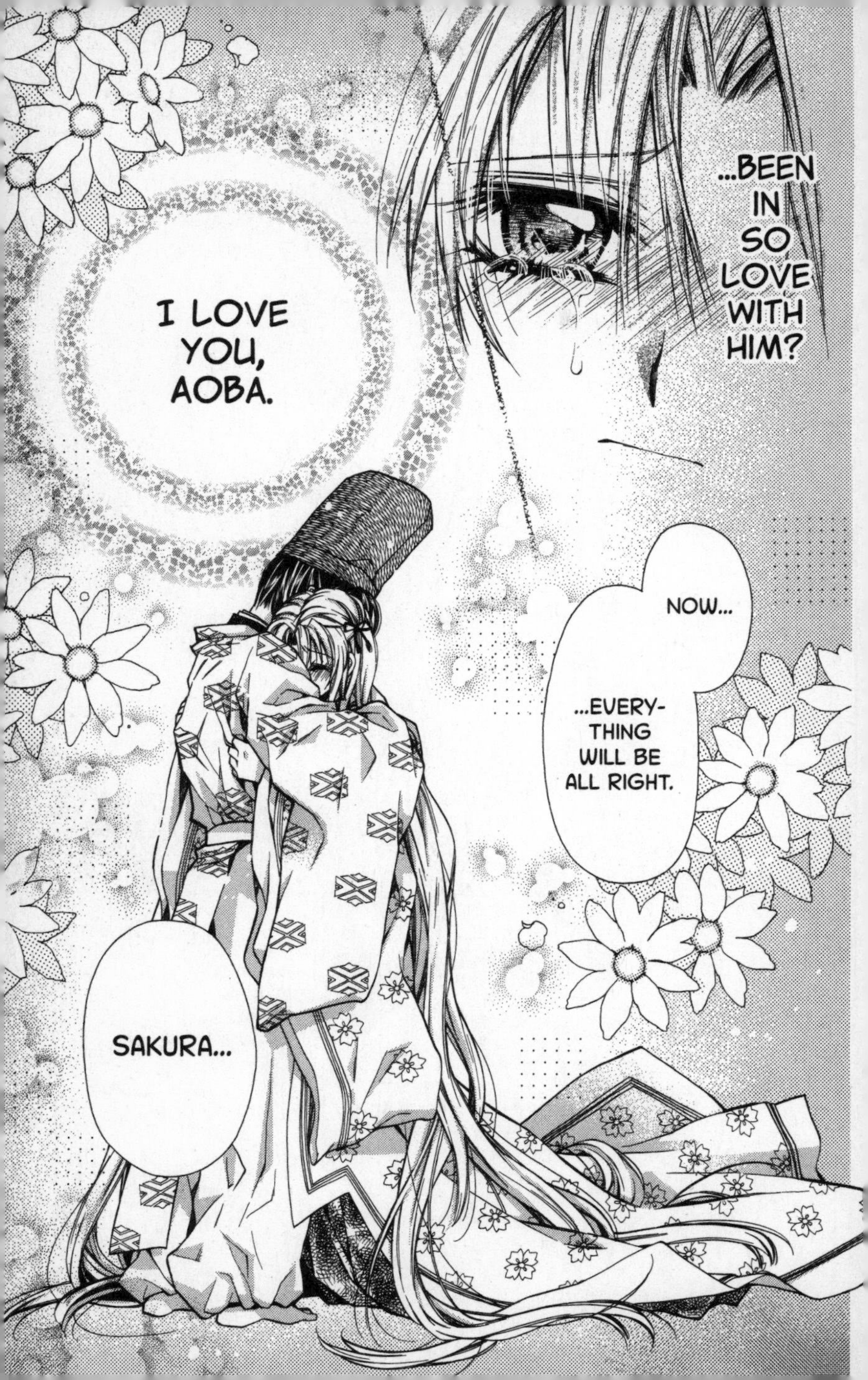
...BEEN IN SO LOVE WITH HIM?
I LOVE YOU, AOBA.
NOW...
...EVERY-THING WILL BE ALL RIGHT.
SAKURA...

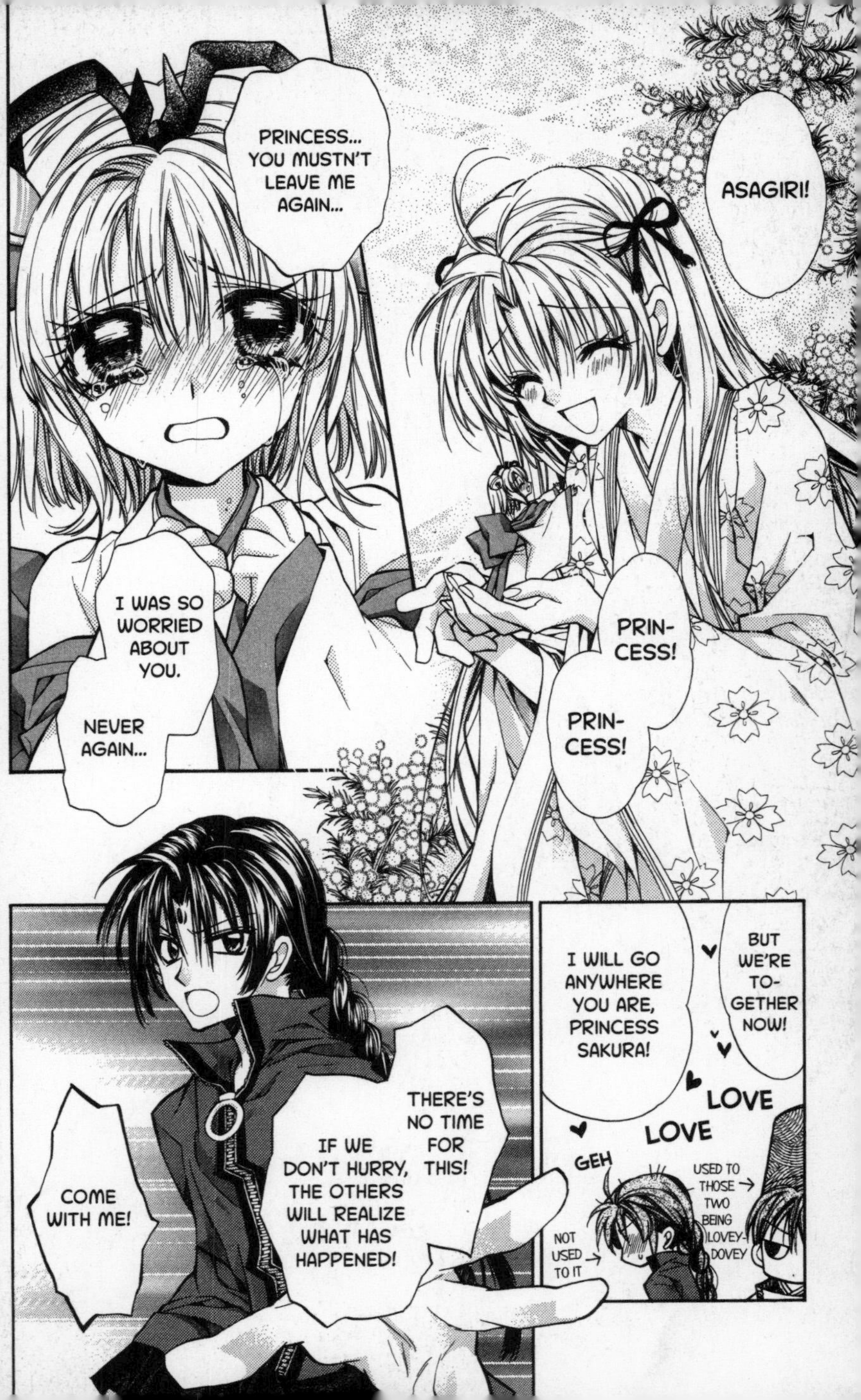
ASAGIRI!
PRINCESS... YOU MUSTN'T LEAVE ME AGAIN...
PRIN-CESS!
PRIN-CESS!
I WAS SO WORRIED ABOUT YOU.
NEVER AGAIN...
BUT WE'RE TO-GETHER NOW!
I WILL GO ANYWHERE YOU ARE, PRINCESS SAKURA!
LOVE
LOVE
GEH
USED TO THOSE TWO BEING LOVEY-DOVEY
NOT USED TO IT
THERE'S NO TIME FOR THIS!
IF WE DON'T HURRY, THE OTHERS WILL REALIZE WHAT HAS HAPPENED!
COME WITH ME!

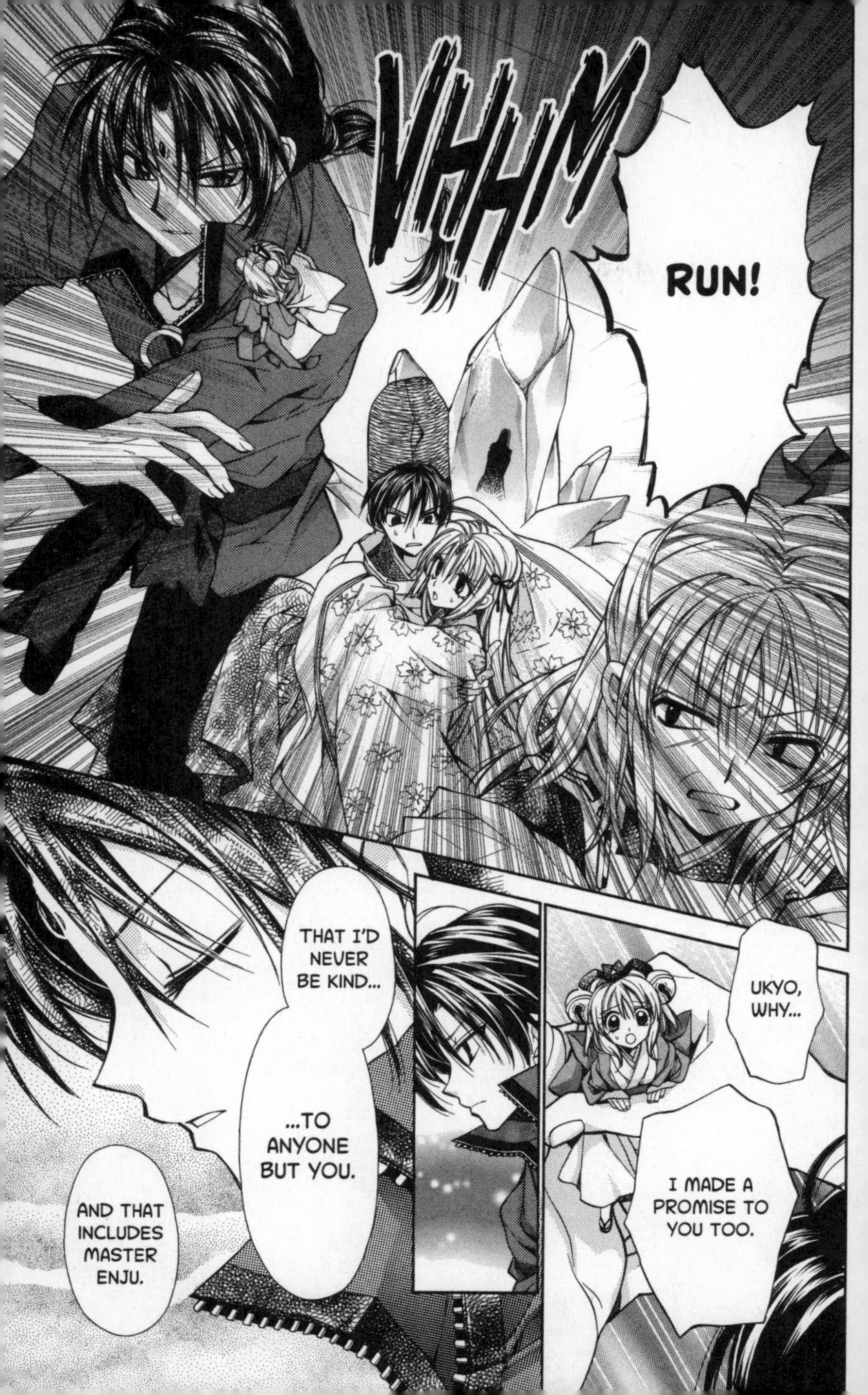
VHHM
RUN!
UKYO, WHY...
I MADE A PROMISE TO YOU TOO.
THAT I'D NEVER BE KIND...
...TO ANYONE BUT YOU.
AND THAT INCLUDES MASTER ENJU.

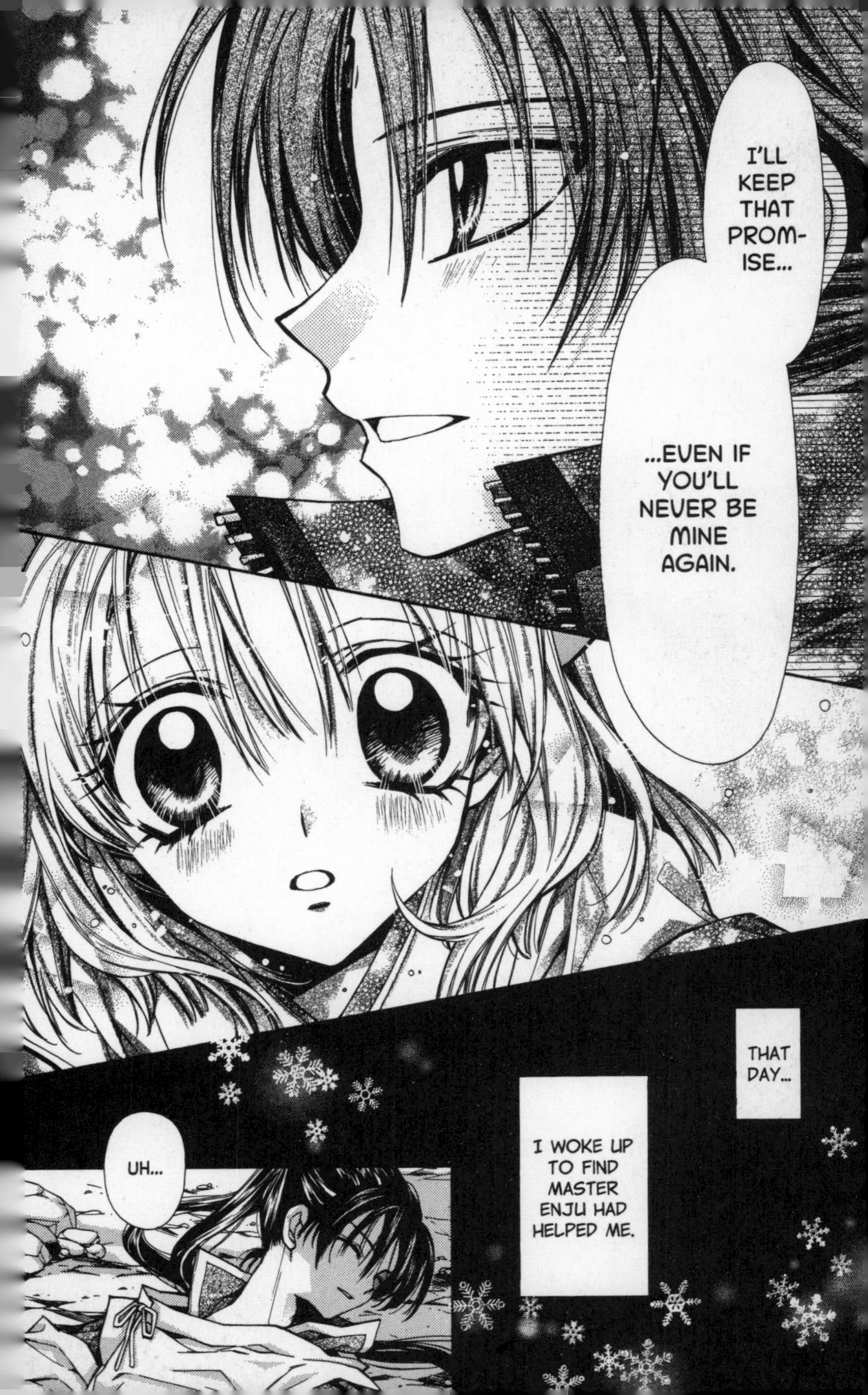
I'LL KEEP THAT PROMISE...
...EVEN IF YOU'LL NEVER BE MINE AGAIN.
THAT DAY...
I WOKE UP TO FIND MASTER ENJU HAD HELPED ME.
UH...

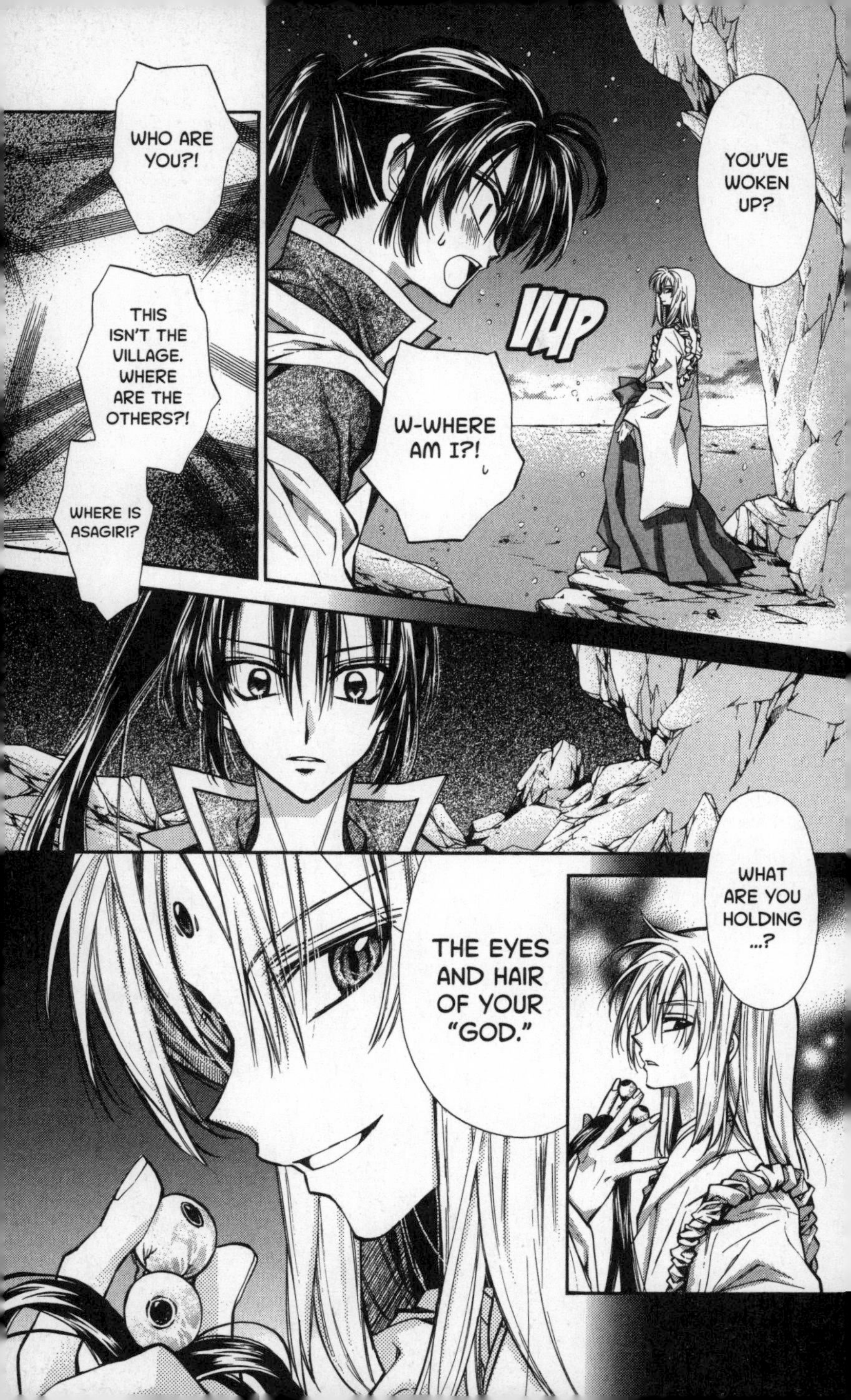
YOU'VE WOKEN UP?
VUP
W-WHERE AM I?!
WHO ARE YOU?!
THIS ISN'T THE VILLAGE. WHERE ARE THE OTHERS?!
WHERE IS ASAGIRI?
WHAT ARE YOU HOLDING ...?
THE EYES AND HAIR OF YOUR "GOD."

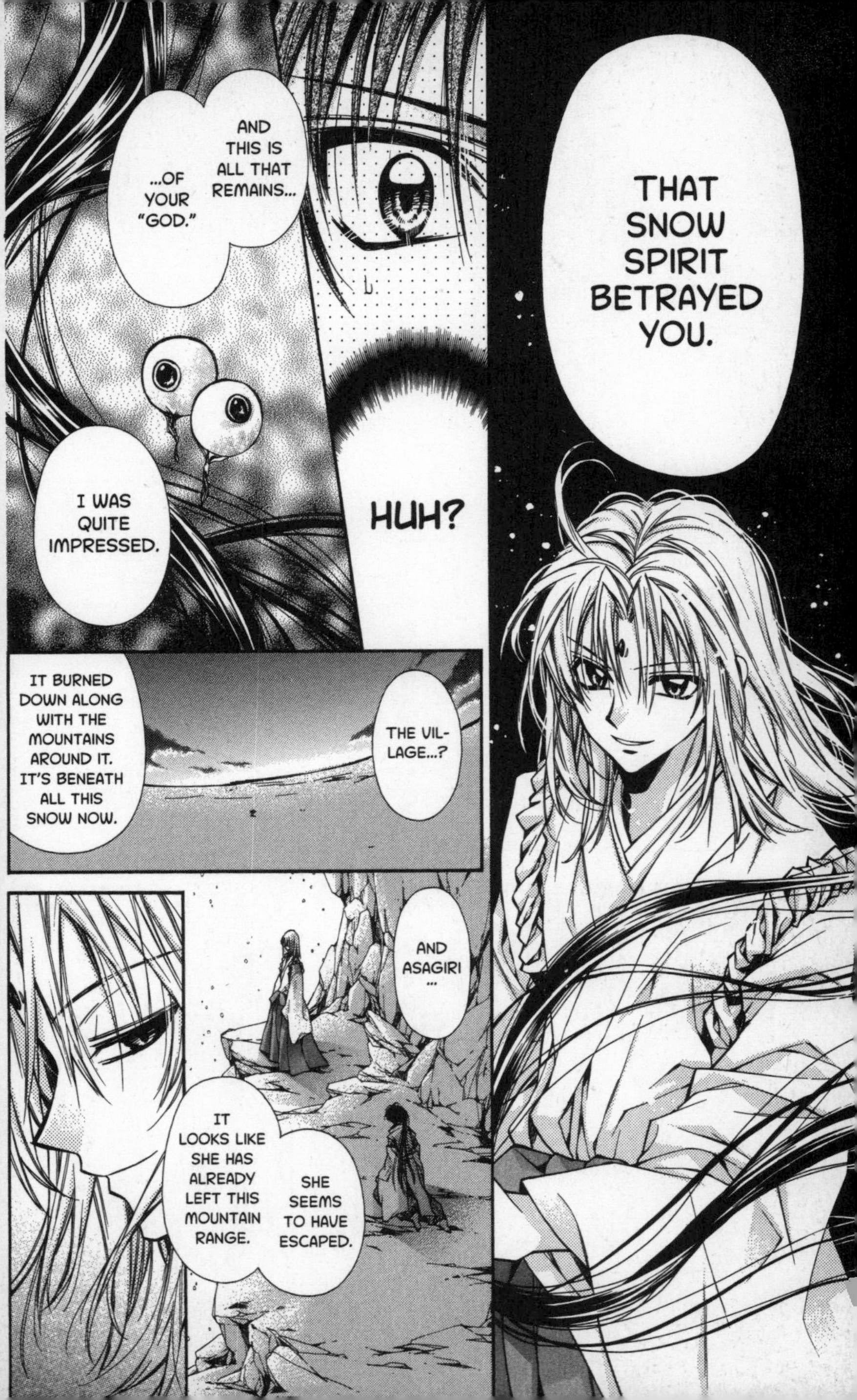
THAT SNOW SPIRIT BETRAYED YOU.
AND THIS IS ALL THAT REMAINS...
...OF YOUR "GOD."
HUH?
I WAS QUITE IMPRESSED.
THE VIL-LAGE...?
IT BURNED DOWN ALONG WITH THE MOUNTAINS AROUND IT. IT'S BENEATH ALL THIS SNOW NOW.
AND ASAGIRI...
SHE SEEMS TO HAVE ESCAPED.
IT LOOKS LIKE SHE HAS ALREADY LEFT THIS MOUNTAIN RANGE.

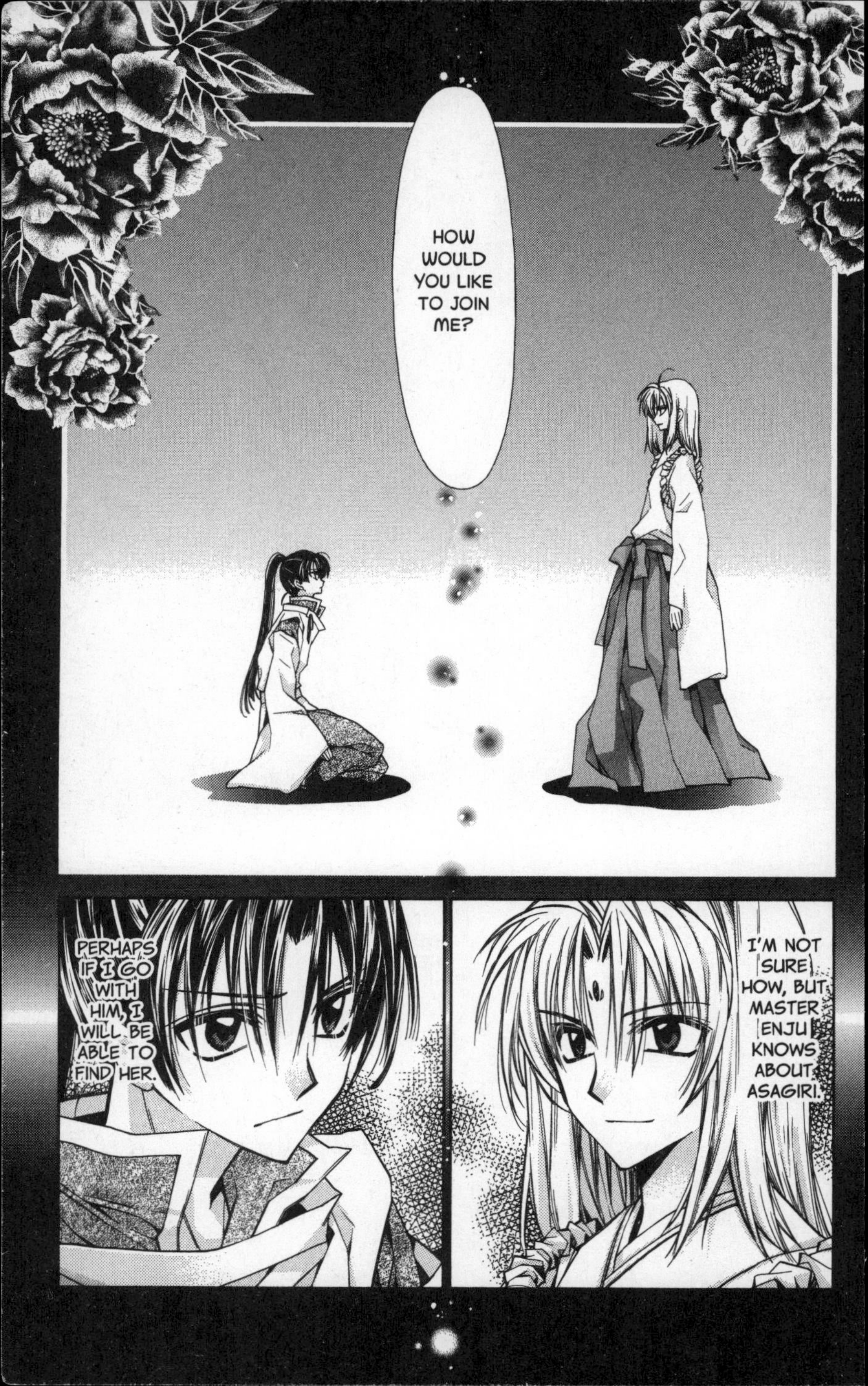
HOW WOULD YOU LIKE TO JOIN ME?
I'M NOT SURE HOW, BUT MASTER ENJU KNOWS ABOUT ASAGIRI.
PERHAPS IF I GO WITH HIM, I WILL BE ABLE TO FIND HER.

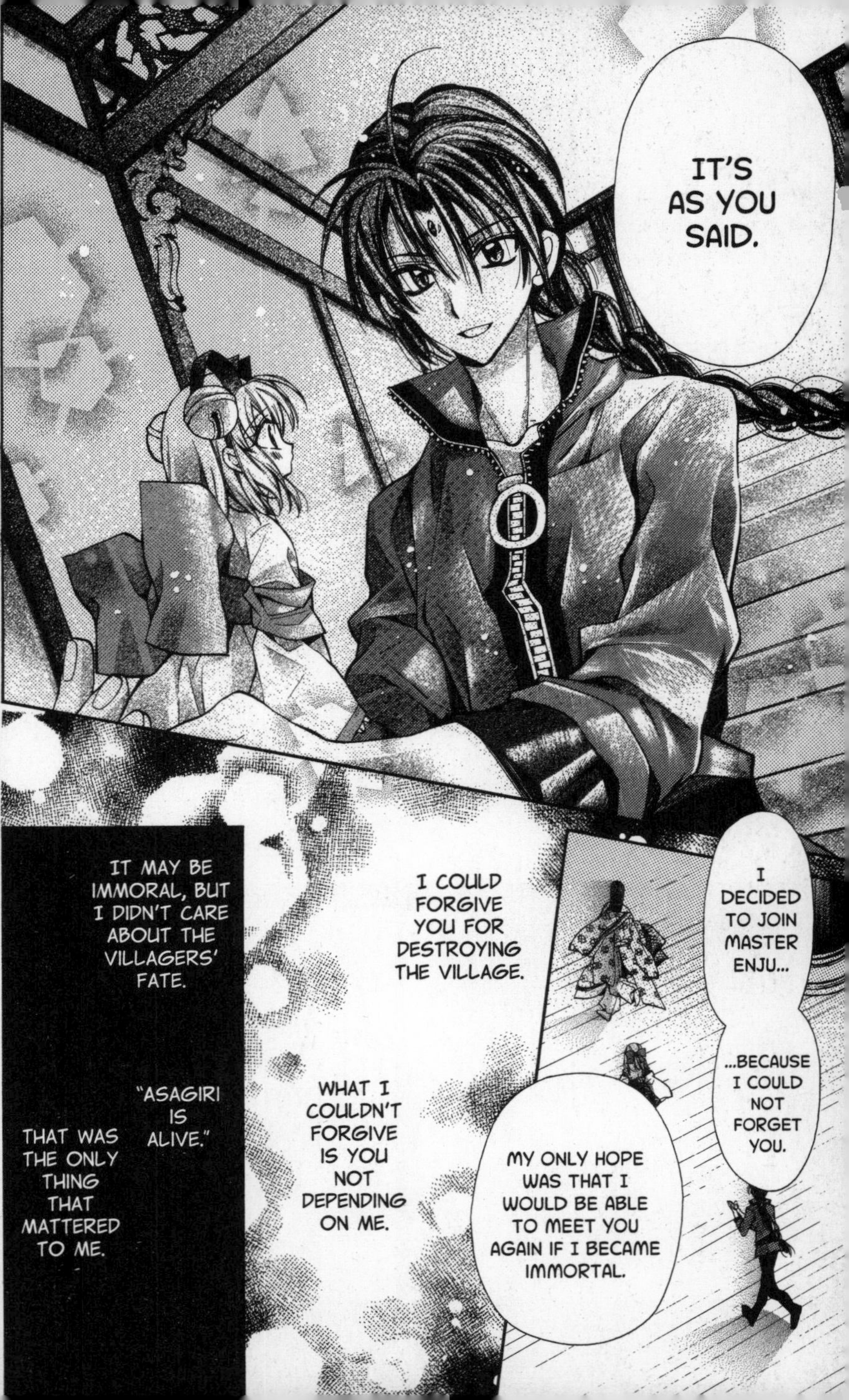
IT'S AS YOU SAID.
I DECIDED TO JOIN MASTER ENJU...
...BECAUSE I COULD NOT FORGET YOU.
MY ONLY HOPE WAS THAT I WOULD BE ABLE TO MEET YOU AGAIN IF I BECAME IMMORTAL.
I COULD FORGIVE YOU FOR DESTROYING THE VILLAGE.
WHAT I COULDN'T FORGIVE IS YOU NOT DEPENDING ON ME.
IT MAY BE IMMORAL, BUT I DIDN'T CARE ABOUT THE VILLAGERS' FATE.
"ASAGIRI IS ALIVE."
THAT WAS THE ONLY THING THAT MATTERED TO ME.

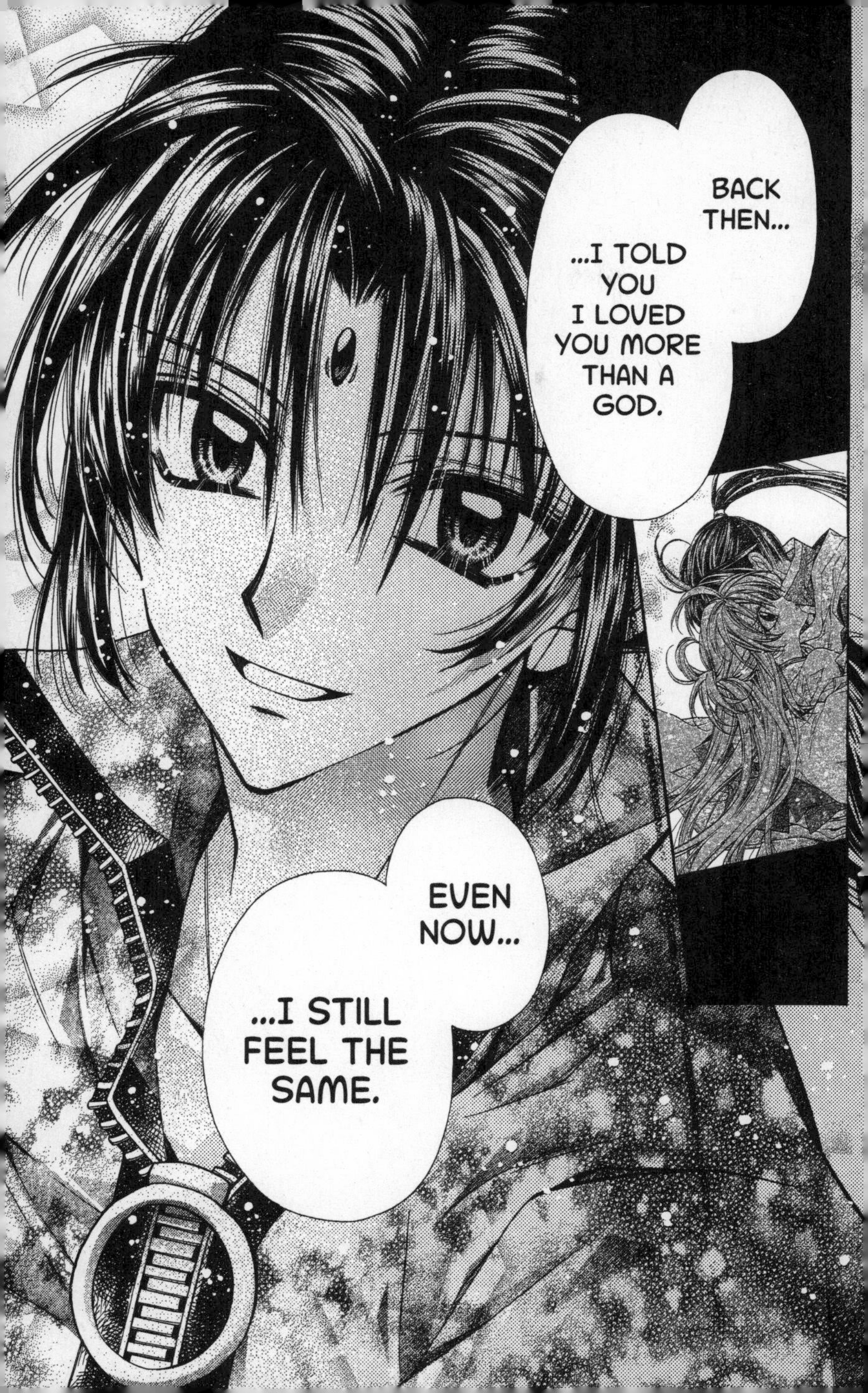
BACK THEN...
...I TOLD YOU I LOVED YOU MORE THAN A GOD.
EVEN NOW...
...I STILL FEEL THE SAME.

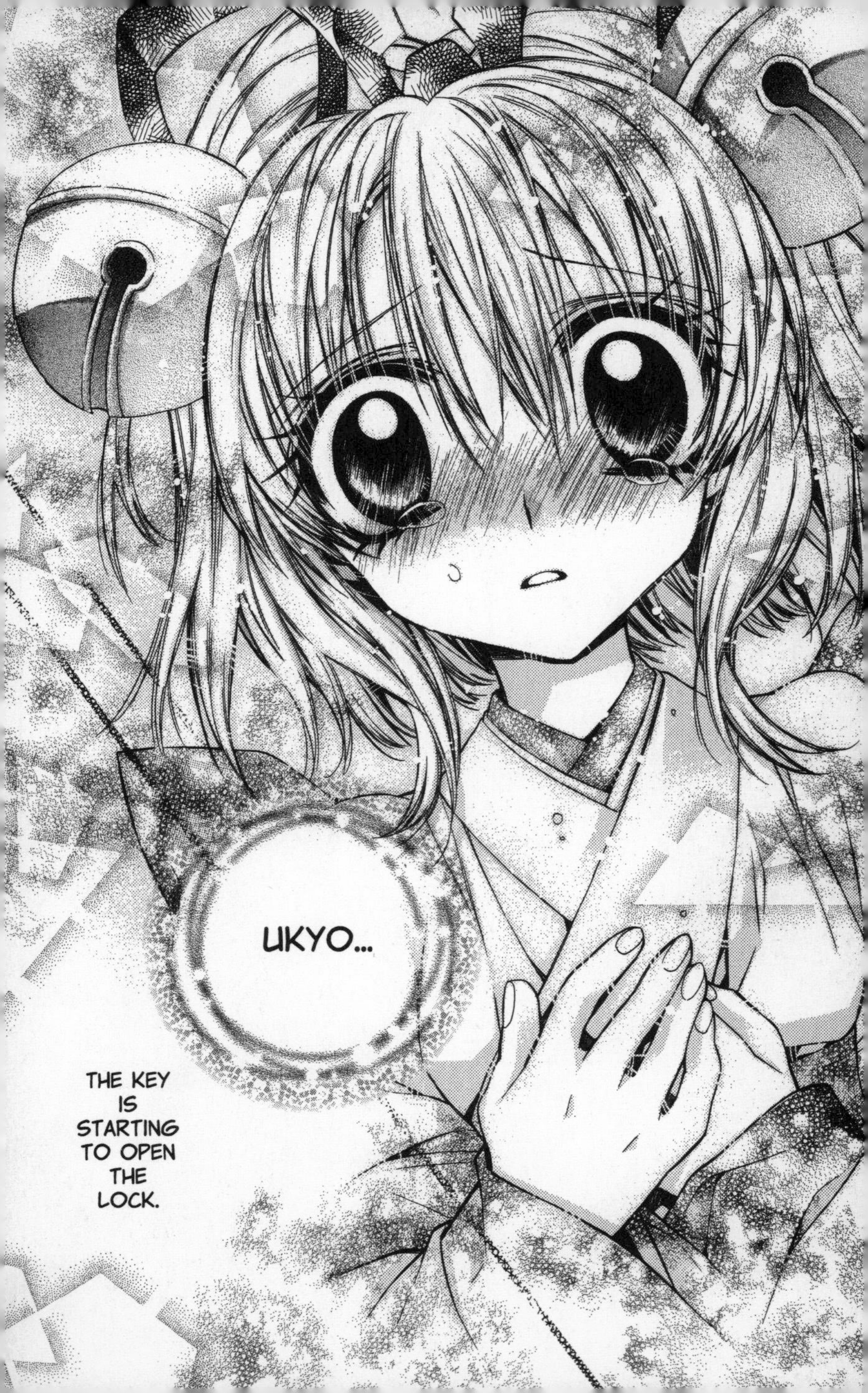
UKYO...
THE KEY IS STARTING TO OPEN THE LOCK.

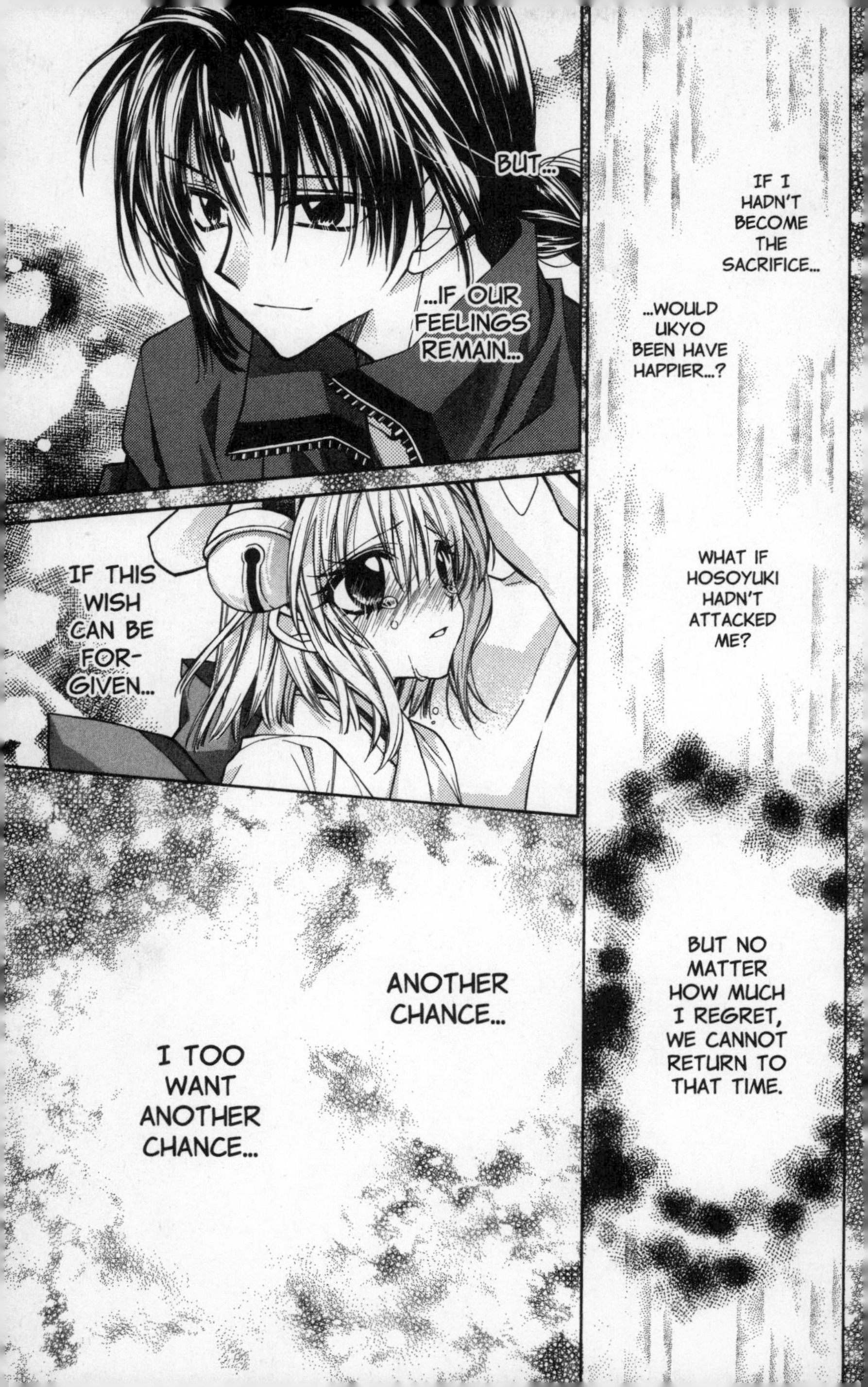
IF I HADN'T BECOME THE SACRIFICE...
...WOULD UKYO BEEN HAVE HAPPIER...?
WHAT IF HOSOYUKI HADN'T ATTACKED ME?
BUT NO MATTER HOW MUCH I REGRET, WE CANNOT RETURN TO THAT TIME.
BUT...
...IF OUR FEELINGS REMAIN...
IF THIS WISH CAN BE FOR-GIVEN...
ANOTHER CHANCE...
I TOO WANT ANOTHER CHANCE...

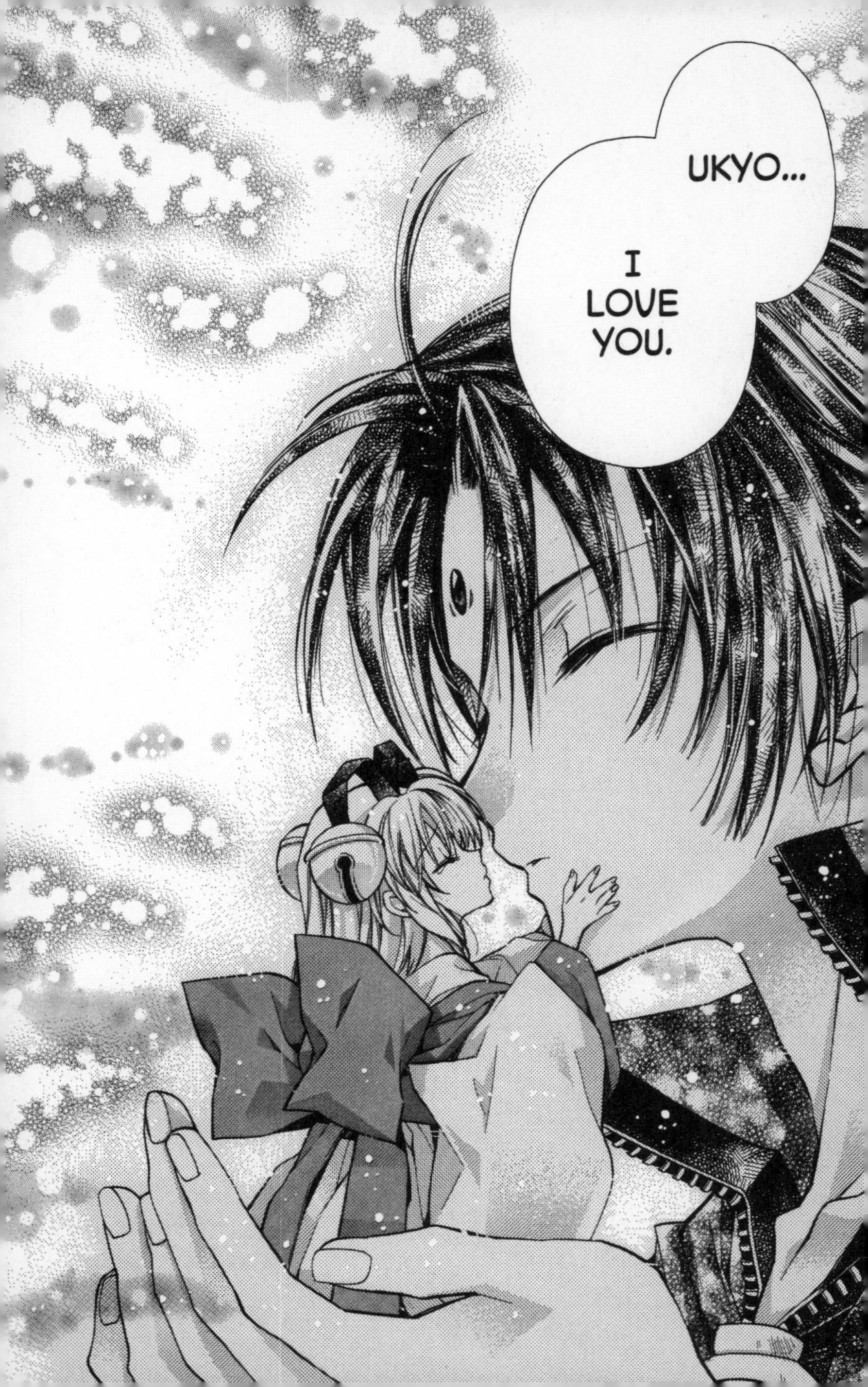
UKYO...
I LOVE YOU.

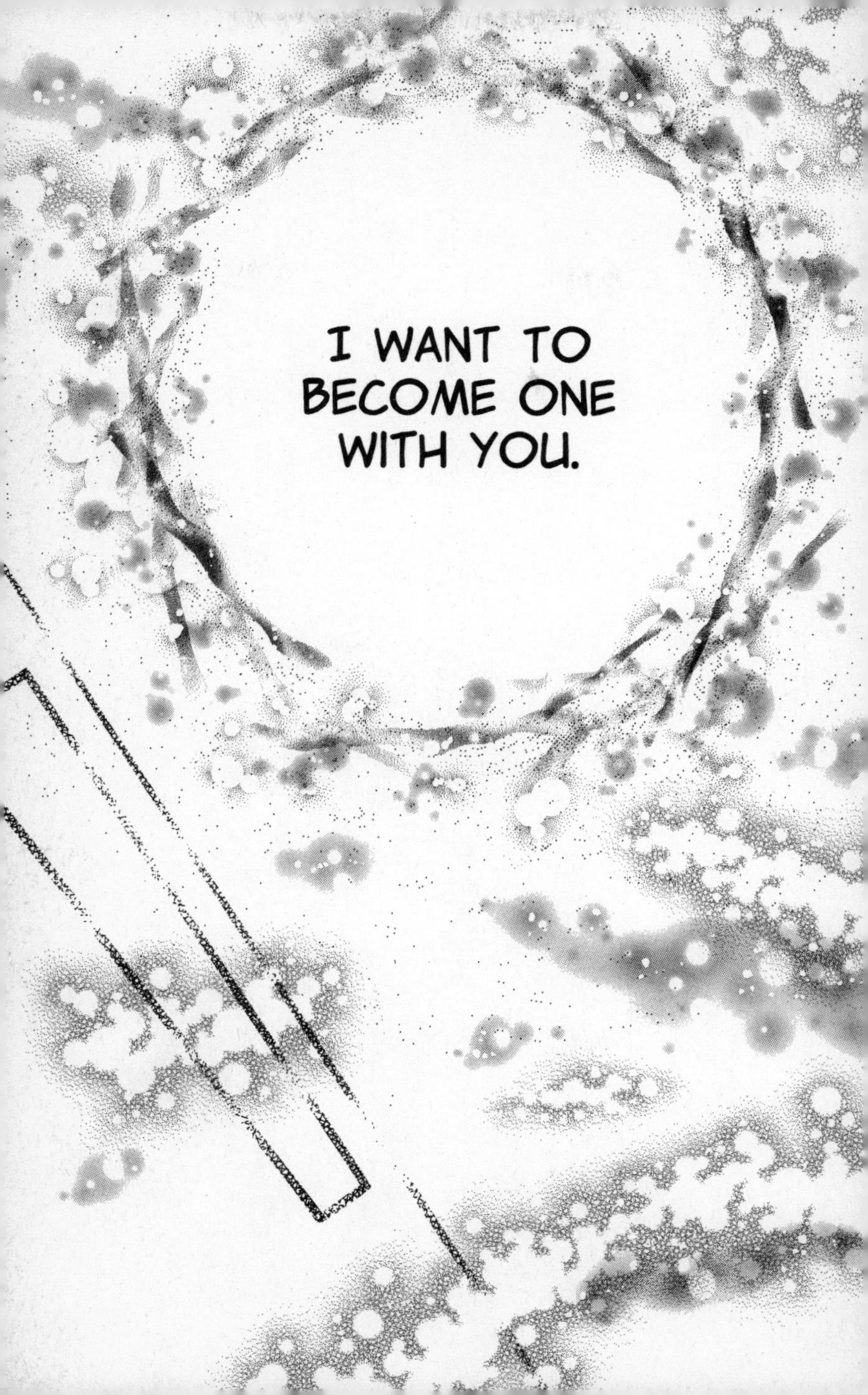
I WANT TO BECOME ONE WITH YOU.

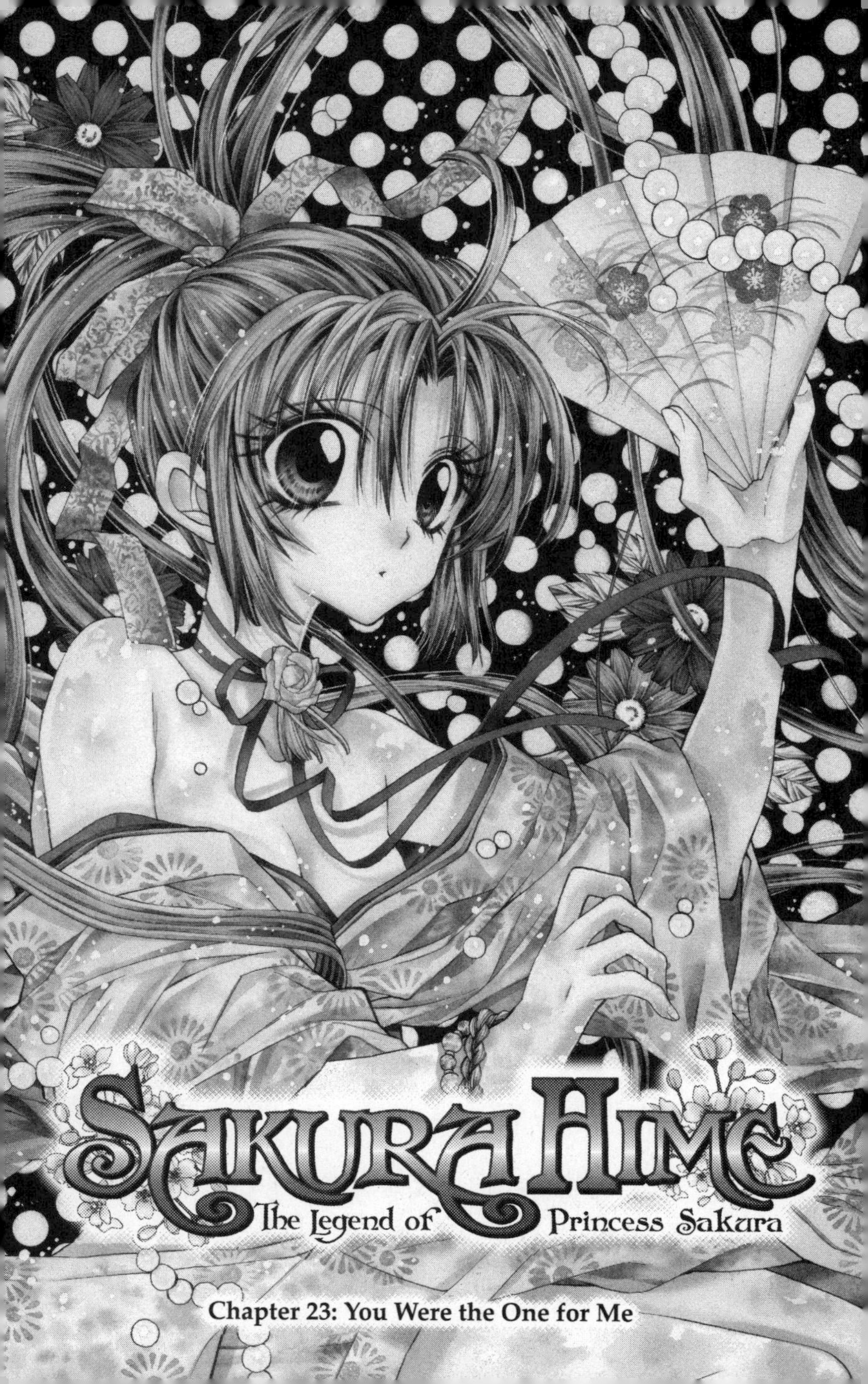
SAKURA HIME
The Legend of Princess Sakura
Chapter 23: You Were the One for Me

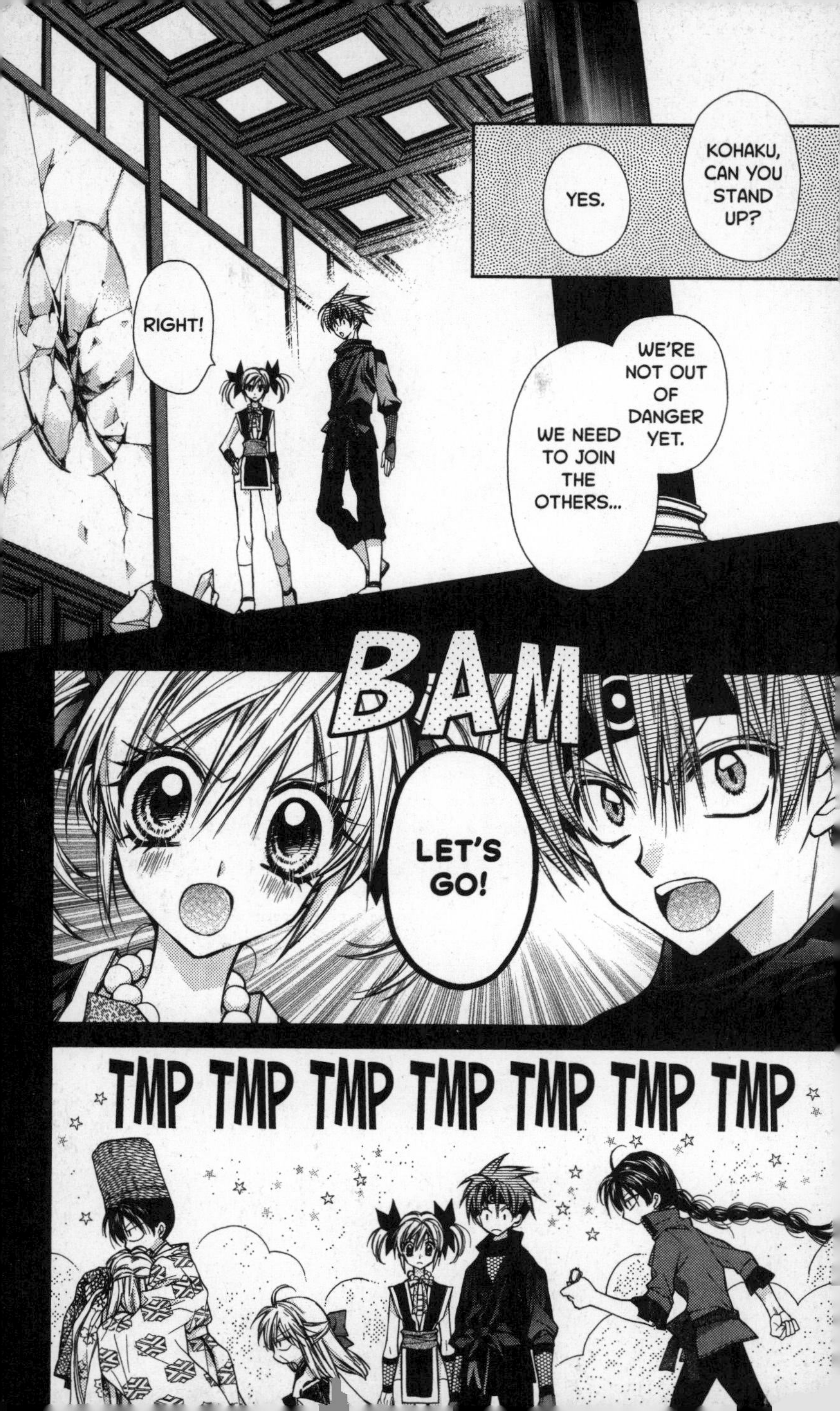
KOHAKU, CAN YOU STAND UP?
YES.
WE'RE NOT OUT OF DANGER YET.
WE NEED TO JOIN THE OTHERS...
RIGHT!
BAM
LET'S GO!
TMP TMP TMP TMP TMP TMP TMP

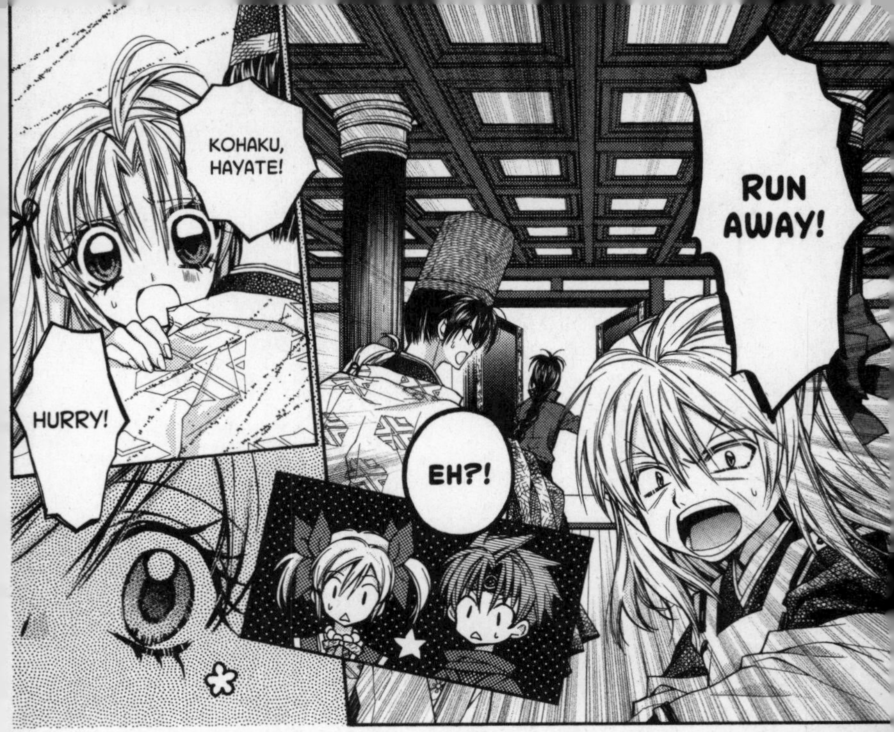
RUN AWAY!
EH?!
KOHAKU, HAYATE!
HURRY!

Chapter 23: You Were the One for Me

☆ I'm giving away the story.

I don't really do it intentionally, but a lot of the chapter titles of *Sakura Hime* tend to be phrases from that chapter.

Not that...it's important or anything. (laugh)

I had some trouble as the creator with Sakura being so hardheaded in this chapter. Enju is a bad guy, so I want her to forget about him, but she just wouldn't hate him...

Well, he is her first love and her only family member... But she couldn't side with what he was doing, so she just kept swaying back and forth.

Being the creator is tough at times like these. I feel bad for the characters, and I am unable to create the story if I'm too close to them. I once heard "mean writers tend to sell better" and I wondered what it meant. Maybe this is what that person was talking about.

A manga with just happy characters isn't any good, so you have to be able to draw the characters experiencing trouble. And you have to enjoy drawing those kind of scenes.

I...just kind of draw them in a daze (laugh), as if I'm watching the scene from far away. I guess I keep a cool head and watch over them like pieces in a game of chess.

Sorry, everyone.

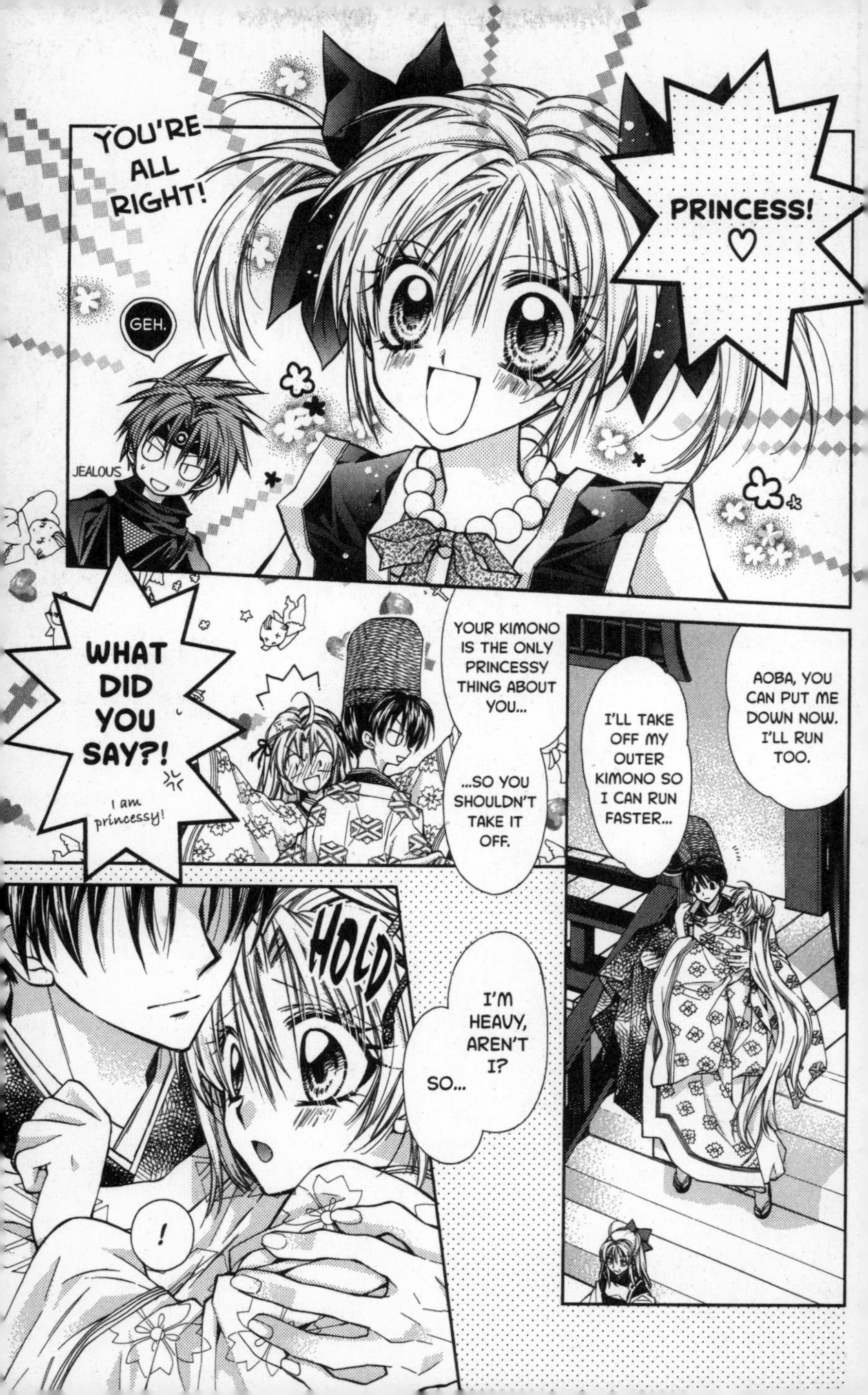
PRINCESS! ♡
YOU'RE ALL RIGHT!
GEH.
JEALOUS
AOBA, YOU CAN PUT ME DOWN NOW. I'LL RUN TOO.
I'LL TAKE OFF MY OUTER KIMONO SO I CAN RUN FASTER...
YOUR KIMONO IS THE ONLY PRINCESSY THING ABOUT YOU...
...SO YOU SHOULDN'T TAKE IT OFF.
WHAT DID YOU SAY?!
I am princessy!
HOLD
I'M HEAVY, AREN'T I? SO...
!

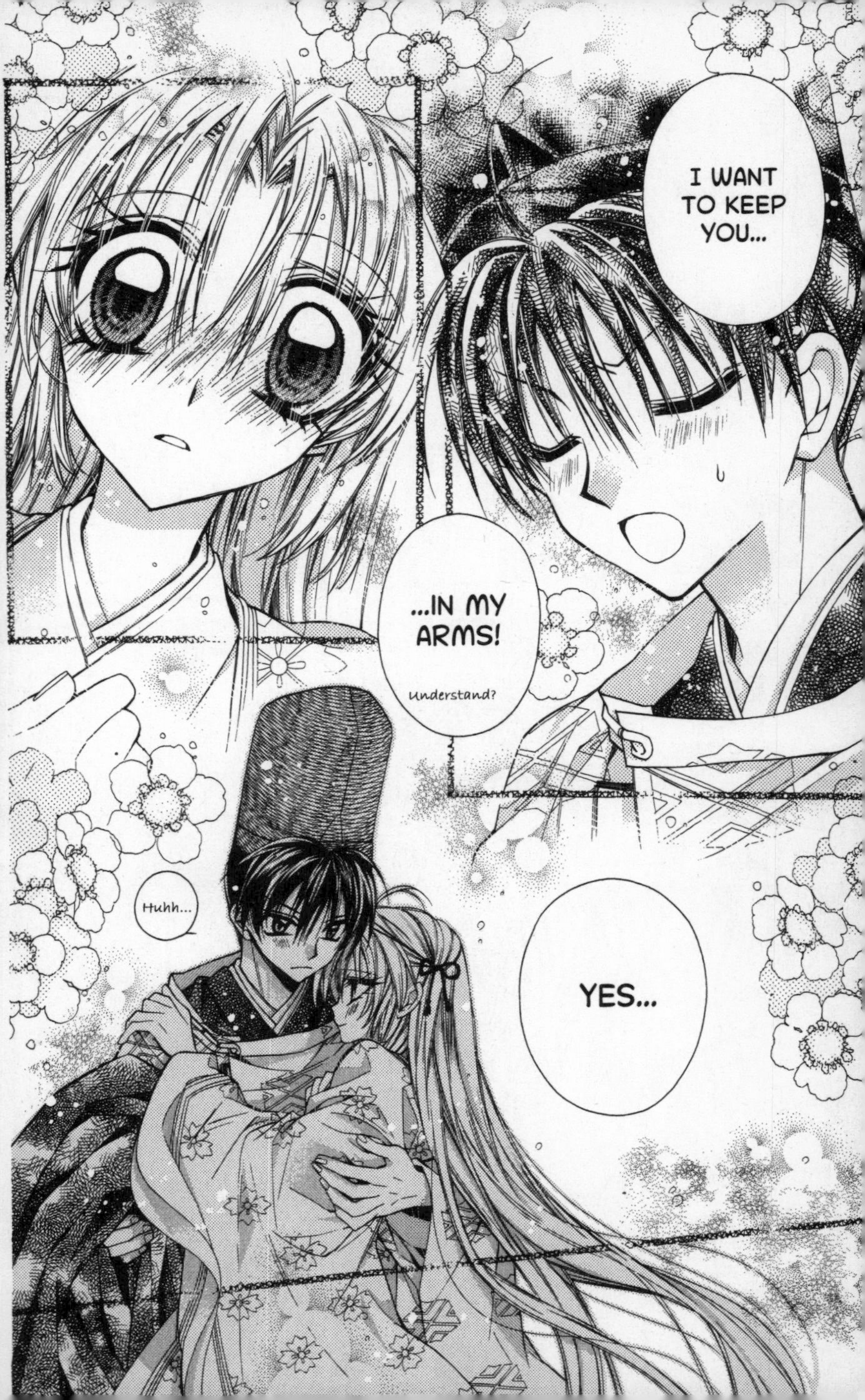
I WANT TO KEEP YOU...
...IN MY ARMS!
Understand?
YES...
Huhh...

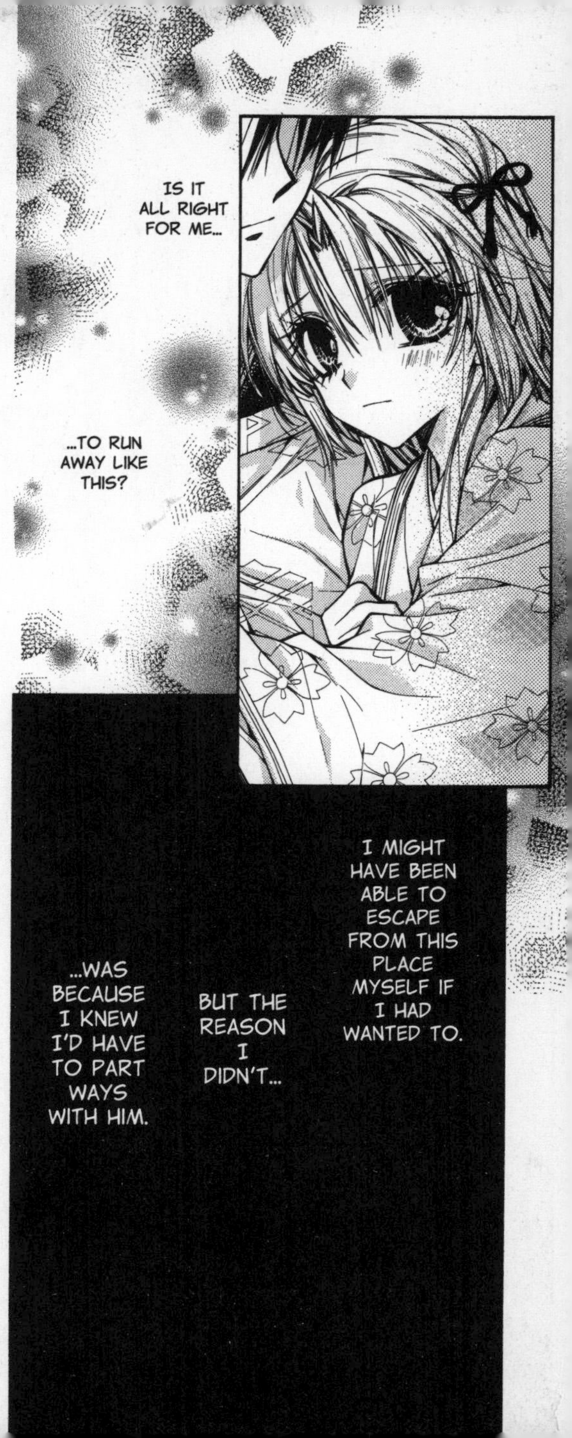
IS IT ALL RIGHT FOR ME...
...TO RUN AWAY LIKE THIS?
I MIGHT HAVE BEEN ABLE TO ESCAPE FROM THIS PLACE MYSELF IF I HAD WANTED TO.
BUT THE REASON I DIDN'T...
...WAS BECAUSE I KNEW I'D HAVE TO PART WAYS WITH HIM.

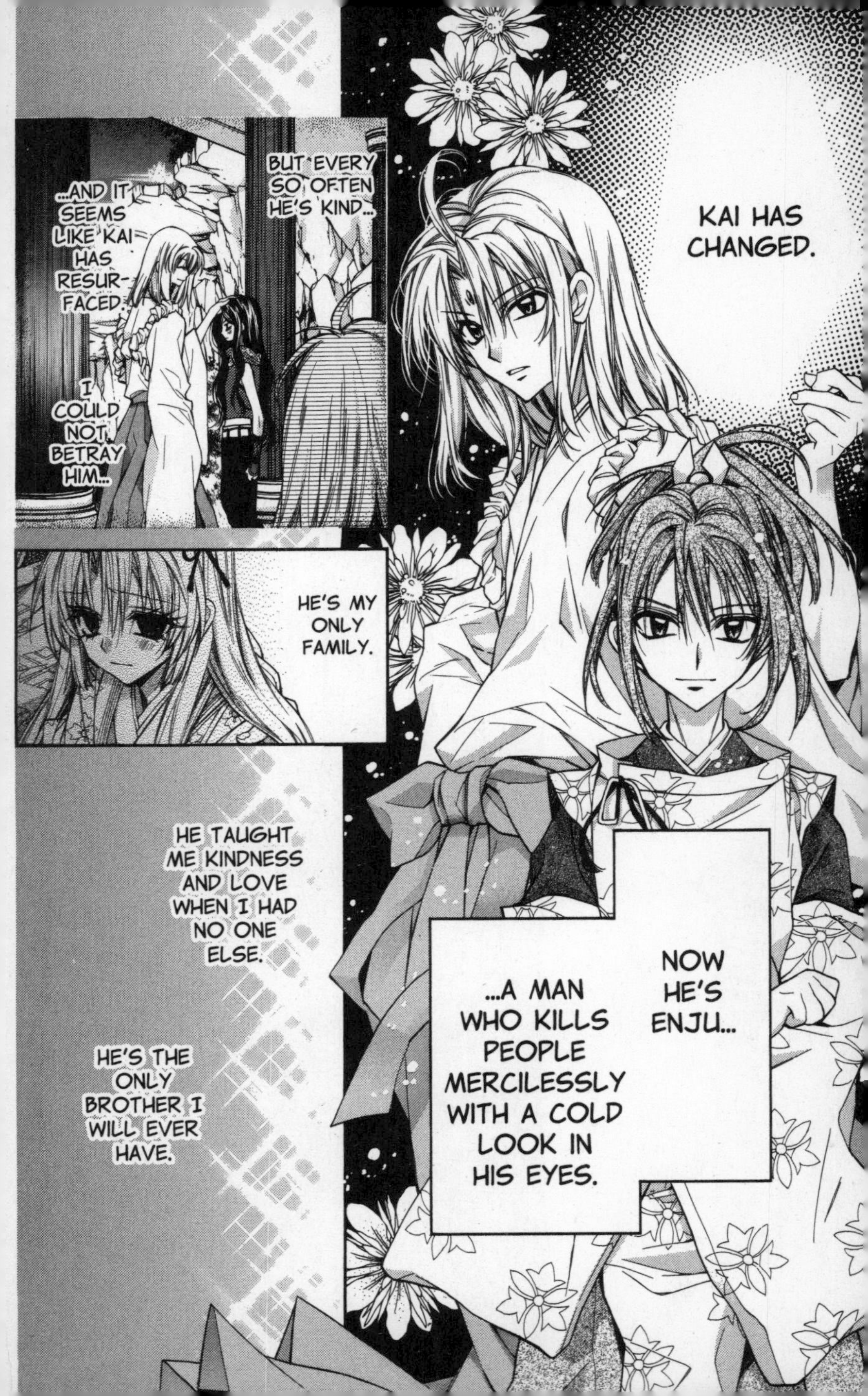
KAI HAS CHANGED.
NOW HE'S ENJU...
...A MAN WHO KILLS PEOPLE MERCILESSLY WITH A COLD LOOK IN HIS EYES.
BUT EVERY SO OFTEN HE'S KIND...
...AND IT SEEMS LIKE KAI HAS RESURFACED.
I COULD NOT BETRAY HIM...
HE'S MY ONLY FAMILY.
HE TAUGHT ME KINDNESS AND LOVE WHEN I HAD NO ONE ELSE.
HE'S THE ONLY BROTHER I WILL EVER HAVE.

Arina Tamemura Works Theme Song CD Production

Um, I am currently self-producing the "Manga Artist Arina Tanemura's 15th Anniversary Theme Songs CD."

I had music created for my manga series, and I wrote the lyrics for the songs.

Let me introduce the songs to you.

There is "Sakura Hime: The Legend of Princess Sakura" for this series.
You all know this one! This is my current series. It's cool Japanese rock music. The lyrics foreshadow what is to come in the story and... Oops.

"Pure Love☆Fortune" for *Mistress☆Fortune*
This is a song for *Mistress☆Fortune*, a three-chapter series. This one is very popular with my assistants. It's a cute, dreamy, and melodious song that sounds like an anime ending theme. I sing it in a slightly high-pitched voice.

"The Sleeping Princess in the Castle of Time" for *Time Stranger Kyoko*
This song is not directly connected to the work itself, and I created the lyrics from a story that came to my head when I listened to the music. Even the introduction is great.

"The Backlit Mademoiselle" for *Kamikaze Kaito Jeanne*
That's right. This for the renowned (?) *Jeanne*. It's a really cool song! I worked hard to sing in a low voice.
Overall it sounded like something a man would sing, so the lyrics were written in Chiaki's point of view.

Continues →

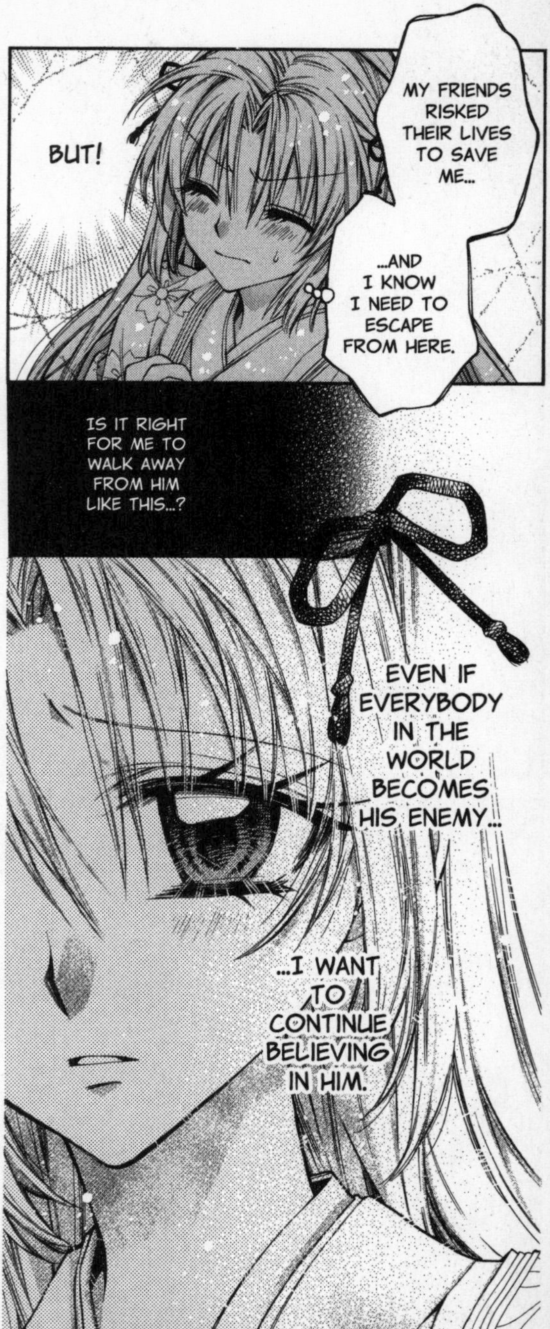
MY FRIENDS RISKED THEIR LIVES TO SAVE ME...
...AND I KNOW I NEED TO ESCAPE FROM HERE.
BUT!
IS IT RIGHT FOR ME TO WALK AWAY FROM HIM LIKE THIS...?
EVEN IF EVERYBODY IN THE WORLD BECOMES HIS ENEMY...
...I WANT TO CONTINUE BELIEVING IN HIM.

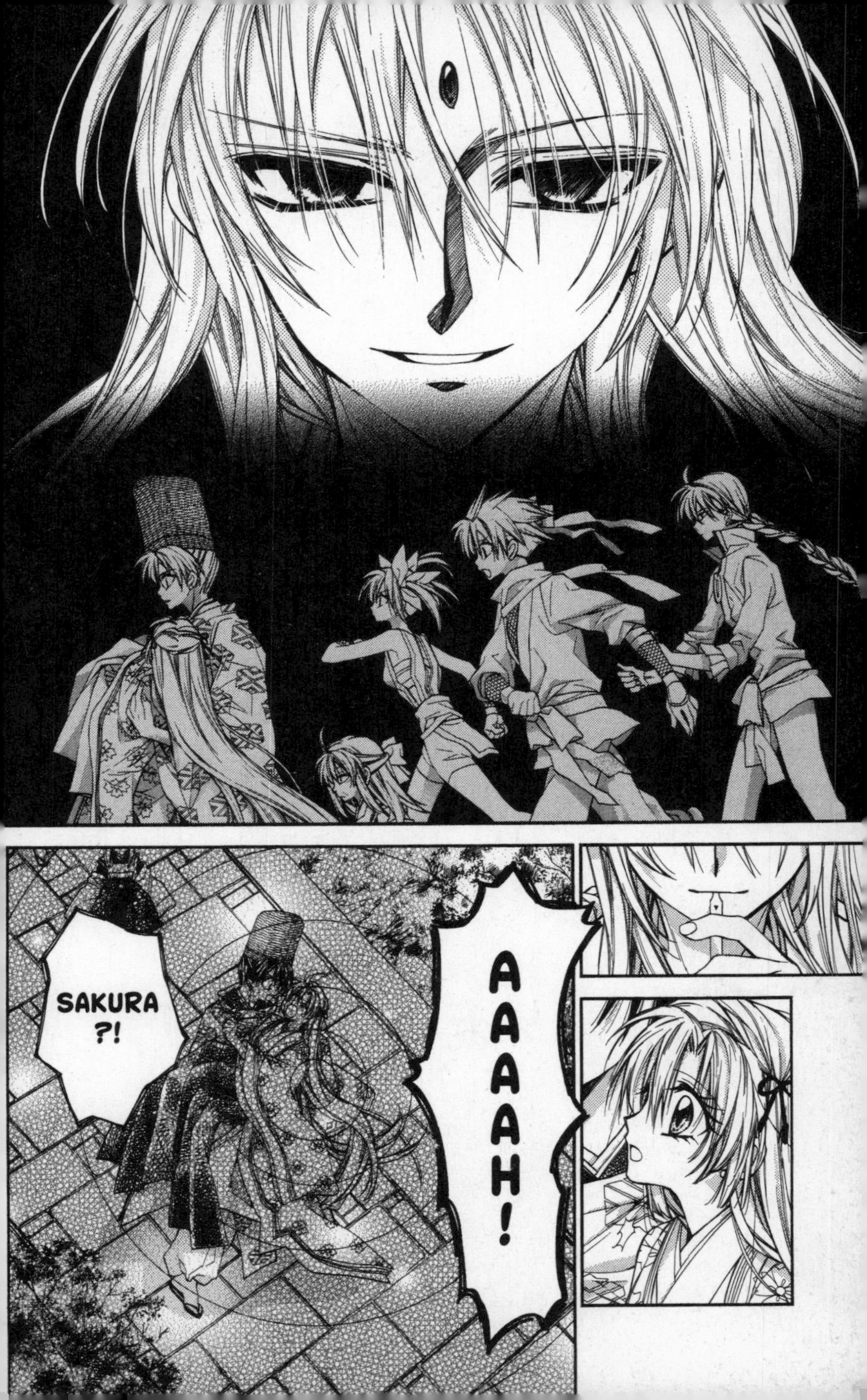
AAAAAH!
SAKURA ?!

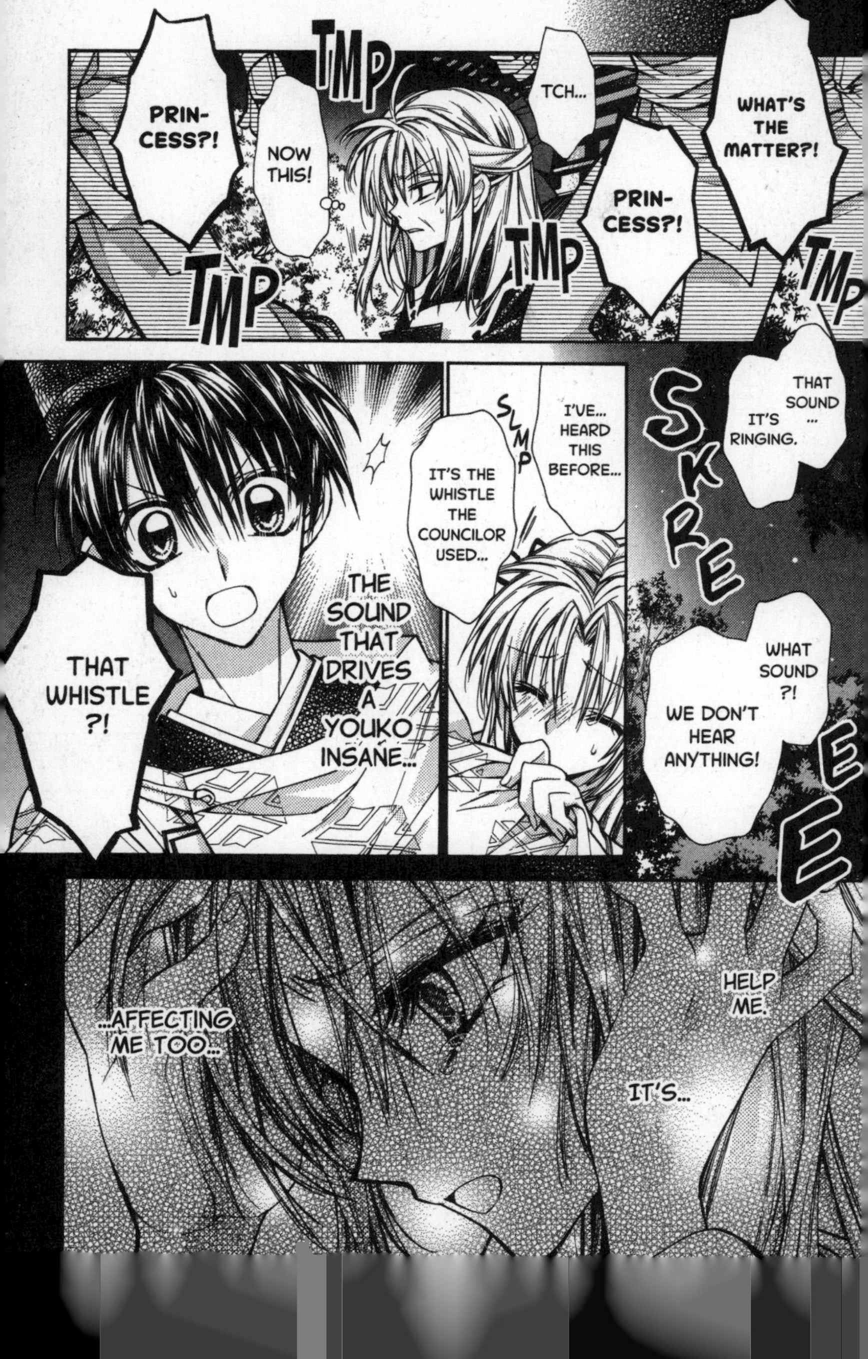
WHAT'S THE MATTER?!
TMP
PRIN-CESS?!
TMP
TCH...
TMP
NOW THIS!
TMP
PRIN-CESS?!
THAT SOUND... IT'S RINGING.
SKREEEE
WHAT SOUND?!
WE DON'T HEAR ANYTHING!
I'VE... HEARD THIS BEFORE...
SLMP
IT'S THE WHISTLE THE COUNCILOR USED...
THE SOUND THAT DRIVES A YOUKO INSANE...
THAT WHISTLE?!
HELP ME.
IT'S...
...AFFECTING ME TOO...

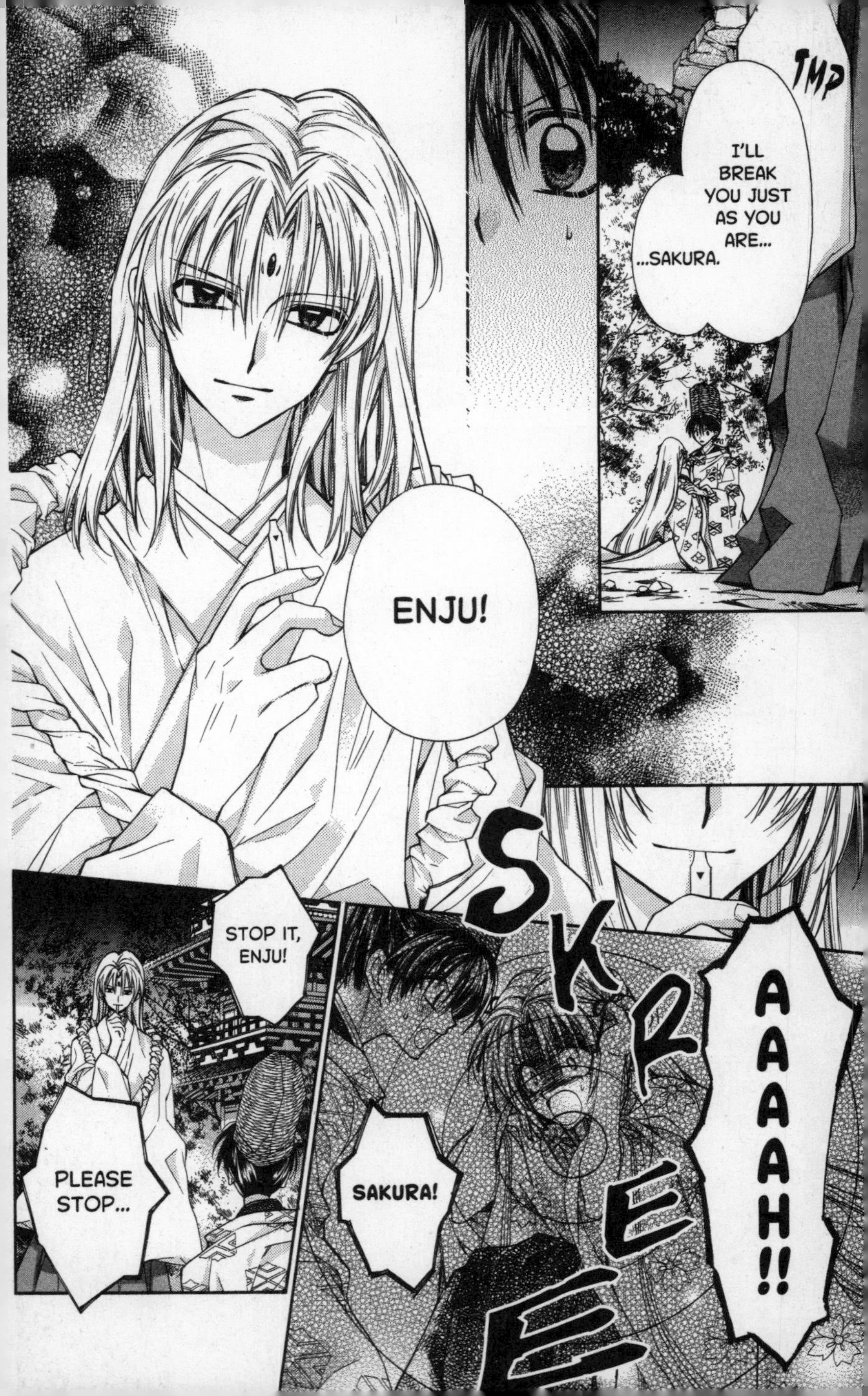
TMP
I'LL BREAK YOU JUST AS YOU ARE... ...SAKURA.
ENJU!
AAAAAH!!
SKREEE
SAKURA!
STOP IT, ENJU!
PLEASE STOP...

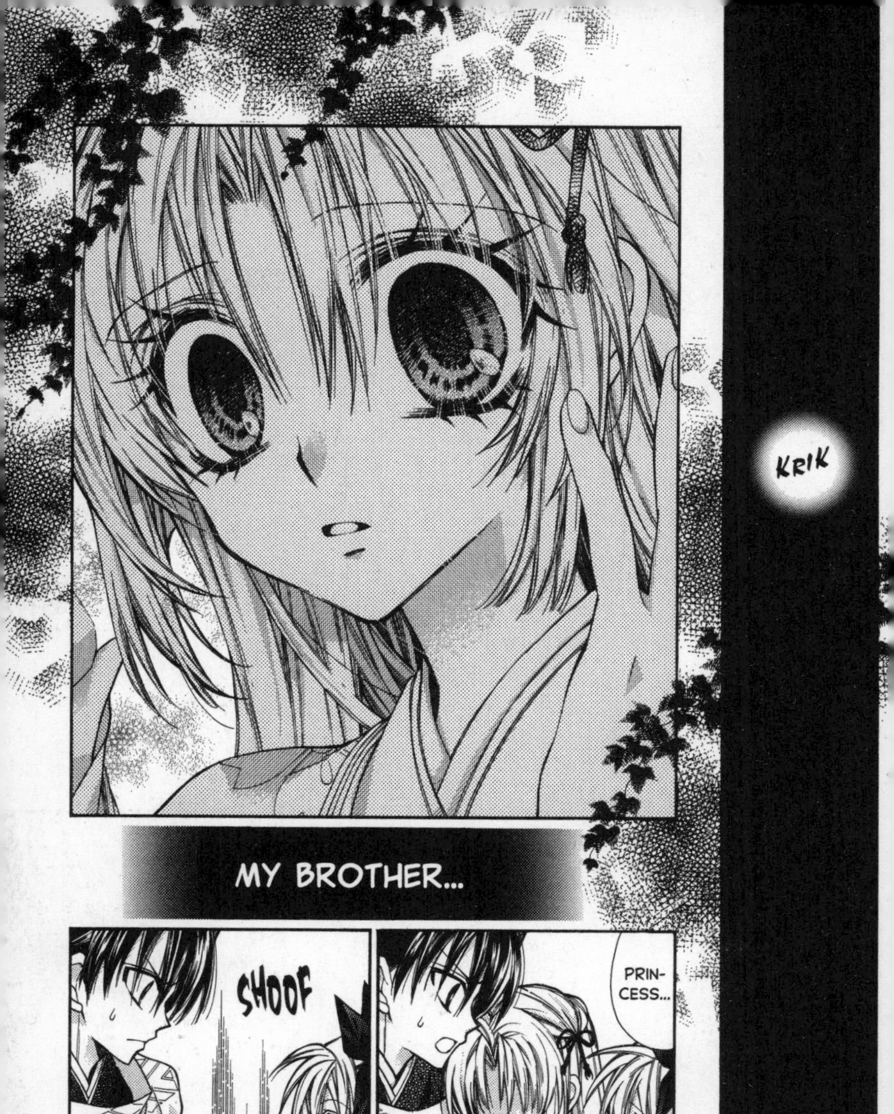
KRIK
MY BROTHER...
PRIN-CESS...
SAKURA?
SHOOF
?!

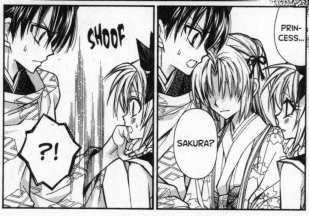

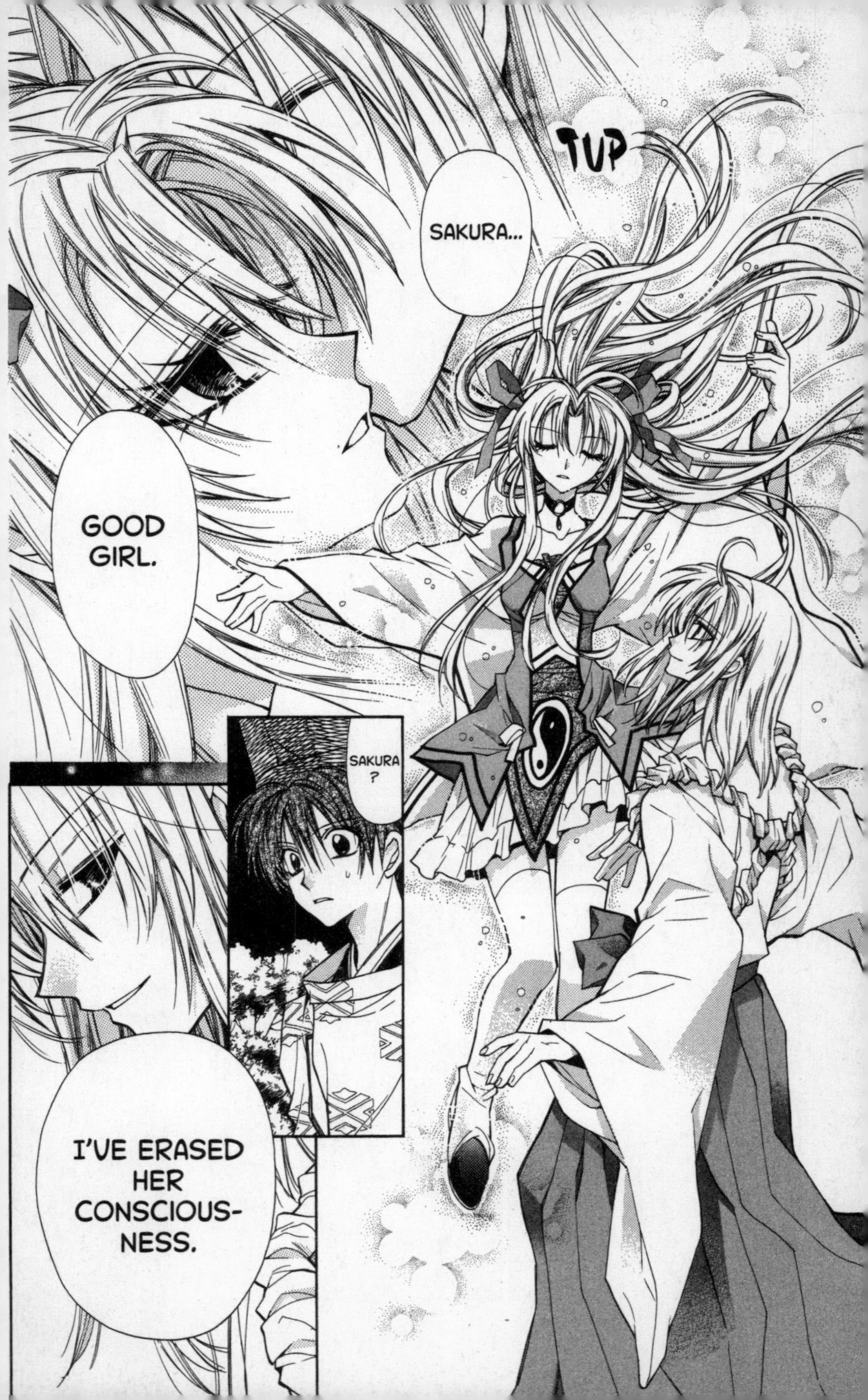
TUP
SAKURA...
GOOD GIRL.
SAKURA ?
I'VE ERASED HER CONSCIOUSNESS.

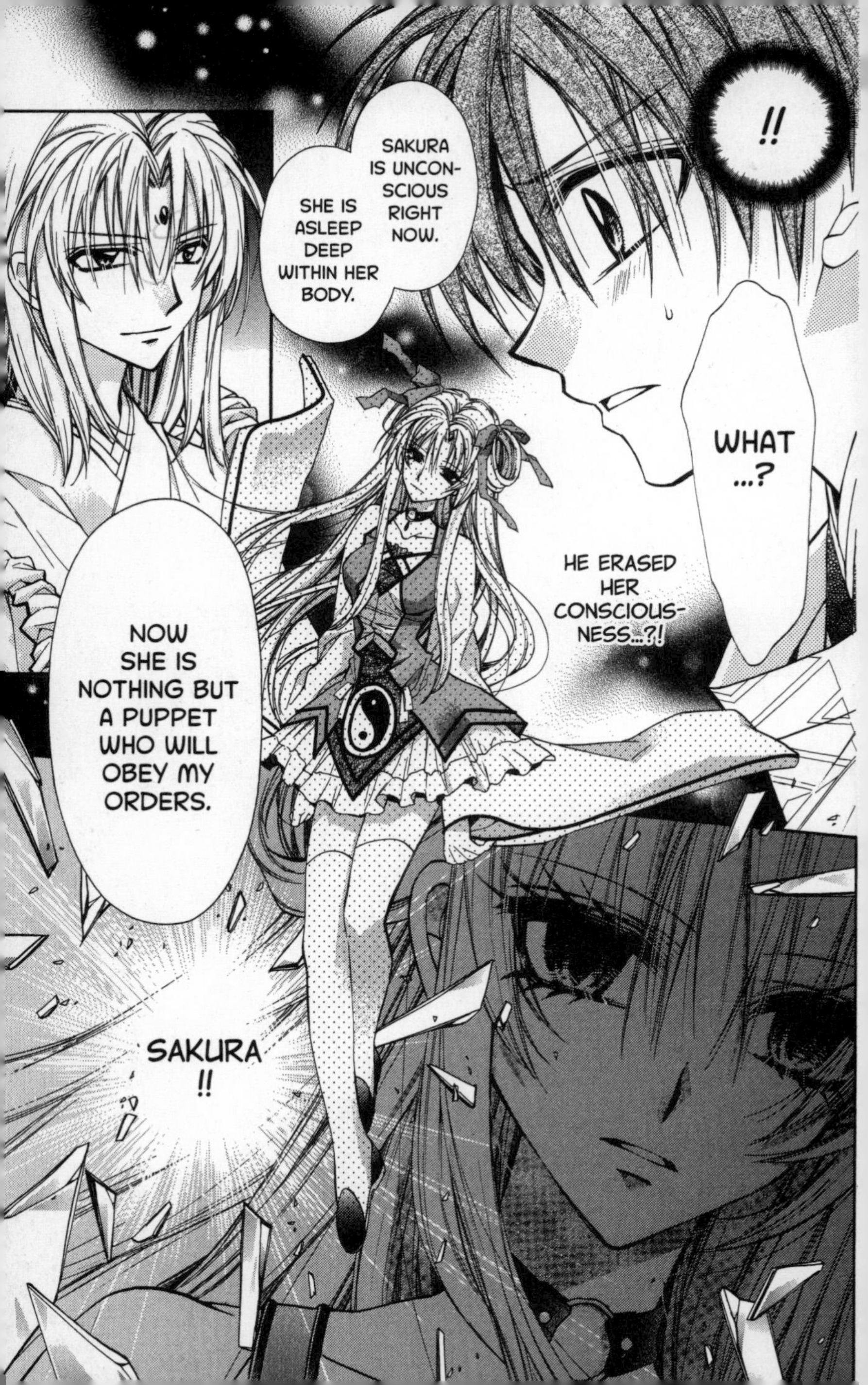
SAKURA IS UNCONSCIOUS RIGHT NOW.
SHE IS ASLEEP DEEP WITHIN HER BODY.
!!
WHAT ...?
HE ERASED HER CONSCIOUSNESS...?!
NOW SHE IS NOTHING BUT A PUPPET WHO WILL OBEY MY ORDERS.
SAKURA !!

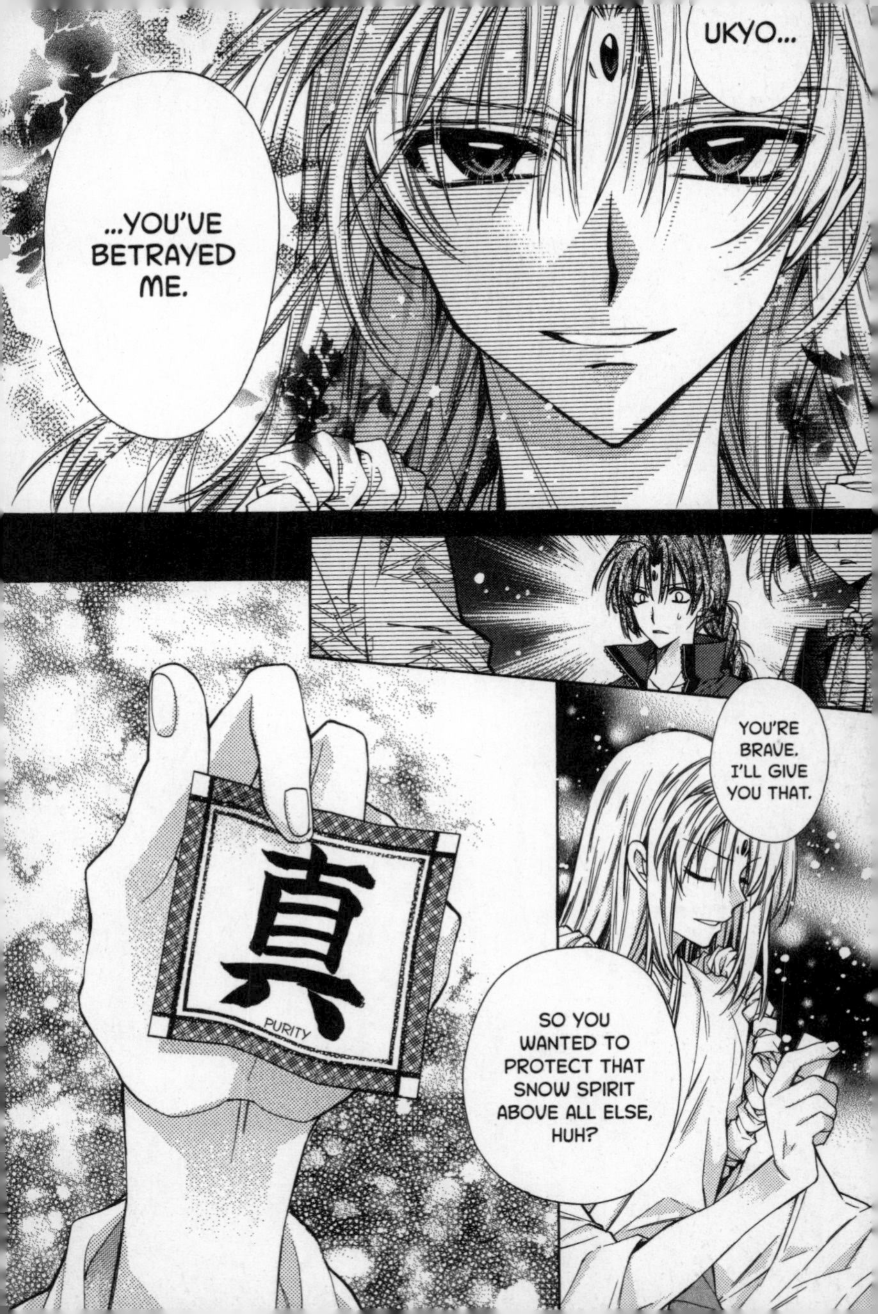
UKYO...
...YOU'VE BETRAYED ME.
YOU'RE BRAVE. I'LL GIVE YOU THAT.
SO YOU WANTED TO PROTECT THAT SNOW SPIRIT ABOVE ALL ELSE, HUH?
真
PURITY

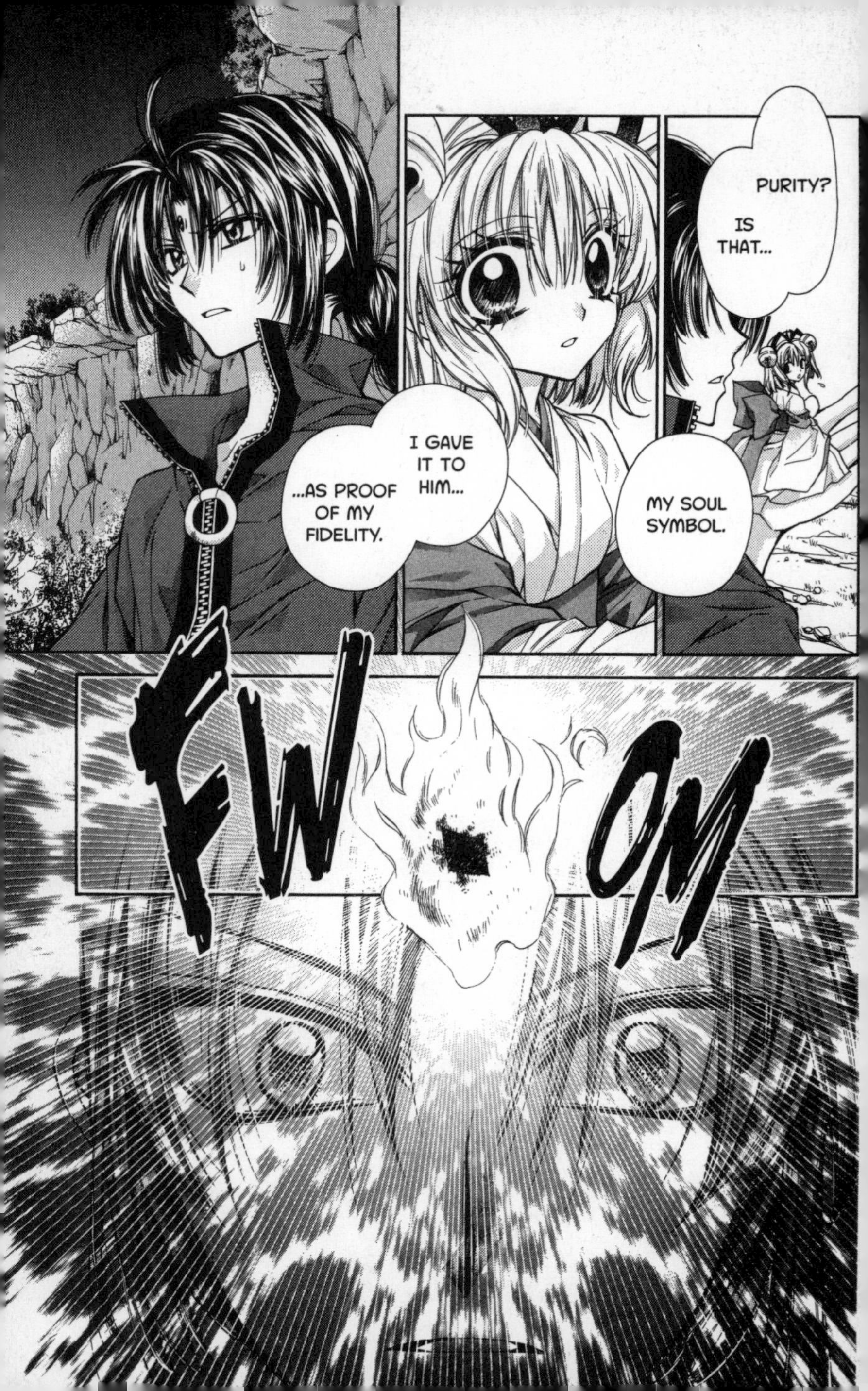
PURITY? IS THAT...
MY SOUL SYMBOL.
I GAVE IT TO HIM...
...AS PROOF OF MY FIDELITY.
FWOOM

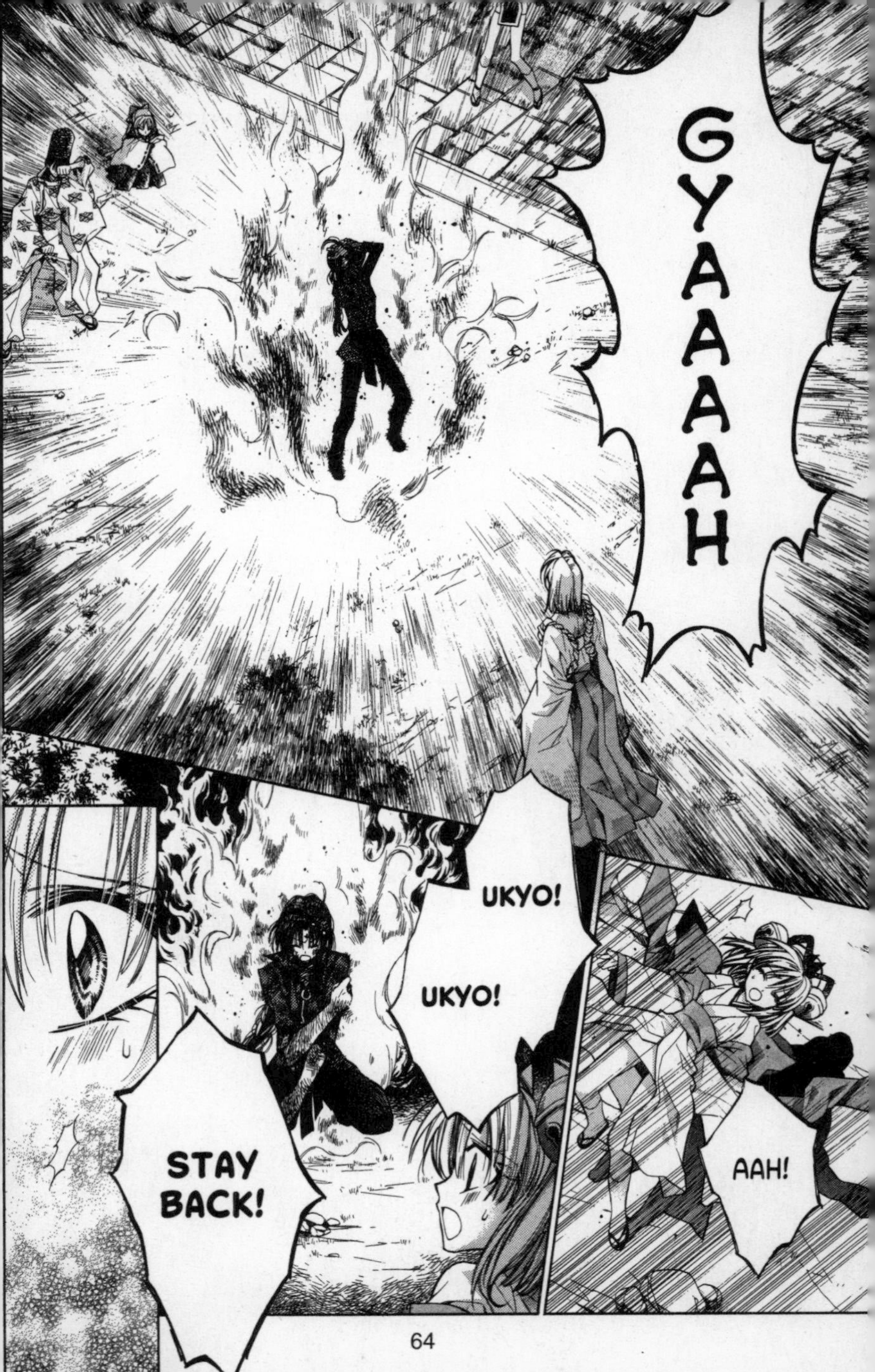
GYAAAAH
AAH!
UKYO!
UKYO!
STAY BACK!

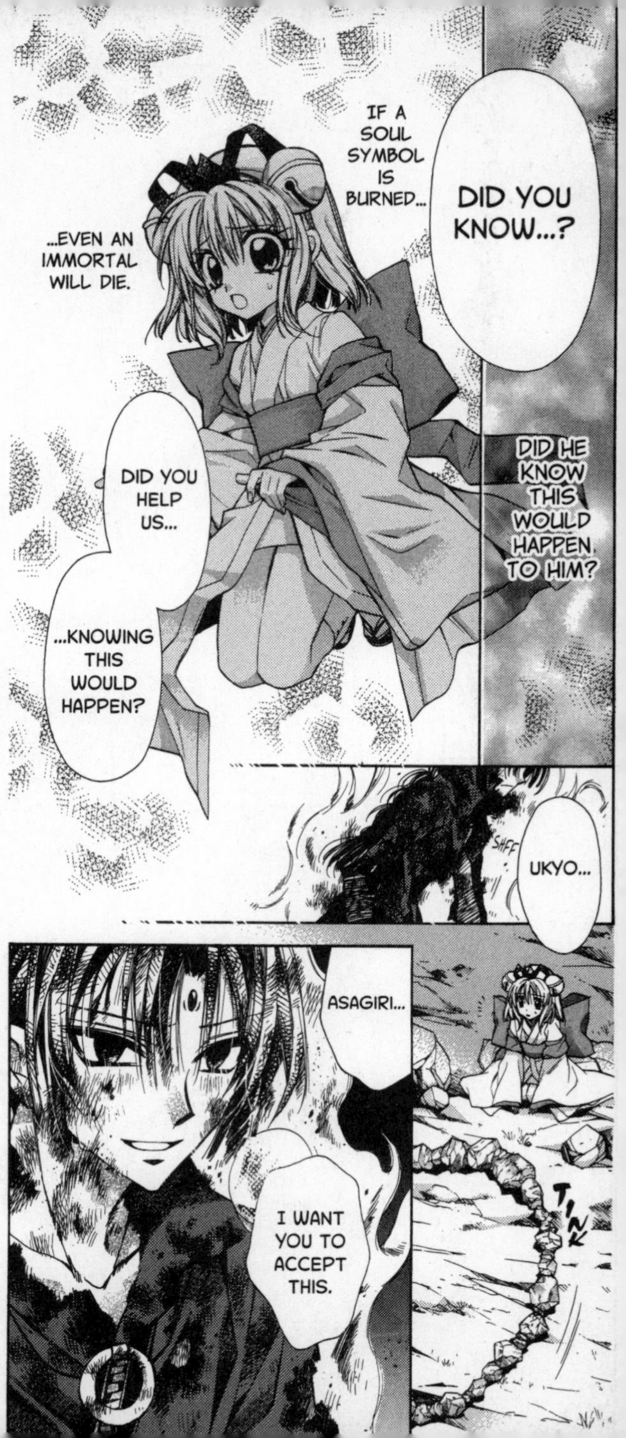
DID YOU KNOW...?
IF A SOUL SYMBOL IS BURNED...
...EVEN AN IMMORTAL WILL DIE.
DID HE KNOW THIS WOULD HAPPEN TO HIM?
DID YOU HELP US...
...KNOWING THIS WOULD HAPPEN?
SHFF
UKYO...
TINK
ASAGIRI...
I WANT YOU TO ACCEPT THIS.

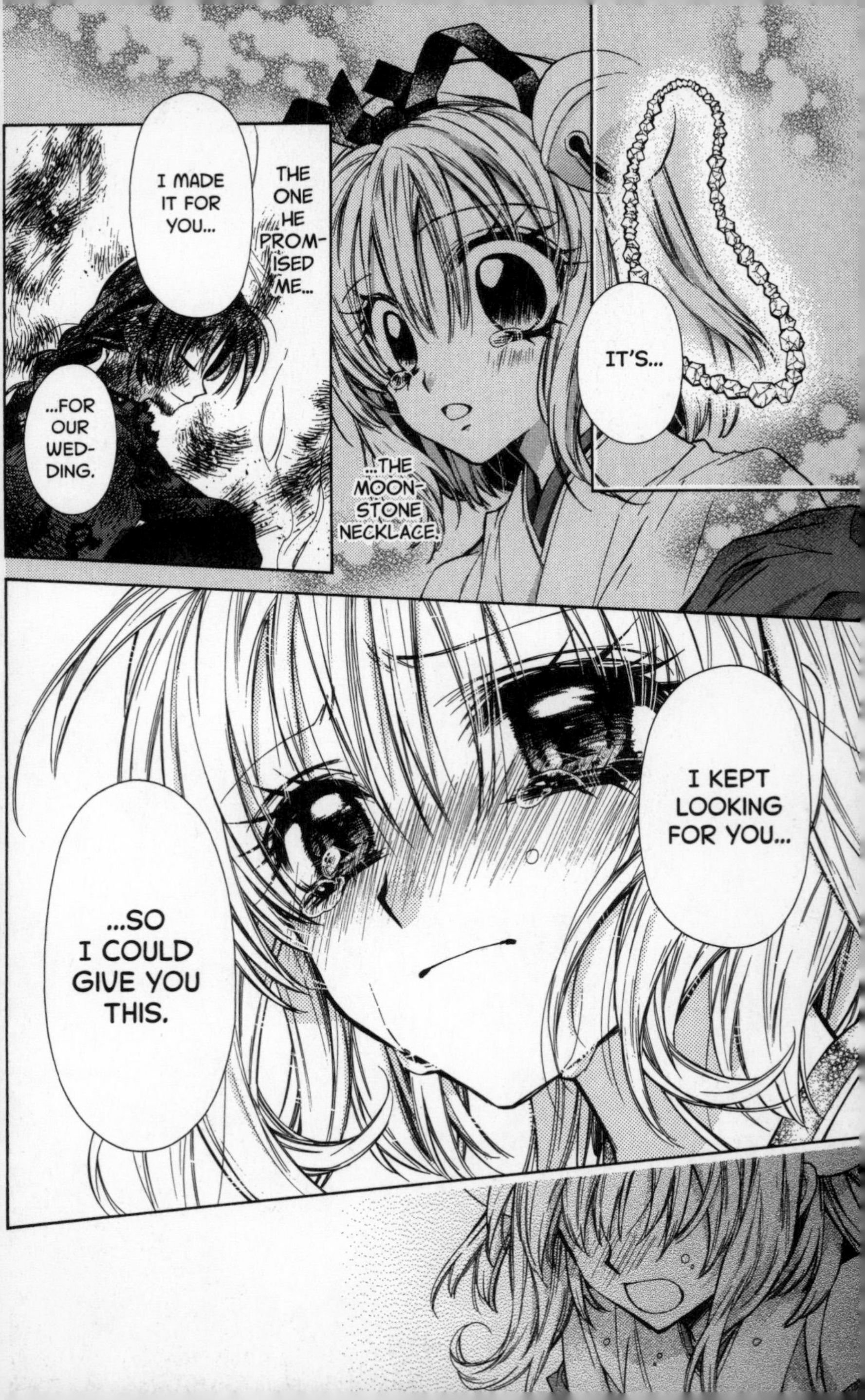
IT'S...
...THE MOON-STONE NECKLACE.
THE ONE HE PROM-ISED ME...
I MADE IT FOR YOU...
...FOR OUR WED-DING.
I KEPT LOOKING FOR YOU...
...SO I COULD GIVE YOU THIS.

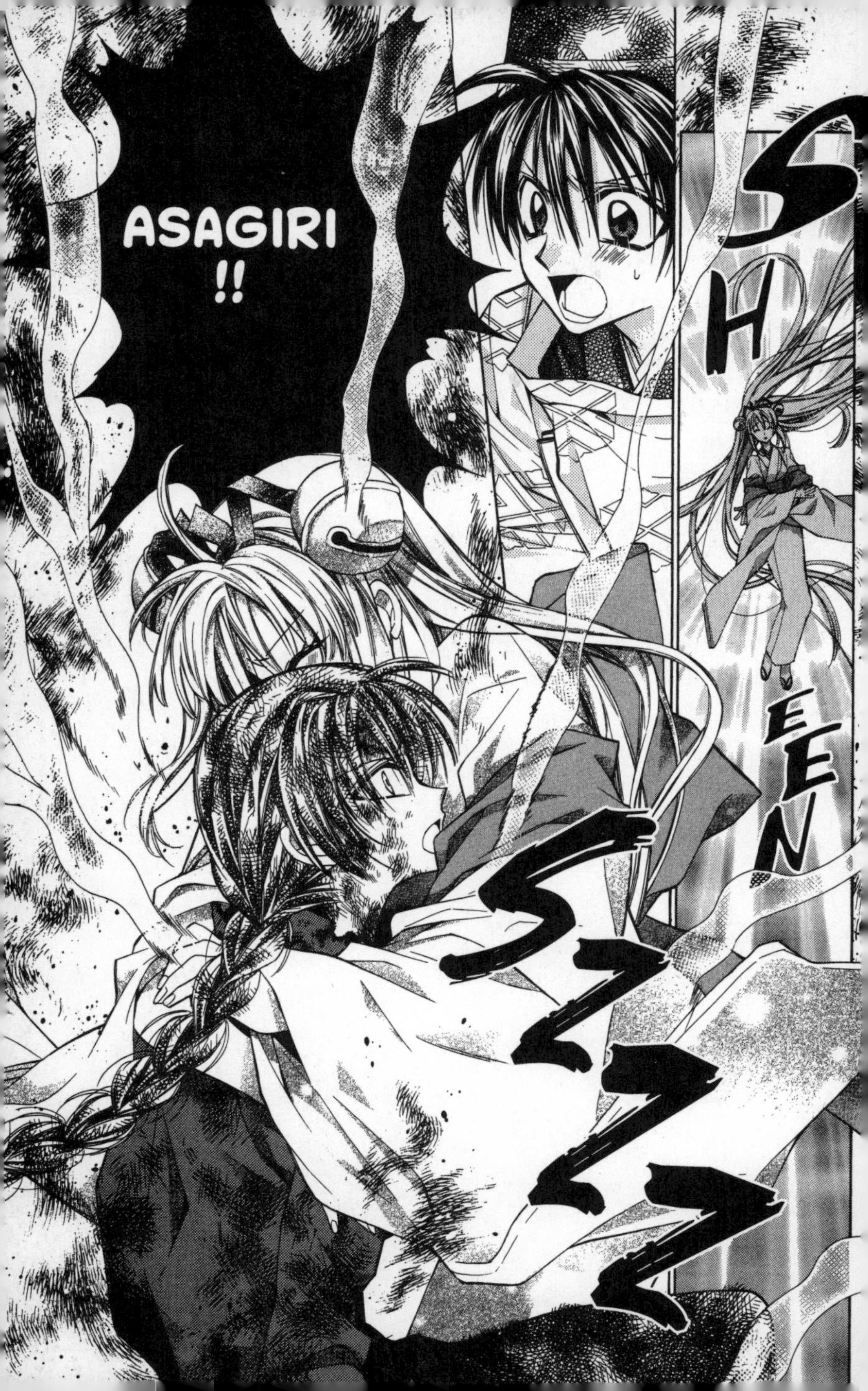
SHEEN
ASAGIRI !!
SSSS

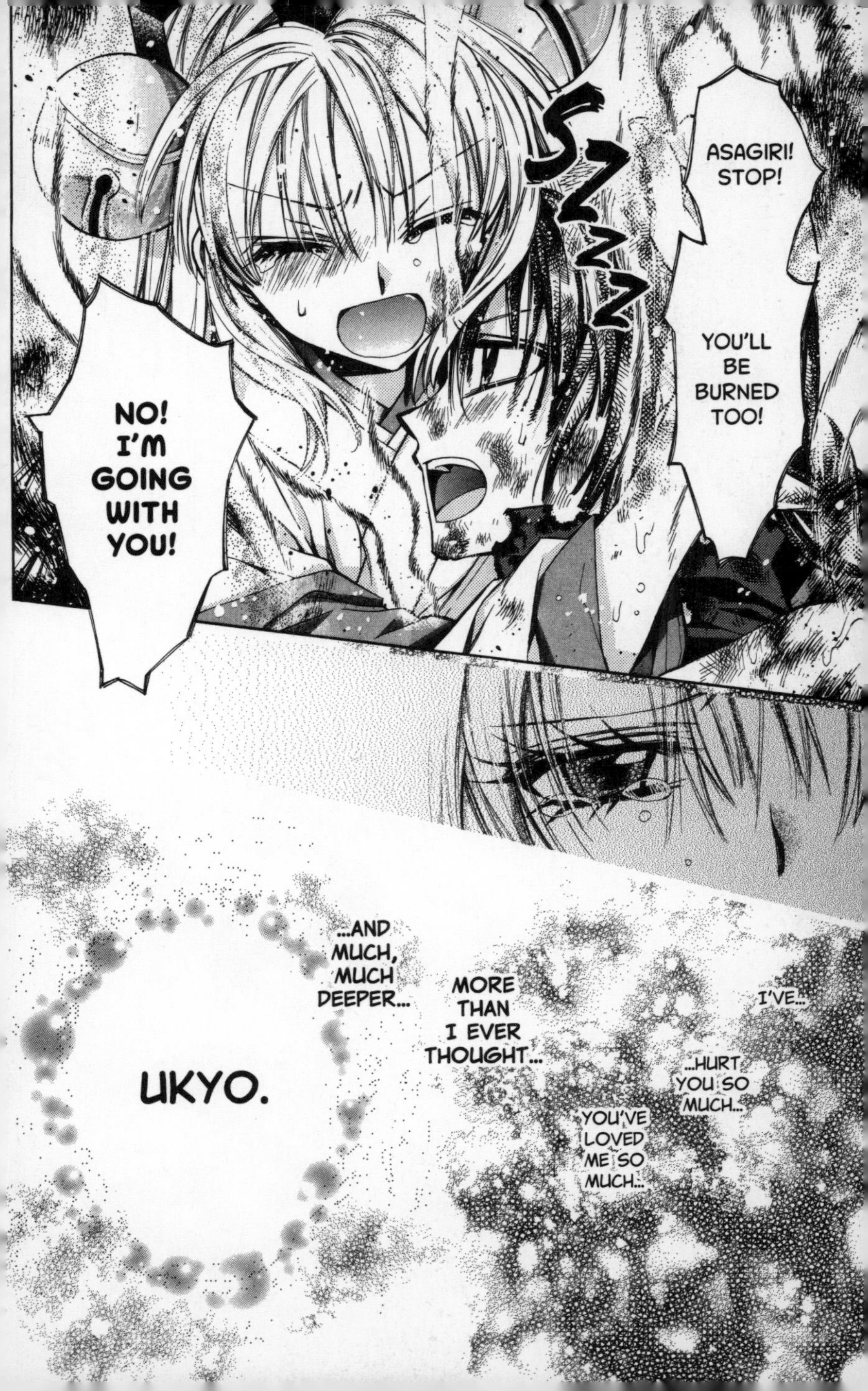
ASAGIRI! STOP!
YOU'LL BE BURNED TOO!
SZZZ
NO! I'M GOING WITH YOU!
I'VE...
...HURT YOU SO MUCH...
YOU'VE LOVED ME SO MUCH...
MORE THAN I EVER THOUGHT...
...AND MUCH, MUCH DEEPER...
UKYO.

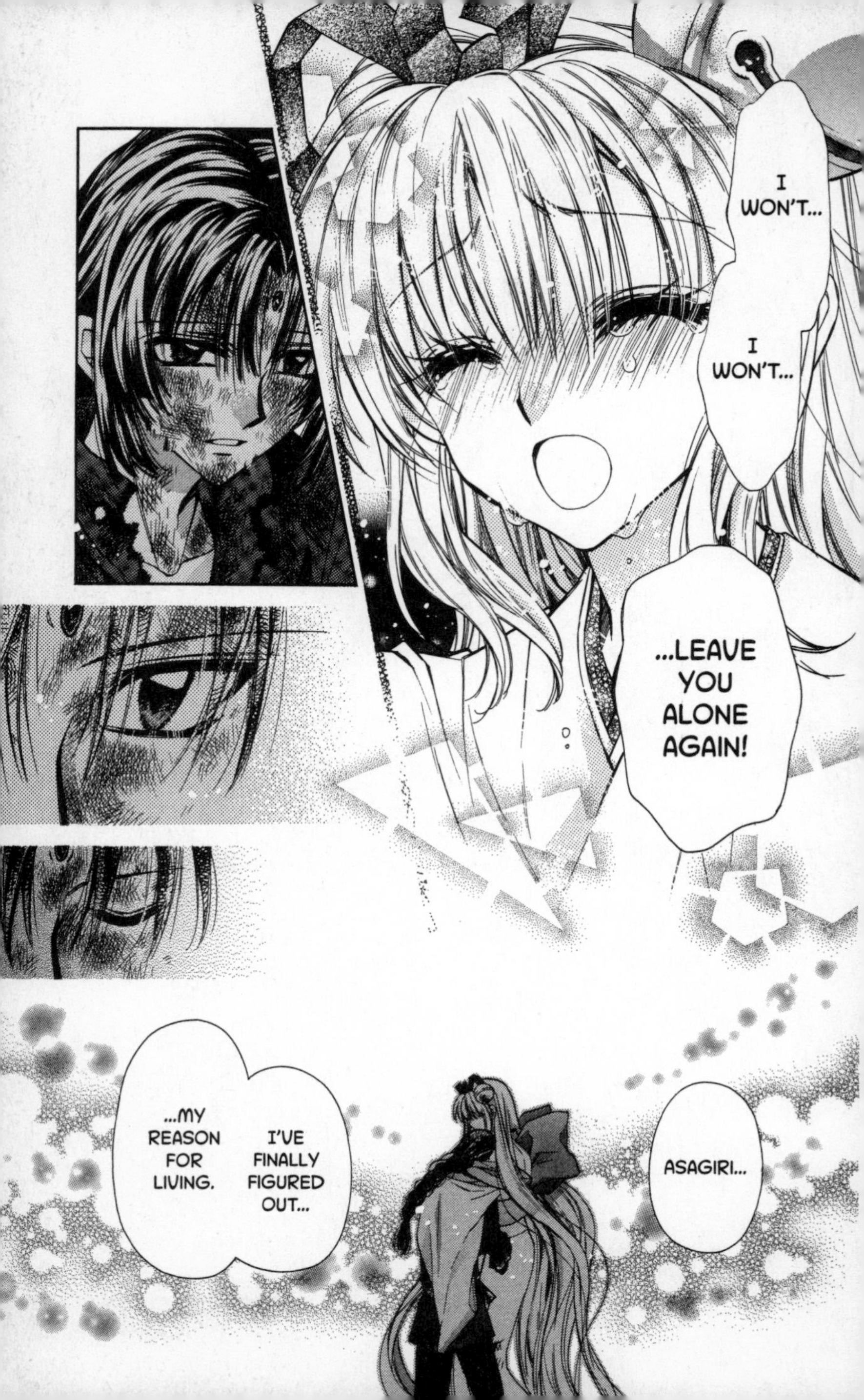
I WON'T...
I WON'T...
...LEAVE YOU ALONE AGAIN!
ASAGIRI...
I'VE FINALLY FIGURED OUT...
...MY REASON FOR LIVING.

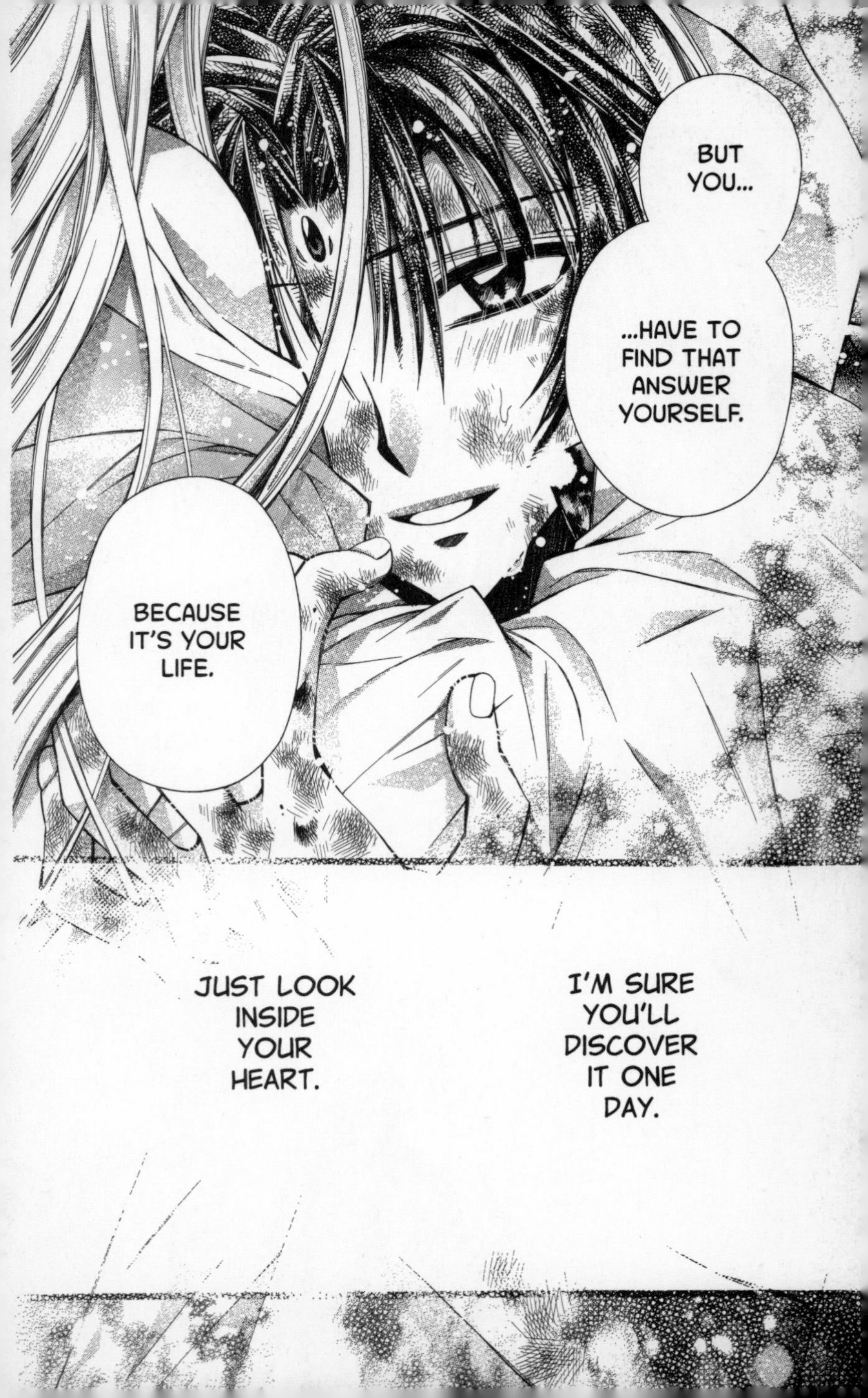
BUT YOU...
...HAVE TO FIND THAT ANSWER YOURSELF.
BECAUSE IT'S YOUR LIFE.
I'M SURE YOU'LL DISCOVER IT ONE DAY.
JUST LOOK INSIDE YOUR HEART.

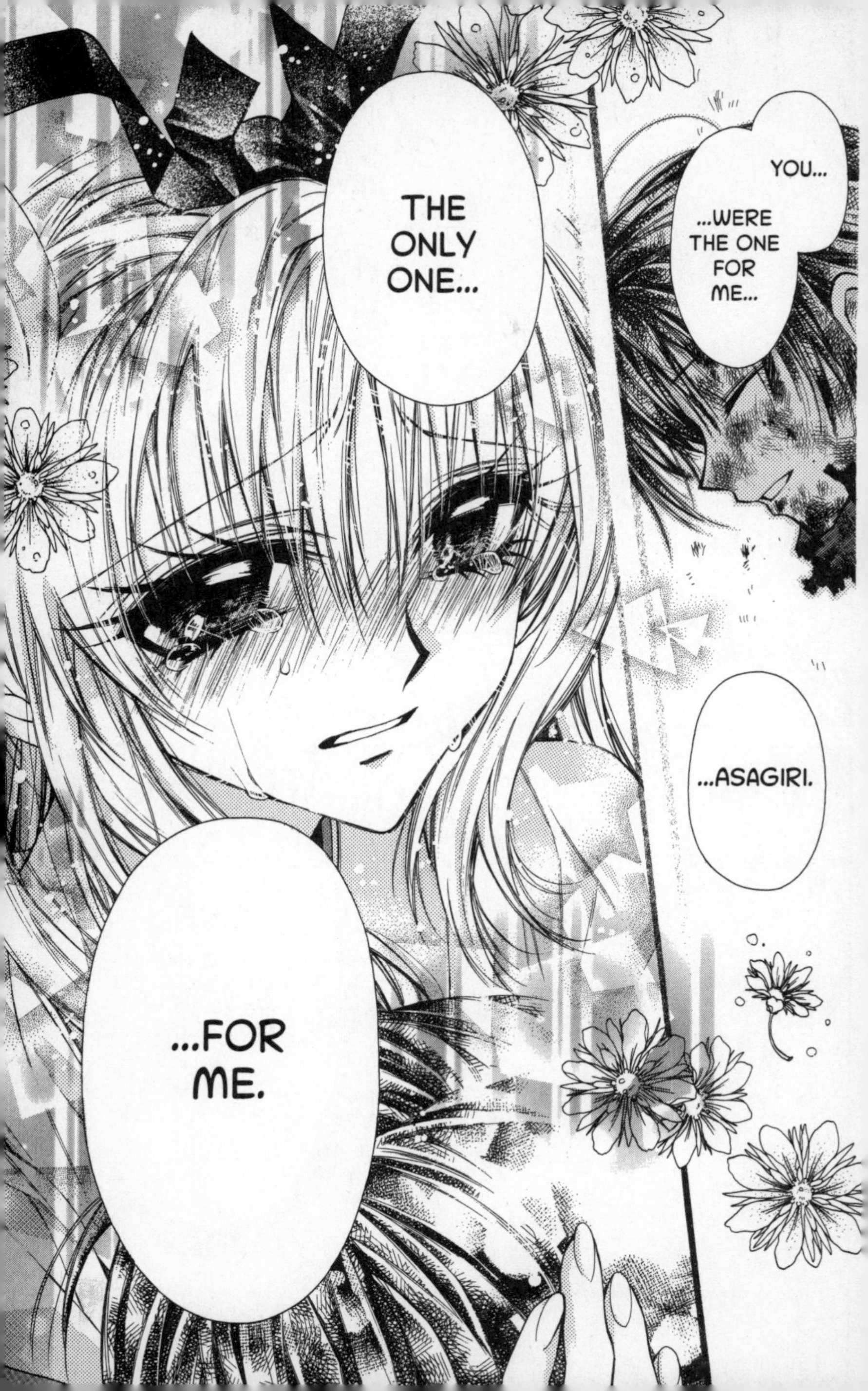
YOU... ...WERE THE ONE FOR ME...
...ASAGIRI.
THE ONLY ONE...
...FOR ME.

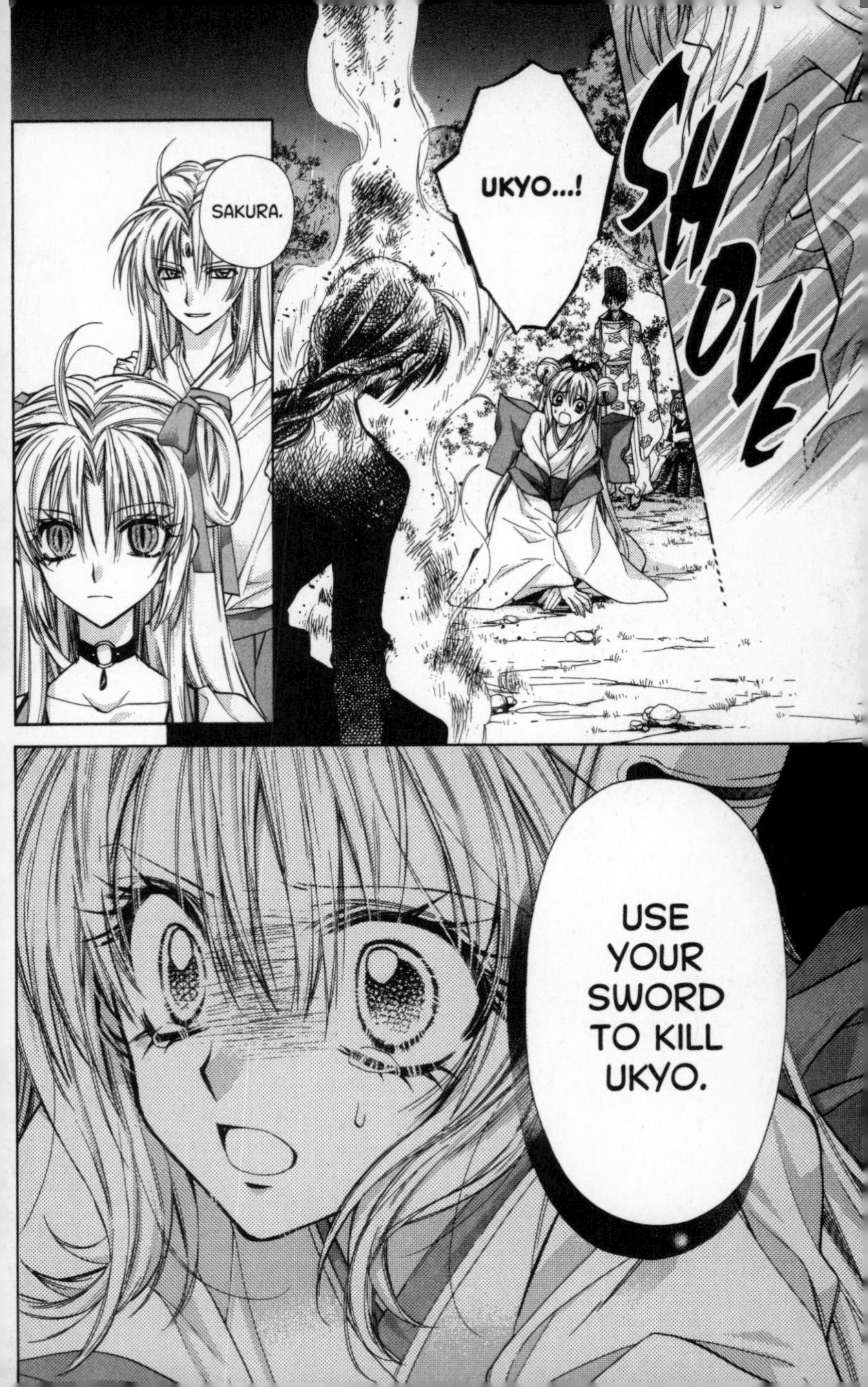
SHOVE
UKYO...!
SAKURA.
USE YOUR SWORD TO KILL UKYO.

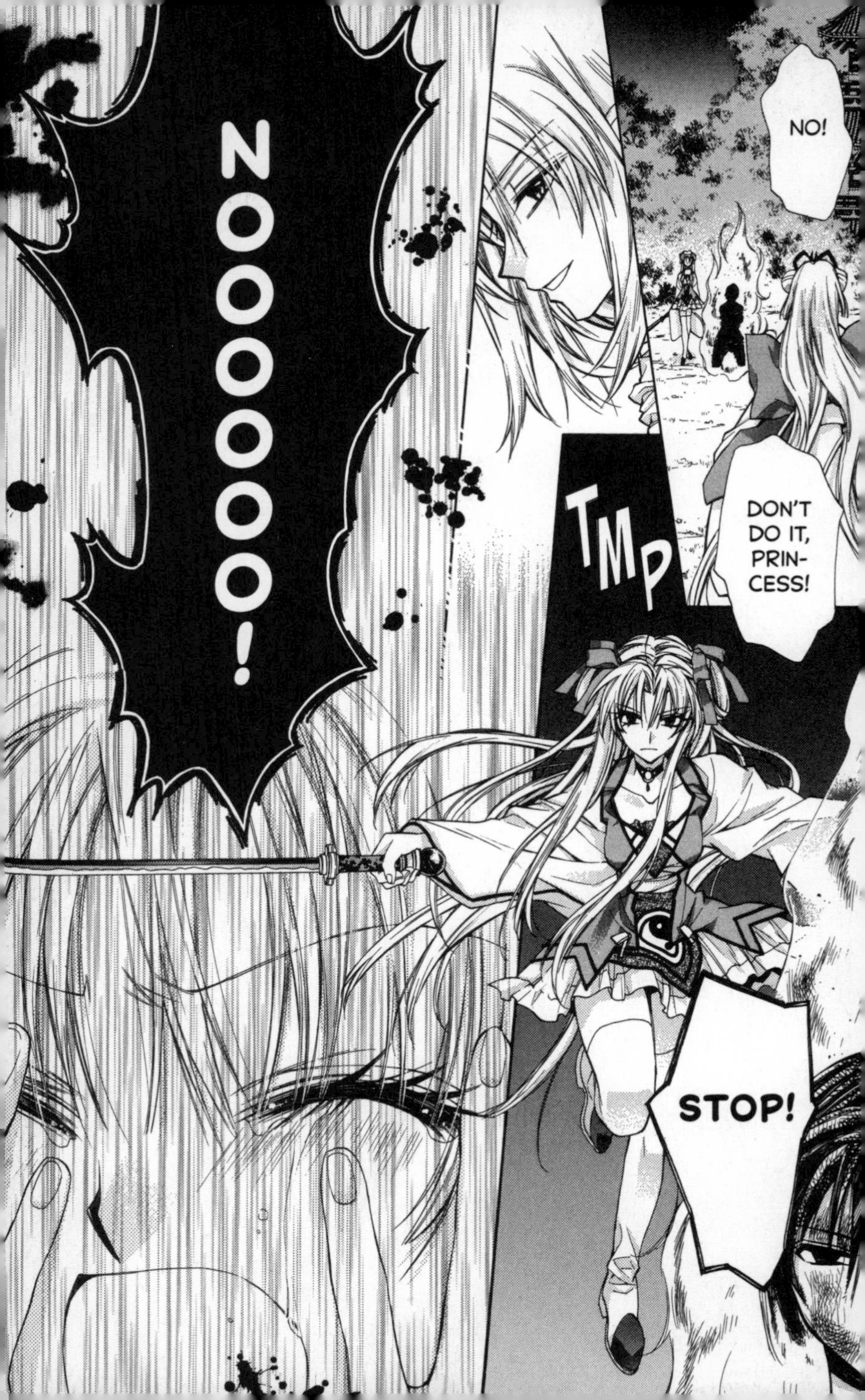
NO!
DON'T DO IT, PRINCESS!
TMP
STOP!
NOOOOOO!

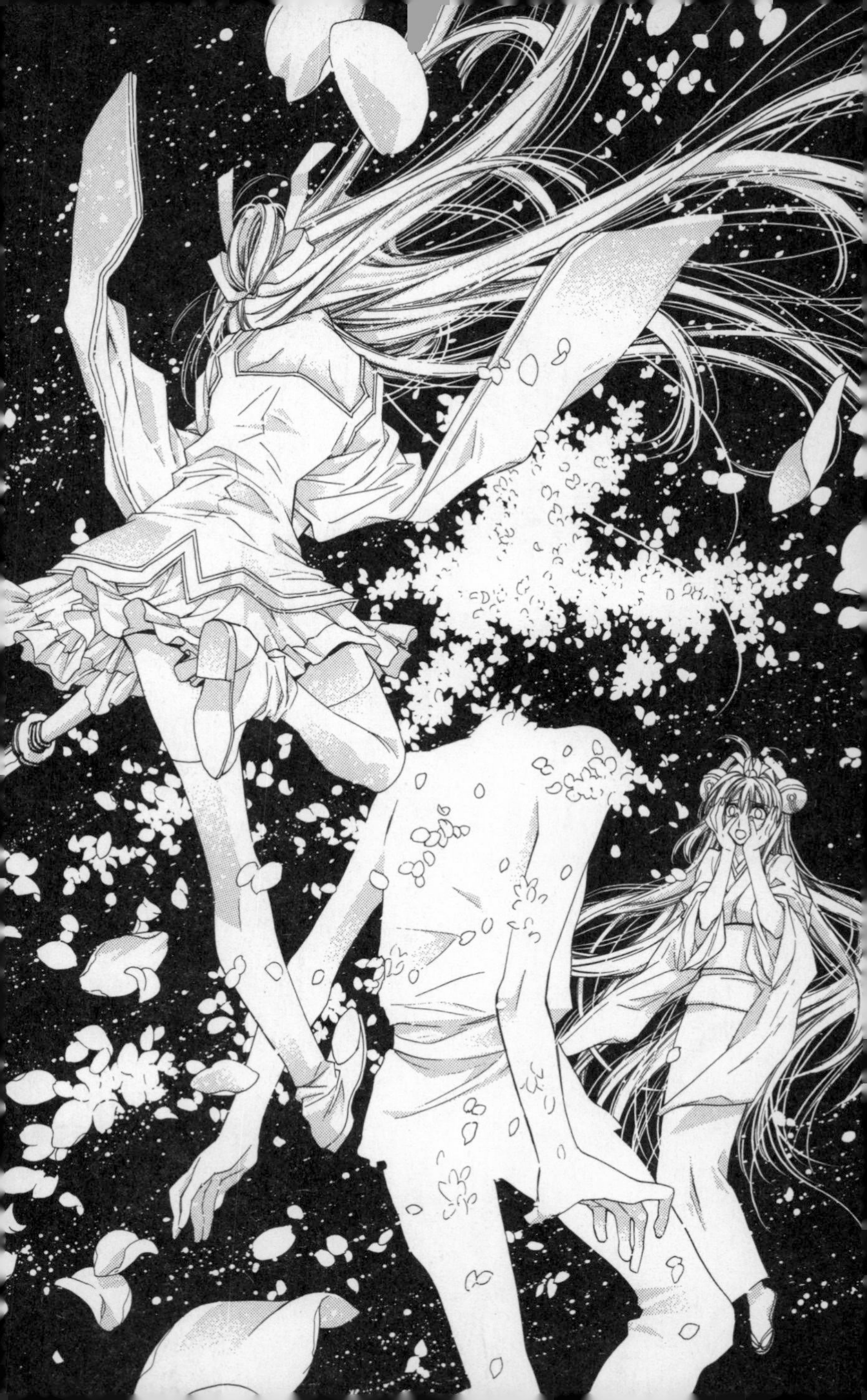

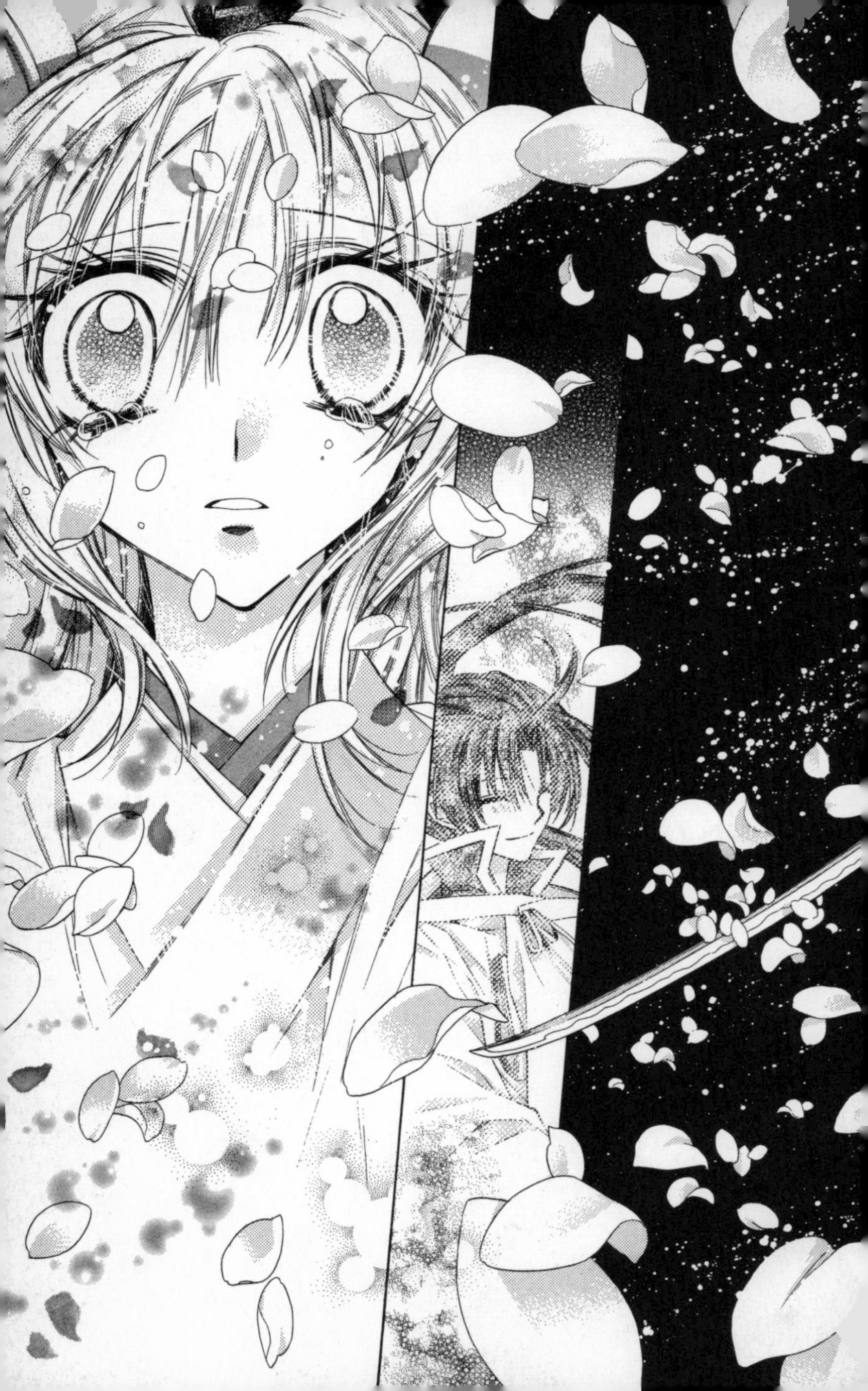

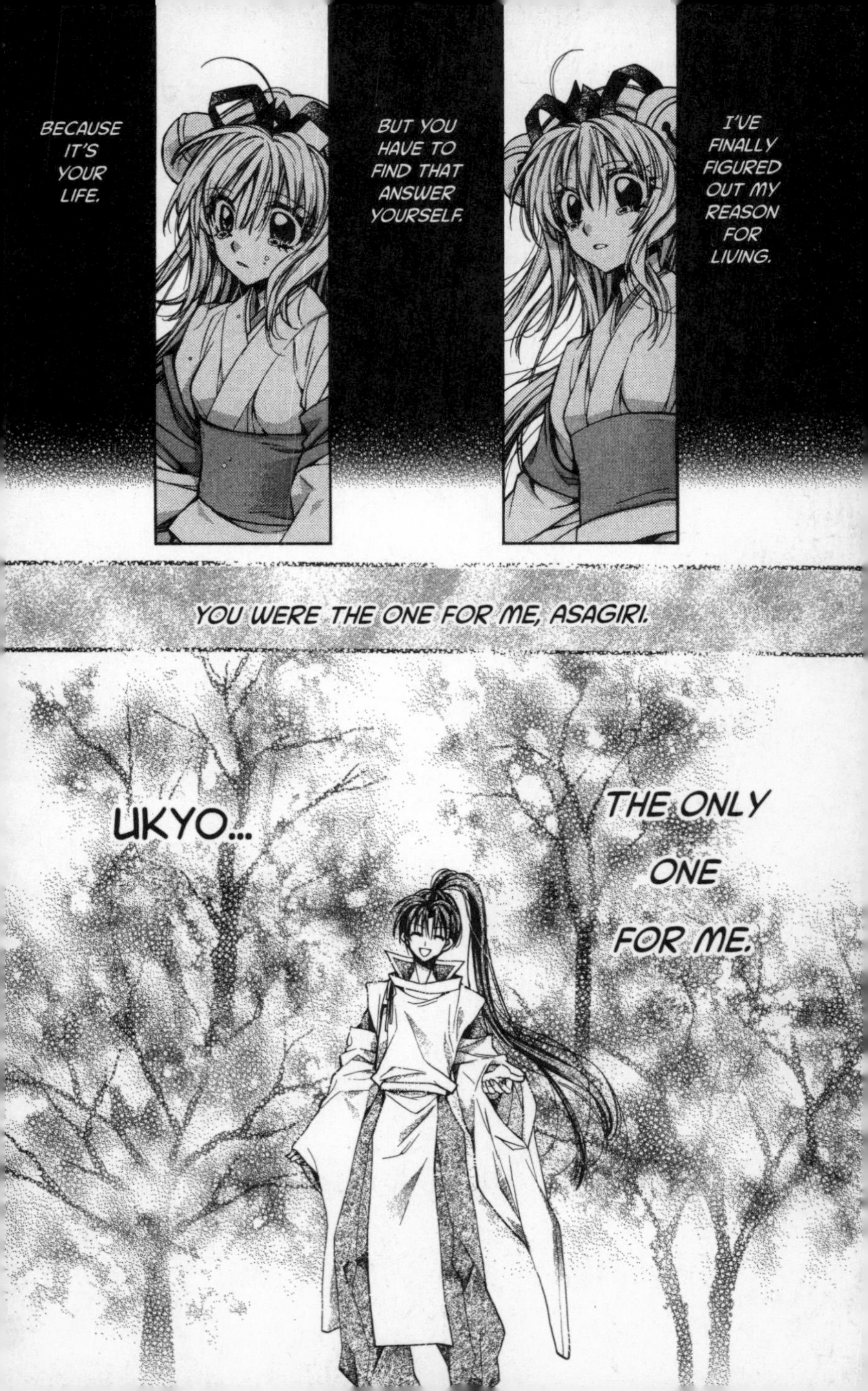

I'VE FINALLY FIGURED OUT MY REASON FOR LIVING.
BUT YOU HAVE TO FIND THAT ANSWER YOURSELF.
BECAUSE IT'S YOUR LIFE.
YOU WERE THE ONE FOR ME, ASAGIRI.
THE ONLY ONE FOR ME.
UKYO...

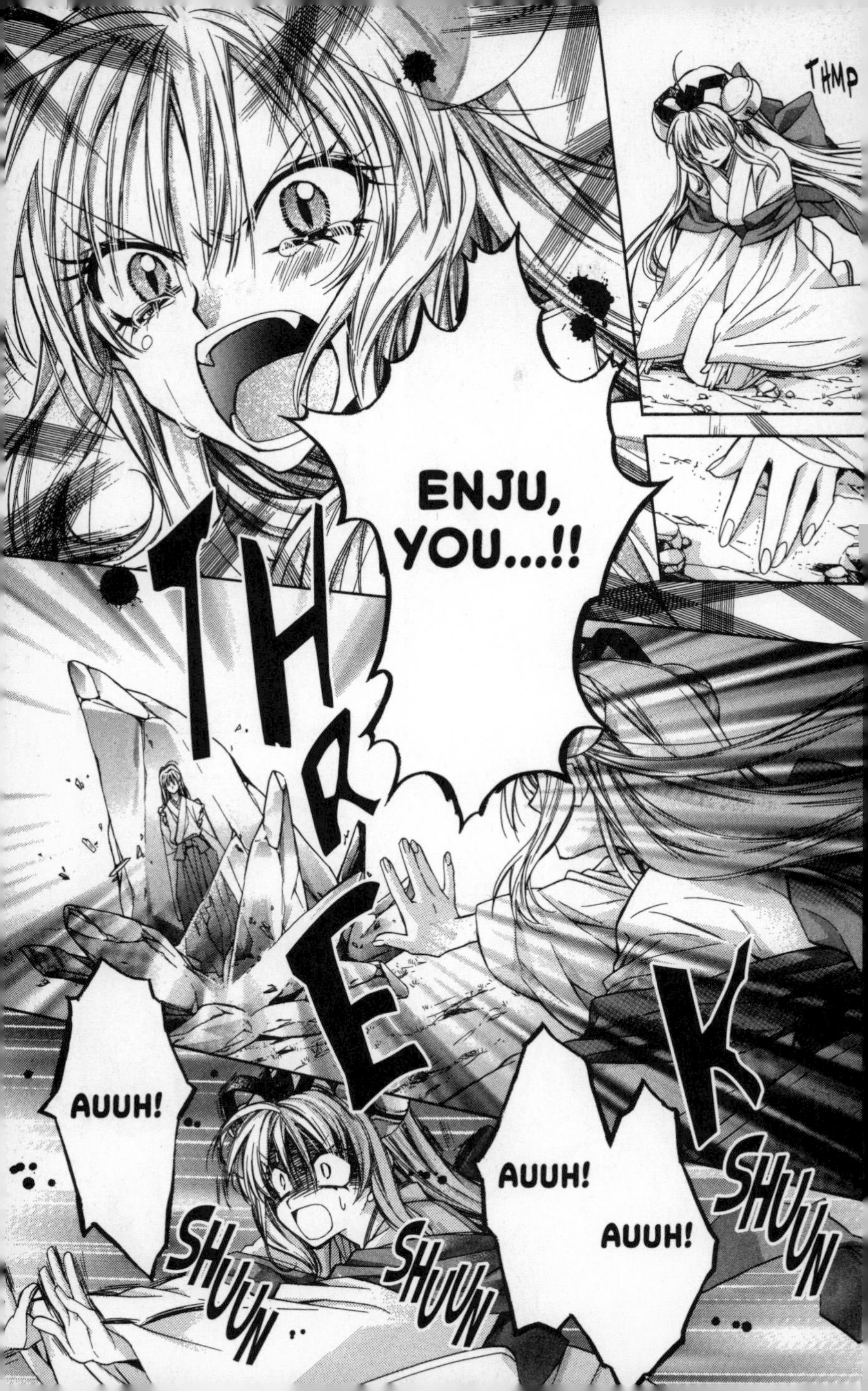
THMP
ENJU, YOU...!!
THREEK
AUUH!
AUUH!
SHUUUN
AUUH!
SHUUUN
SHUUUN

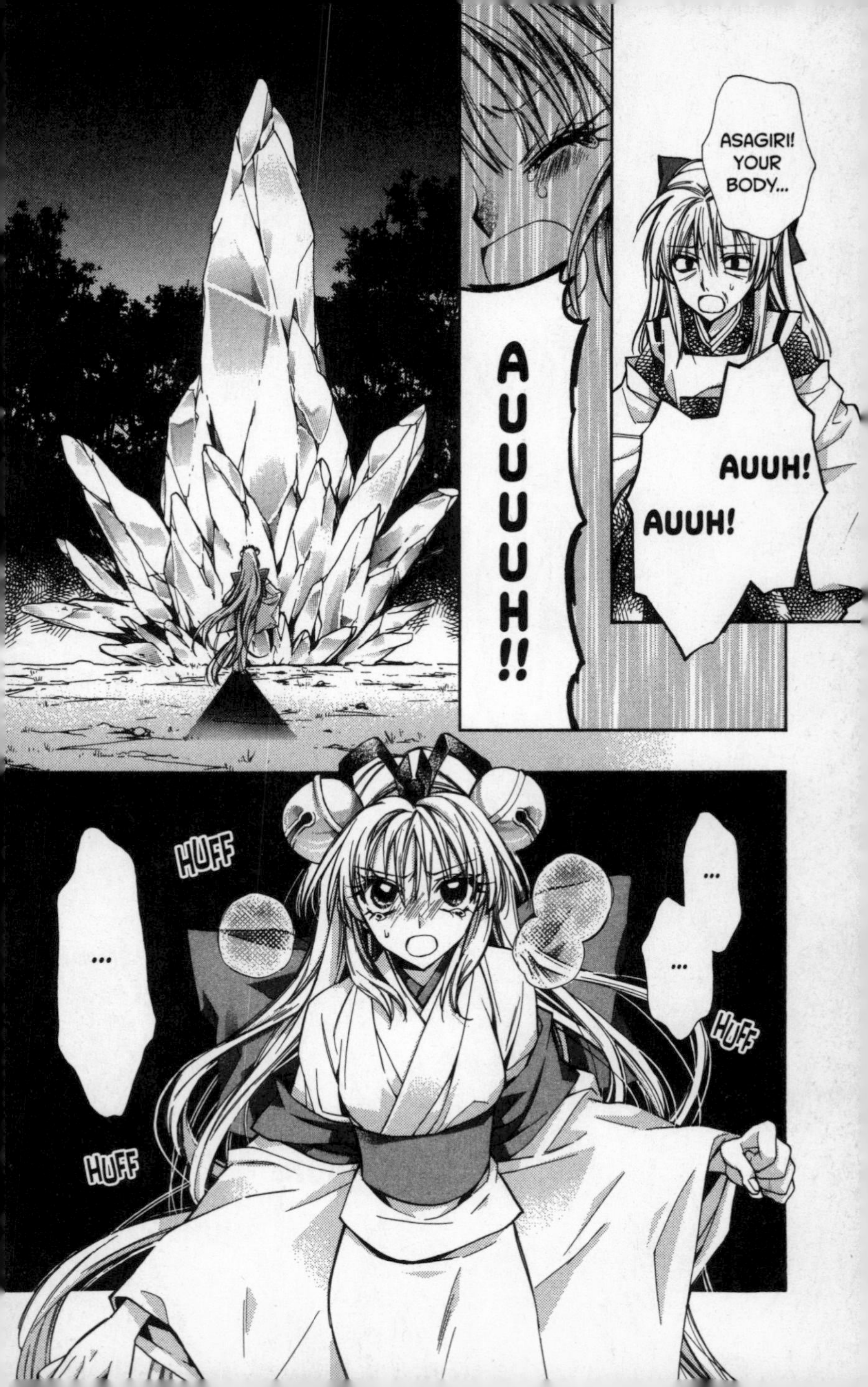
ASAGIRI! YOUR BODY...
AUUH!
AUUH!
AUUUUUH!!
...
...
HUFF
HUFF
...
HUFF

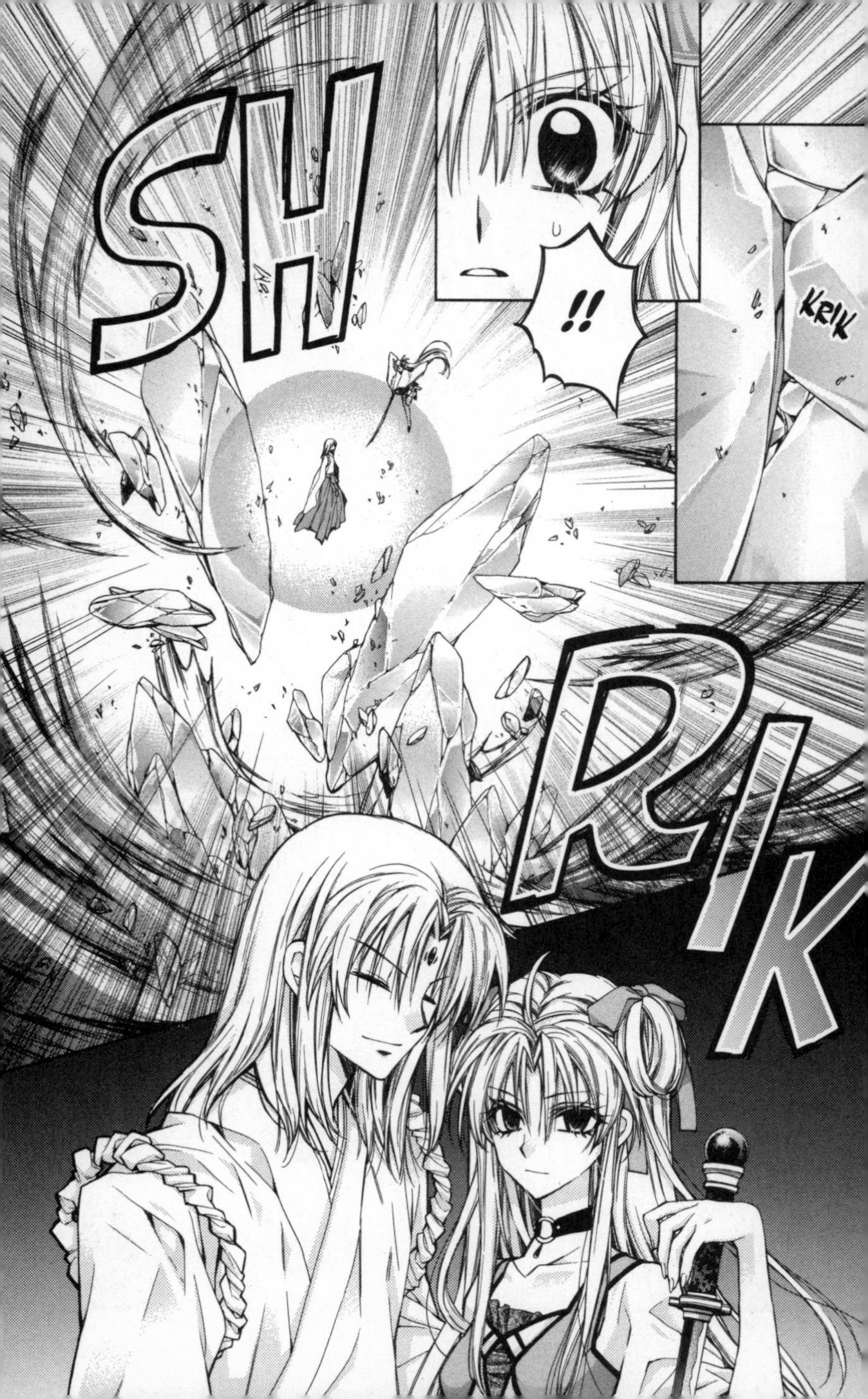
KRIK
!!
SHRIK

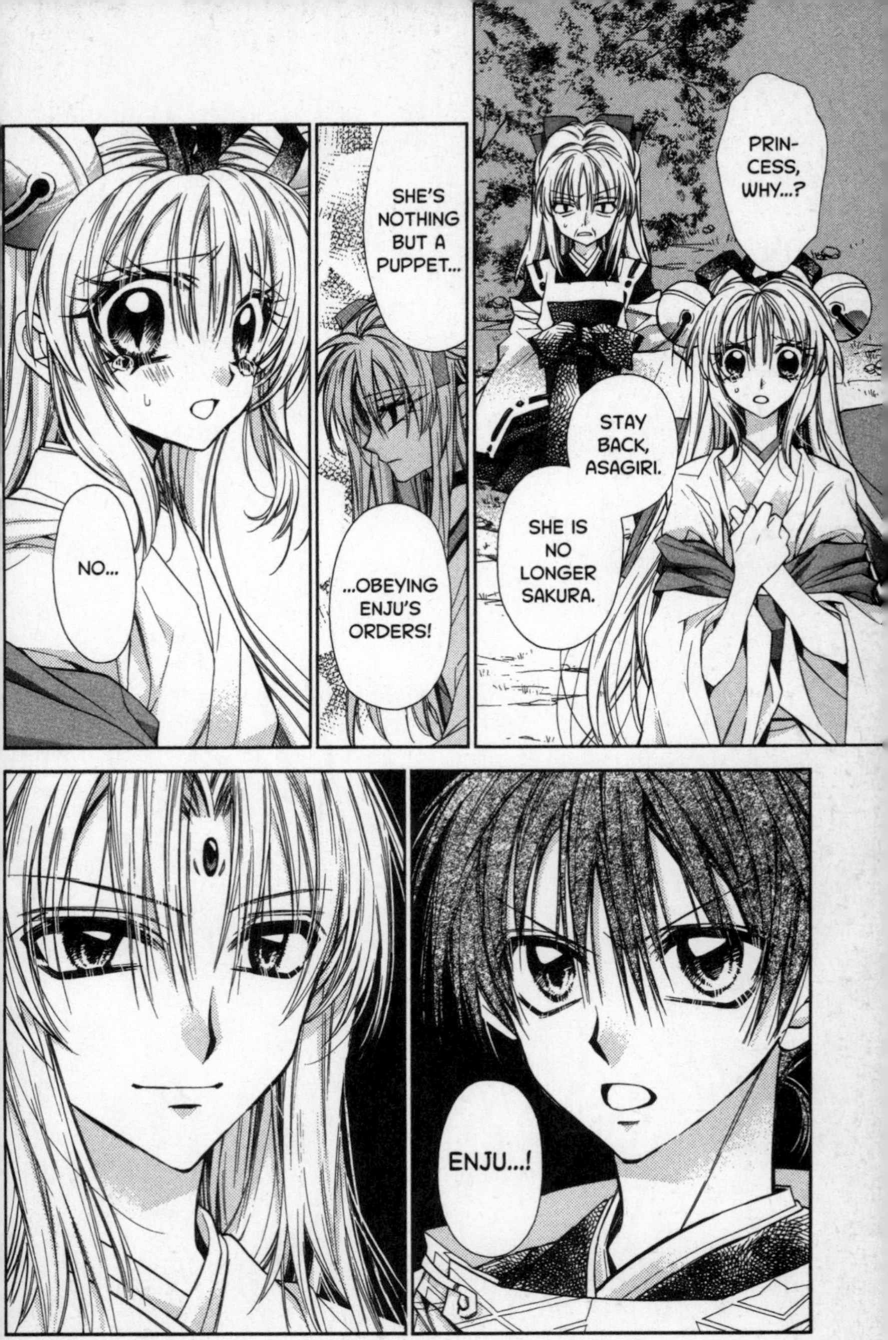
PRIN-CESS, WHY...?
STAY BACK, ASAGIRI.
SHE IS NO LONGER SAKURA.
SHE'S NOTHING BUT A PUPPET...
...OBEYING ENJU'S ORDERS!
NO...
ENJU...!

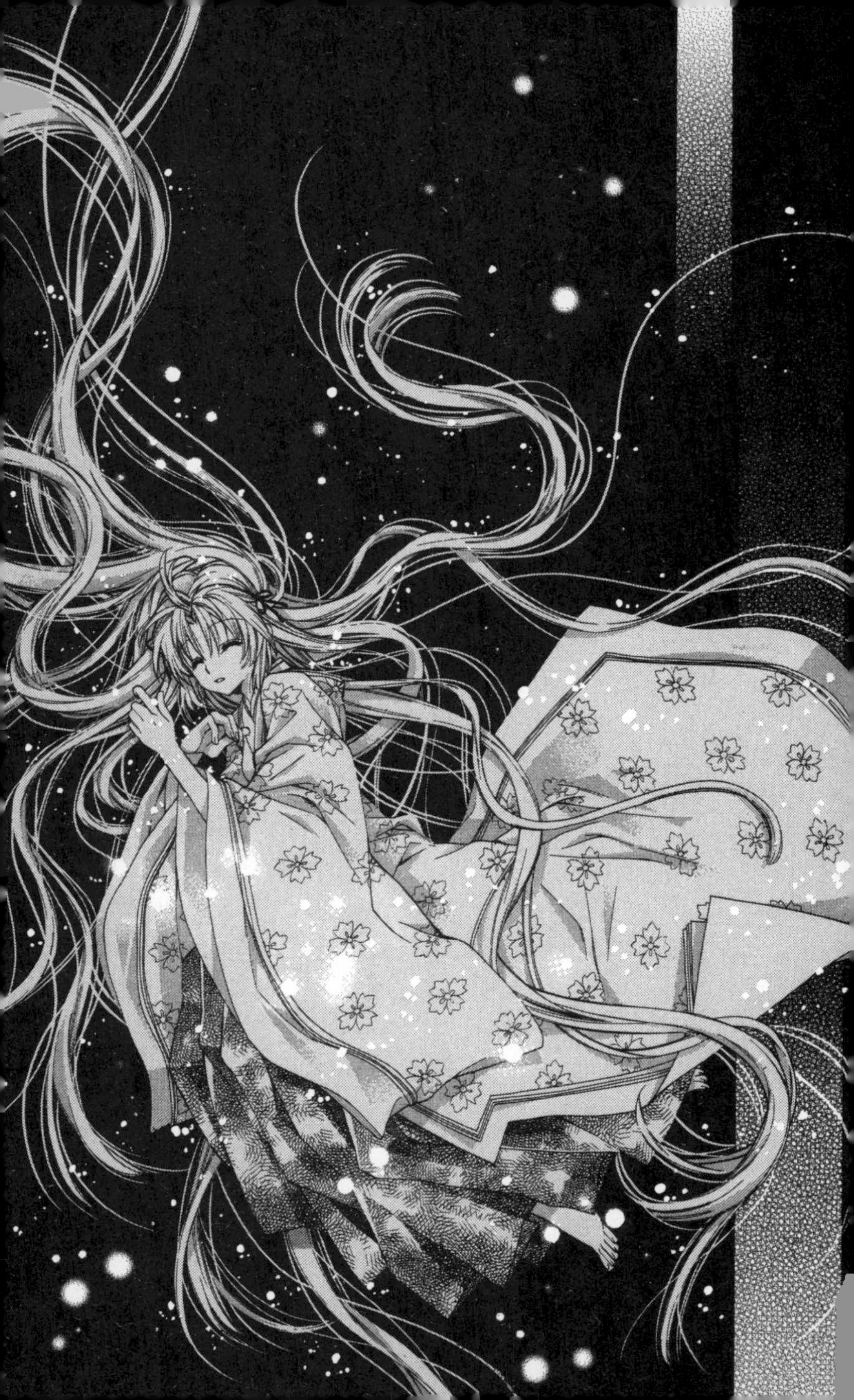

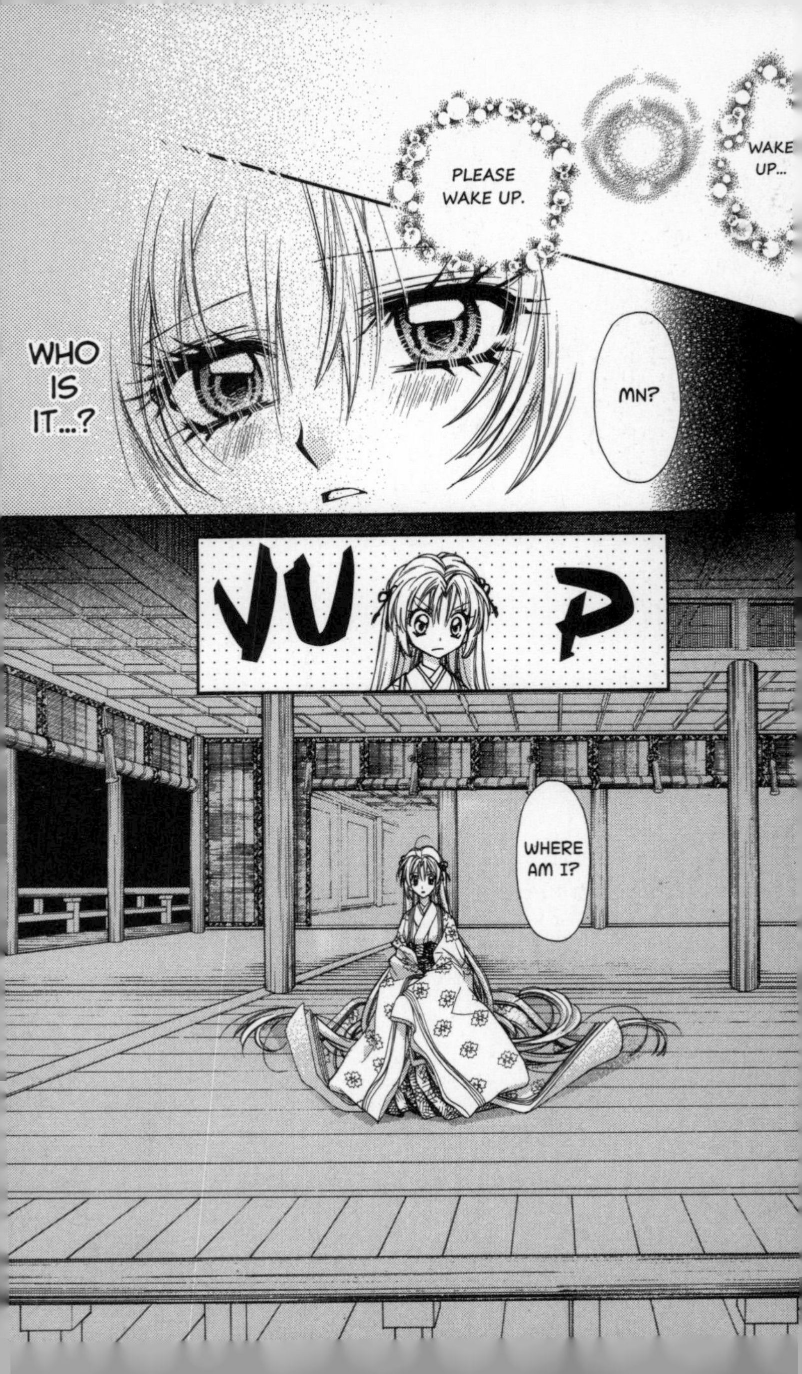
WAKE UP...
PLEASE WAKE UP.
MN?
WHO IS IT...?
VU P
WHERE AM I?

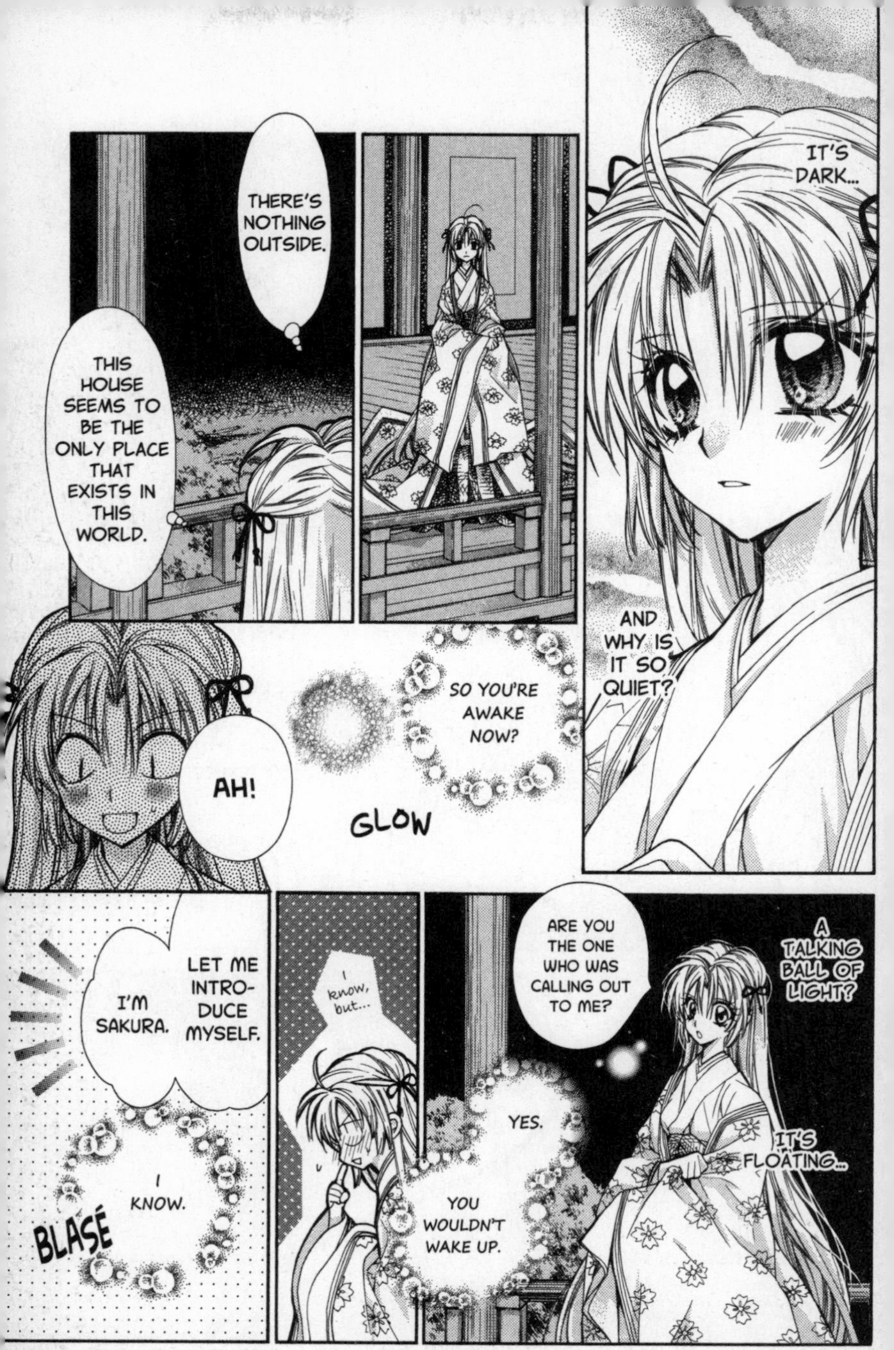
IT'S DARK...
AND WHY IS IT SO QUIET?
THERE'S NOTHING OUTSIDE.
THIS HOUSE SEEMS TO BE THE ONLY PLACE THAT EXISTS IN THIS WORLD.
SO YOU'RE AWAKE NOW?
GLOW
AH!
A TALKING BALL OF LIGHT?
ARE YOU THE ONE WHO WAS CALLING OUT TO ME?
YES.
IT'S FLOATING...
YOU WOULDN'T WAKE UP.
I know, but...
LET ME INTRO-DUCE MYSELF.
I'M SAKURA.
I KNOW.
BLASÉ

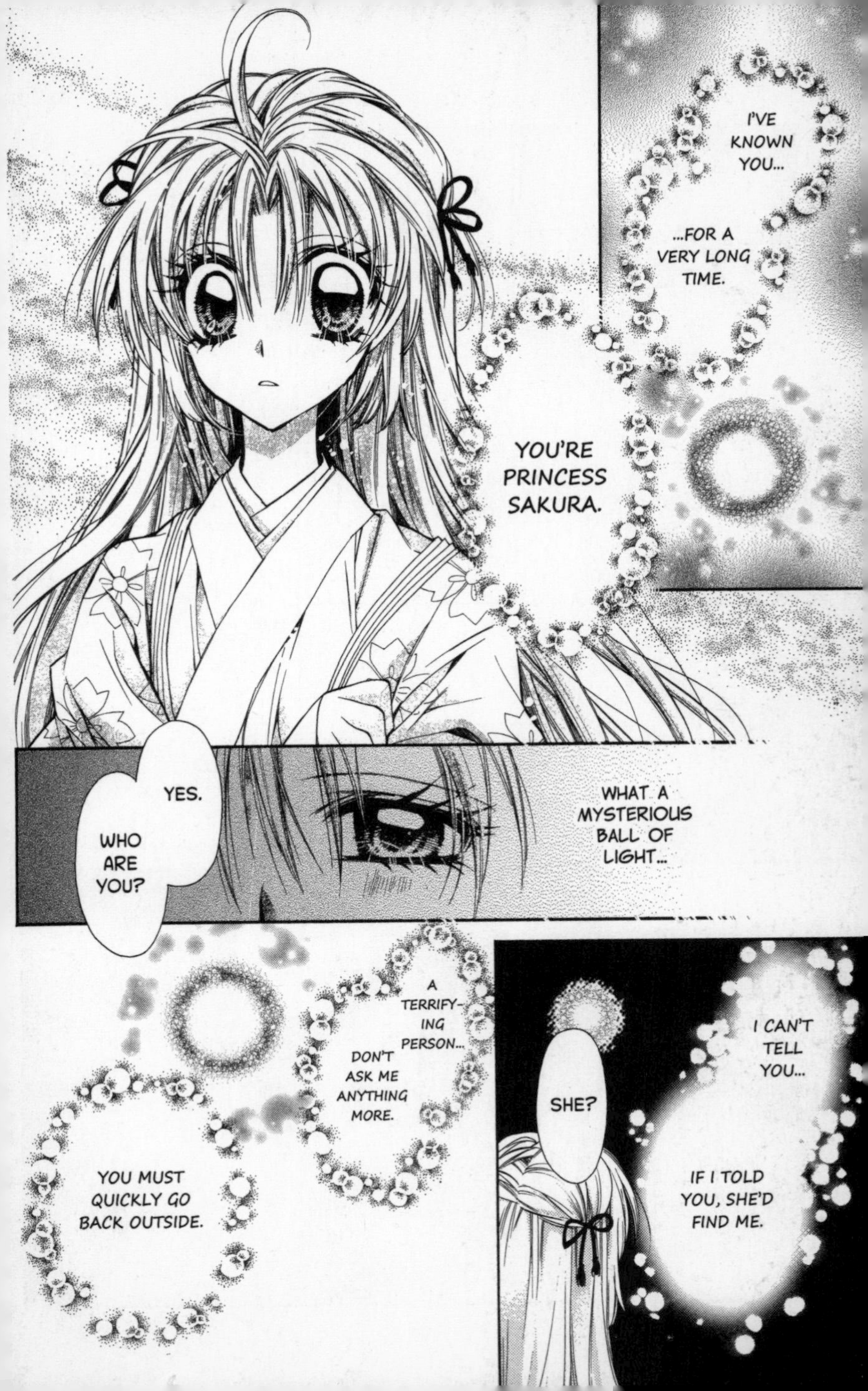
I'VE KNOWN YOU...
...FOR A VERY LONG TIME.
YOU'RE PRINCESS SAKURA.
WHAT A MYSTERIOUS BALL OF LIGHT...
YES.
WHO ARE YOU?
I CAN'T TELL YOU...
IF I TOLD YOU, SHE'D FIND ME.
SHE?
A TERRIFY-ING PERSON...
DON'T ASK ME ANYTHING MORE.
YOU MUST QUICKLY GO BACK OUTSIDE.

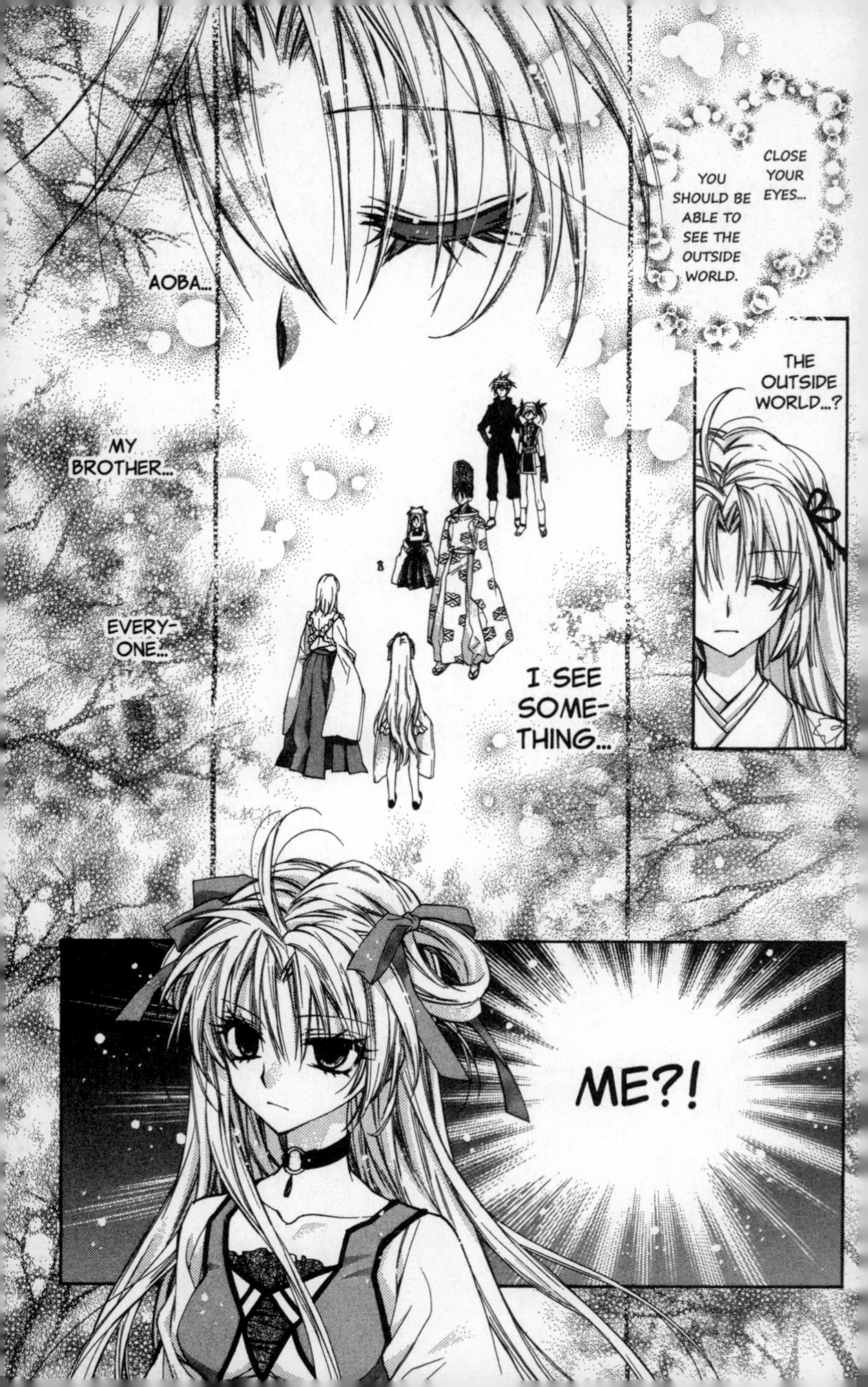
CLOSE YOUR EYES...
YOU SHOULD BE ABLE TO SEE THE OUTSIDE WORLD.
THE OUTSIDE WORLD...?
I SEE SOME-THING...
AOBA...
MY BROTHER...
EVERY-ONE...
ME?!

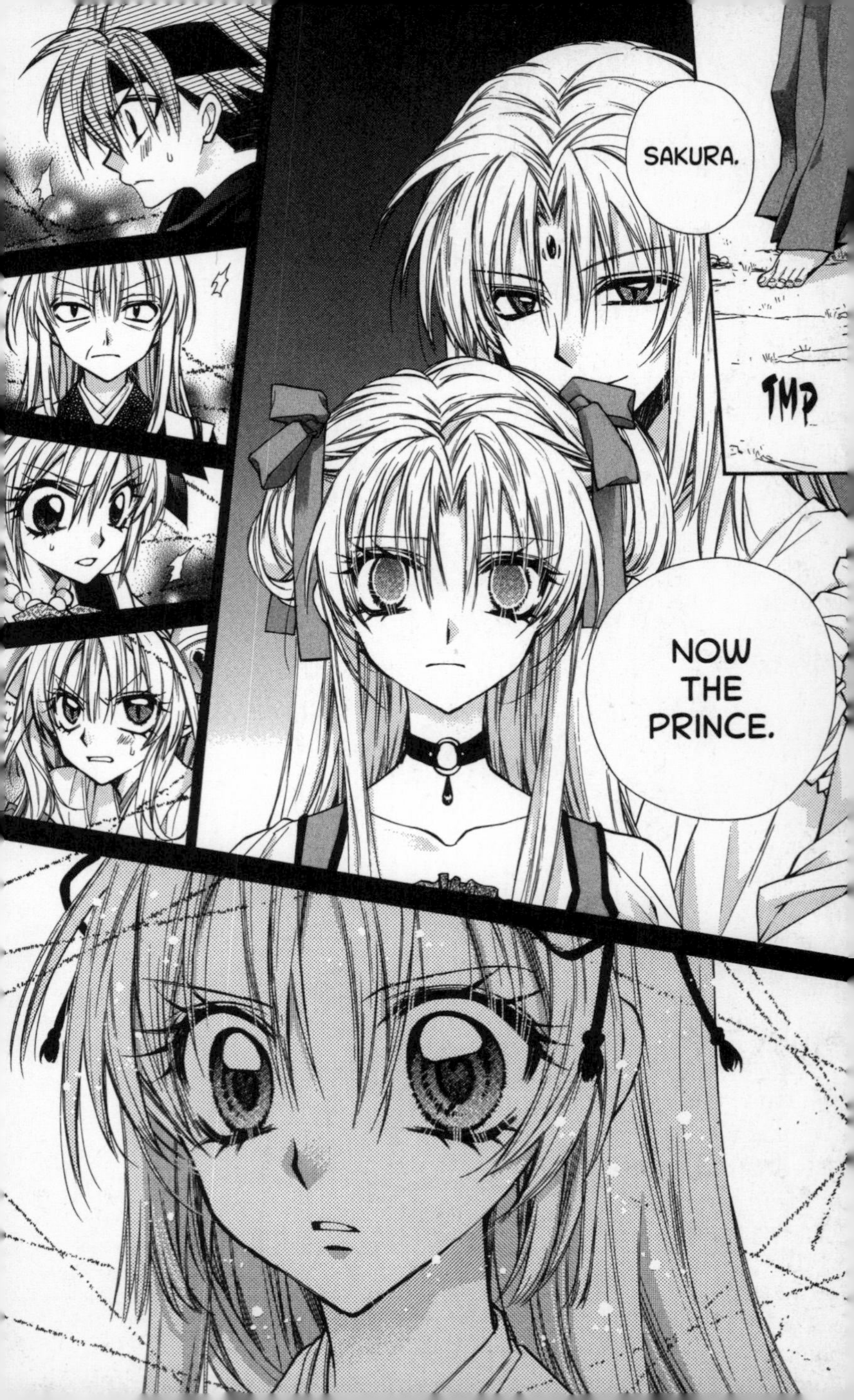
TMP
SAKURA.
NOW THE PRINCE.

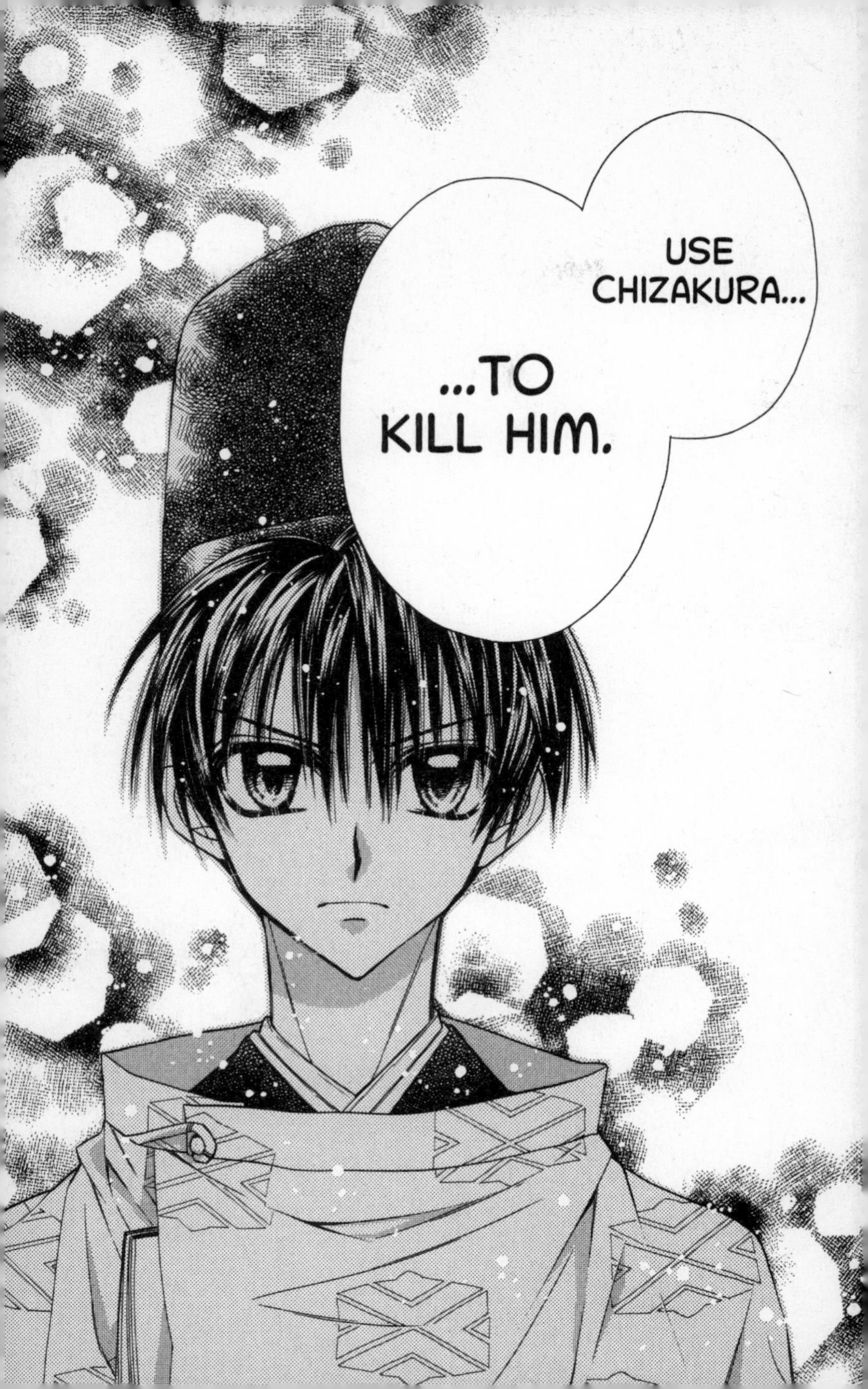
USE CHIZAKURA...
...TO KILL HIM.

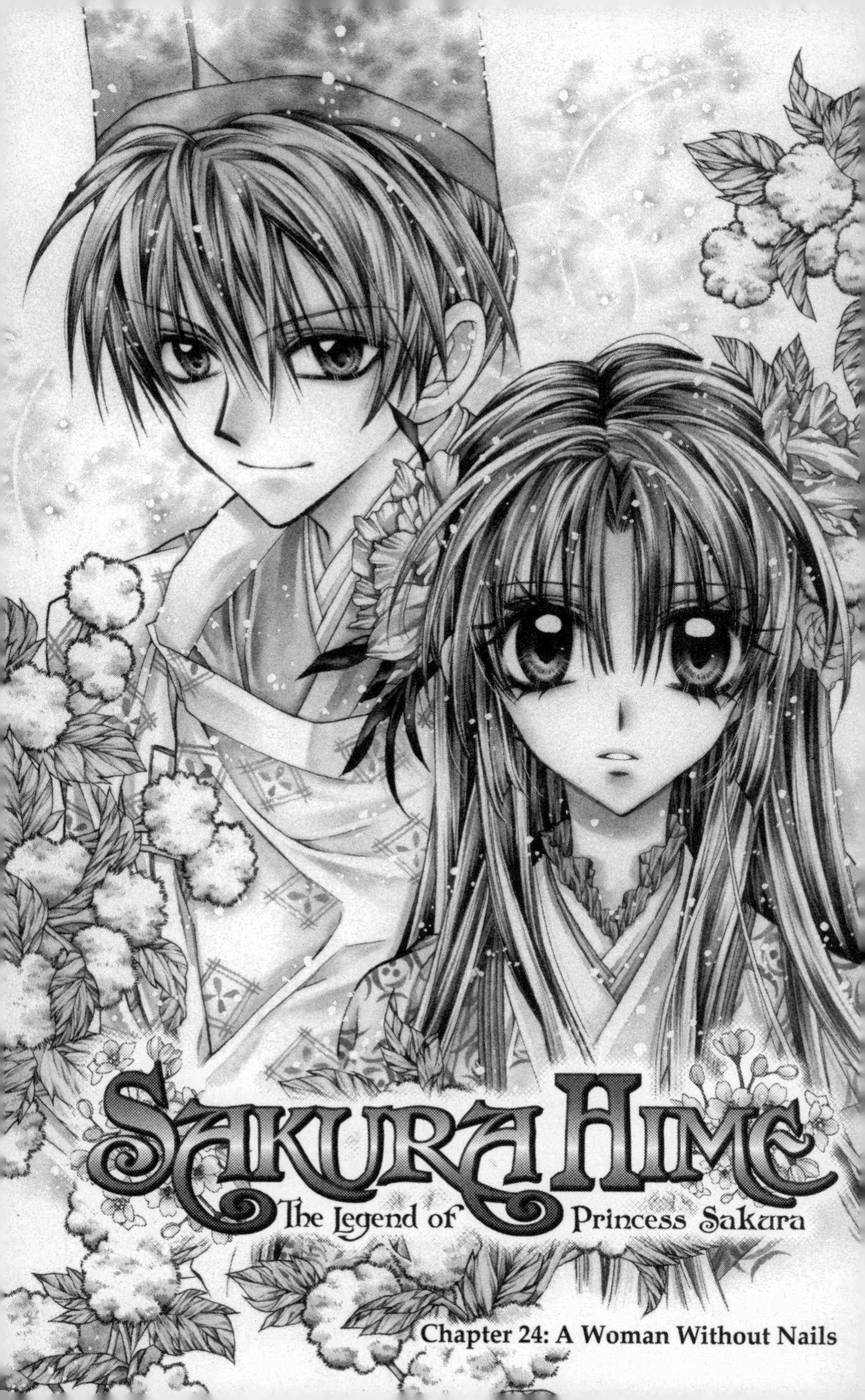
SAKURA HIME
The Legend of Princess Sakura
Chapter 24: A Woman Without Nails

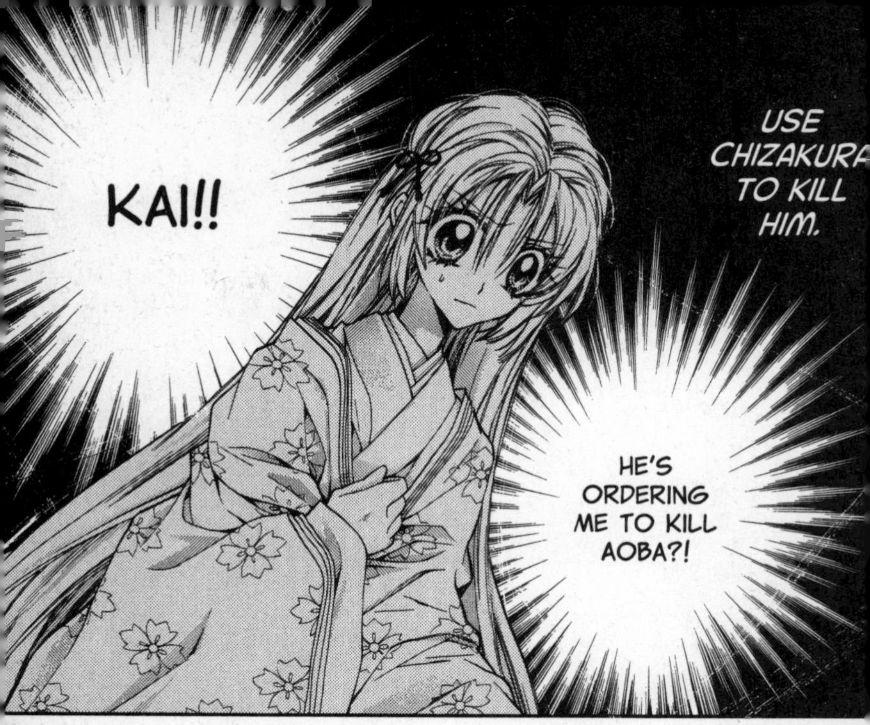
USE CHIZAKURA TO KILL HIM.
KAI!!
HE'S ORDERING ME TO KILL AOBA?!

Chapter 24: A Woman Without Nails ※ I'm giving away the story.

I was finally able to do something about the scene in the preview. (A month before this series started, a six-page manga preview was in *Ribon* magazine.)

I had been looking forward to doing a scene with "that woman," but my assistants said, "It's scary! It's scary!!" Is it scary?

I thought it was a very *Sakura Hime*-like scene.

Oh, the chapter title is about "that woman" having no nails. Before working on that scene, I was really relieved that I have shown hands often. (It wouldn't make sense if my artwork lacked details like nails to begin with.)
The identity of the ball of light is revealed in the second half of the chapter. Most of my readers hadn't figured out who it was.

(And for some reason, they thanked me after it was revealed.)

I was very happy that the readers remembered her...
The clue was that the ball of light called Enju "Kai."
I had not drawn that character for a while, but I really like her design...
I hope I get the chance to draw her again in an illustration or something.

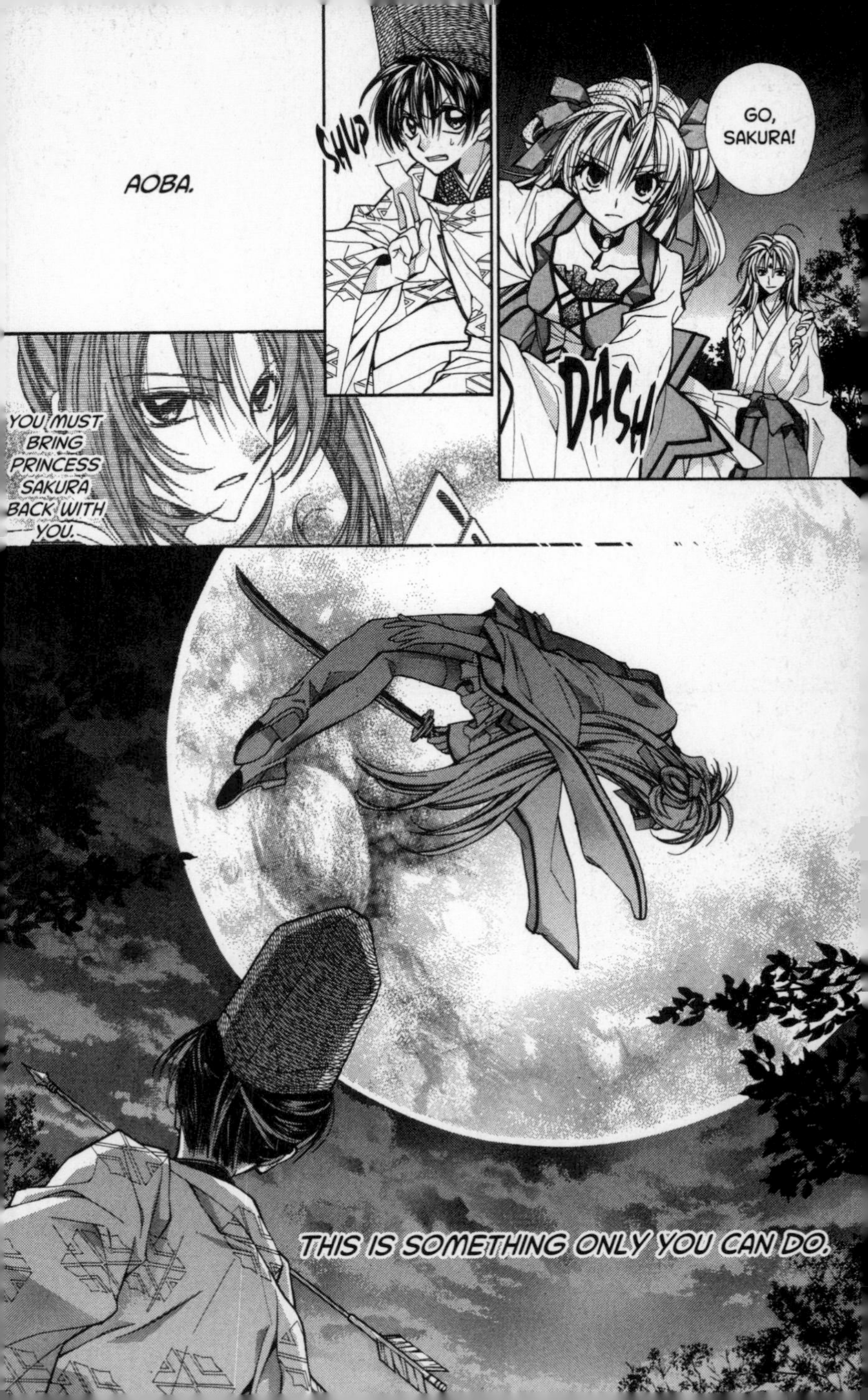
GO, SAKURA!
DASH
SHUP
AOBA.
YOU MUST BRING PRINCESS SAKURA BACK WITH YOU.
THIS IS SOMETHING ONLY YOU CAN DO.

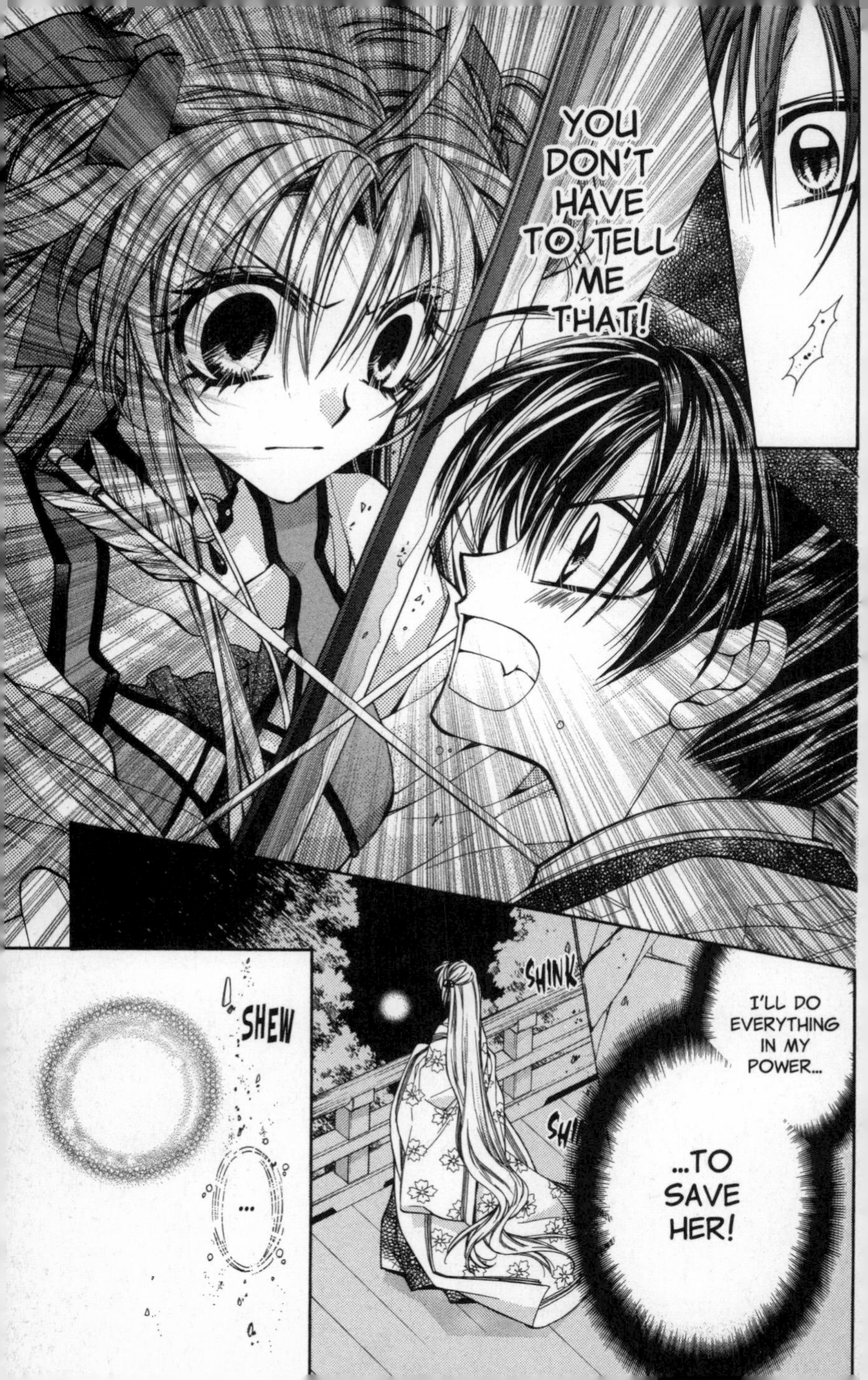
YOU DON'T HAVE TO TELL ME THAT!
I'LL DO EVERYTHING IN MY POWER...
SHINK
...TO SAVE HER!
SHEW
...

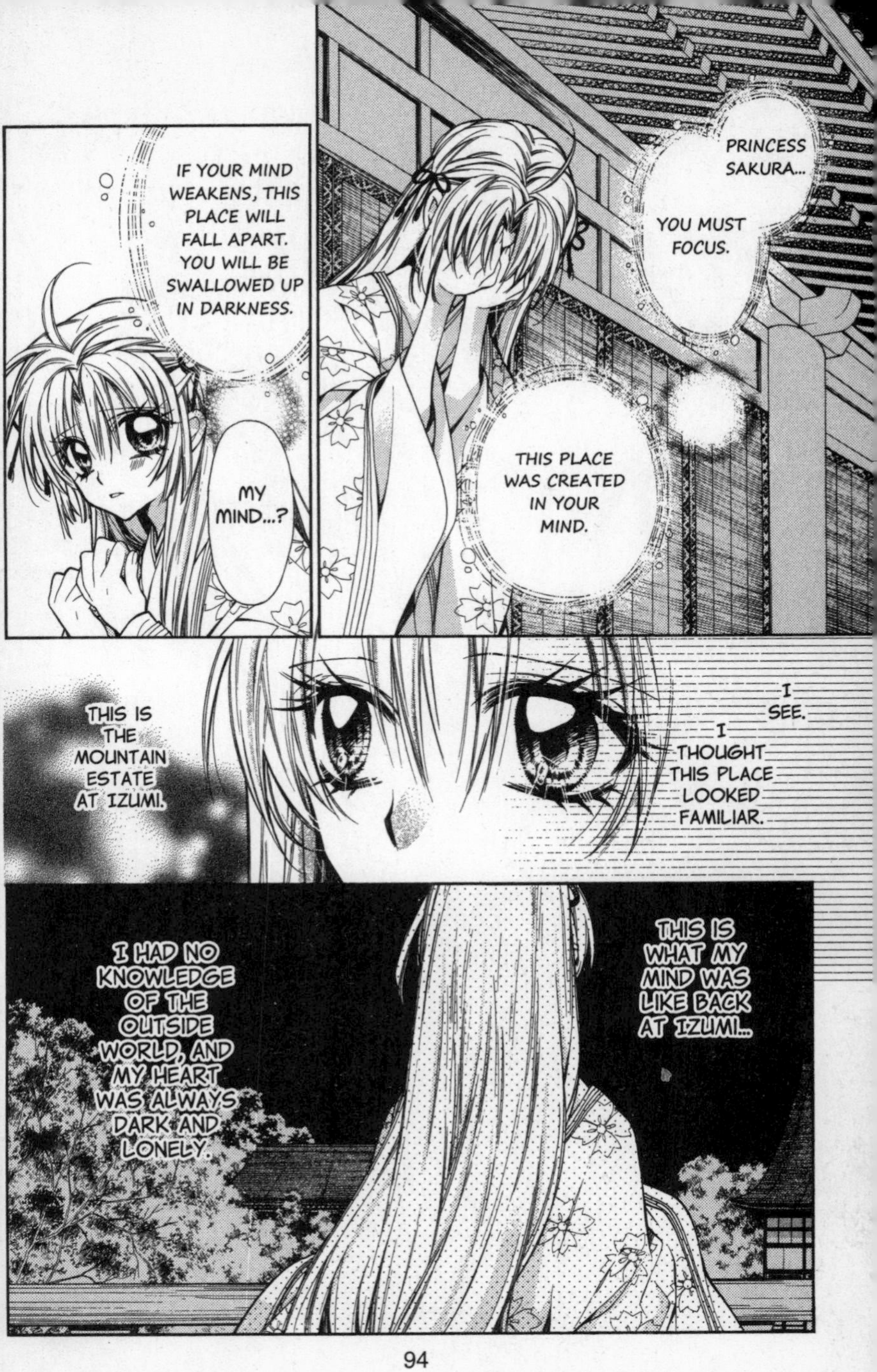
PRINCESS SAKURA...
YOU MUST FOCUS.
THIS PLACE WAS CREATED IN YOUR MIND.
IF YOUR MIND WEAKENS, THIS PLACE WILL FALL APART. YOU WILL BE SWALLOWED UP IN DARKNESS.
MY MIND...?
I SEE.
I THOUGHT THIS PLACE LOOKED FAMILIAR.
THIS IS THE MOUNTAIN ESTATE AT IZUMI.
THIS IS WHAT MY MIND WAS LIKE BACK AT IZUMI...
I HAD NO KNOWLEDGE OF THE OUTSIDE WORLD, AND MY HEART WAS ALWAYS DARK AND LONELY.

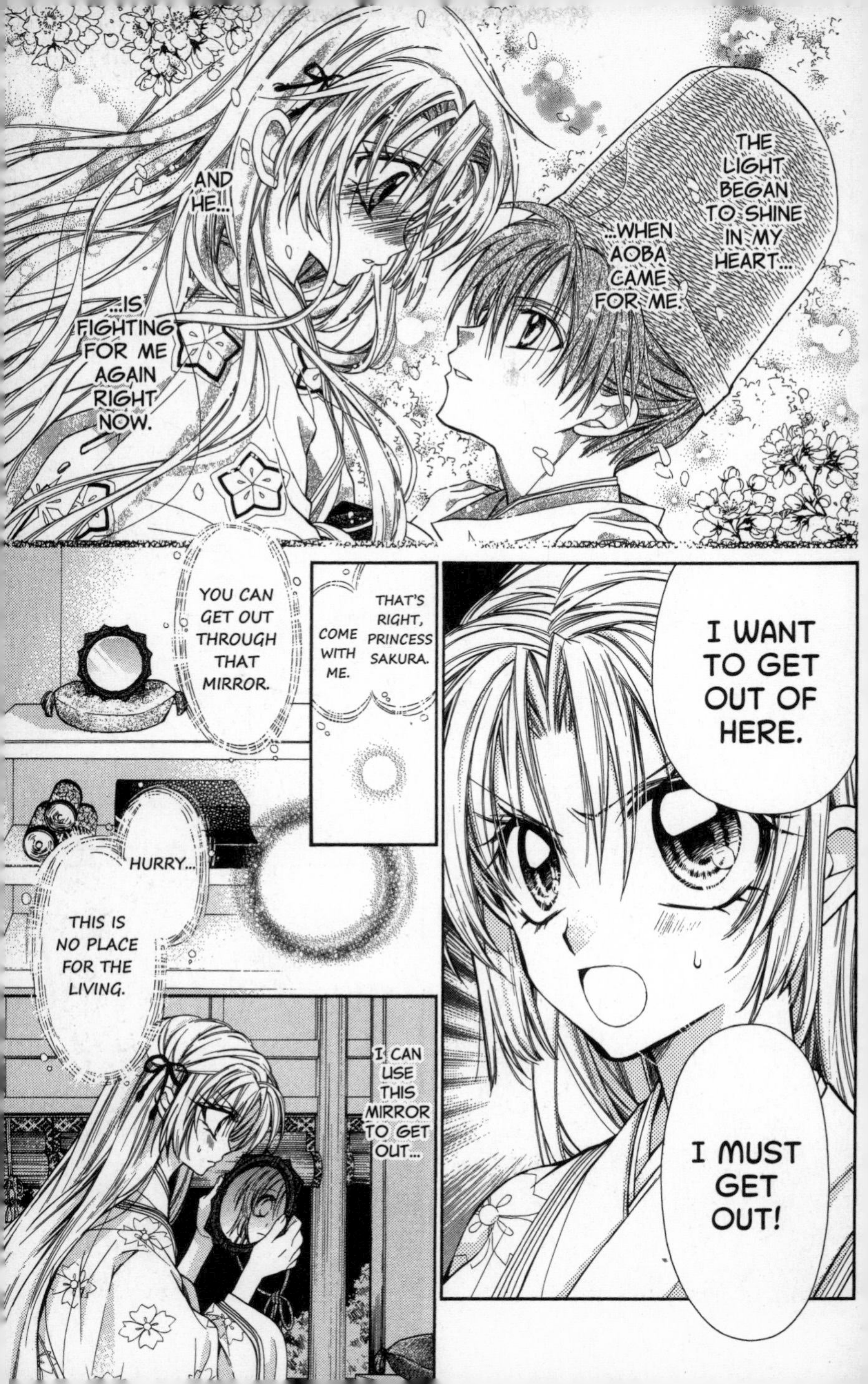
THE LIGHT BEGAN TO SHINE IN MY HEART...
...WHEN AOBA CAME FOR ME.
AND HE...
...IS FIGHTING FOR ME AGAIN RIGHT NOW.
I WANT TO GET OUT OF HERE.
I MUST GET OUT!
THAT'S RIGHT, PRINCESS SAKURA.
COME WITH ME.
YOU CAN GET OUT THROUGH THAT MIRROR.
HURRY...
THIS IS NO PLACE FOR THE LIVING.
I CAN USE THIS MIRROR TO GET OUT...

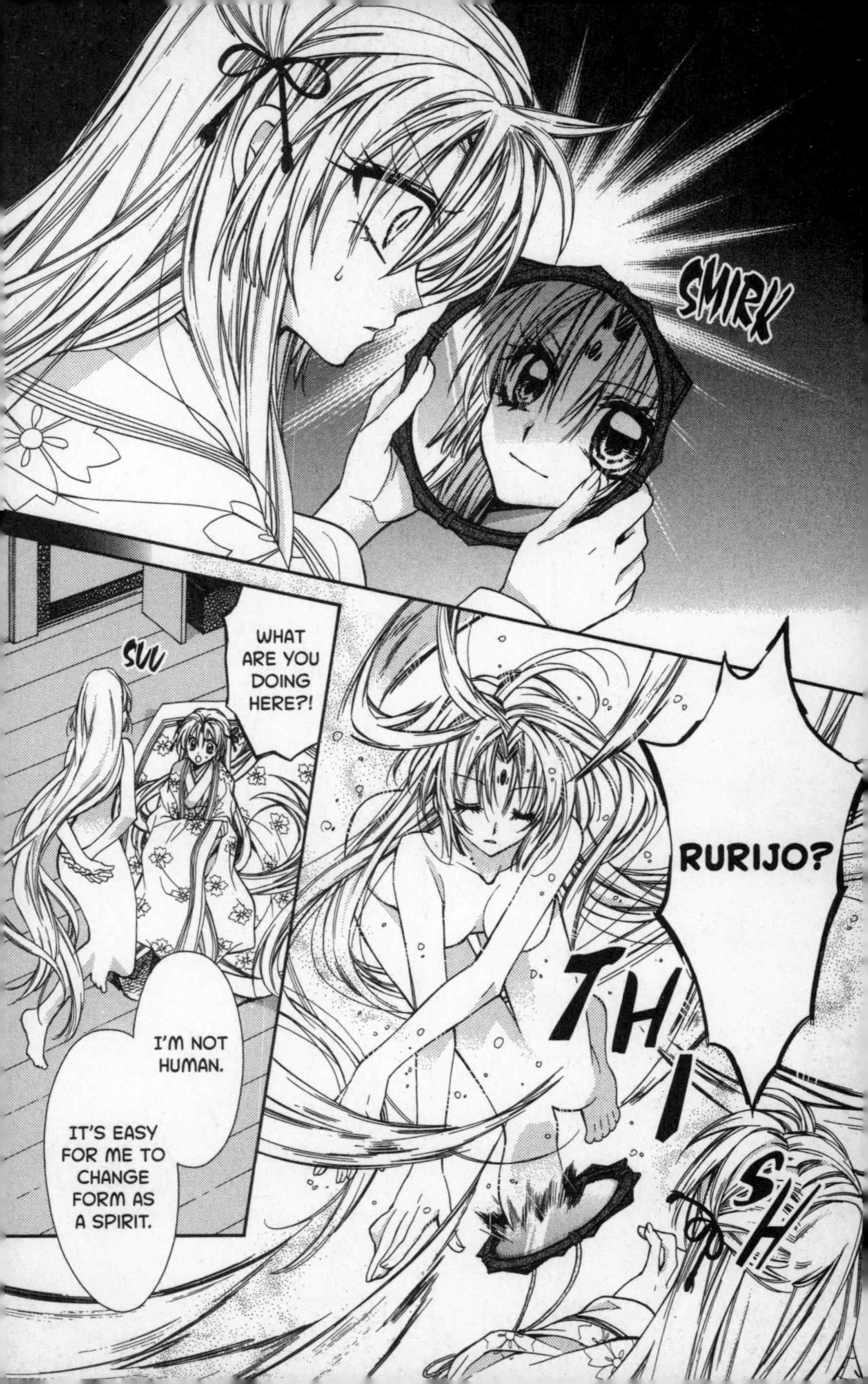
SMIRK
RURIJO?
THISH
SUU
WHAT ARE YOU DOING HERE?!
I'M NOT HUMAN.
IT'S EASY FOR ME TO CHANGE FORM AS A SPIRIT.

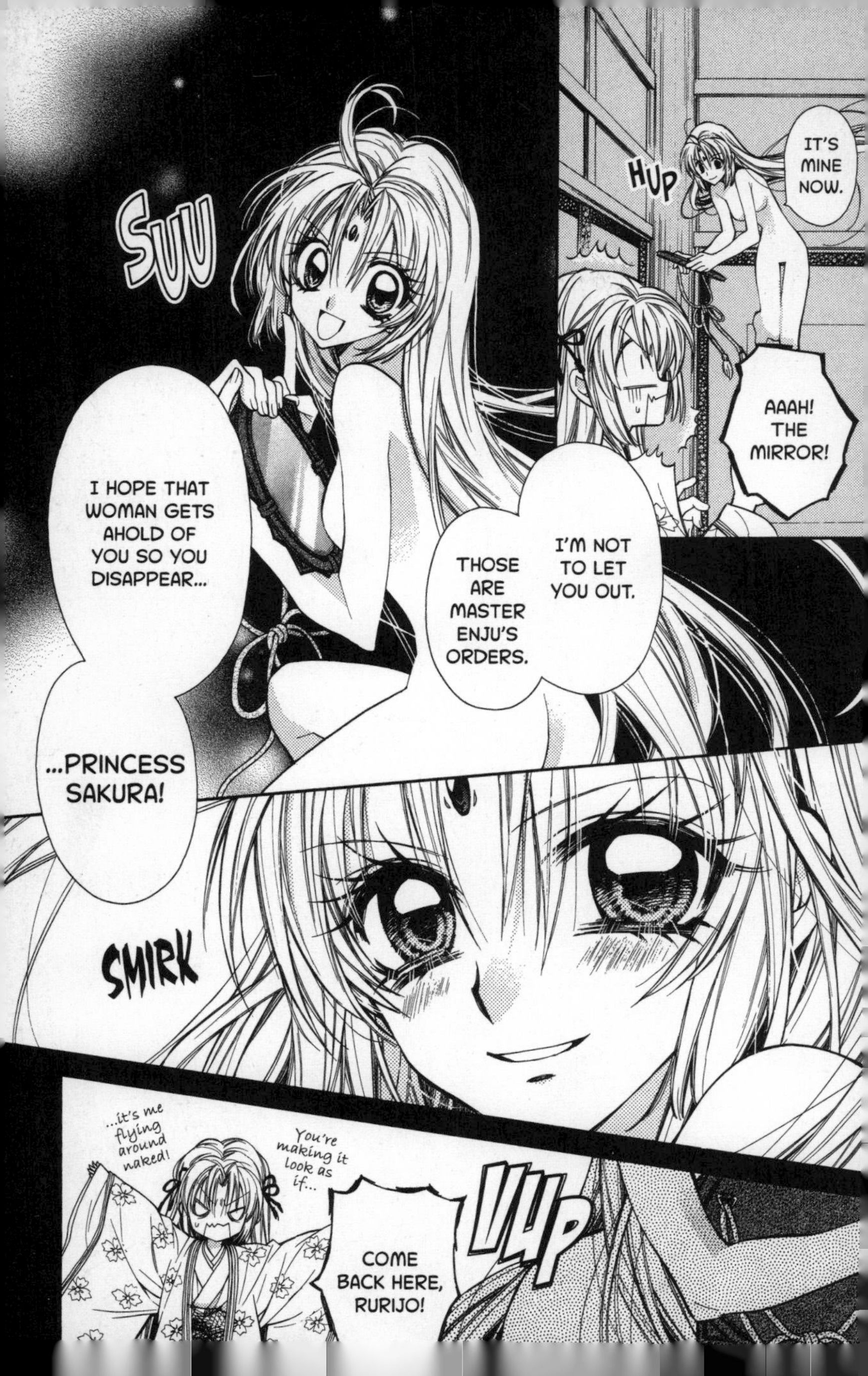
IT'S MINE NOW.
HUP
AAAH! THE MIRROR!
I'M NOT TO LET YOU OUT.
THOSE ARE MASTER ENJU'S ORDERS.
SUU
I HOPE THAT WOMAN GETS AHOLD OF YOU SO YOU DISAPPEAR...
...PRINCESS SAKURA!
SMIRK
VUP
COME BACK HERE, RURIJO!
You're making it look as if...
...it's me flying around naked!

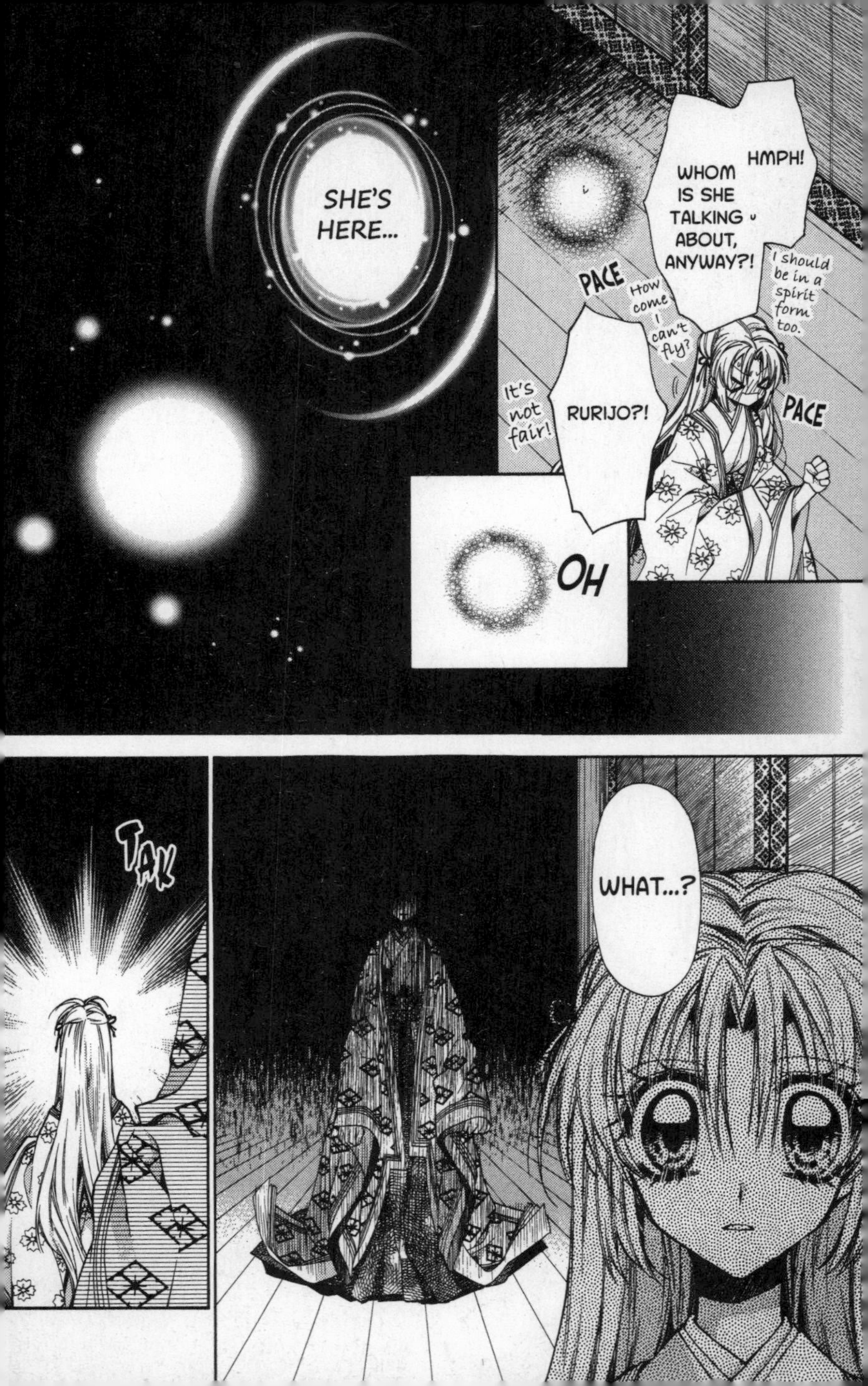
HMPH!
WHOM IS SHE TALKING ABOUT, ANYWAY?!
I should be in a spirit form too.
PACE
How come I can't fly?
PACE
It's not fair!
RURIJO?!
OH
SHE'S HERE...
WHAT...?
TAK

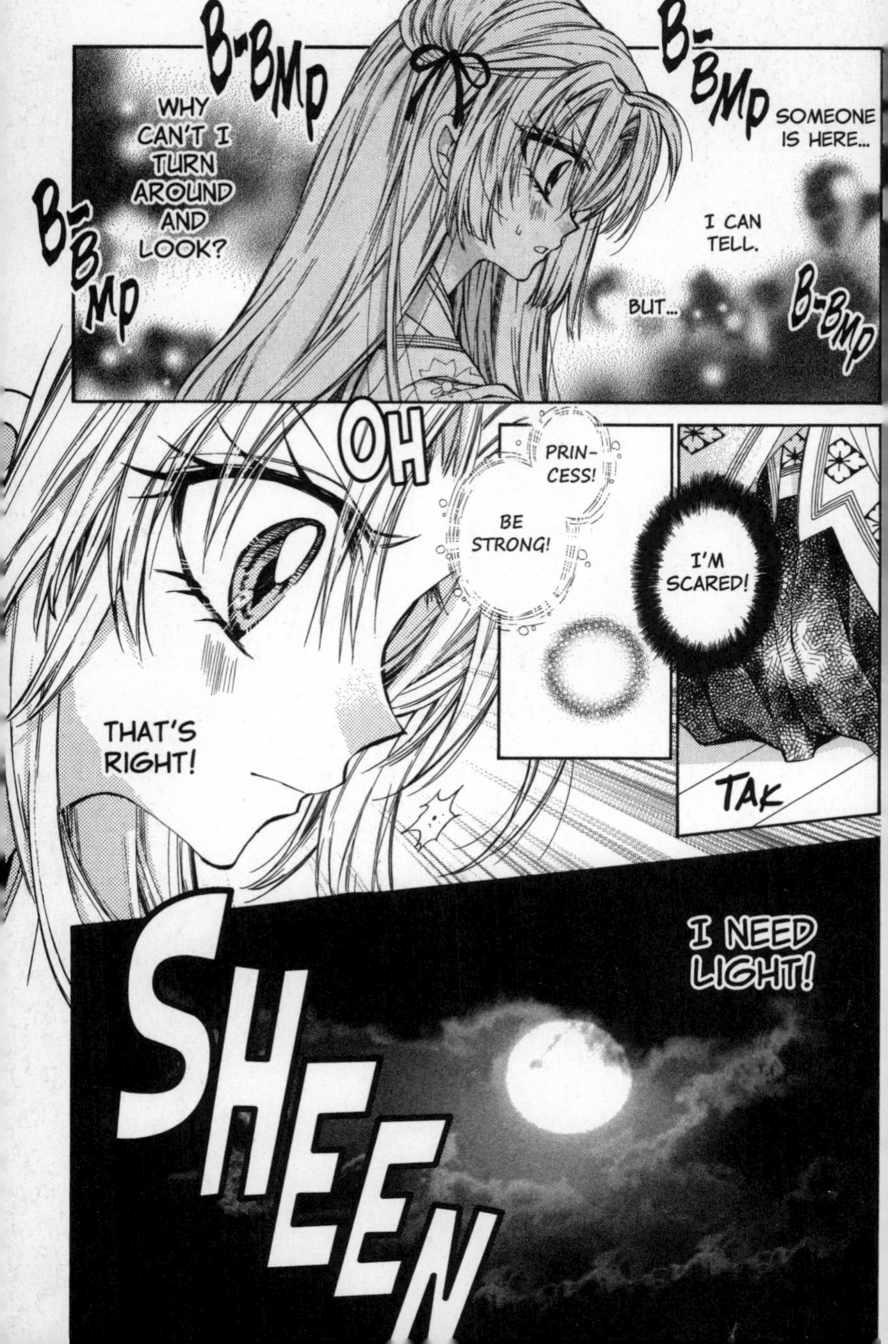
B-BMP
SOMEONE IS HERE...
I CAN TELL.
B-BMP
BUT...
B-BMP
WHY CAN'T I TURN AROUND AND LOOK?
B-BMP
I'M SCARED!
TAK
PRIN-CESS!
BE STRONG!
OH
THAT'S RIGHT!
I NEED LIGHT!
SHEEN

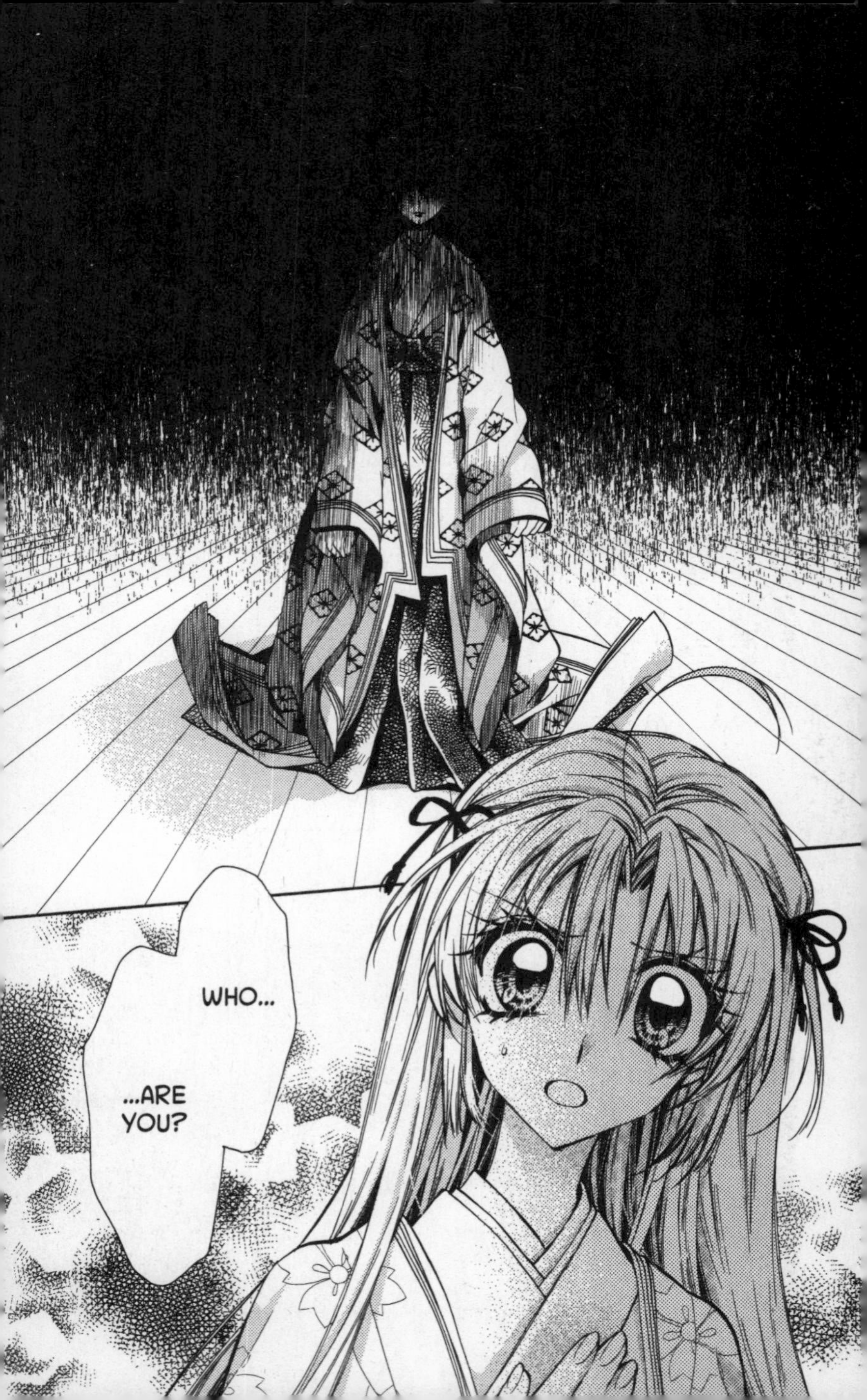
WHO...
...ARE YOU?

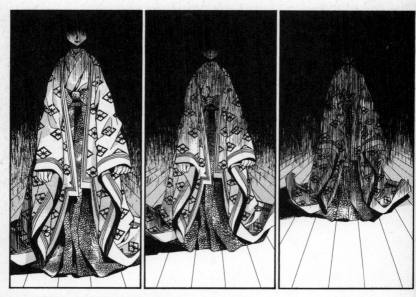

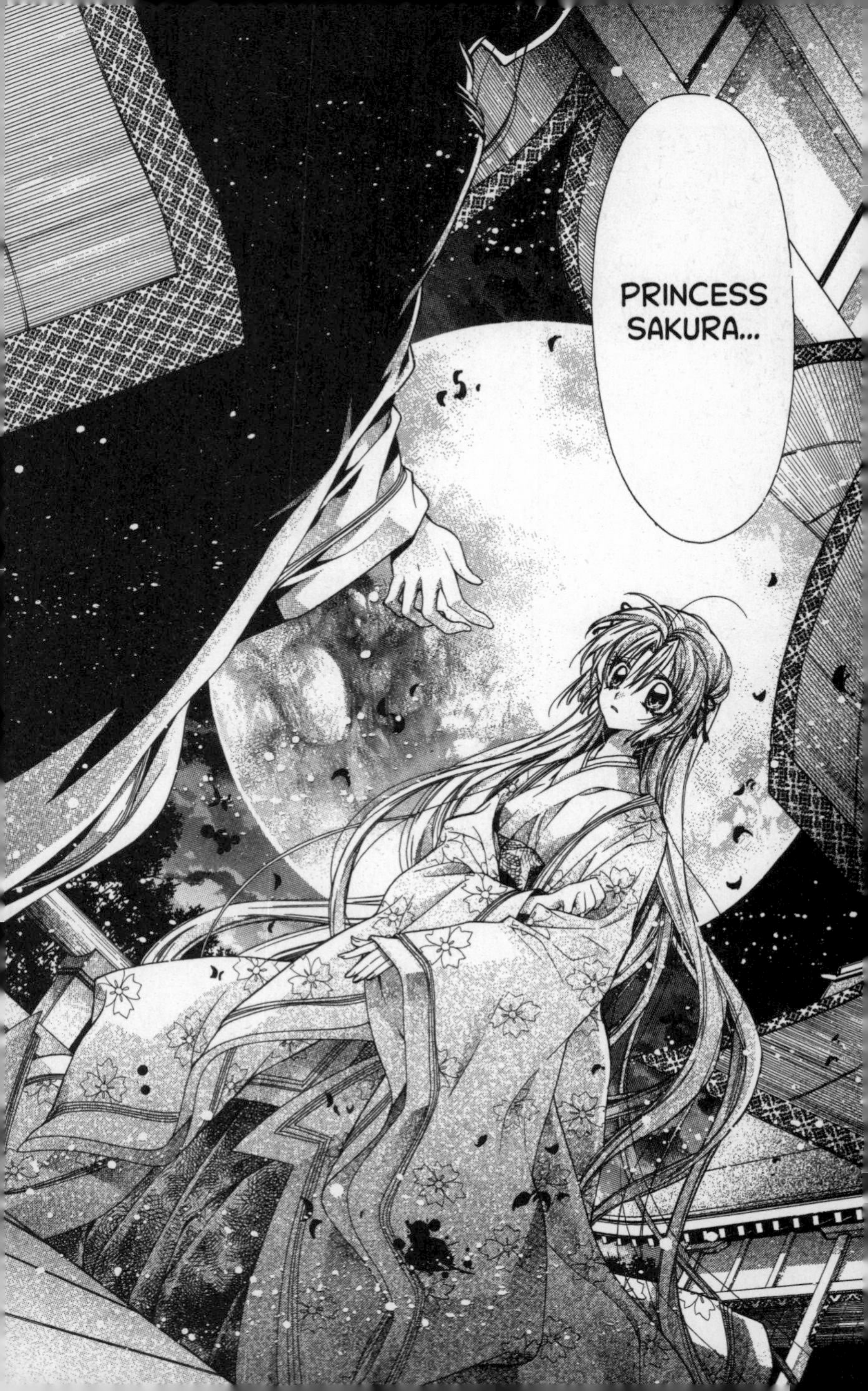
PRINCESS SAKURA...

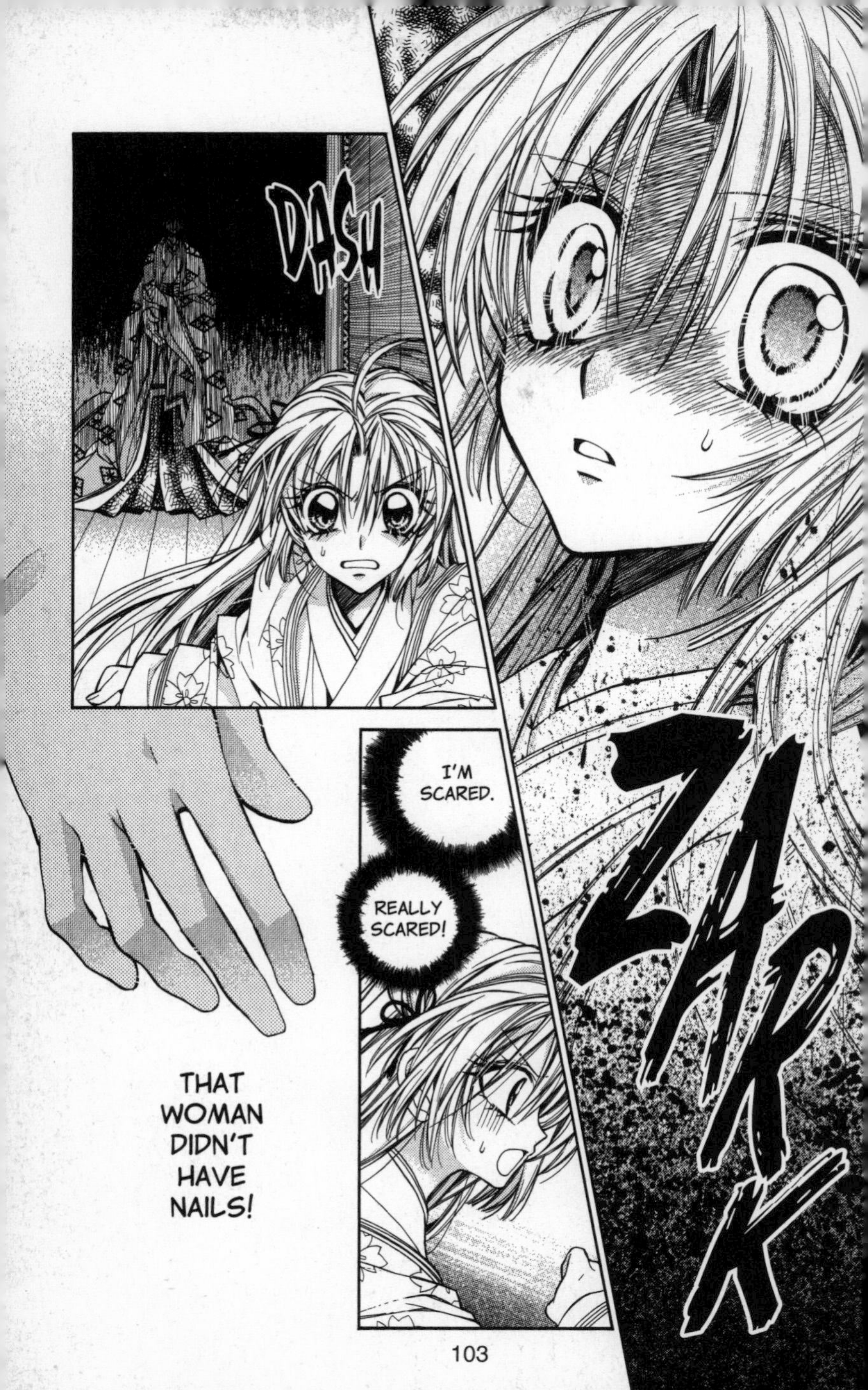
DASH
I'M SCARED.
REALLY SCARED!
THAT WOMAN DIDN'T HAVE NAILS!

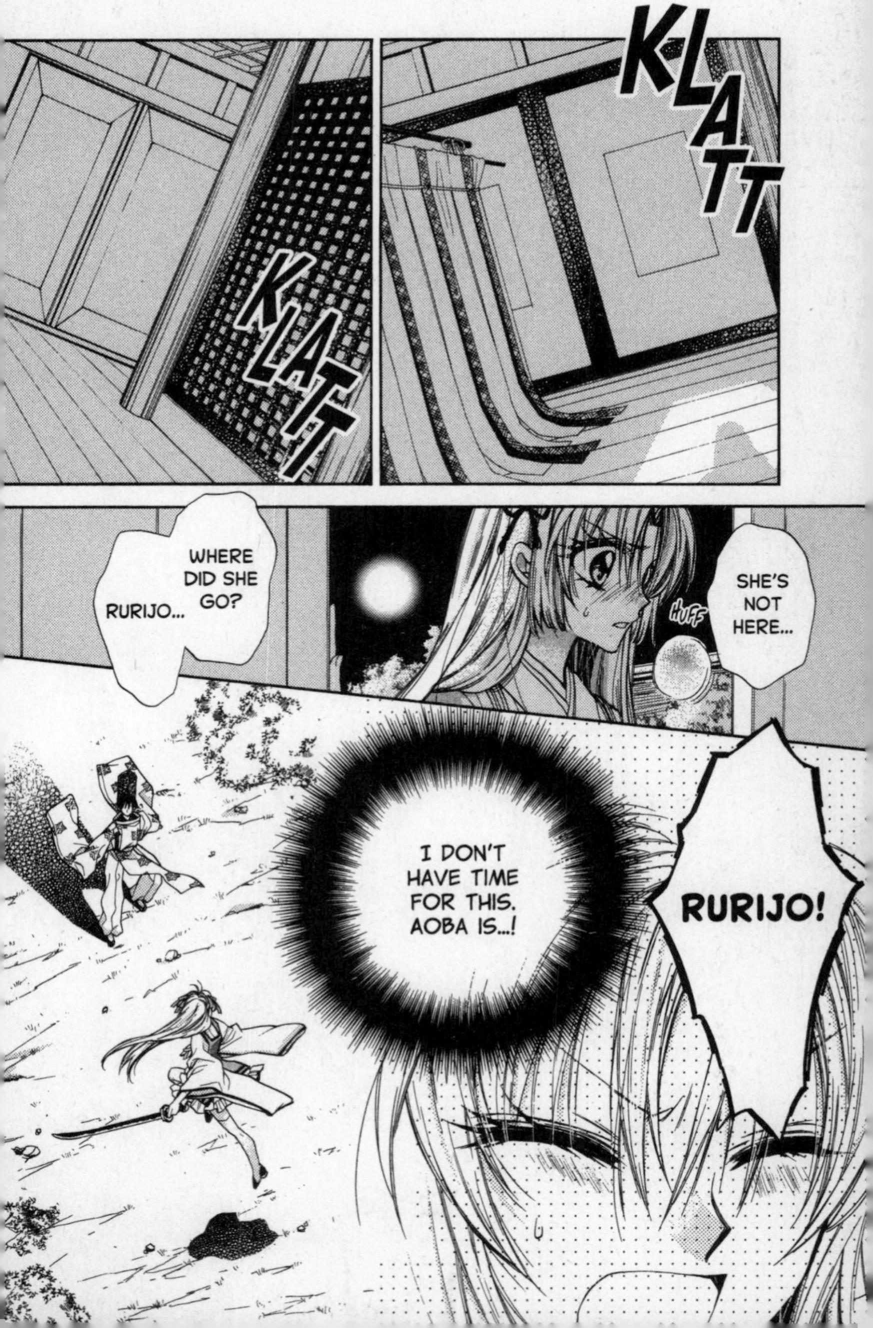
KLATT
KLATT
SHE'S NOT HERE...
HUFF
RURIJO... WHERE DID SHE GO?
RURIJO!
I DON'T HAVE TIME FOR THIS. AOBA IS...!

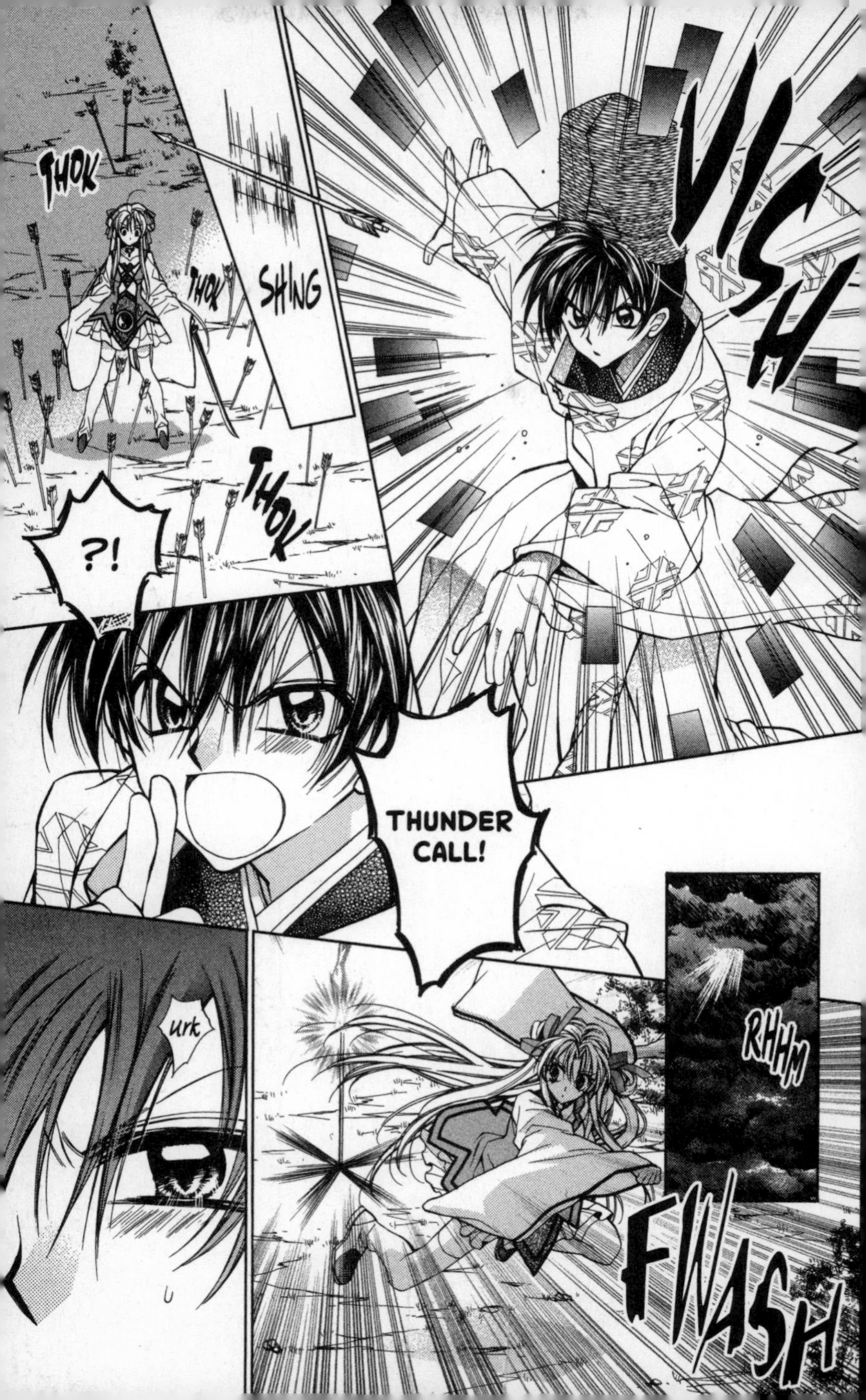
VISH
SHING
THOK
THOK
THOK
?!
THUNDER CALL!
RHHM
FLASH
urk

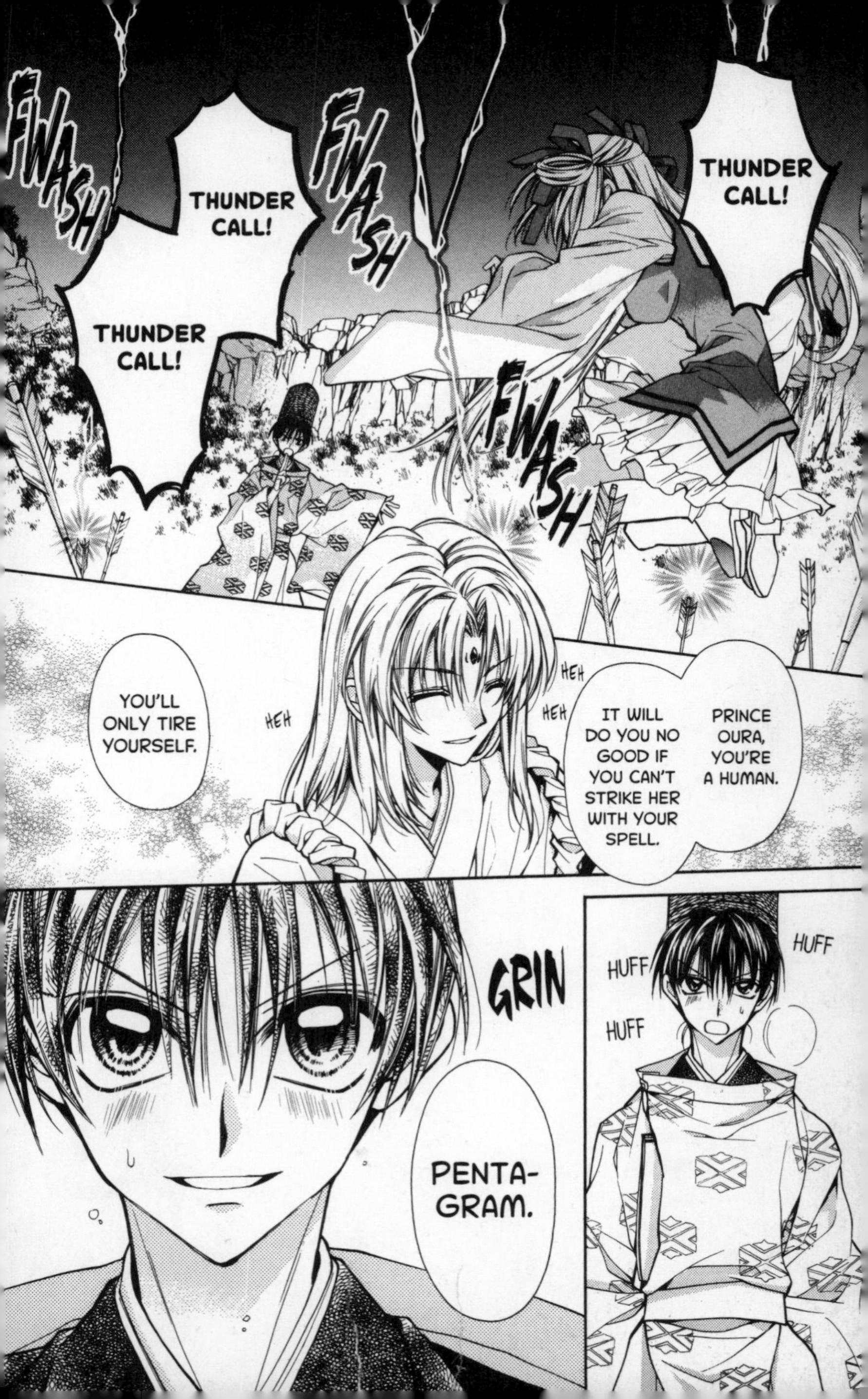
THUNDER CALL!
FWASH
FWASH
THUNDER CALL!
FWASH
THUNDER CALL!
PRINCE OURA, YOU'RE A HUMAN.
IT WILL DO YOU NO GOOD IF YOU CAN'T STRIKE HER WITH YOUR SPELL.
HEH
HEH
HEH
YOU'LL ONLY TIRE YOURSELF.
HUFF
HUFF
HUFF
GRIN
PENTA-GRAM.

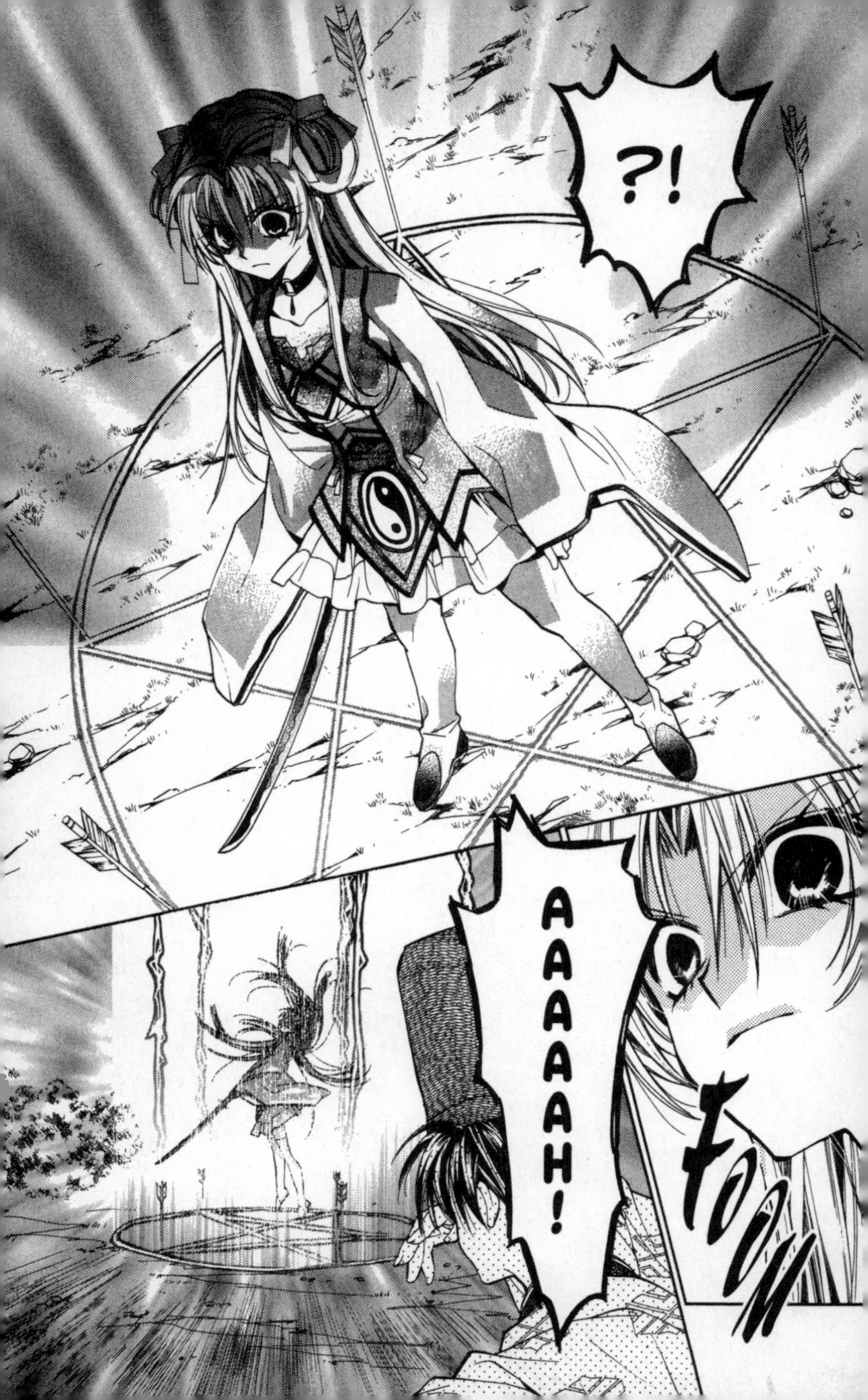
?!
AAAAAAH!
FOOM

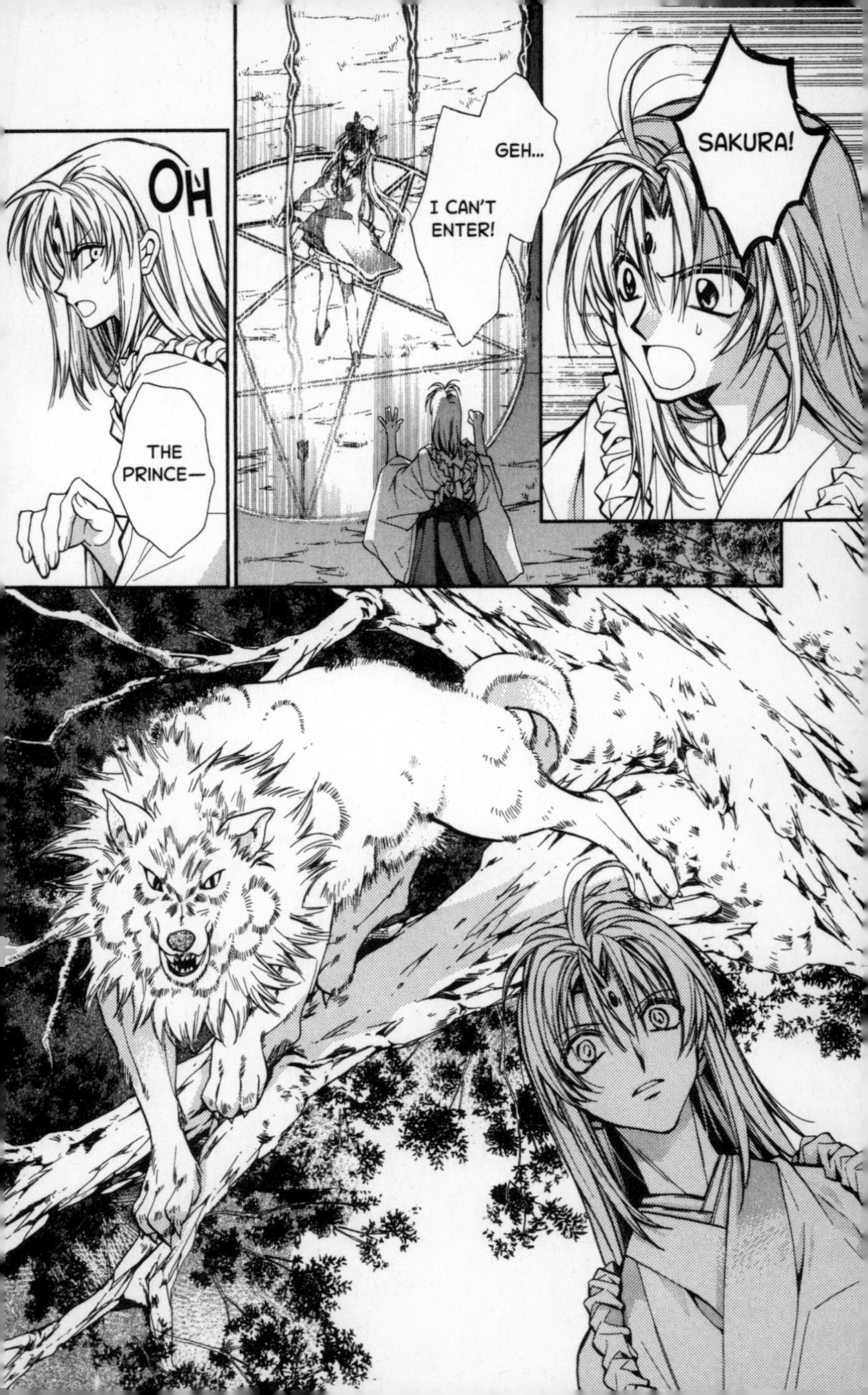
SAKURA!
GEH...
I CAN'T ENTER!
OH
THE PRINCE—

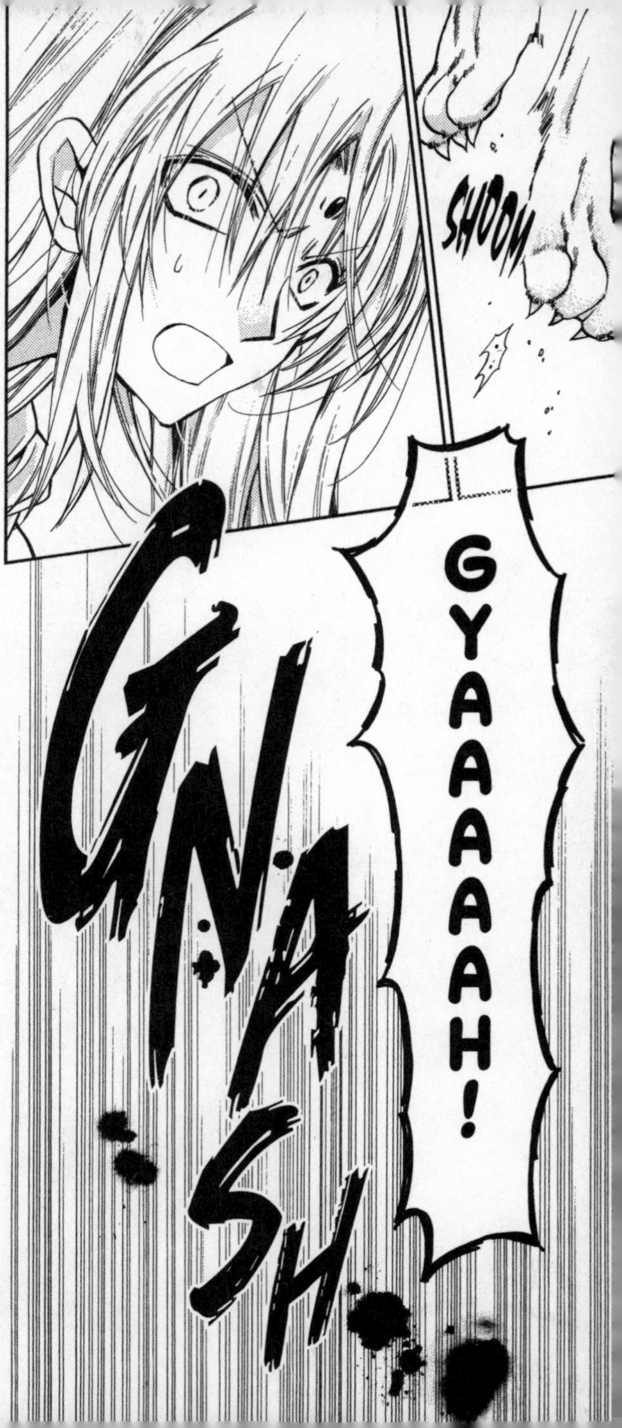
SHOOM
GYAAAAAH!
GNASH

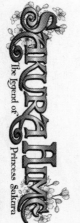

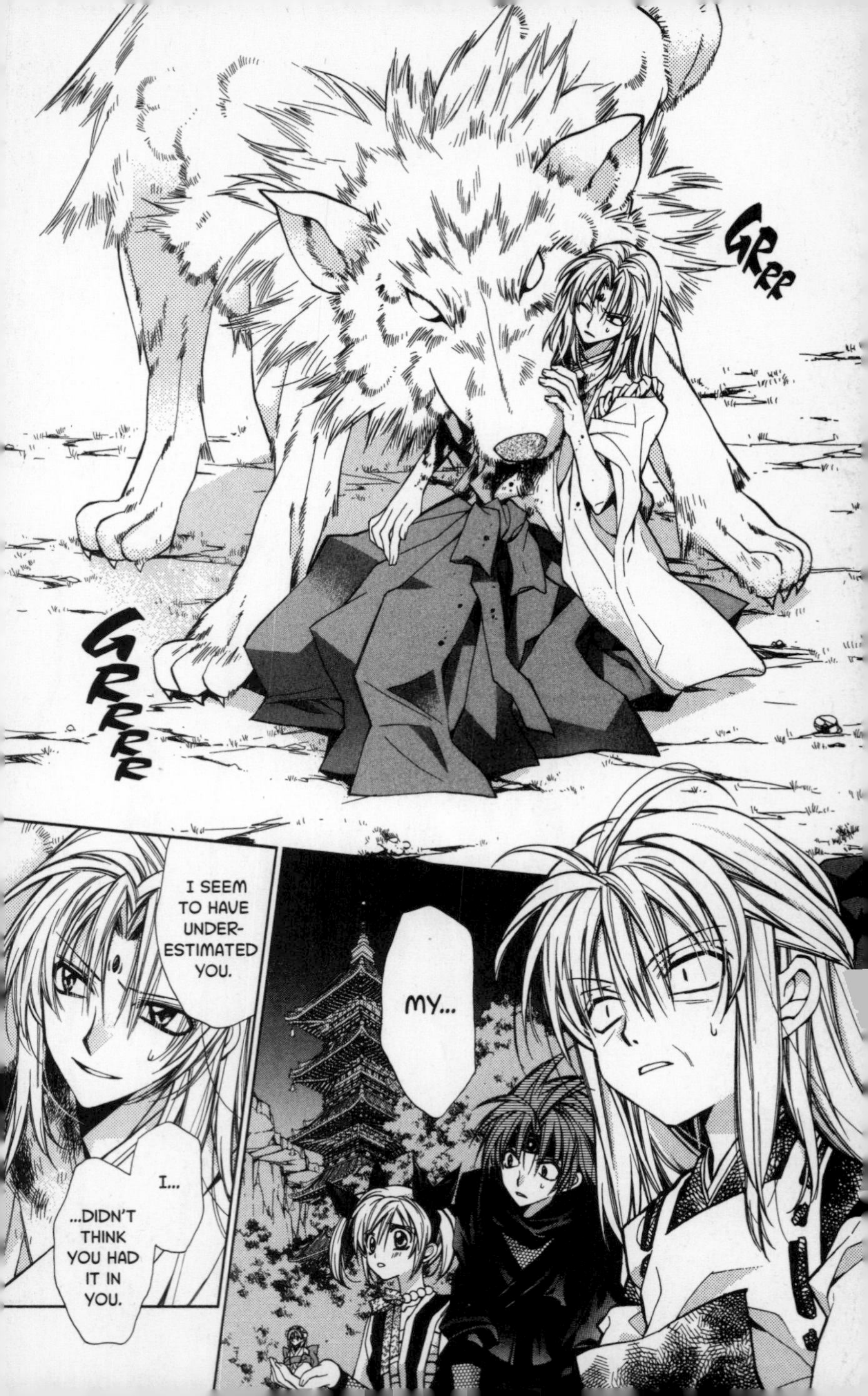
GRRR
GRRRR
MY...
I SEEM TO HAVE UNDER-ESTIMATED YOU.
I...
...DIDN'T THINK YOU HAD IT IN YOU.

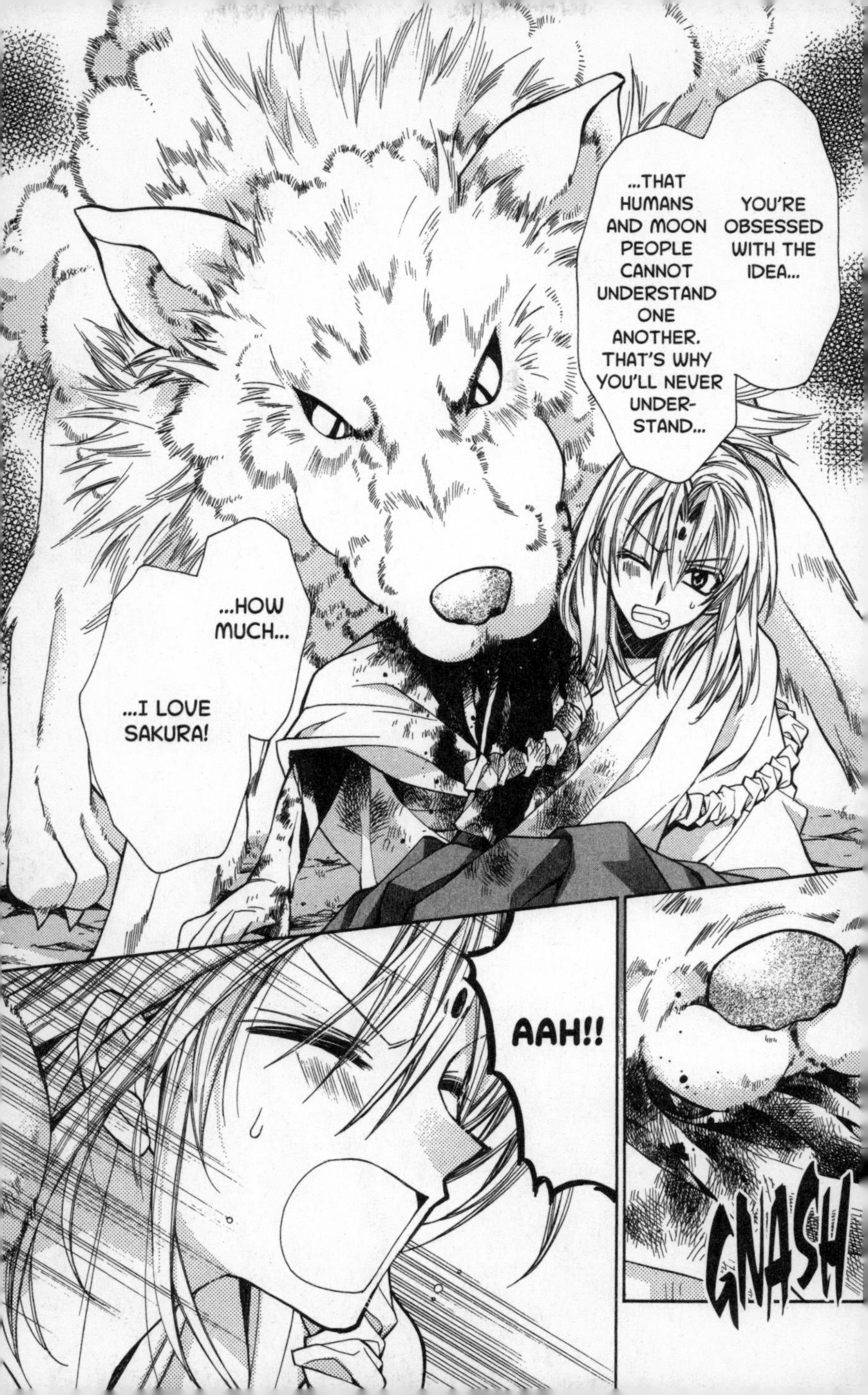
YOU'RE OBSESSED WITH THE IDEA...
...THAT HUMANS AND MOON PEOPLE CANNOT UNDERSTAND ONE ANOTHER. THAT'S WHY YOU'LL NEVER UNDER-STAND...
...HOW MUCH...
...I LOVE SAKURA!
GNASH
AAH!!

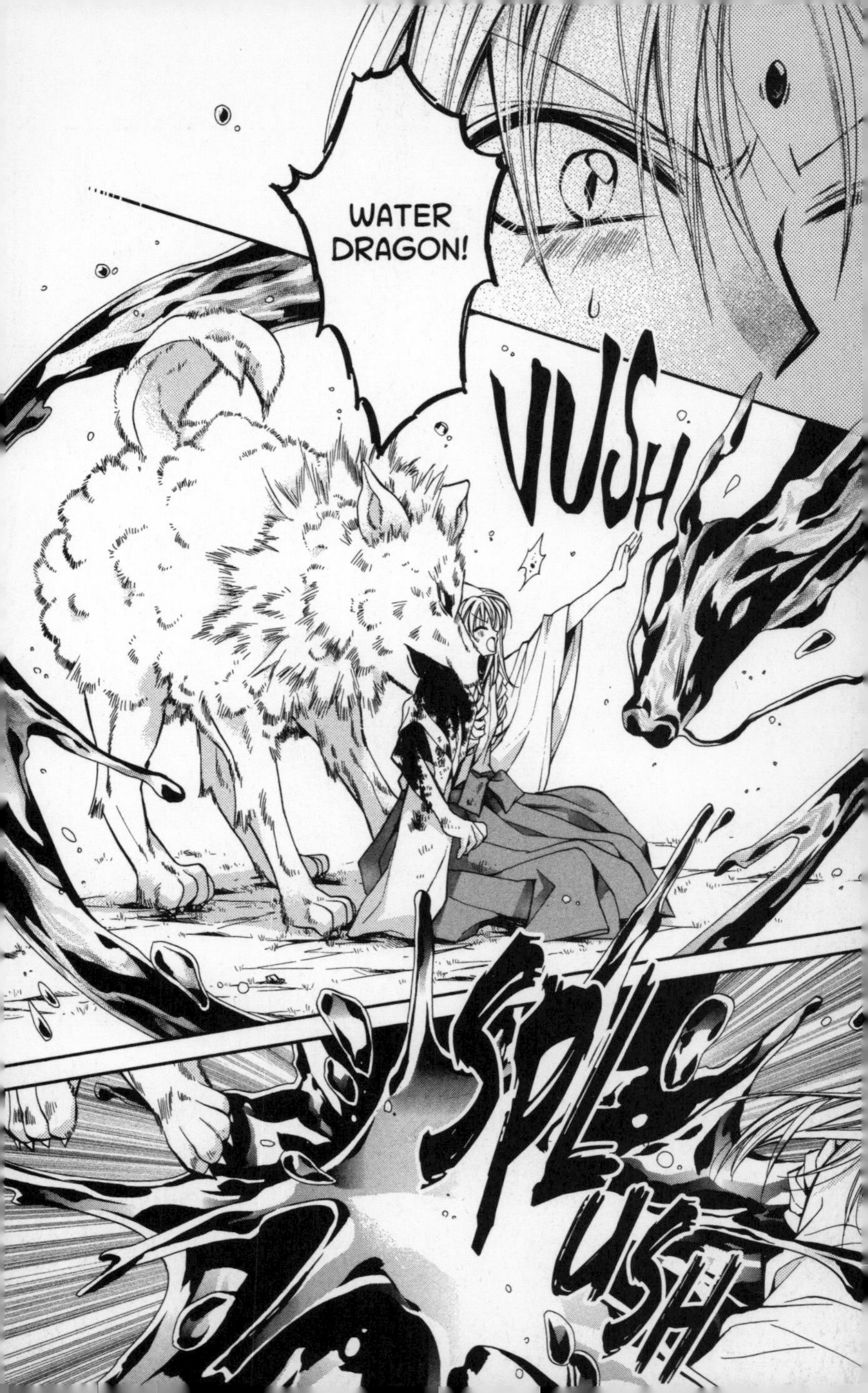
WATER DRAGON!
VUSH
SPLASH
USH

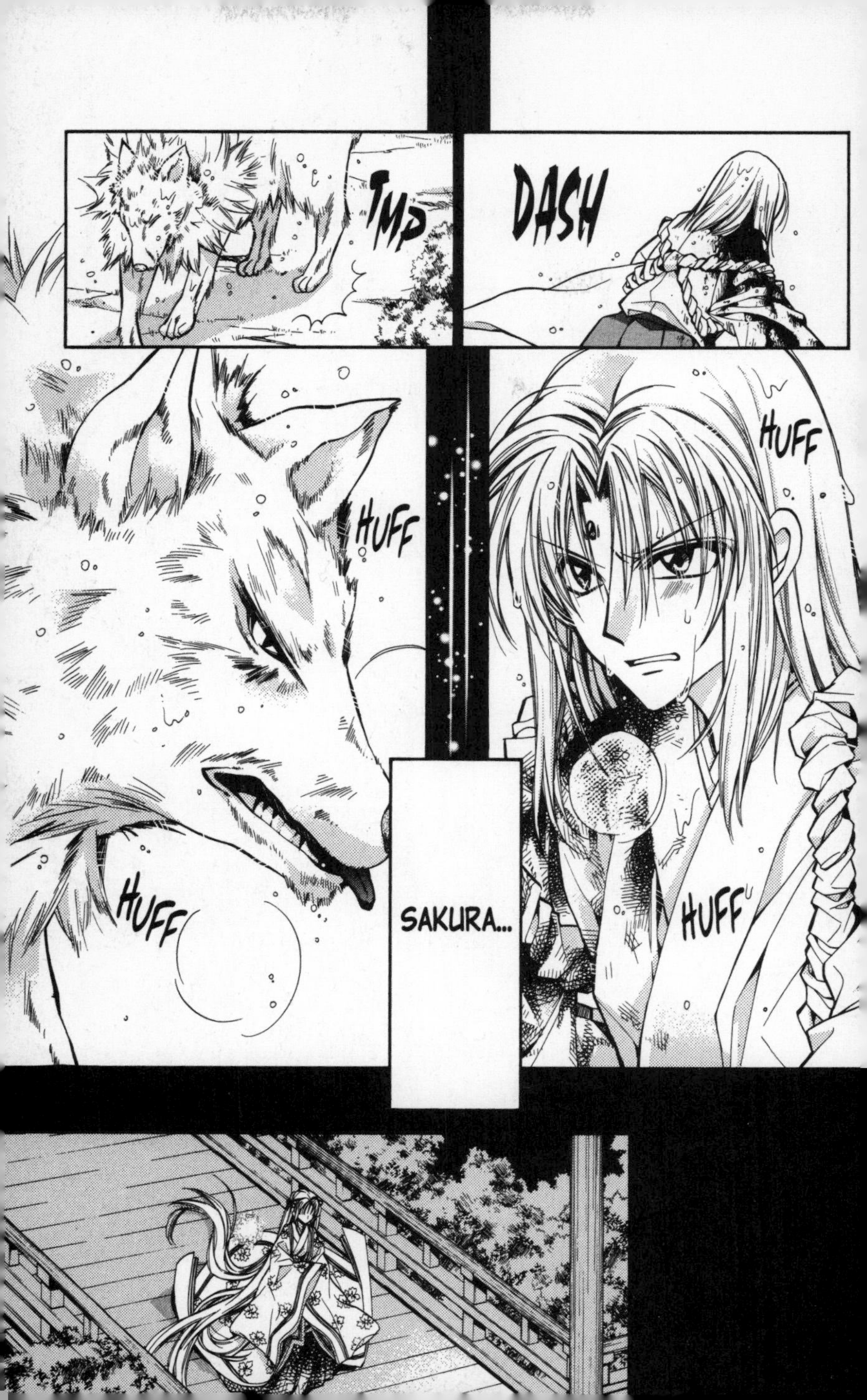

DASH
TMP
HUFF
HUFF
SAKURA...
HUFF
HUFF

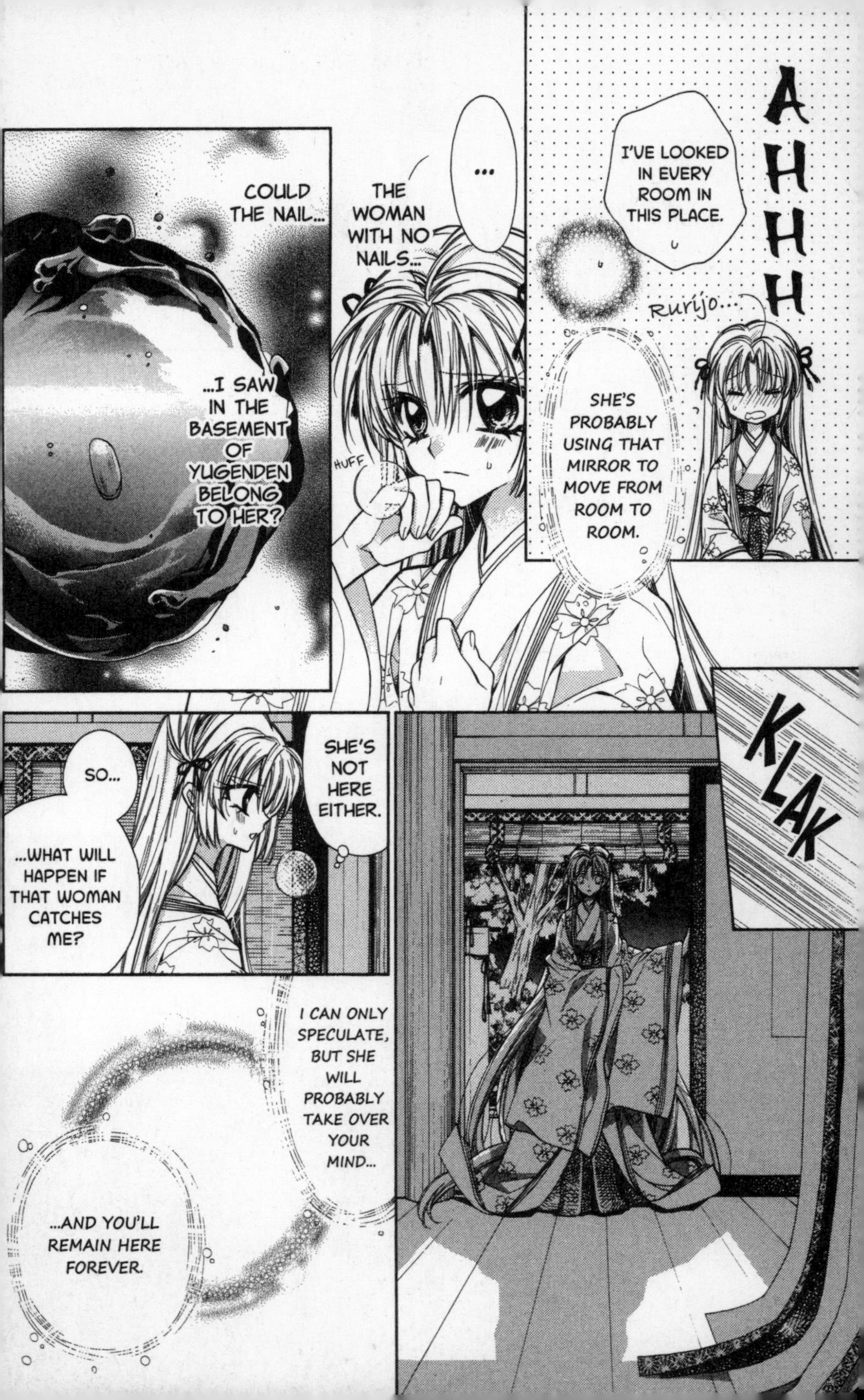
AHHH
I'VE LOOKED IN EVERY ROOM IN THIS PLACE.
Rurijo...
SHE'S PROBABLY USING THAT MIRROR TO MOVE FROM ROOM TO ROOM.
...
THE WOMAN WITH NO NAILS...
HUFF
COULD THE NAIL...
...I SAW IN THE BASEMENT OF YUGENDEN BELONG TO HER?
KLAK
SHE'S NOT HERE EITHER.
SO...
...WHAT WILL HAPPEN IF THAT WOMAN CATCHES ME?
I CAN ONLY SPECULATE, BUT SHE WILL PROBABLY TAKE OVER YOUR MIND...
...AND YOU'LL REMAIN HERE FOREVER.

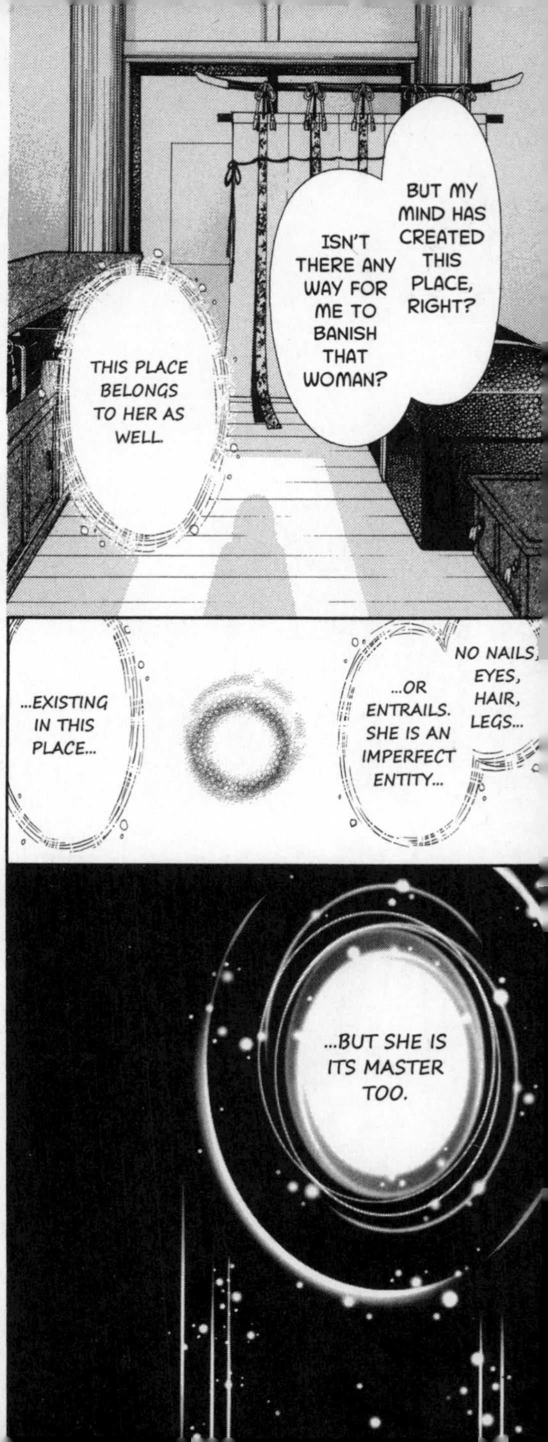
BUT MY MIND HAS CREATED THIS PLACE, RIGHT?
ISN'T THERE ANY WAY FOR ME TO BANISH THAT WOMAN?
THIS PLACE BELONGS TO HER AS WELL.
NO NAILS, EYES, HAIR, LEGS...
...OR ENTRAILS. SHE IS AN IMPERFECT ENTITY...
...EXISTING IN THIS PLACE...
...BUT SHE IS ITS MASTER TOO.

"Rainy Afternoons Are for Romantic Heroines" for *Rainy Afternoons are for Romantic Heroines*
This was my second one-shot since my debut as a manga artist. The song holds special meaning for me as my assistant Miichi had sent me a fan letter about the series. She also told me I should create a CD! I wrote the song lyrics for her. This is my favorite song.

"The Three-Second Miracle" for *I·O·N*
This manga was my very first series and the first book that was published. This brings back memories... I created a one-shot sequel for *I·O·N* recently after 13 years, so I included some of the phrases from the new work. It may sound a bit cheesy, but I tried to create a song that was straightforward and refreshing.

"The Fish's Silver Screen Movie Theater" for *This Love Is Nonfiction*
This was my fourth piece of work. It was placed at the very beginning of a special issue of *Ribon*. I wrote sweet-sounding lyrics for this song because this manga is romantic. The manga takes place in an aquarium, as you may be able to assume from the song's title, but the song is about a fish inside the tank watching the love story outside unfold like a movie.

"Flower Transformation" for *Short-Tempered Melancholic*
My third work and the first that was put in *Ribon* magazine! This story is about a girl ninja. The story is about a girl whose heart sways between two boys, so the first part of the lyrics are aimed towards one boy, and the second part to the other. The people around me loved the last part of the song, so please listen to it.

Continues →

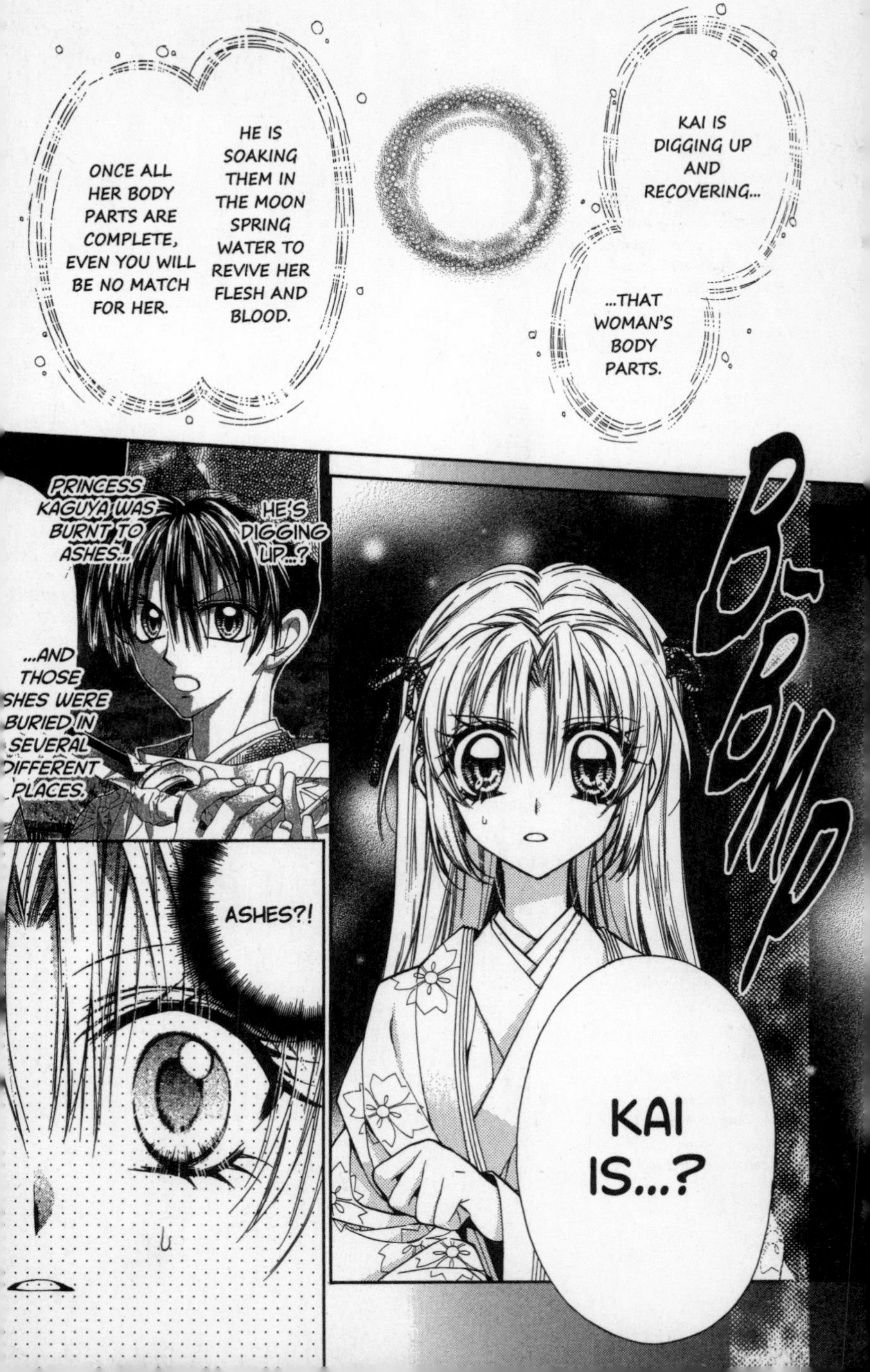
KAI IS DIGGING UP AND RECOVERING...
...THAT WOMAN'S BODY PARTS.
HE IS SOAKING THEM IN THE MOON SPRING WATER TO REVIVE HER FLESH AND BLOOD.
ONCE ALL HER BODY PARTS ARE COMPLETE, EVEN YOU WILL BE NO MATCH FOR HER.
KAI IS...?
HE'S DIGGING UP...?
PRINCESS KAGUYA WAS BURNT TO ASHES...
...AND THOSE SHES WERE BURIED IN SEVERAL IFFERENT PLACES.
ASHES?!

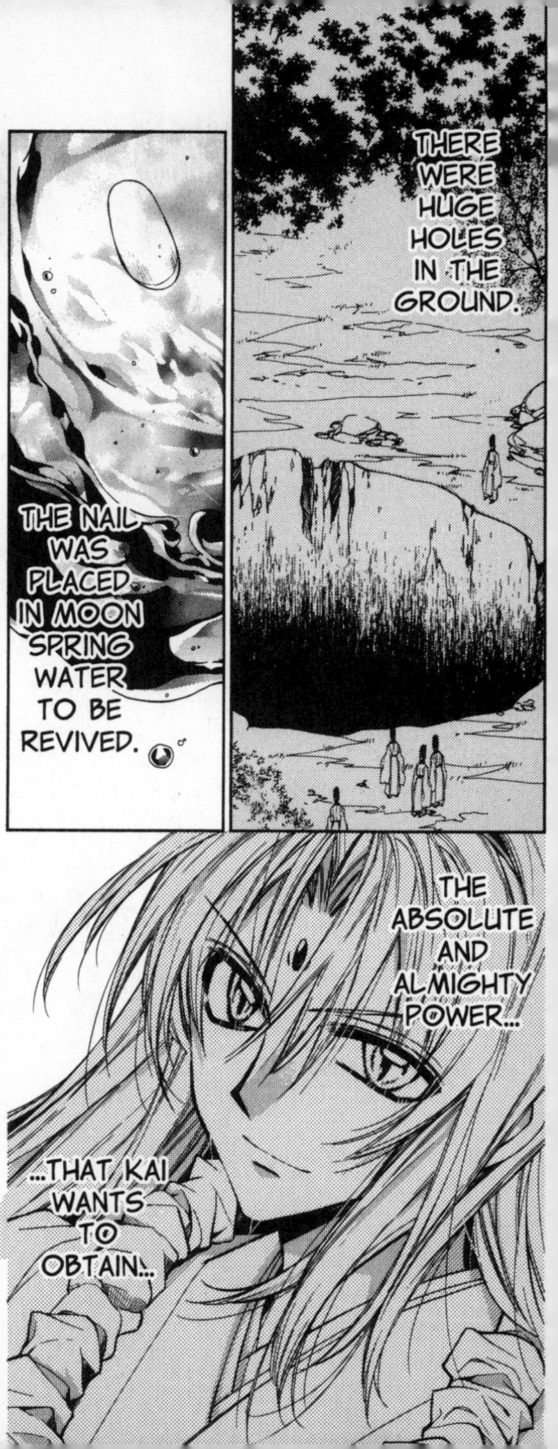
THERE WERE HUGE HOLES IN THE GROUND.
THE NAIL WAS PLACED IN MOON SPRING WATER TO BE REVIVED.
THE ABSOLUTE AND ALMIGHTY POWER...
...THAT KAI WANTS TO OBTAIN...

"Full Moon" for *Full Moon*
The moment I heard the music, I thought, "This is a song about Mitsuki and Eichi!" I wrote lyrics about their ephemeral and crystal-clear love for each other.
I was very happy because a lot of people liked it. (Serious-sounding lyrics are harder to write.)

"The Forbidden Cross Game" for *The Gentlemen's Alliance Cross*
The title is meant to be a pun in Japanese: "Close Game" and "Cross Game." The manga contains intertwining feelings and unrequited loves, so I tried to create the lyrics with that in mind. The music has a very mysterious sound to it that is perfect for *The Gentlemen's Alliance*.
I really am grateful.

This self-produced CD will be sold on December 29, 2010, at the Winter Comike at Tokyo Big Sight.
You will also be able to buy the CD at Animate all over Japan starting at the end of January.
You should be able to buy the CD online at Animate too, so please look into it.

(I would recommend people buy the CD at Comike or have a friend buy it for them. I am thinking about handing out a book about the production of the CD at Comike.)
You can only get this book at the event. I'm sorry.
There will be a limited number of books, so they will be handed out on a first-come-first-served basis.
The books are free.

And... I'm sorry
I'm a bad singer.
(BLUNT)

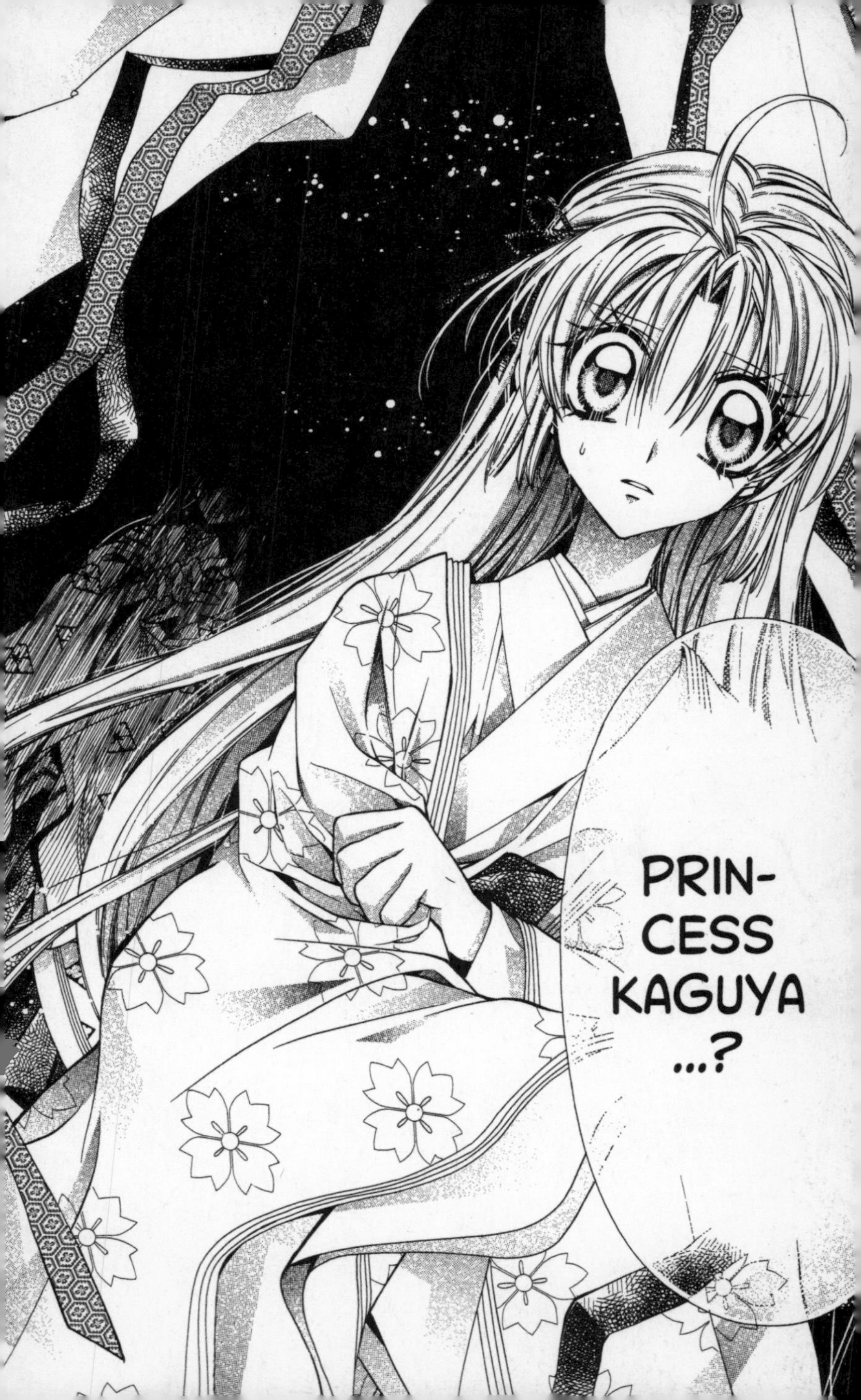
PRIN-CESS KAGUYA ...?

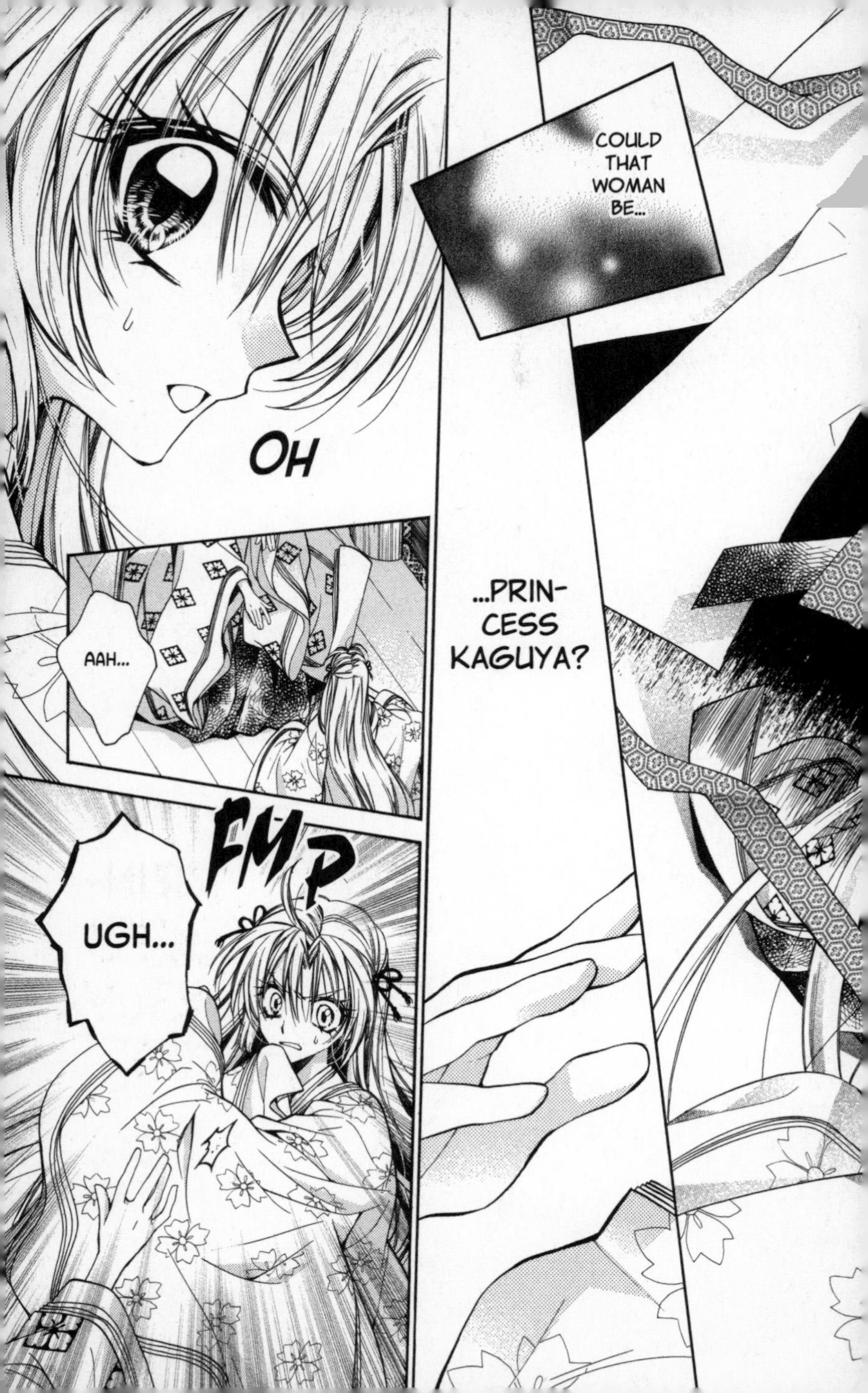
COULD THAT WOMAN BE...
...PRIN-CESS KAGUYA?
OH
AAH...
FMP
UGH...

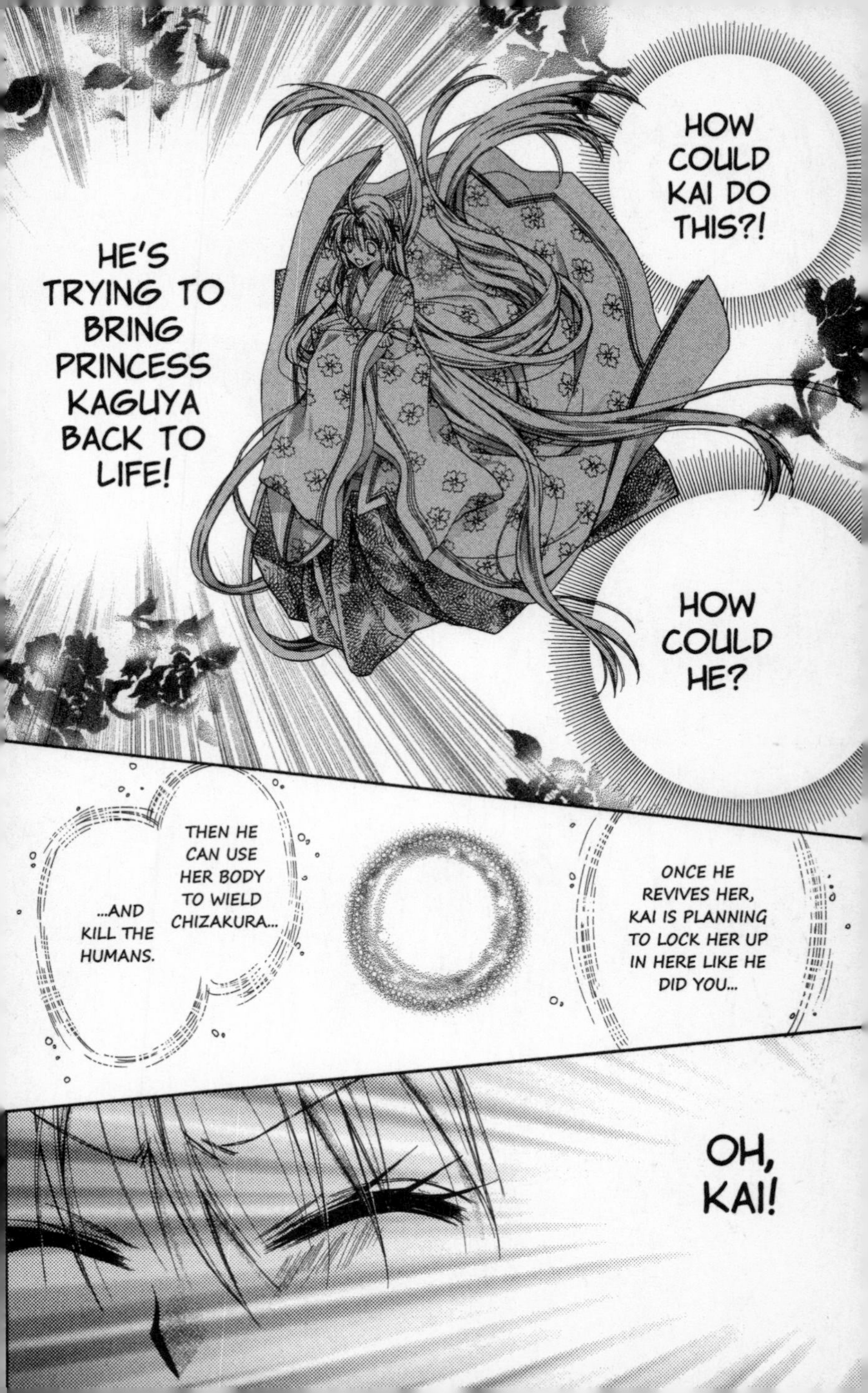
HOW COULD KAI DO THIS?!
HE'S TRYING TO BRING PRINCESS KAGUYA BACK TO LIFE!
HOW COULD HE?
ONCE HE REVIVES HER, KAI IS PLANNING TO LOCK HER UP IN HERE LIKE HE DID YOU...
THEN HE CAN USE HER BODY TO WIELD CHIZAKURA...
...AND KILL THE HUMANS.
OH, KAI!

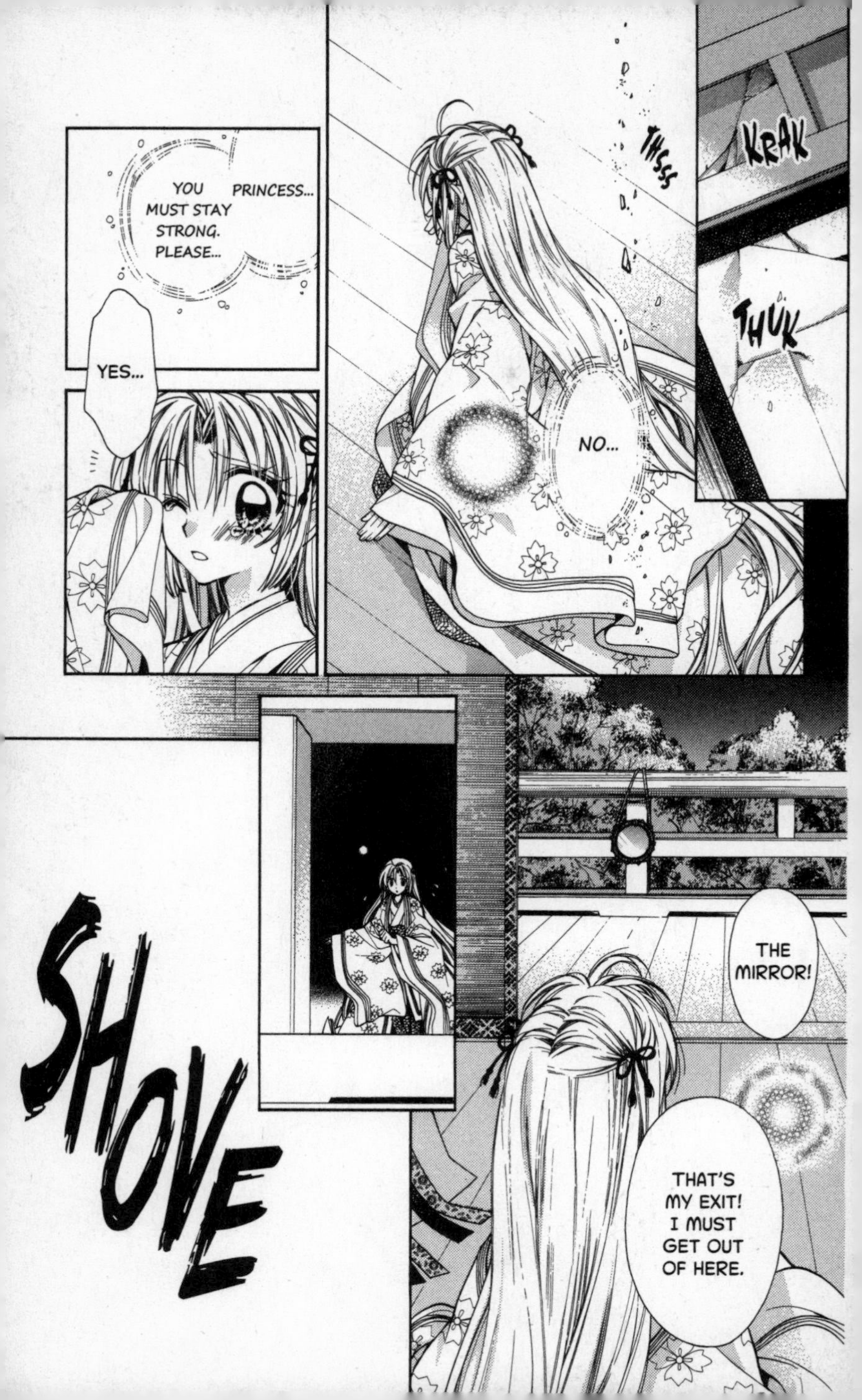
KRAK
THUK
THSSS
NO...
PRINCESS... YOU MUST STAY STRONG. PLEASE...
YES...
THE MIRROR!
THAT'S MY EXIT! I MUST GET OUT OF HERE.
SHOVE

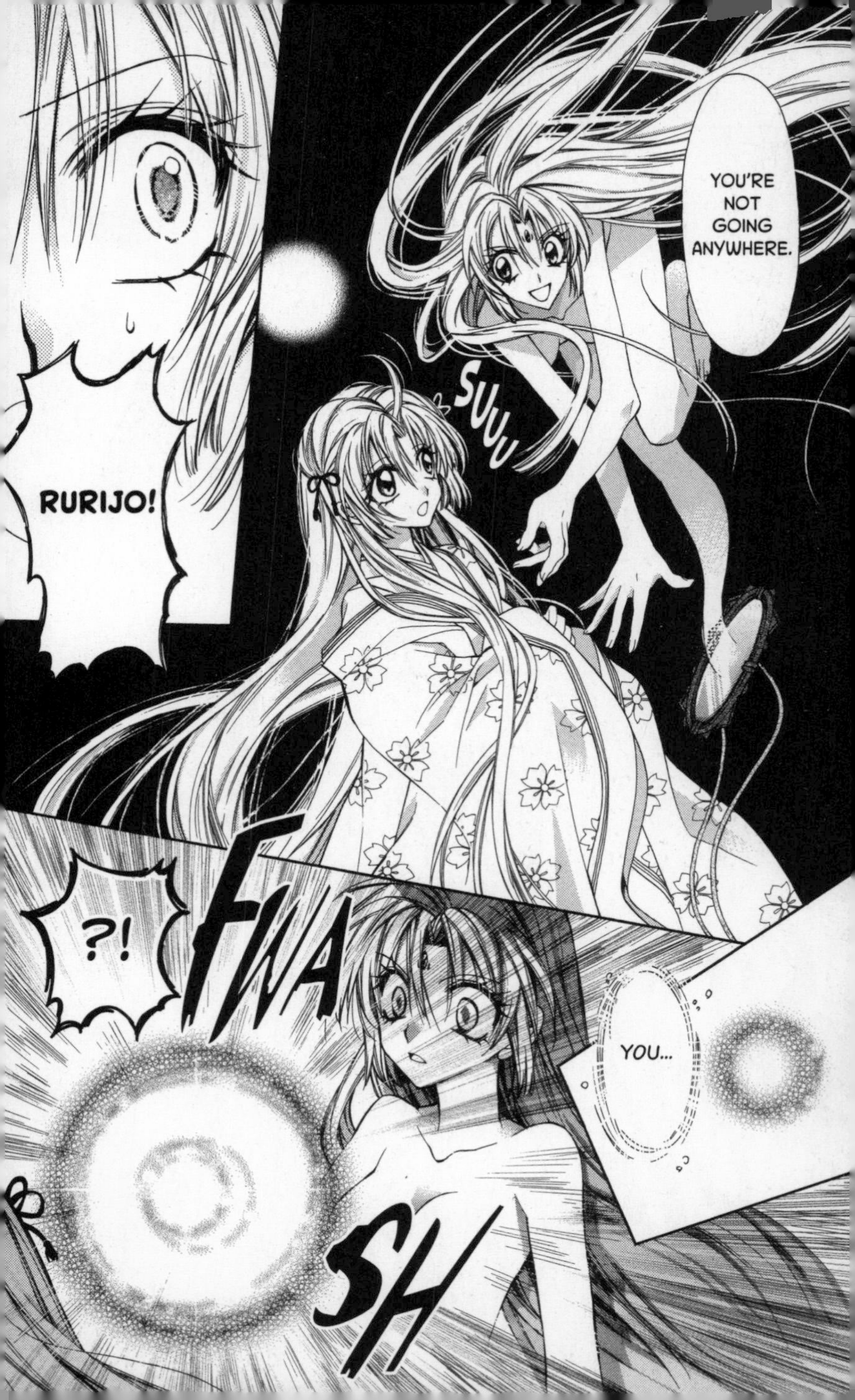
YOU'RE NOT GOING ANYWHERE.
SUUU
RURIJO!
FWA
?!
YOU...
SH

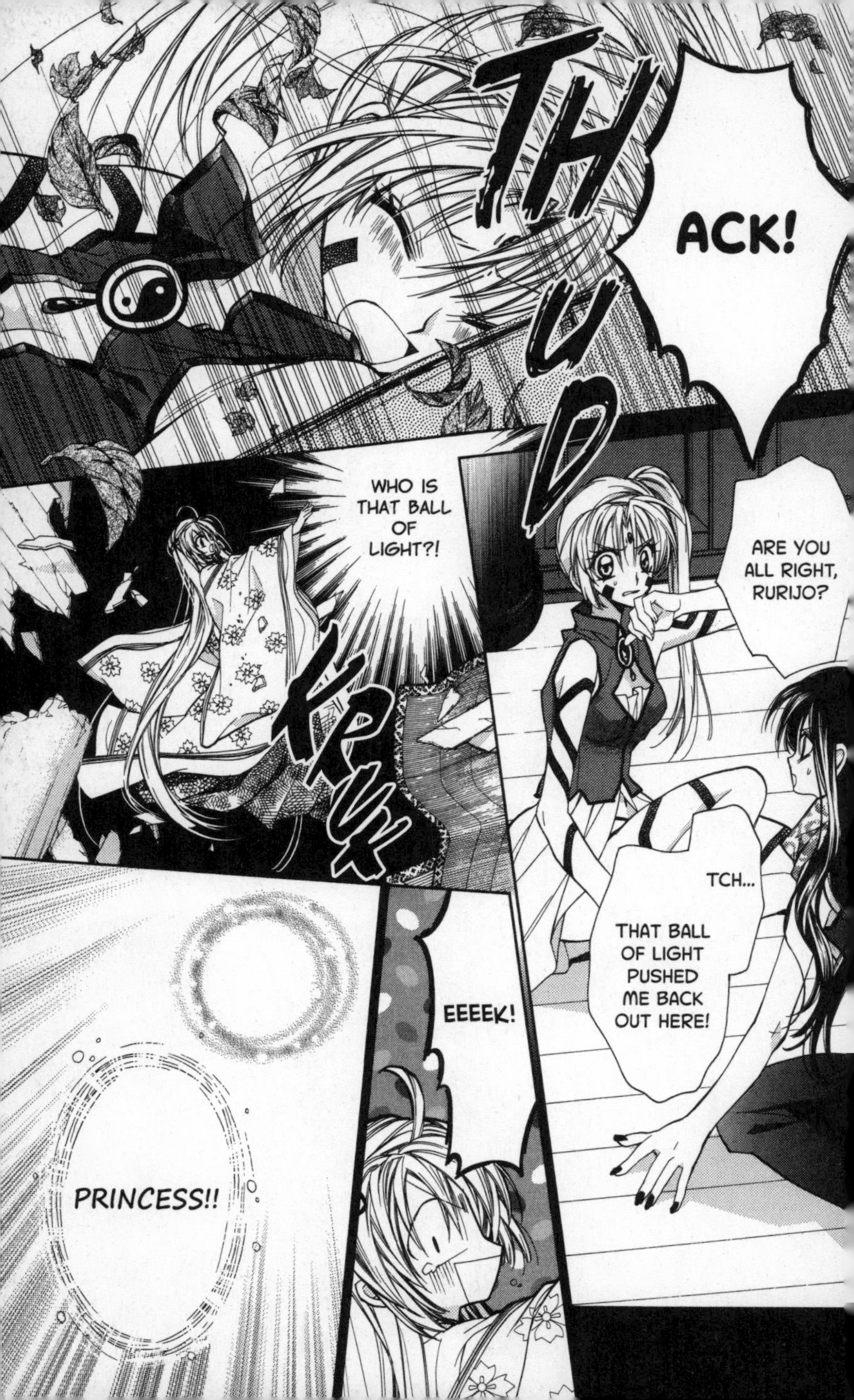
THUD
ACK!
ARE YOU ALL RIGHT, RURIJO?
TCH...
THAT BALL OF LIGHT PUSHED ME BACK OUT HERE!
WHO IS THAT BALL OF LIGHT?!
KRUK
EEEEK!
PRINCESS!!

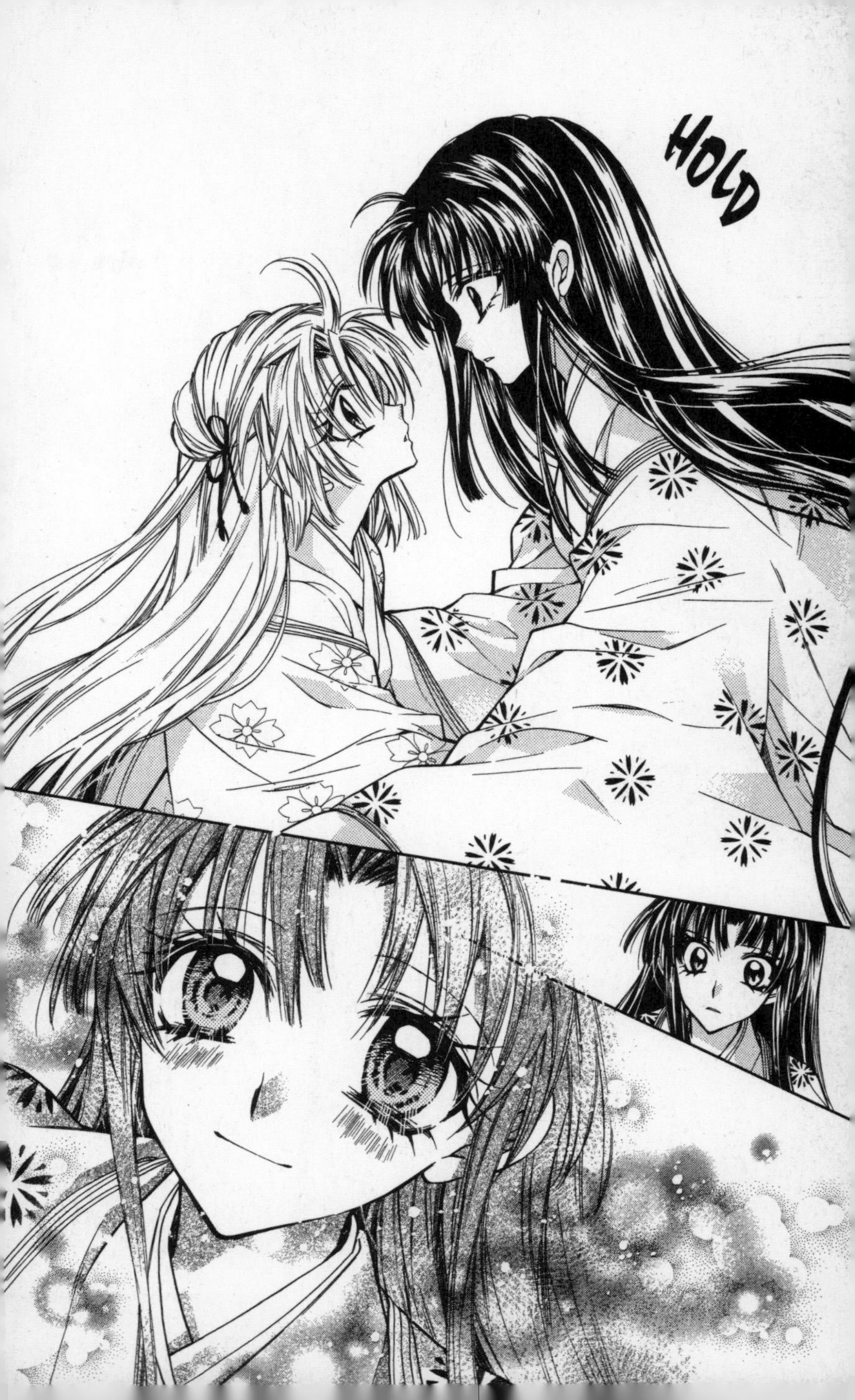
HOLD

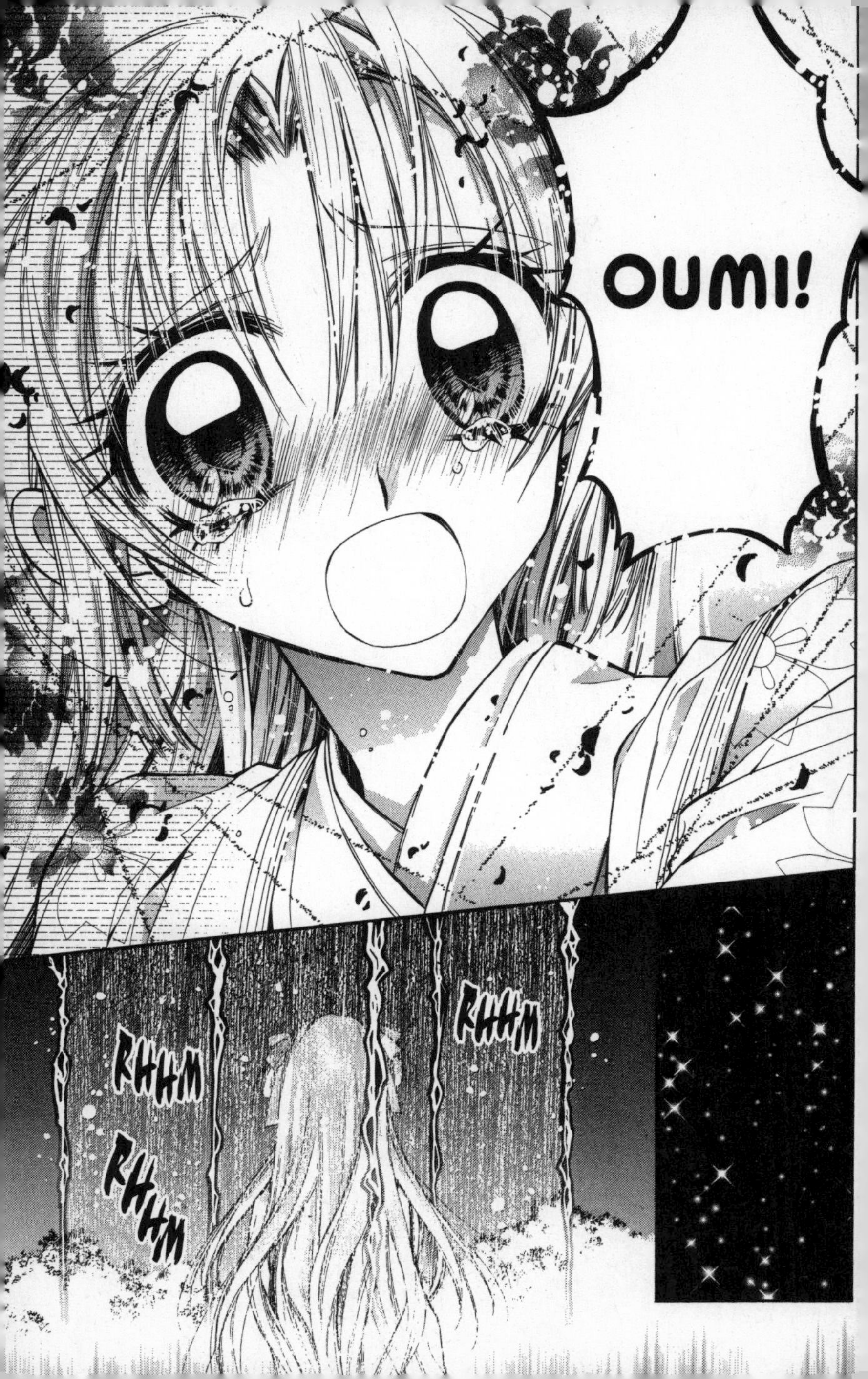
OUMI!
RHHM
RHHM
RHHM

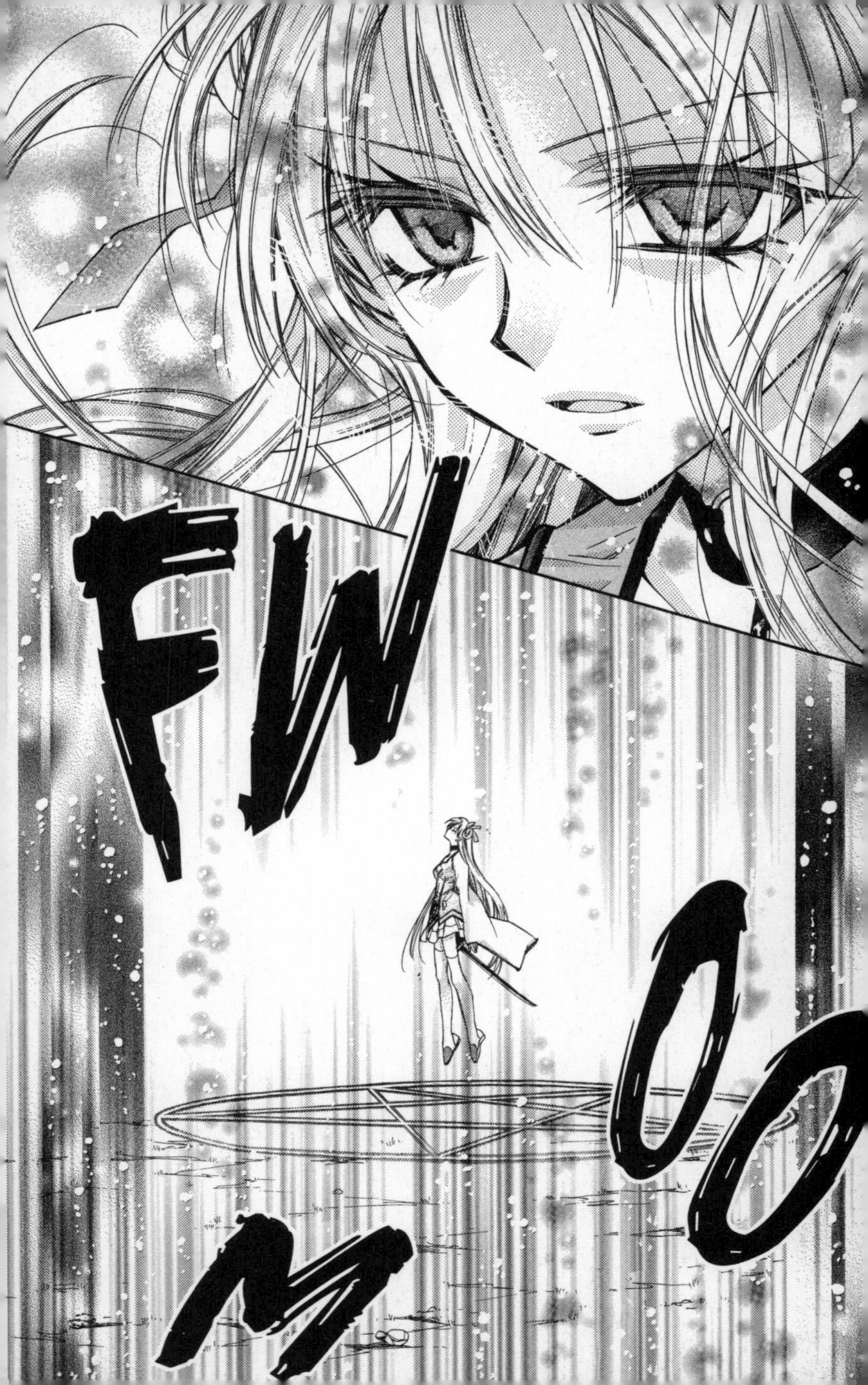
FWOOM

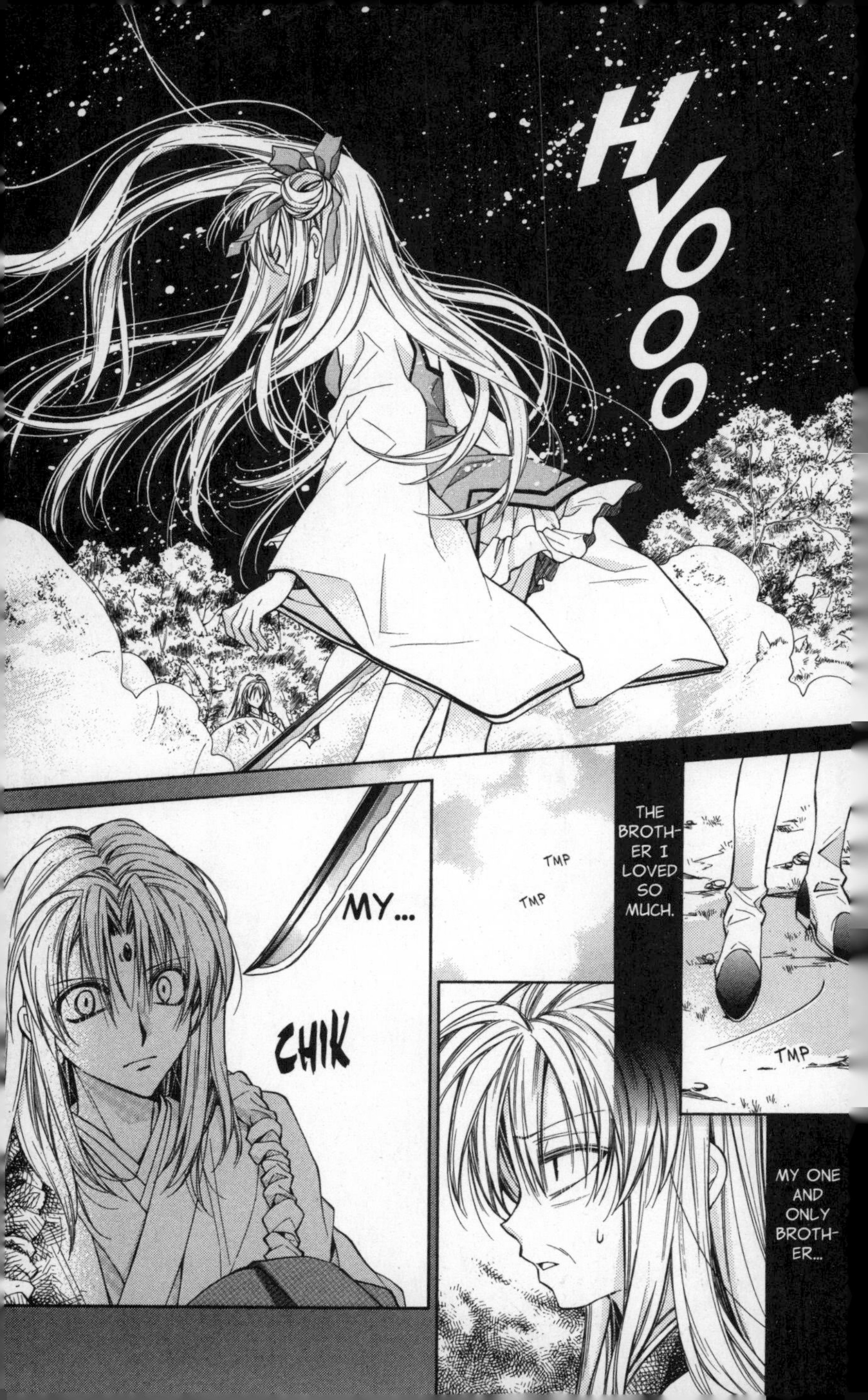
HYOOO
THE BROTH-ER I LOVED SO MUCH.
TMP
TMP
TMP
MY...
CHIK
MY ONE AND ONLY BROTH-ER...

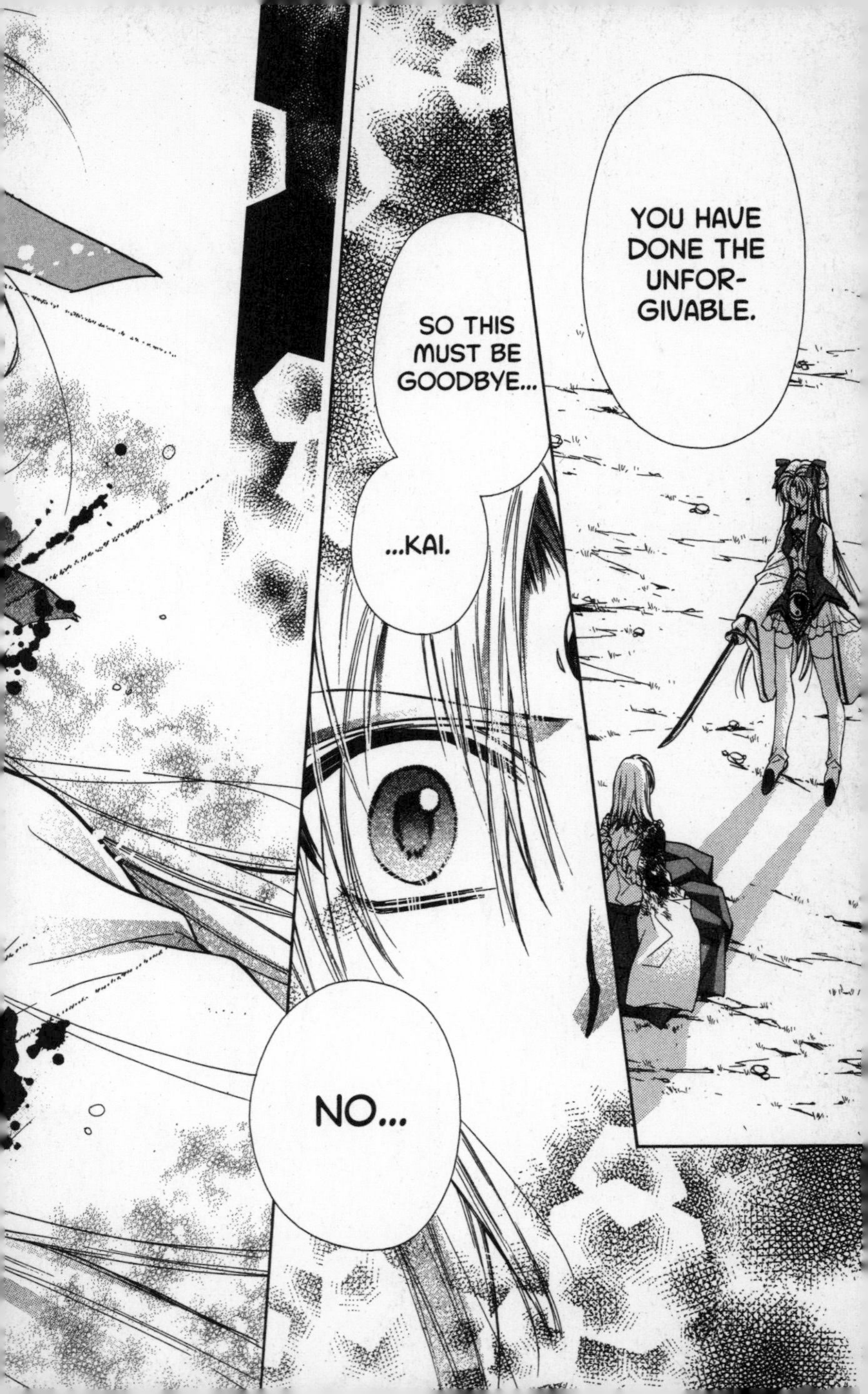
YOU HAVE DONE THE UNFOR-GIVABLE.
SO THIS MUST BE GOODBYE...
...KAI.
NO...

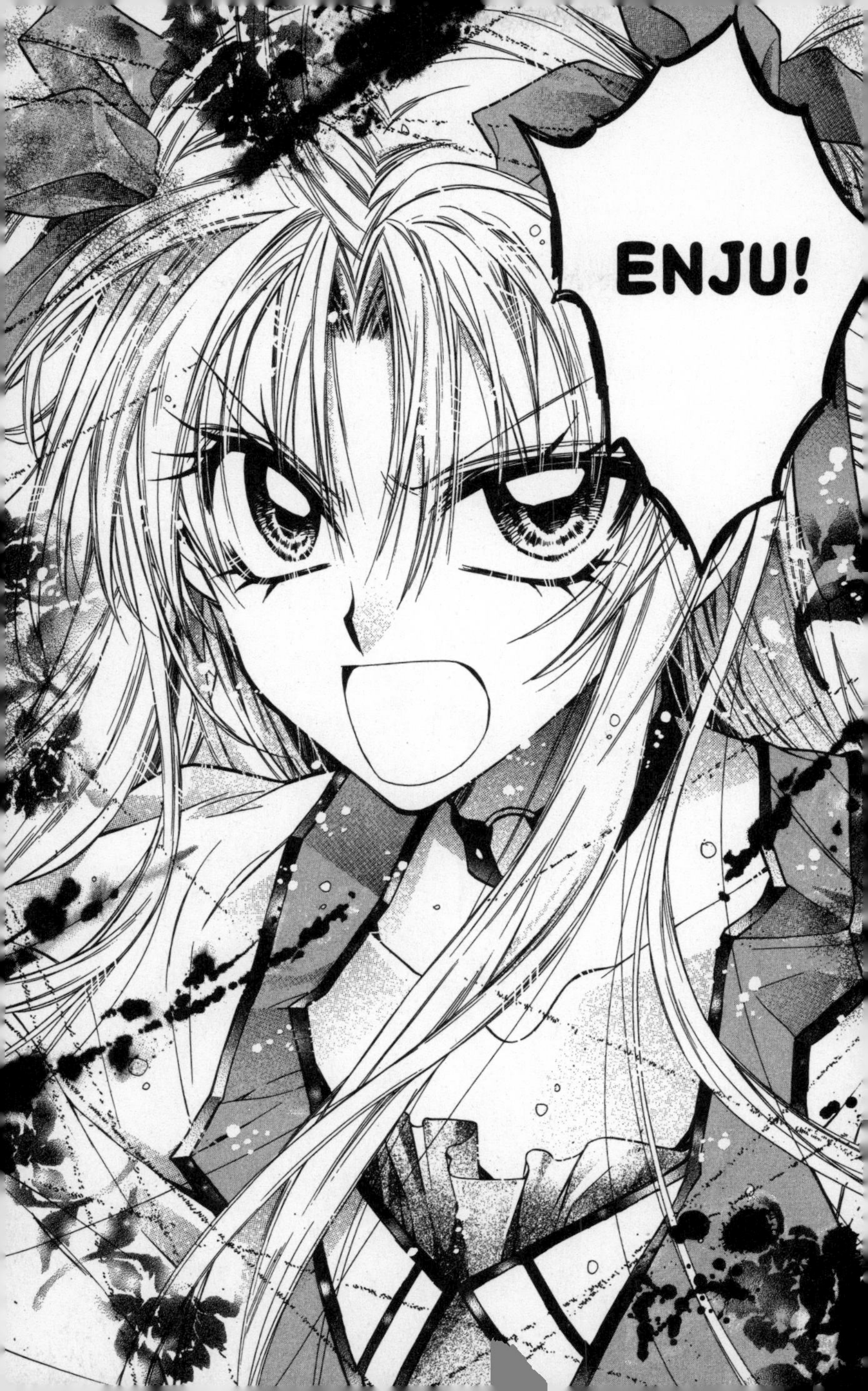
ENJU!

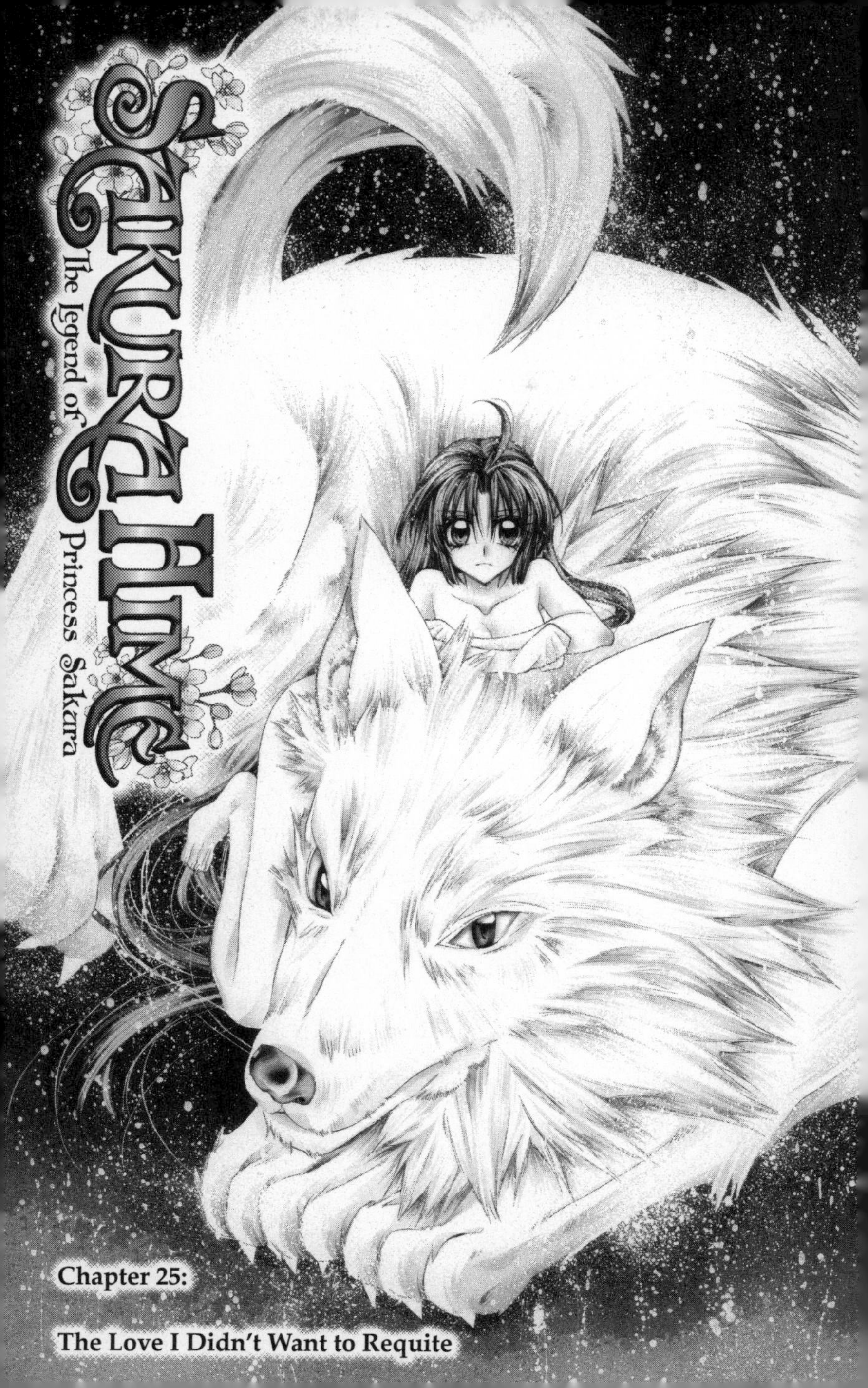
Sakura Hime
The Legend of Princess Sakura

Chapter 25:

The Love I Didn't Want to Requite

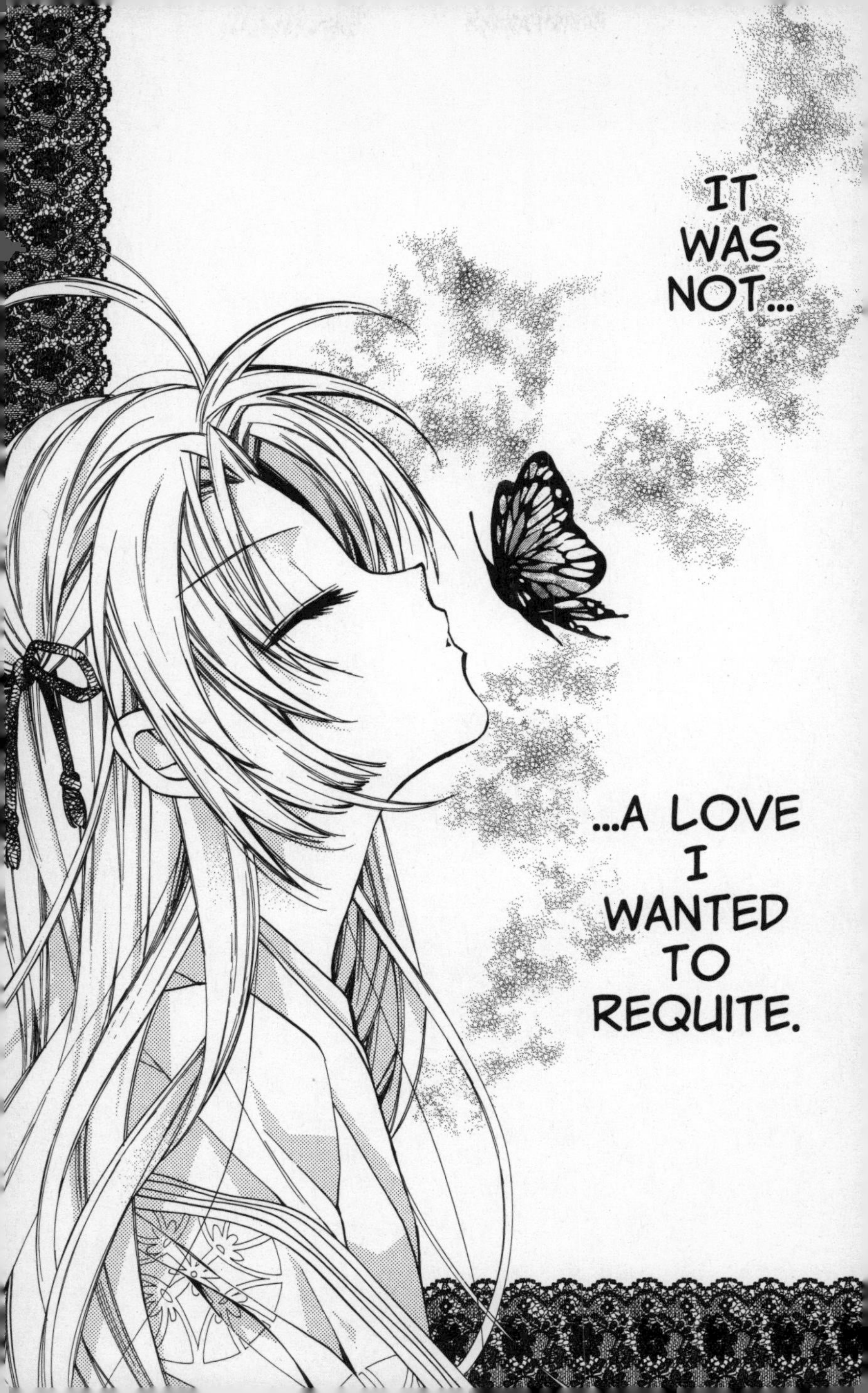
IT WAS NOT...
...A LOVE I WANTED TO REQUITE.

Chapter 25: The Love I Didn't Want to Requite

※ I'm giving away the story.

This is the last chapter of the Shura Yugenden arc.
You get to see a lot of Fujimurasaki scenes as if he's trying to get rid of his frustration for not being able to appear in the manga all this time.
"The Love I Didn't Want to Requite" may sound strange. After all, you fall in love because you want to make it come true.
Sakura probably knew the love she had for him would never be realized, but she still couldn't restrain those feelings. I think that is fine. But the person she was in love with was "Kai," not "Enju." It's as if she's chasing his shadow...
He's her first love whom she can't forget. The way she loves Aoba is a more real kind of love.
The scene with Fujimurasaki and Sakura at the edge of the cliff and the two-page spread at the very end were scenes I had really looked forward to drawing, so I'm glad I finally reached that point.
That was a very important line for Fujimurasaki. (I wonder when I'll be able to do the one-shot about Fujimurasaki... Maybe I'll just include it in the main story if I can't get around to doing it.)
Anyway, the story will take a new turn in the next volume.
Maybe Sakura will finally start having a proper romantic relationship?
Please look forward to it, and please keep supporting this series. ♪

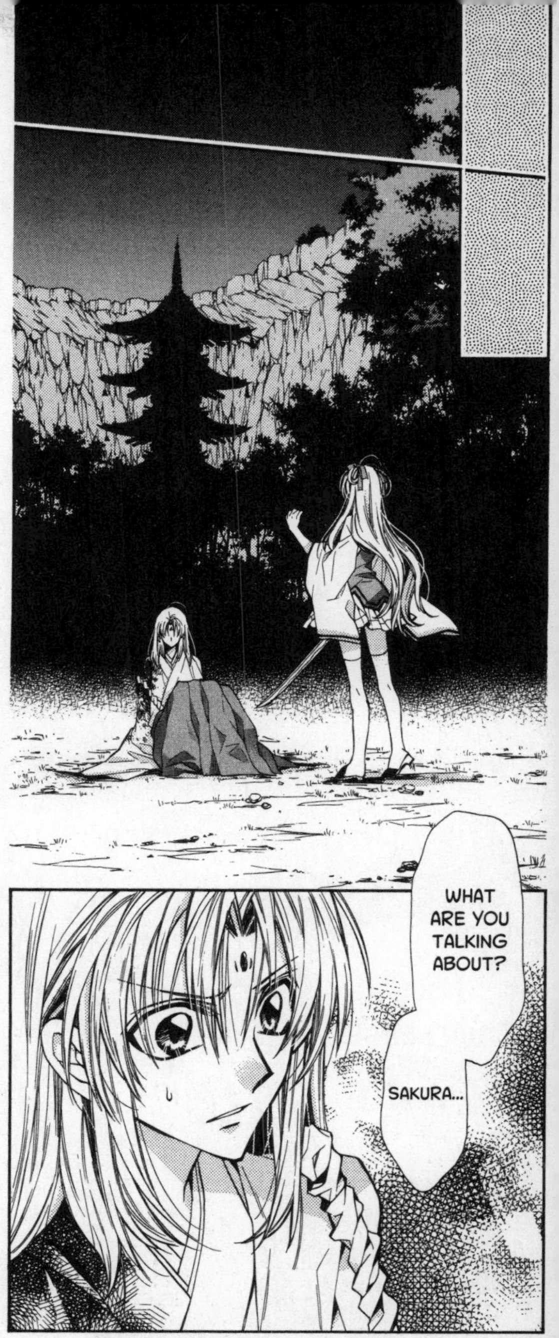
WHAT ARE YOU TALKING ABOUT?
SAKURA...

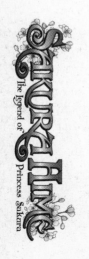

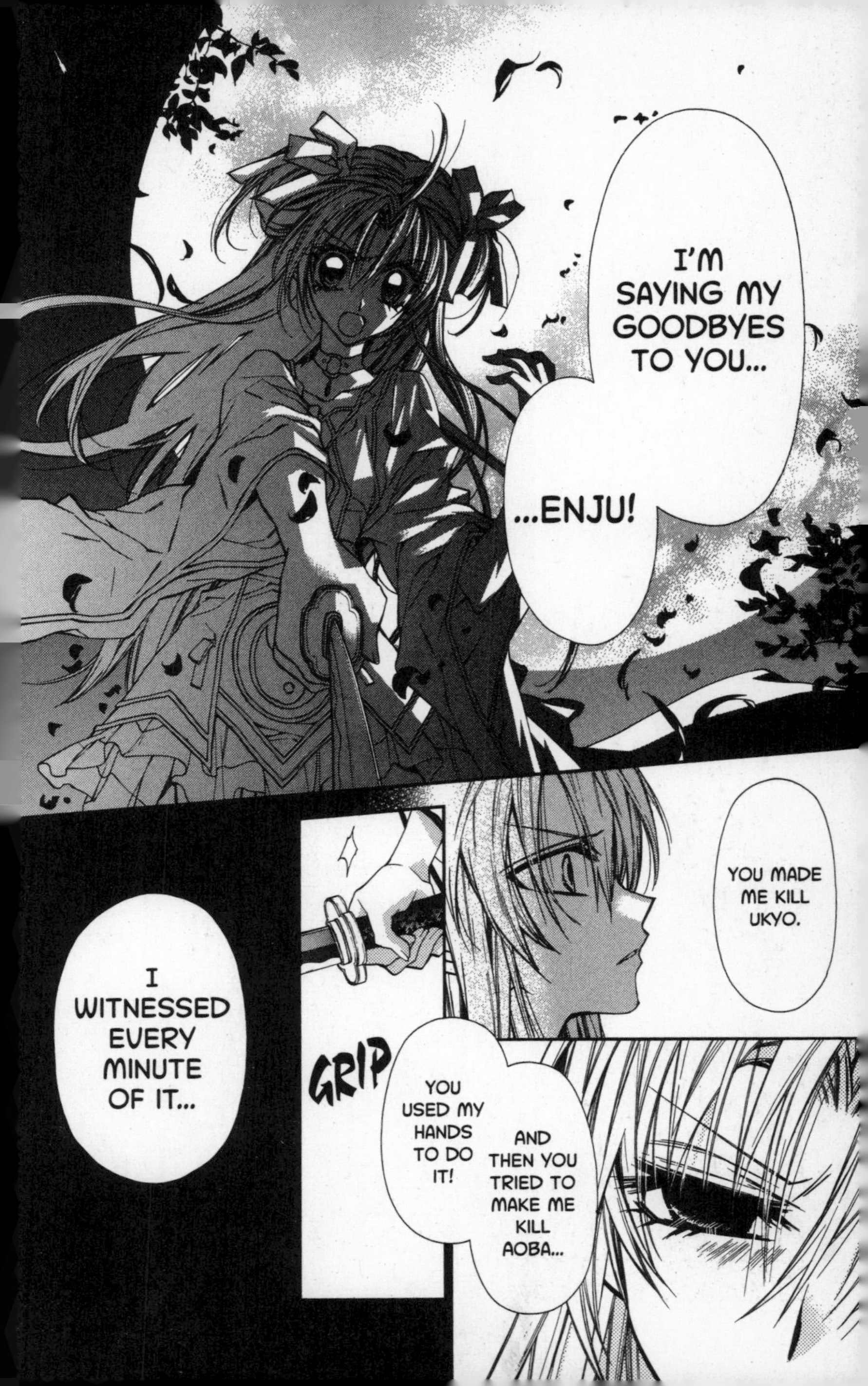
I'M SAYING MY GOODBYES TO YOU...
...ENJU!
YOU MADE ME KILL UKYO.
GRIP
YOU USED MY HANDS TO DO IT!
AND THEN YOU TRIED TO MAKE ME KILL AOBA...
I WITNESSED EVERY MINUTE OF IT...

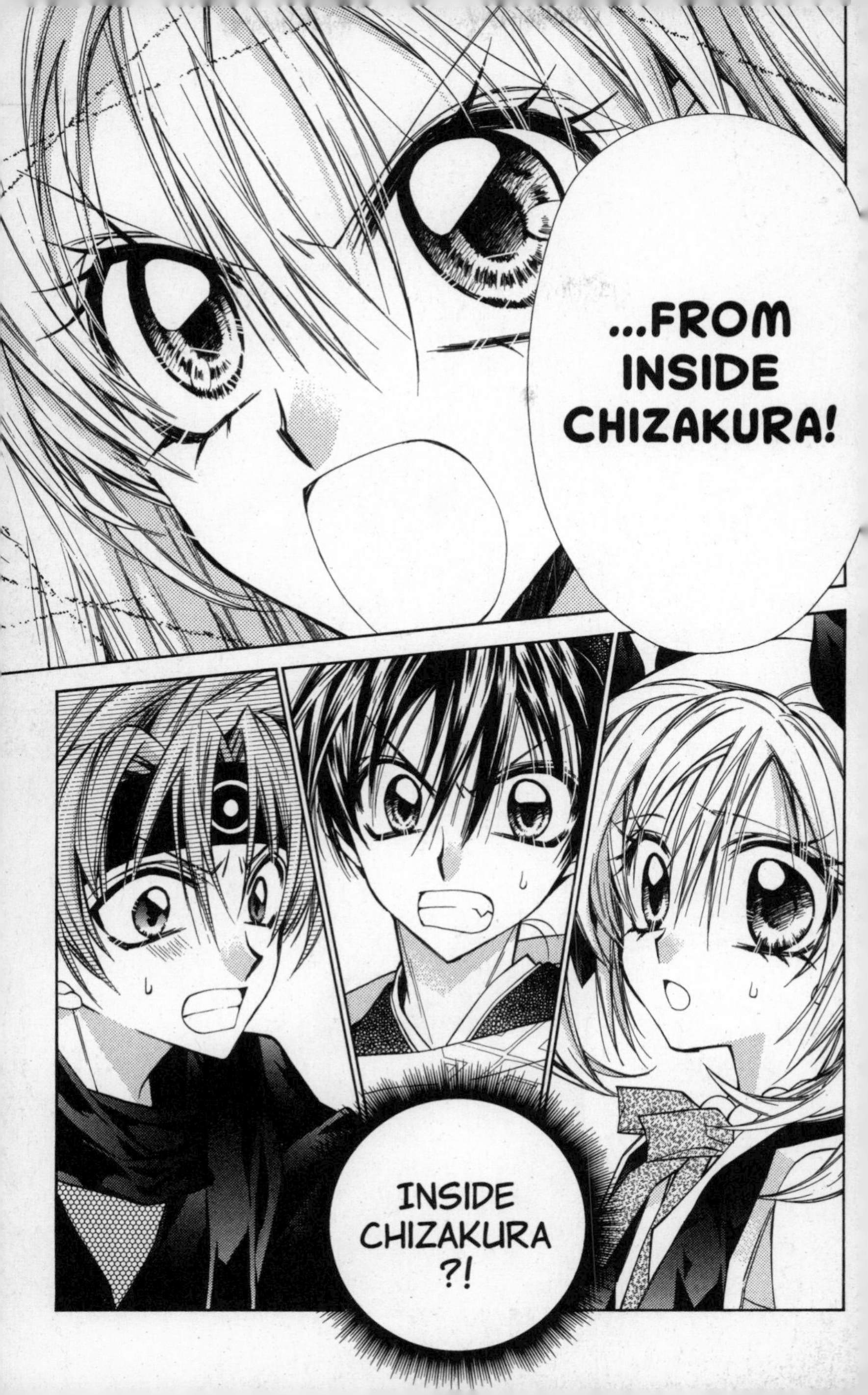
...FROM INSIDE CHIZAKURA!
INSIDE CHIZAKURA ?!

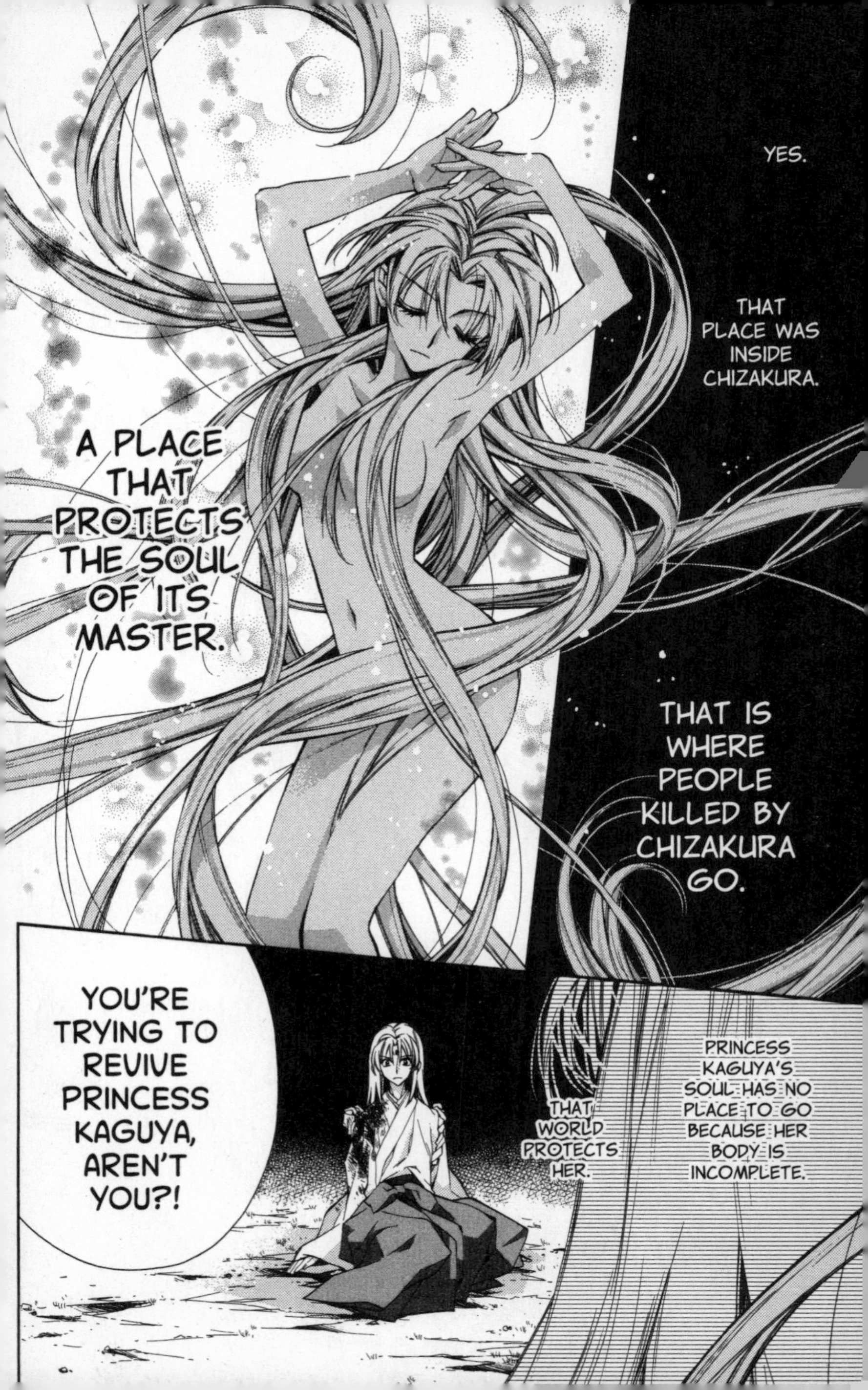
YES.
THAT PLACE WAS INSIDE CHIZAKURA.
A PLACE THAT PROTECTS THE SOUL OF ITS MASTER.
THAT IS WHERE PEOPLE KILLED BY CHIZAKURA GO.
PRINCESS KAGUYA'S SOUL HAS NO PLACE TO GO BECAUSE HER BODY IS INCOMPLETE.
THAT WORLD PROTECTS HER.
YOU'RE TRYING TO REVIVE PRINCESS KAGUYA, AREN'T YOU?!

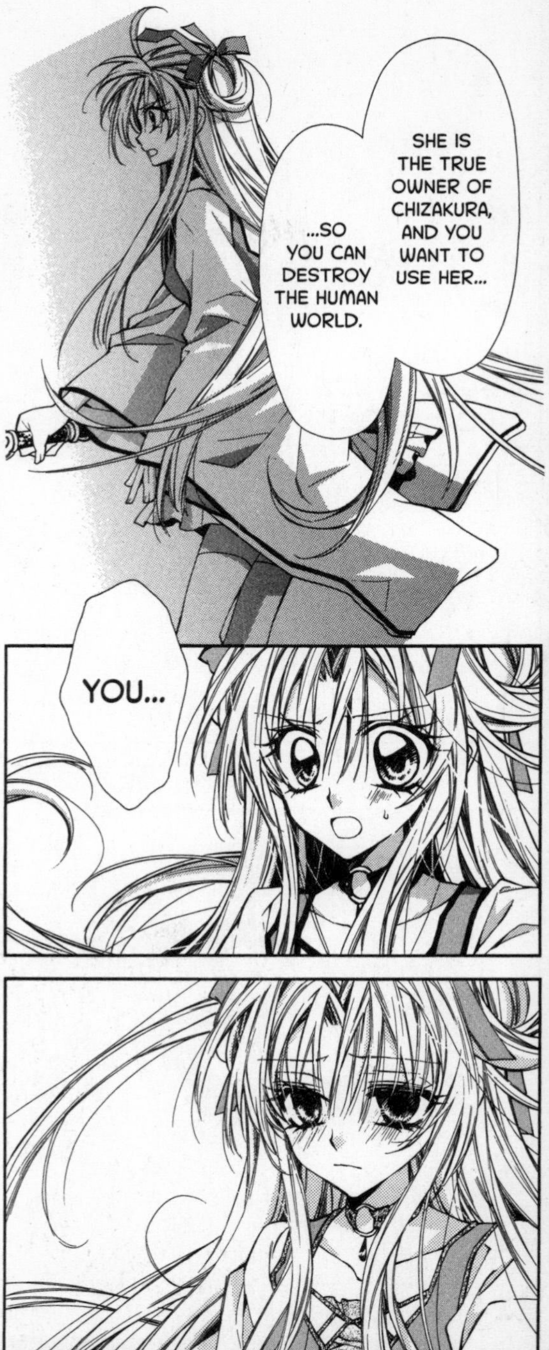
SHE IS THE TRUE OWNER OF CHIZAKURA, AND YOU WANT TO USE HER...
...SO YOU CAN DESTROY THE HUMAN WORLD.
YOU...

GOODBYE

Monster Hunter Portable 3rd (video game) will be out soon.

I'm going to be playing it all the time with my friends at the end of this year and beginning of the next.

We'll have a sleepover!!

I made friends with a lot of people this year.

I hope next year will be filled with many joys as well.☆

Thank you, and see you in volume 8.

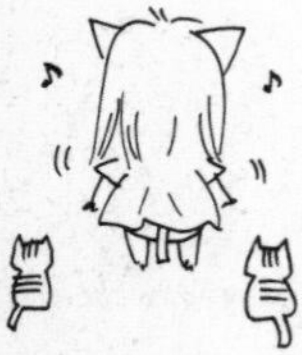

☆ Special Thanks ☆

Nakame
Itakura-san
Kawanishi-san
Kawamura-san
Momo-chan

Miichi
Hina-chan
Ikurun
Momo-san
Yuki-chan
Naho Minami-chan
Nakazawa-san
Kyomoto-san
Konako

Shueisha
Ribon Editorial Department

Ammonite, Inc.

Kawatani-san
(Kawatani Design)

Sobisha

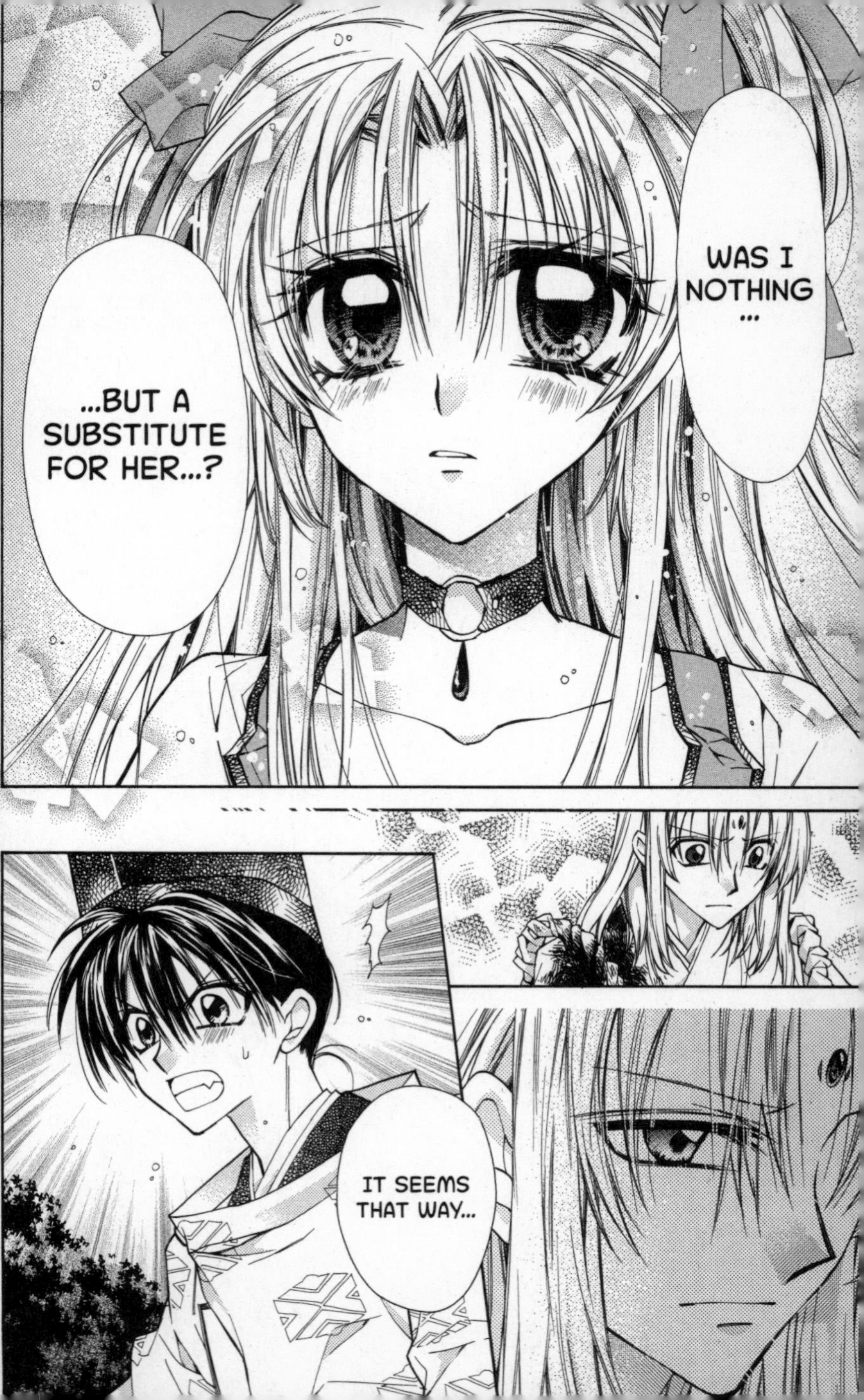
WAS I NOTHING ...
...BUT A SUBSTITUTE FOR HER...?
IT SEEMS THAT WAY...

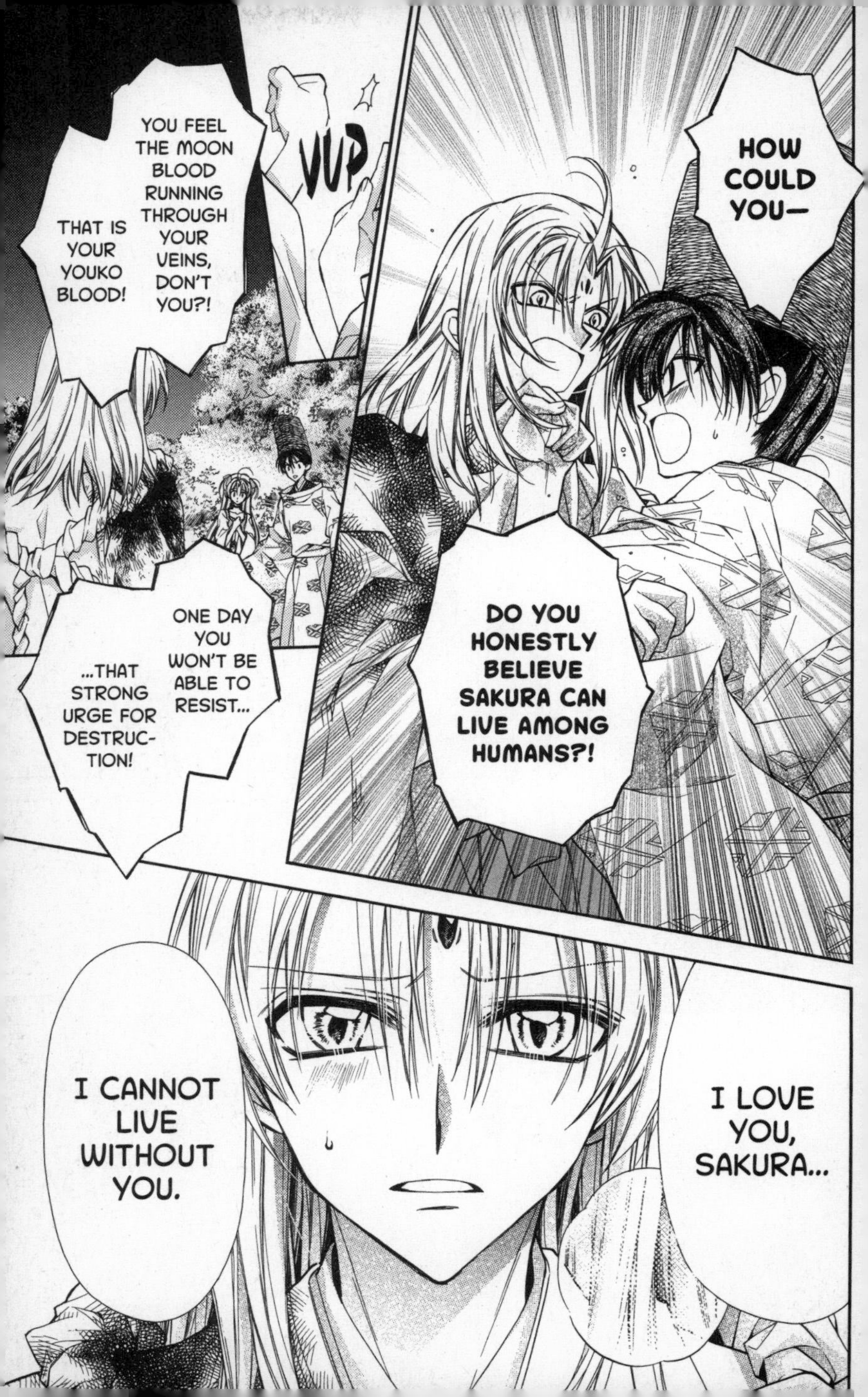
HOW COULD YOU—
DO YOU HONESTLY BELIEVE SAKURA CAN LIVE AMONG HUMANS?!
VUP
YOU FEEL THE MOON BLOOD RUNNING THROUGH YOUR VEINS, DON'T YOU?!
THAT IS YOUR YOUKO BLOOD!
ONE DAY YOU WON'T BE ABLE TO RESIST...
...THAT STRONG URGE FOR DESTRUC-TION!
I LOVE YOU, SAKURA...
I CANNOT LIVE WITHOUT YOU.

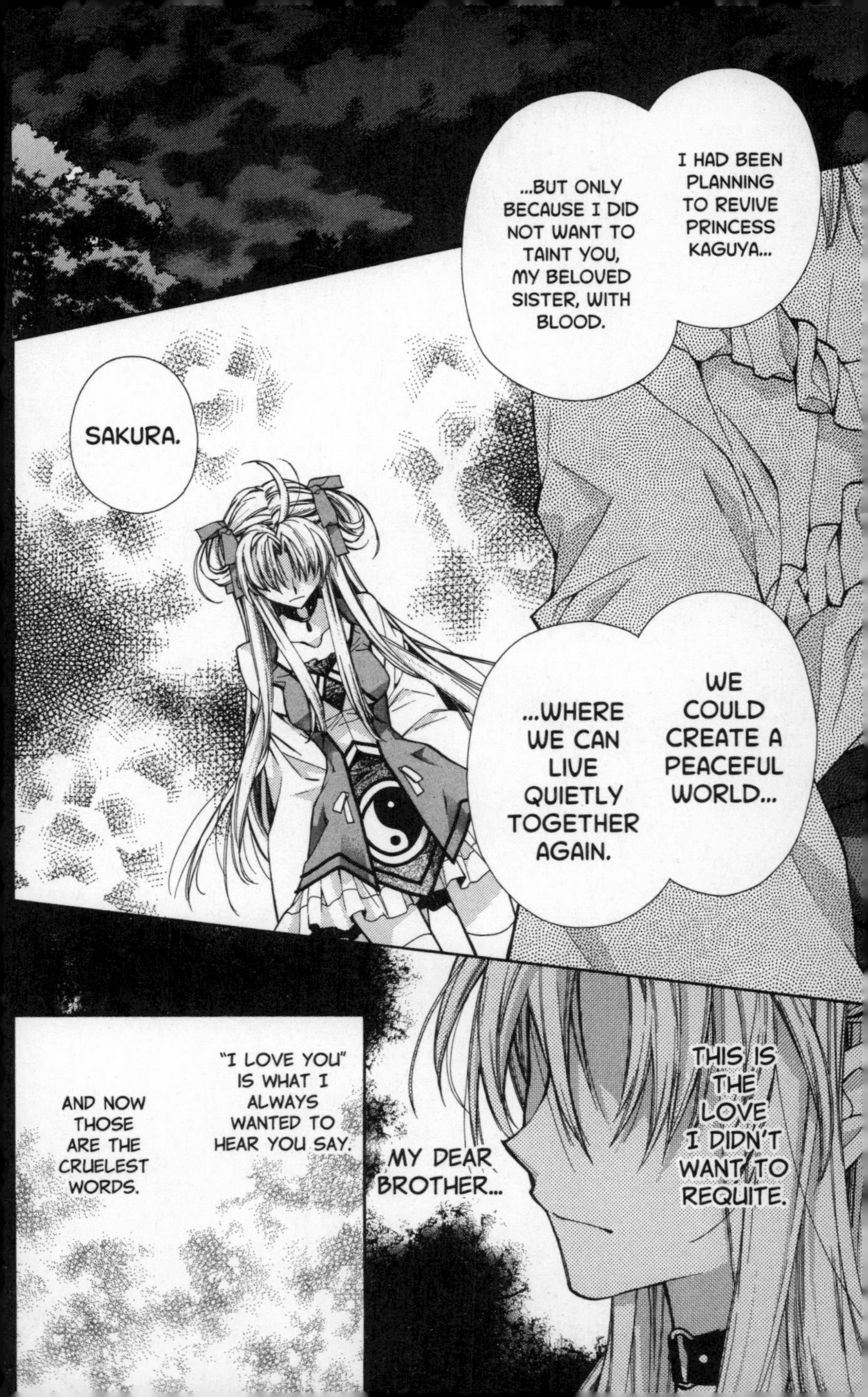
I HAD BEEN PLANNING TO REVIVE PRINCESS KAGUYA...
...BUT ONLY BECAUSE I DID NOT WANT TO TAINT YOU, MY BELOVED SISTER, WITH BLOOD.
SAKURA.
WE COULD CREATE A PEACEFUL WORLD...
...WHERE WE CAN LIVE QUIETLY TOGETHER AGAIN.
THIS IS THE LOVE I DIDN'T WANT TO REQUITE.
MY DEAR BROTHER...
"I LOVE YOU" IS WHAT I ALWAYS WANTED TO HEAR YOU SAY.
AND NOW THOSE ARE THE CRUELEST WORDS.

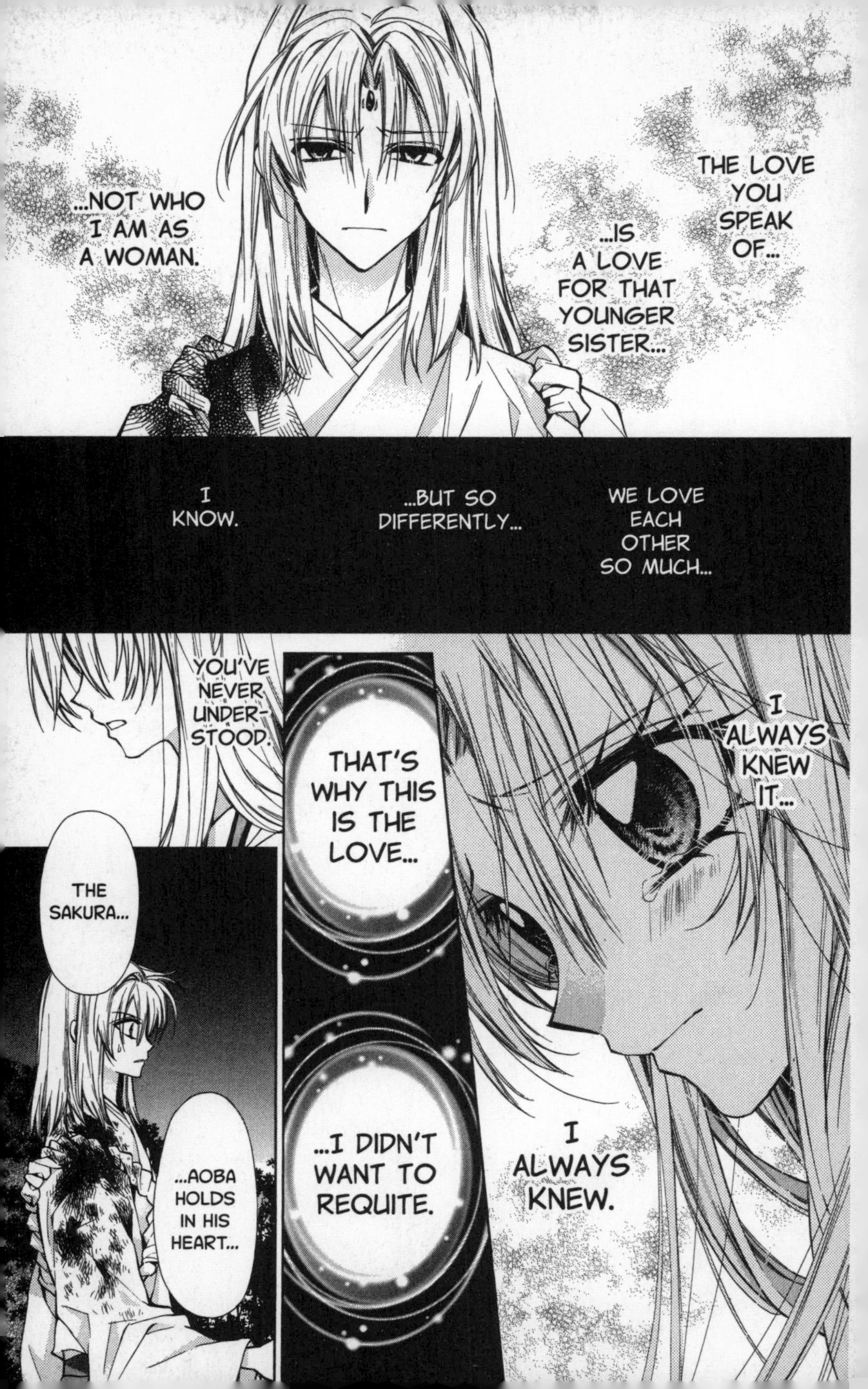
THE LOVE YOU SPEAK OF...
...IS A LOVE FOR THAT YOUNGER SISTER...
...NOT WHO I AM AS A WOMAN.
WE LOVE EACH OTHER SO MUCH...
...BUT SO DIFFERENTLY...
I KNOW.
I ALWAYS KNEW IT...
I ALWAYS KNEW.
THAT'S WHY THIS IS THE LOVE...
...I DIDN'T WANT TO REQUITE.
YOU'VE NEVER UNDER-STOOD.
THE SAKURA...
...AOBA HOLDS IN HIS HEART...

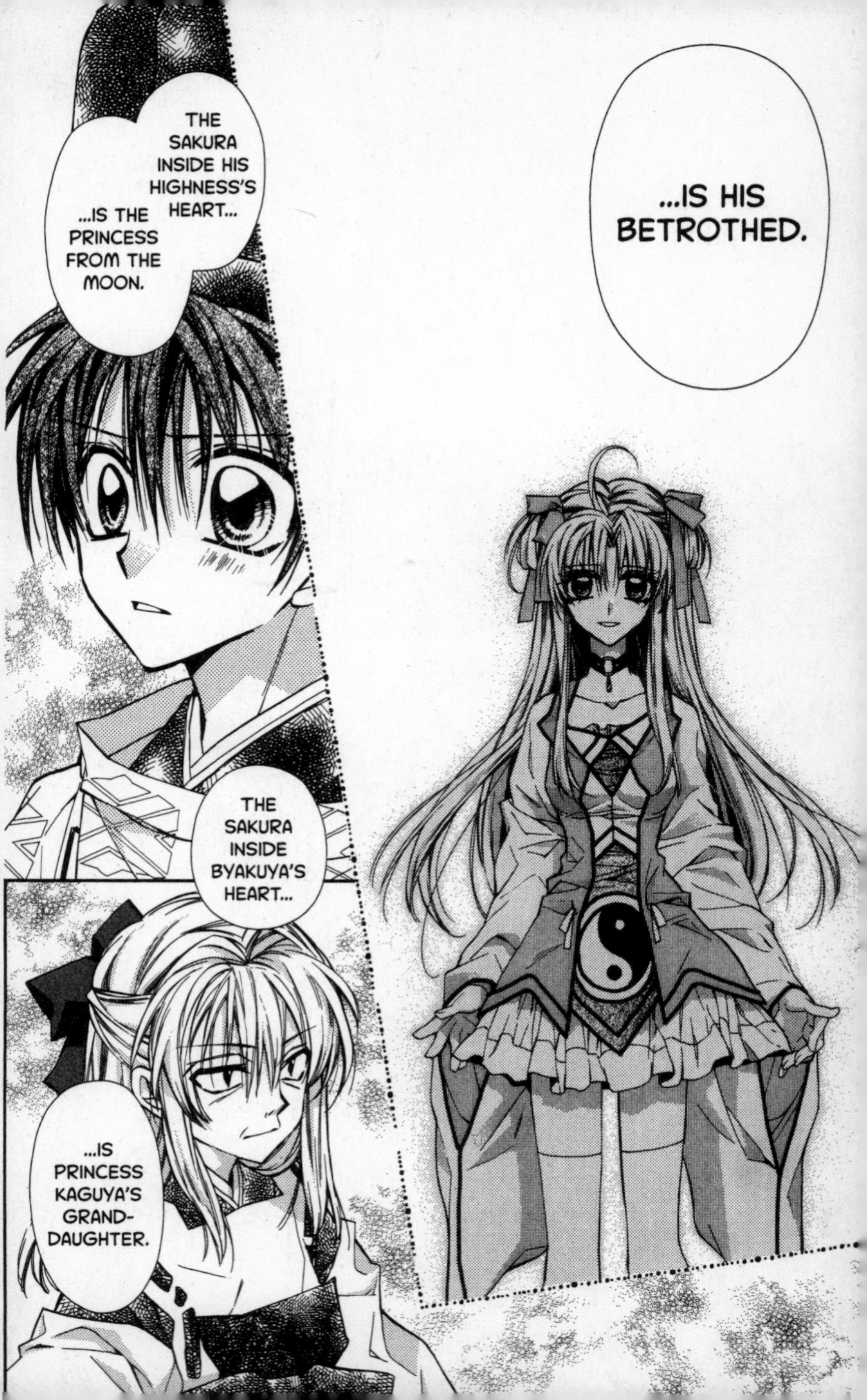
...IS HIS BETROTHED.
THE SAKURA INSIDE HIS HIGHNESS'S HEART...
...IS THE PRINCESS FROM THE MOON.
THE SAKURA INSIDE BYAKUYA'S HEART...
...IS PRINCESS KAGUYA'S GRAND-DAUGHTER.

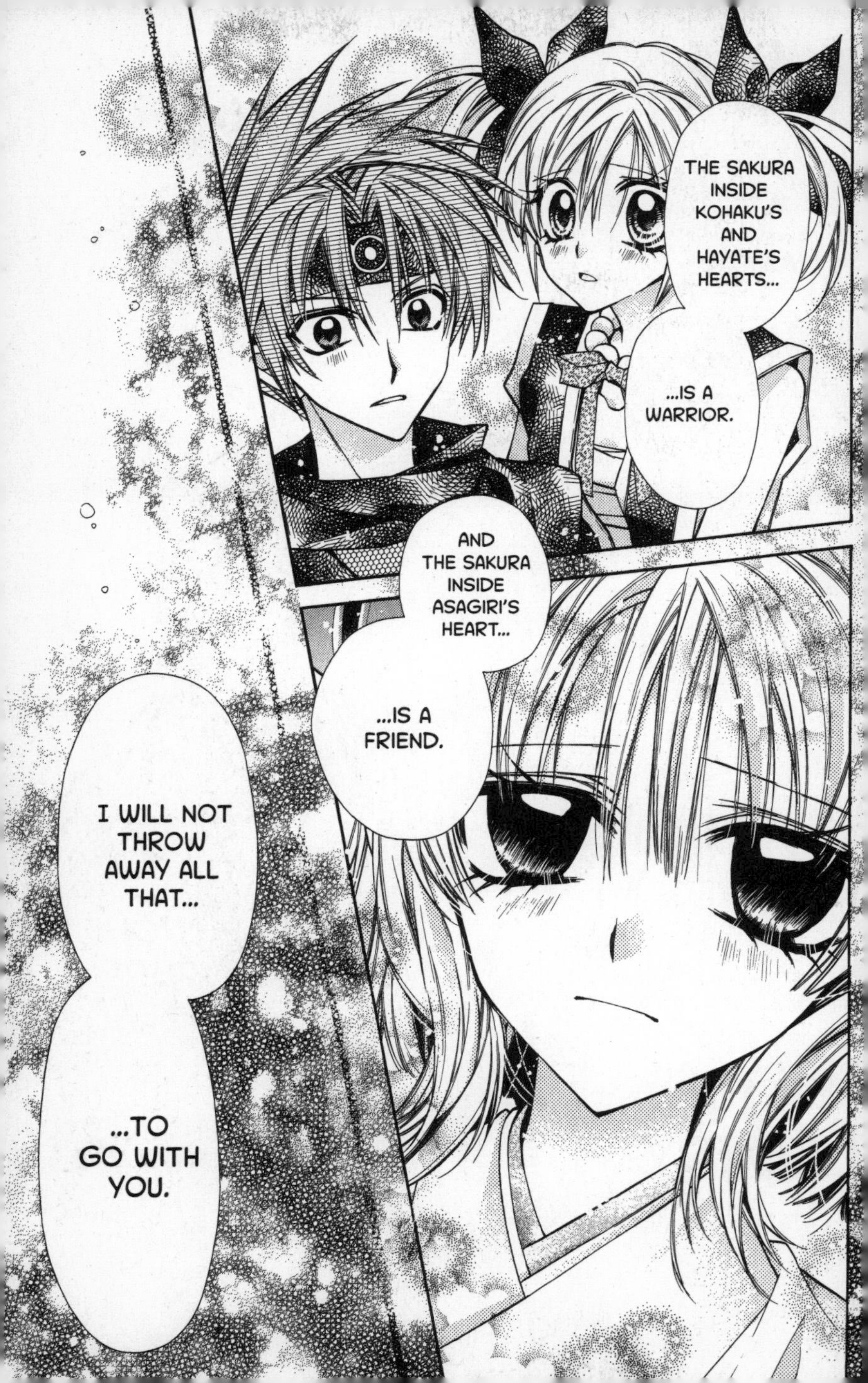
THE SAKURA INSIDE KOHAKU'S AND HAYATE'S HEARTS...
...IS A WARRIOR.
AND THE SAKURA INSIDE ASAGIRI'S HEART...
...IS A FRIEND.
I WILL NOT THROW AWAY ALL THAT...
...TO GO WITH YOU.

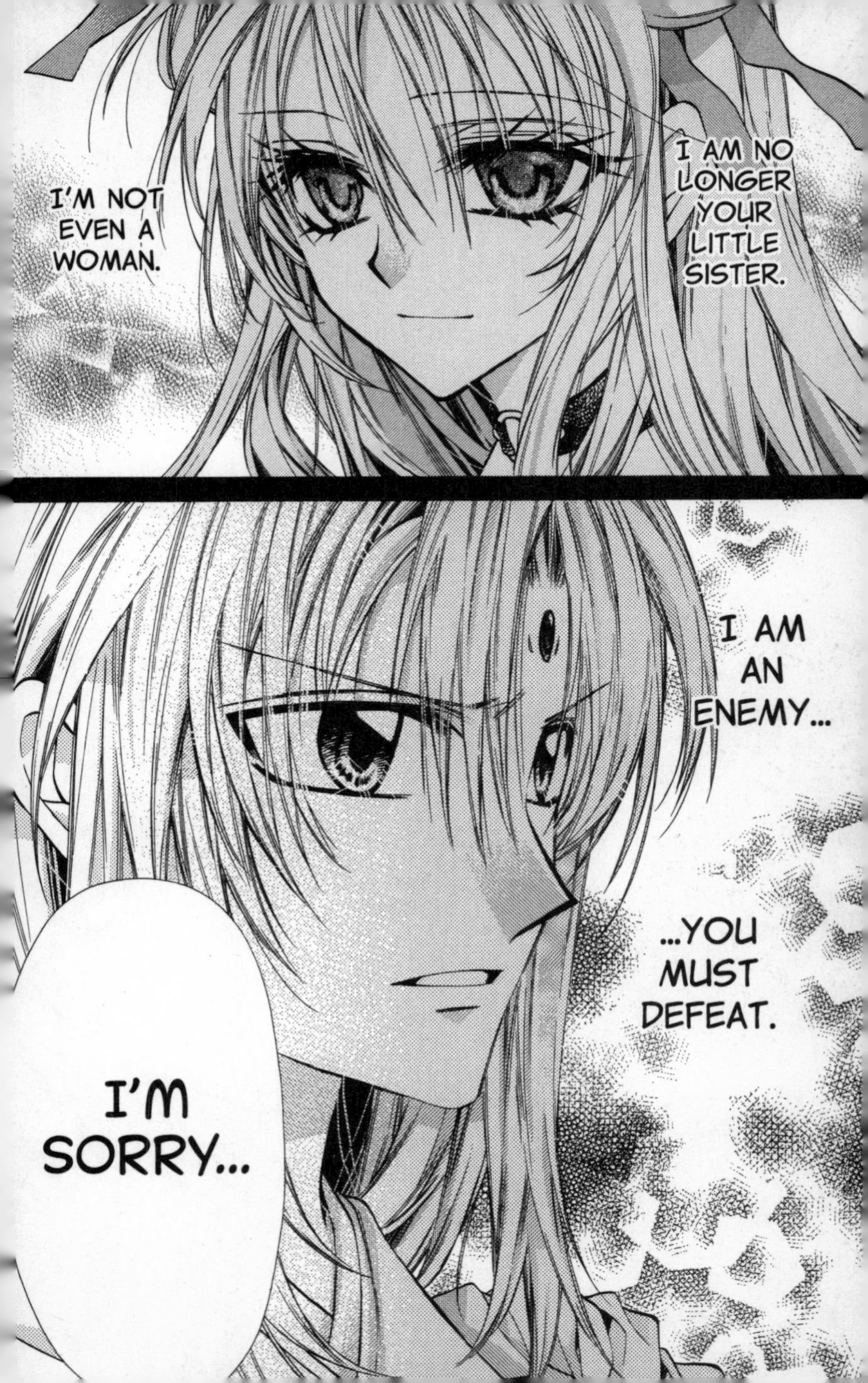
I AM NO LONGER YOUR LITTLE SISTER.
I'M NOT EVEN A WOMAN.
I AM AN ENEMY...
...YOU MUST DEFEAT.
I'M SORRY...

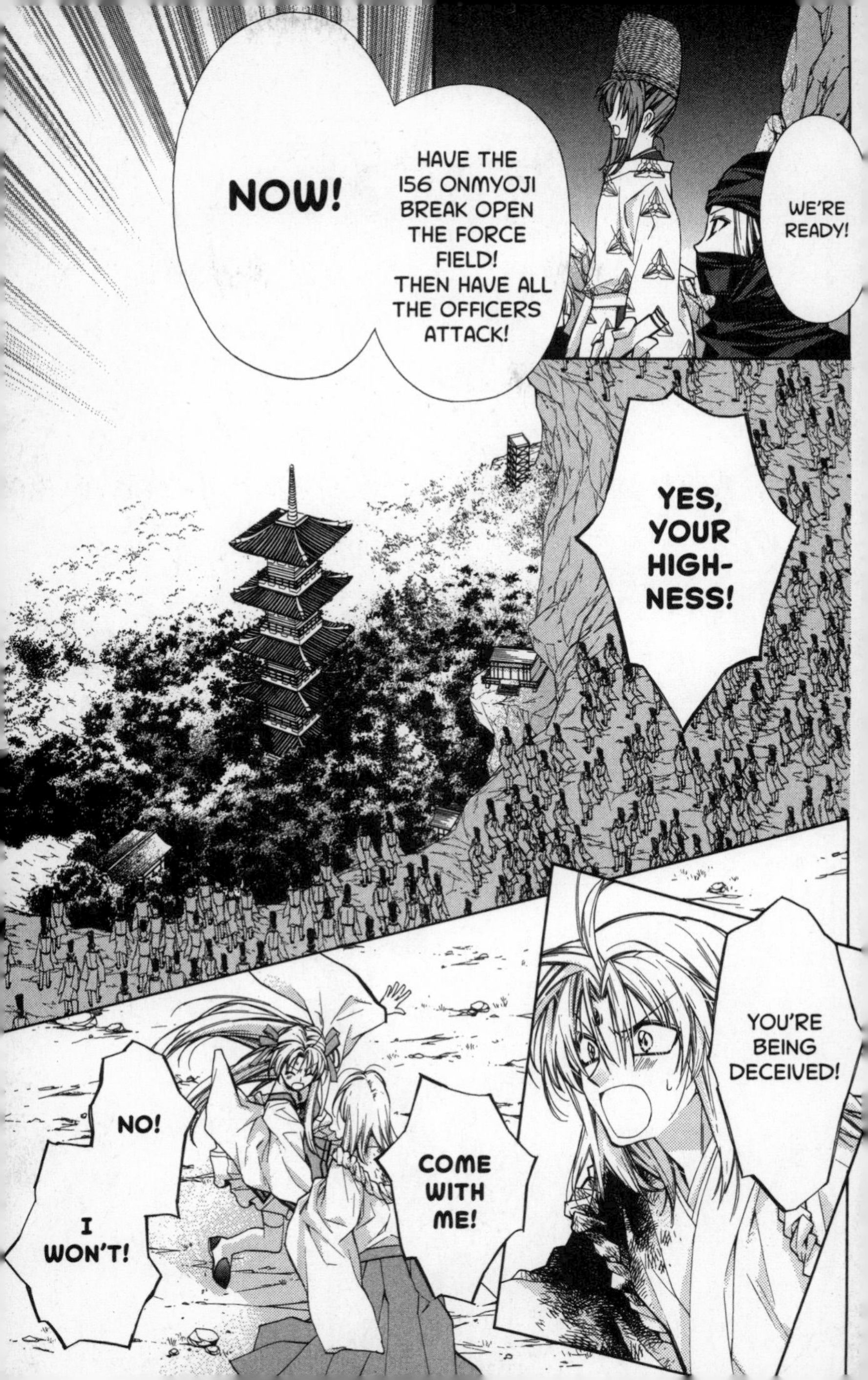
WE'RE READY!
NOW!
HAVE THE 156 ONMYOJI BREAK OPEN THE FORCE FIELD! THEN HAVE ALL THE OFFICERS ATTACK!
YES, YOUR HIGH-NESS!
YOU'RE BEING DECEIVED!
COME WITH ME!
NO!
I WON'T!

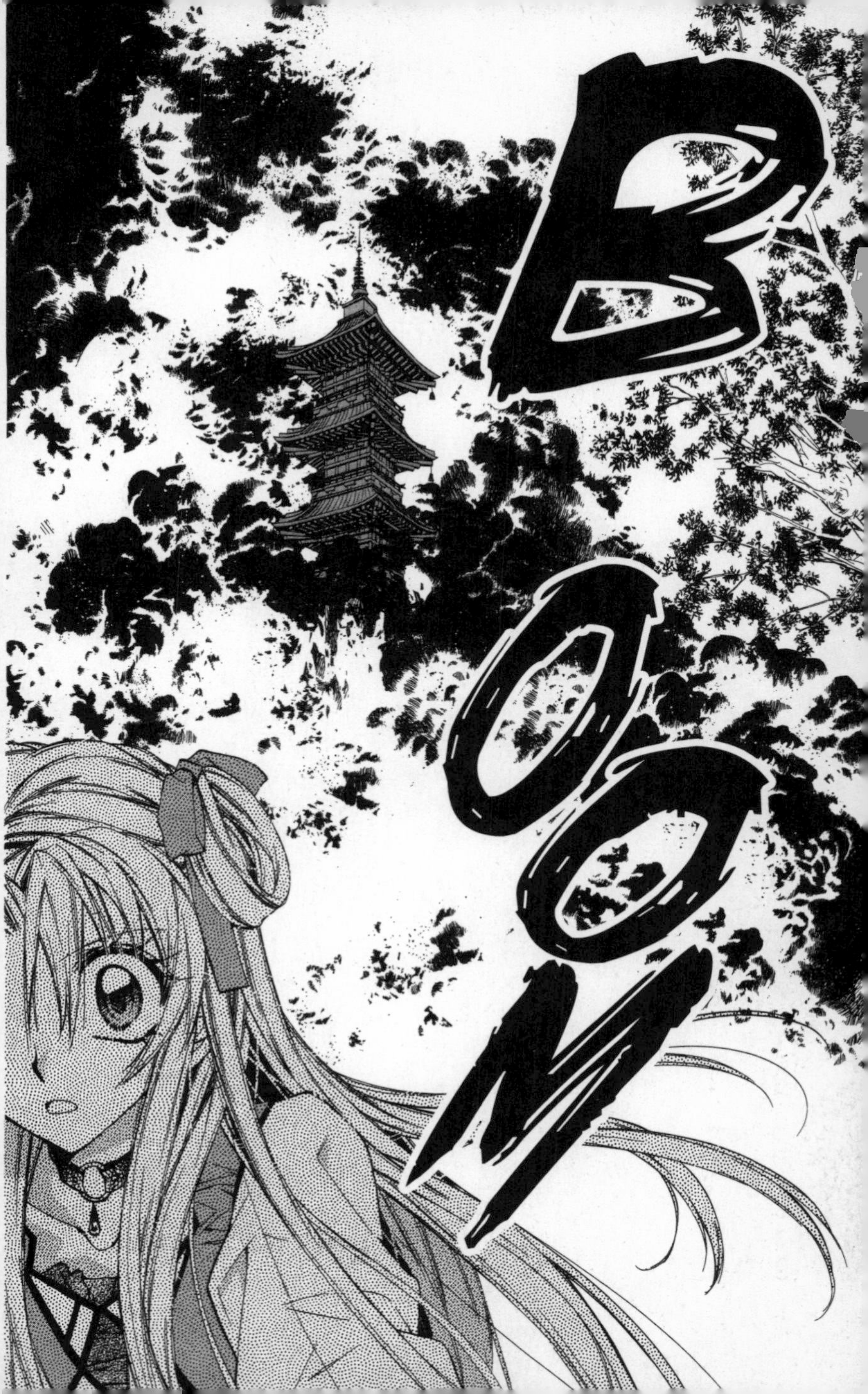
BOOOM

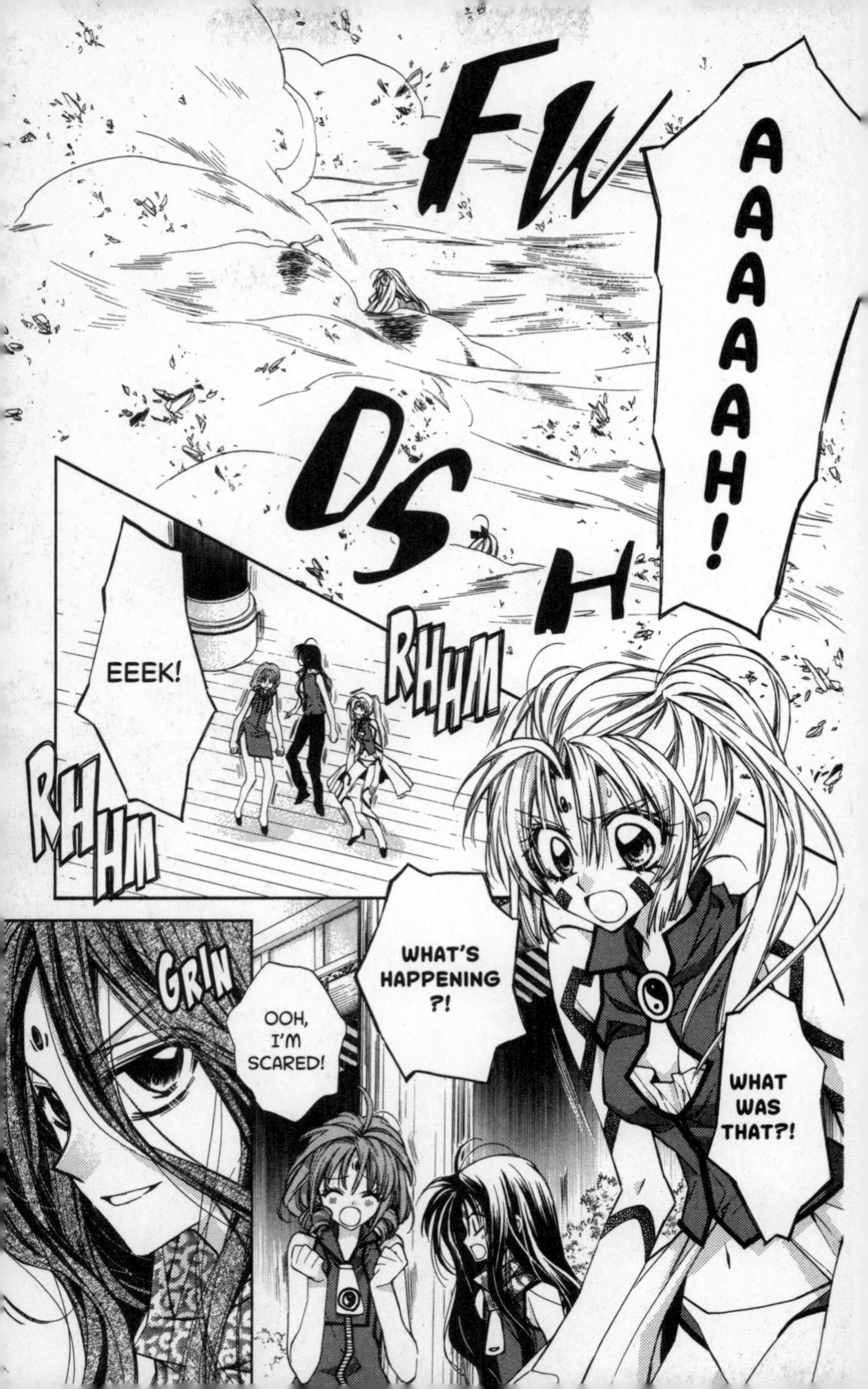
AAAAAH!
FWDSH
WHAT'S HAPPENING?!
WHAT WAS THAT?!
RHHM
EEEK!
RHHM
OOH, I'M SCARED!
GRIN

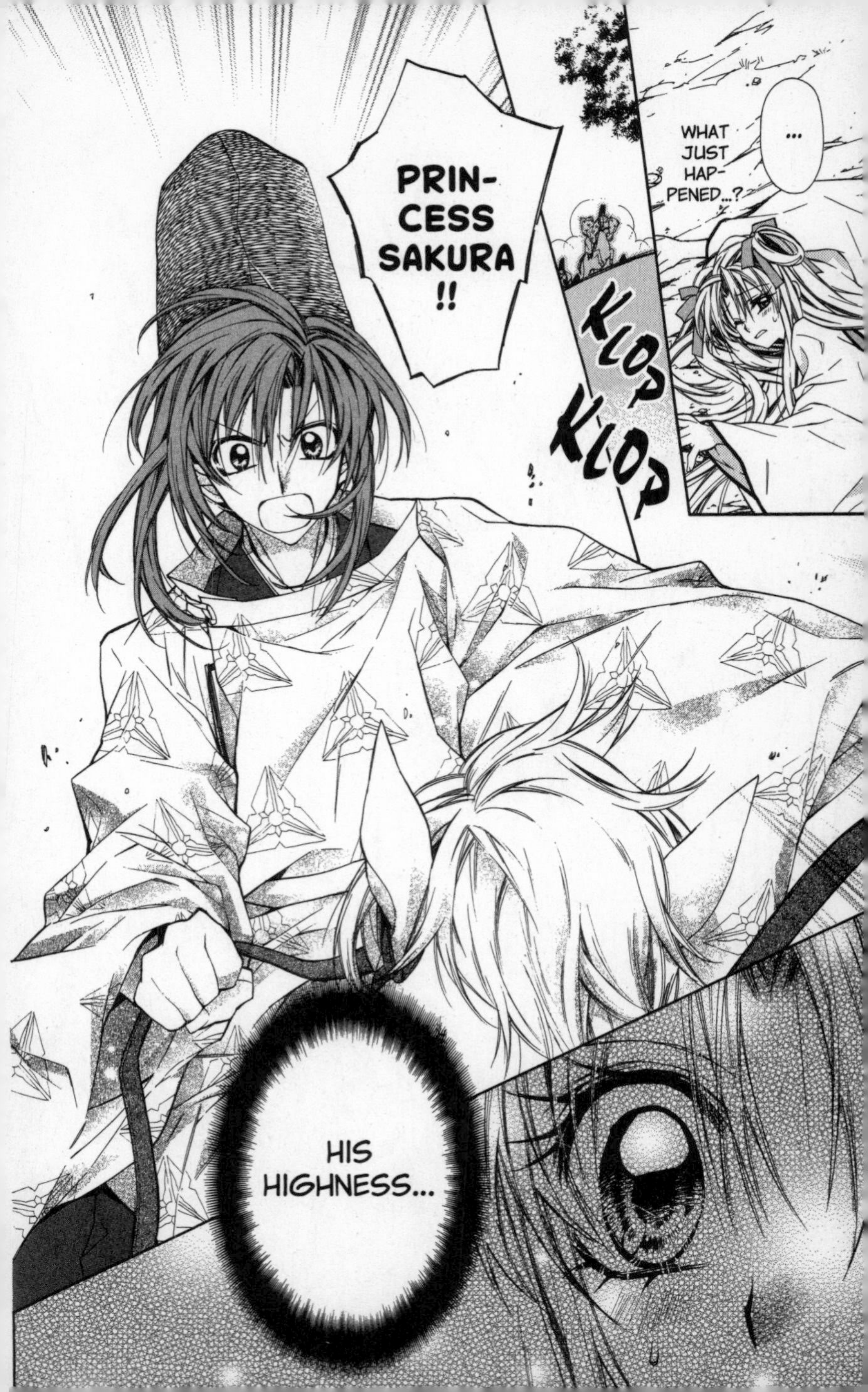
...
WHAT JUST HAPPENED...?
KLOP KLOP
PRINCESS SAKURA!!
HIS HIGHNESS...

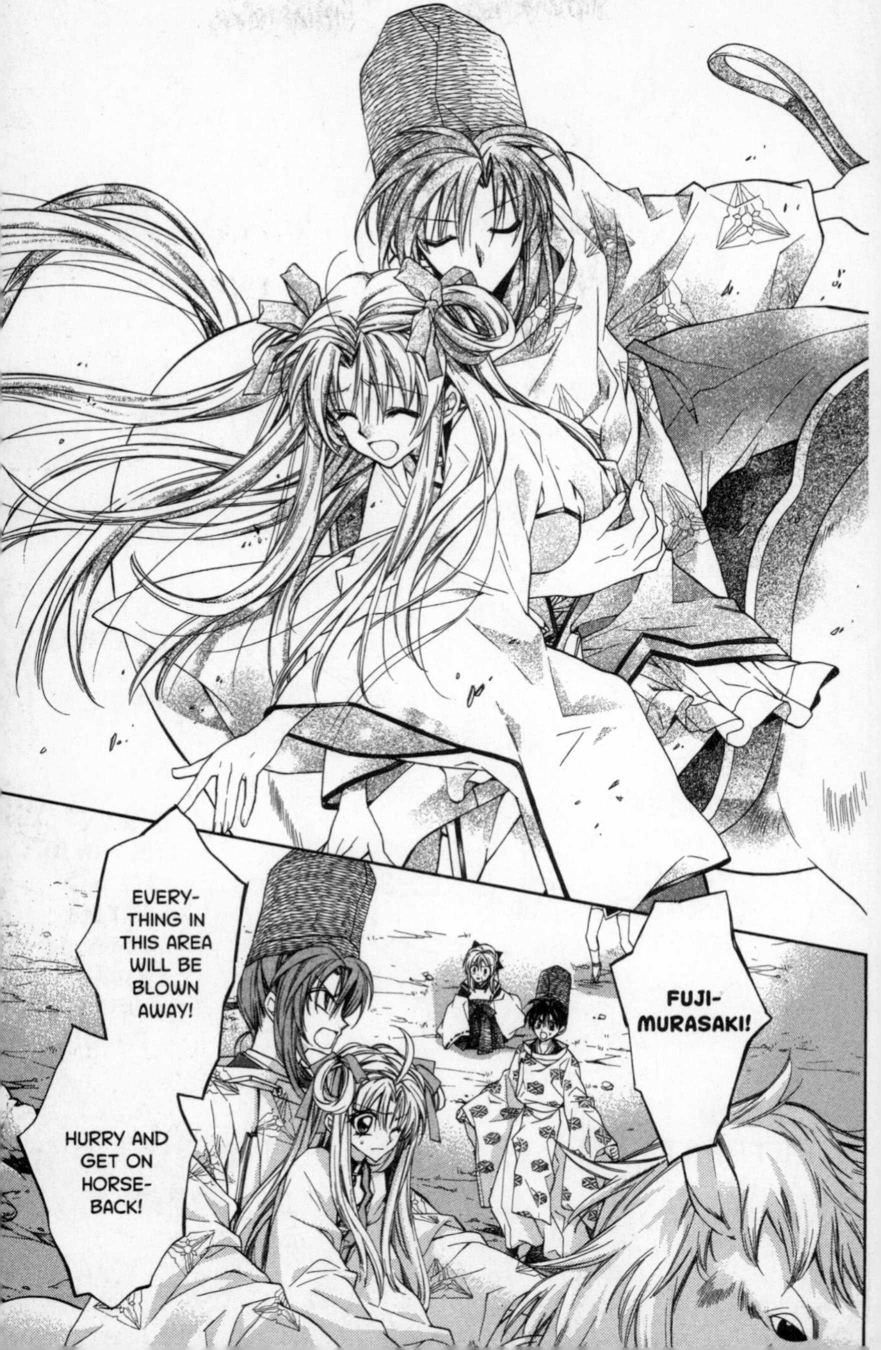
FUJI-MURASAKI!
EVERY-THING IN THIS AREA WILL BE BLOWN AWAY!
HURRY AND GET ON HORSE-BACK!

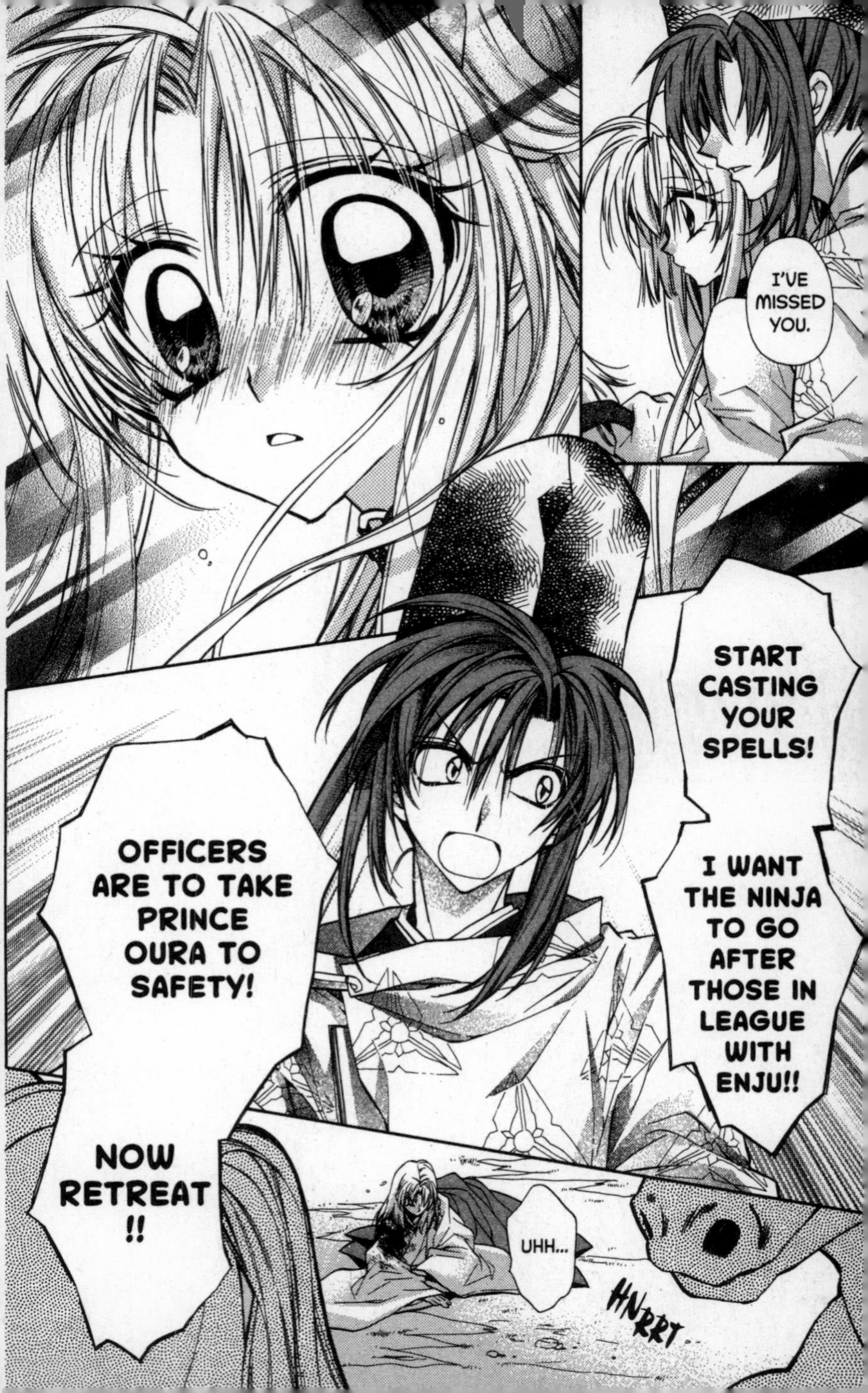
I'VE MISSED YOU.
START CASTING YOUR SPELLS!
I WANT THE NINJA TO GO AFTER THOSE IN LEAGUE WITH ENJU!!
OFFICERS ARE TO TAKE PRINCE OURA TO SAFETY!
NOW RETREAT !!
UHH...
HNRRT

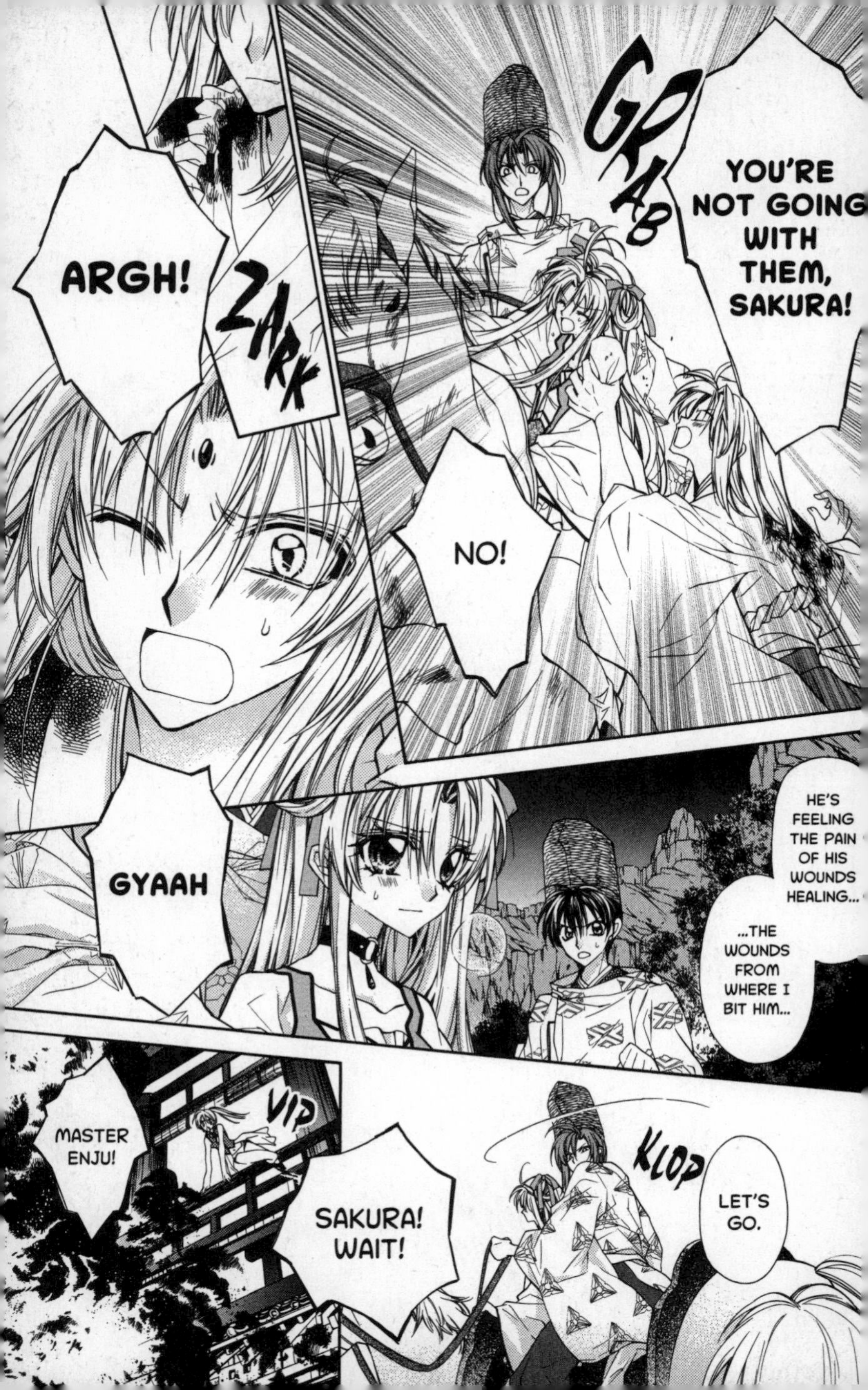
GRAB
YOU'RE NOT GOING WITH THEM, SAKURA!
NO!
ZARK
ARGH!
HE'S FEELING THE PAIN OF HIS WOUNDS HEALING...
...THE WOUNDS FROM WHERE I BIT HIM...
GYAAH
LET'S GO.
KLOP
SAKURA! WAIT!
VIP
MASTER ENJU!

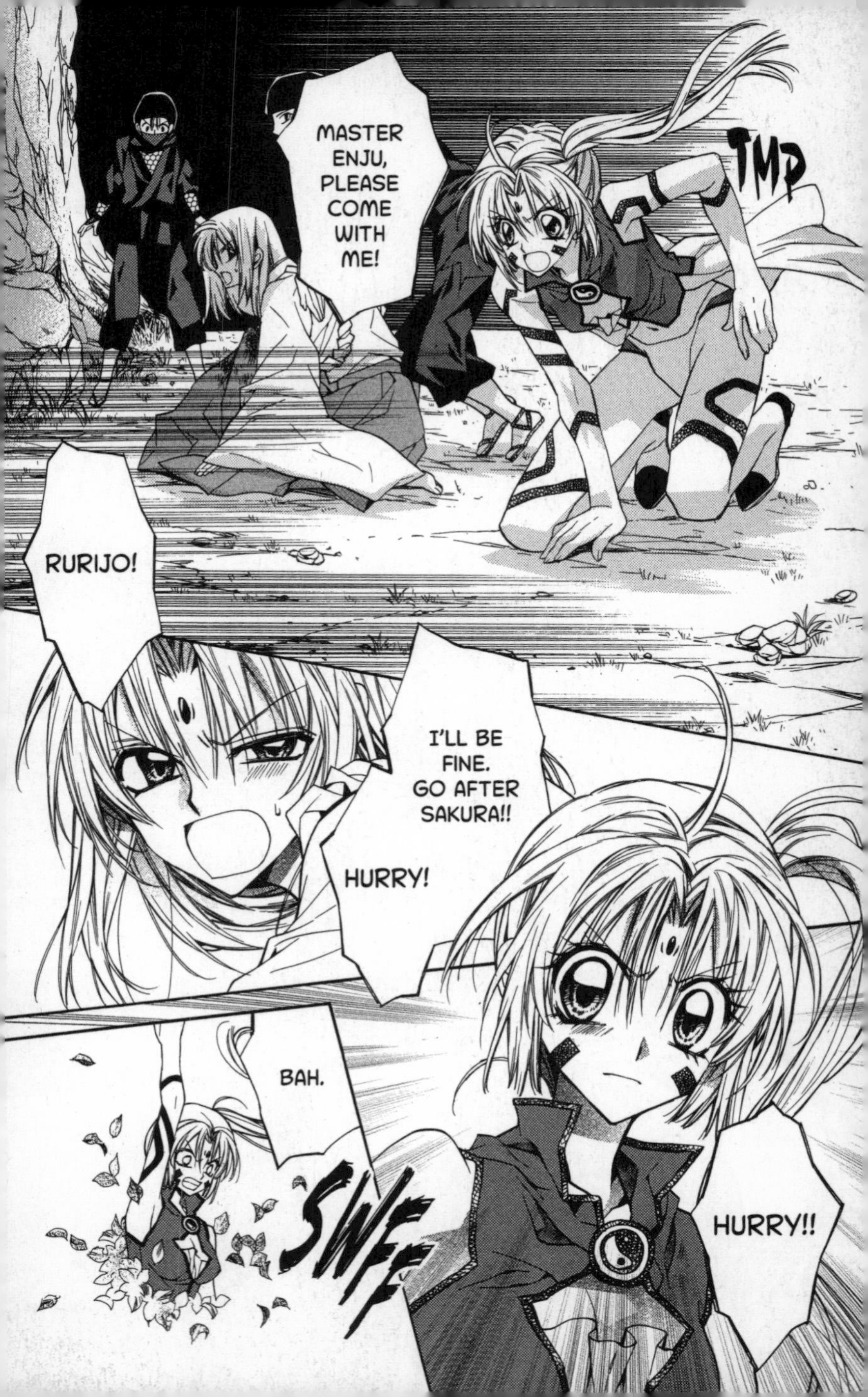
TMP
MASTER ENJU, PLEASE COME WITH ME!
RURIJO!
I'LL BE FINE. GO AFTER SAKURA!!
HURRY!
HURRY!!
BAH.
SWF

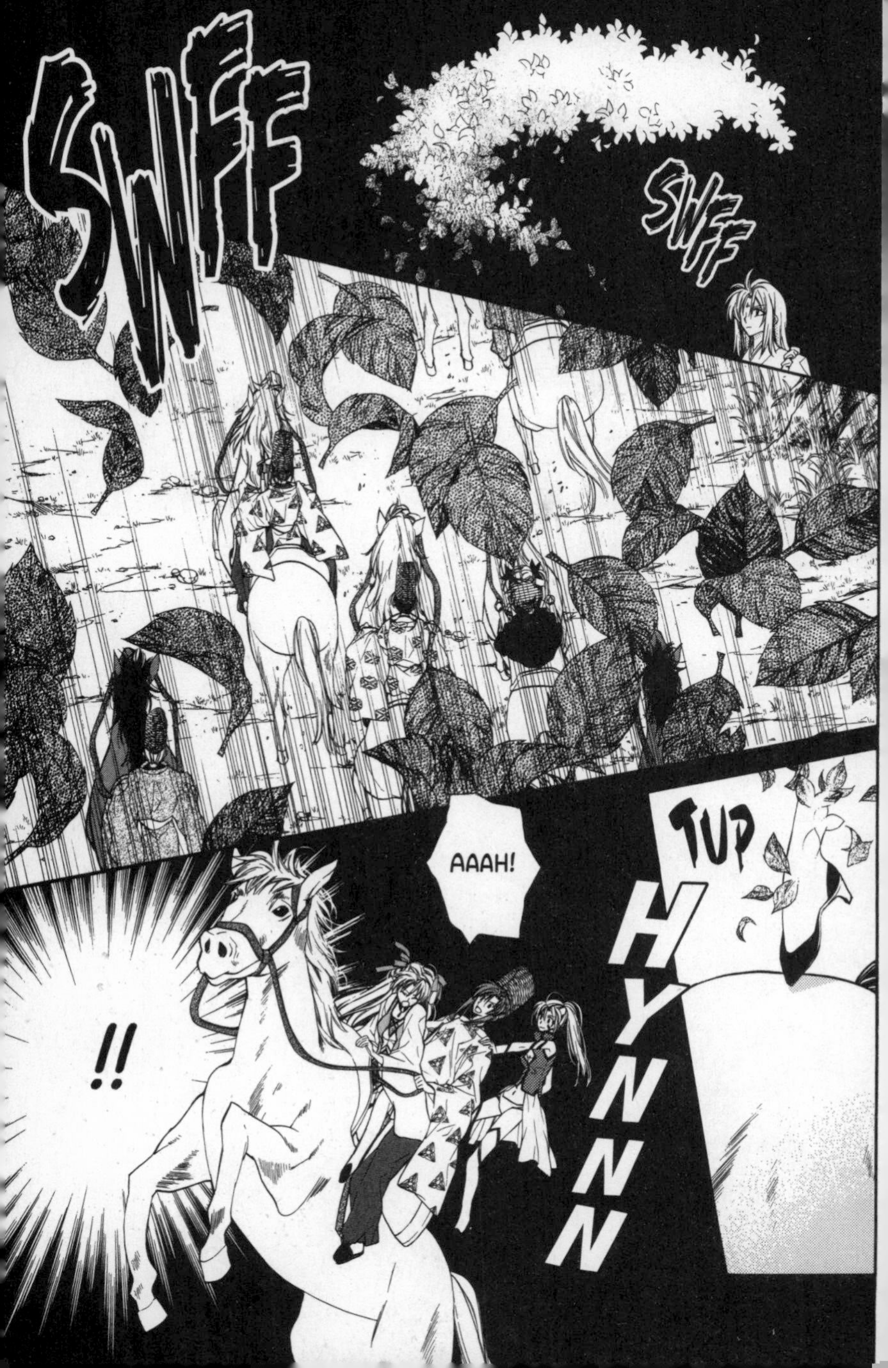
SWFF
SWFF
TUP
AAAH!
HYYNNN
!!

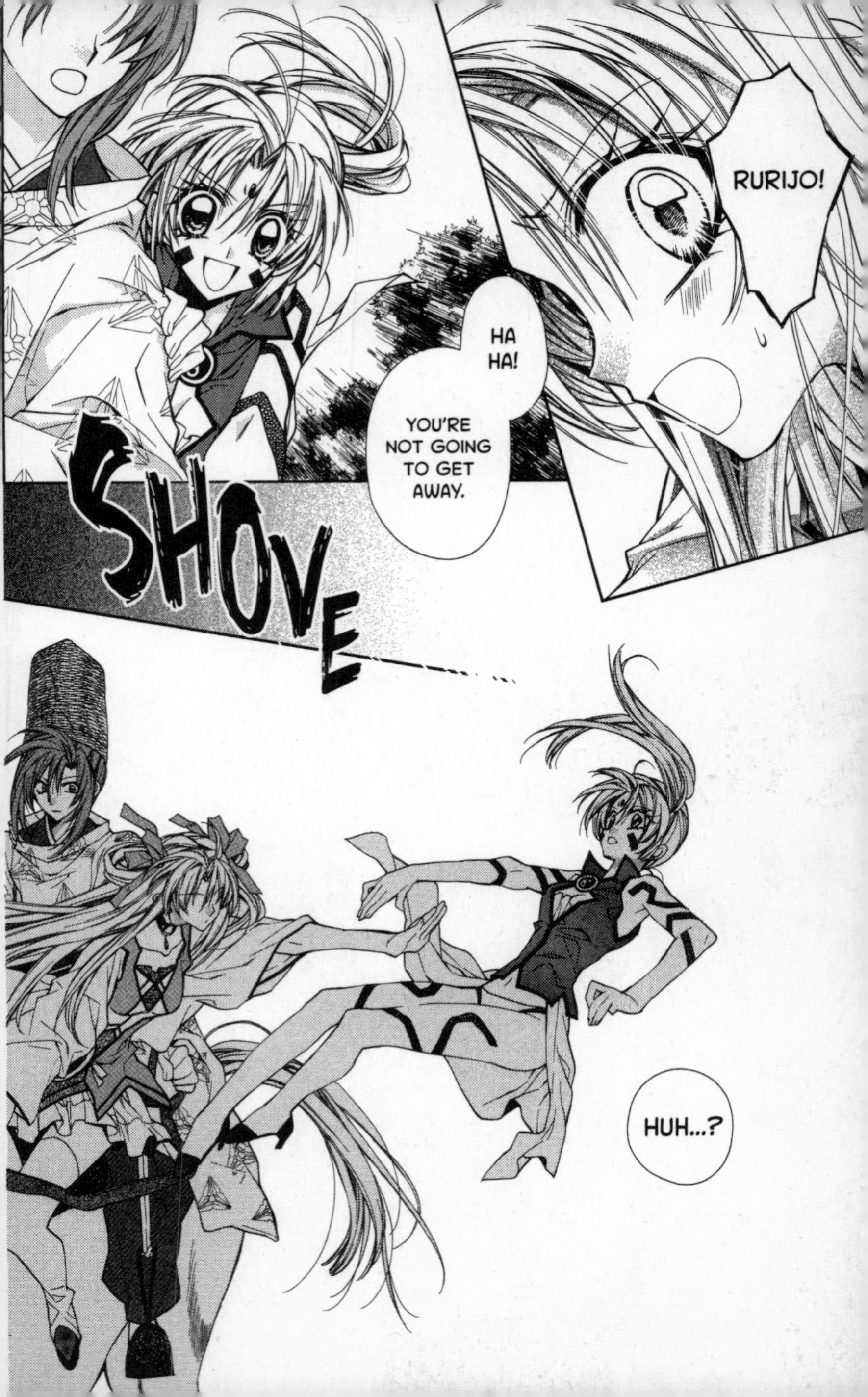
RURIJO!
HA HA!
YOU'RE NOT GOING TO GET AWAY.
SHOVE
HUH...?

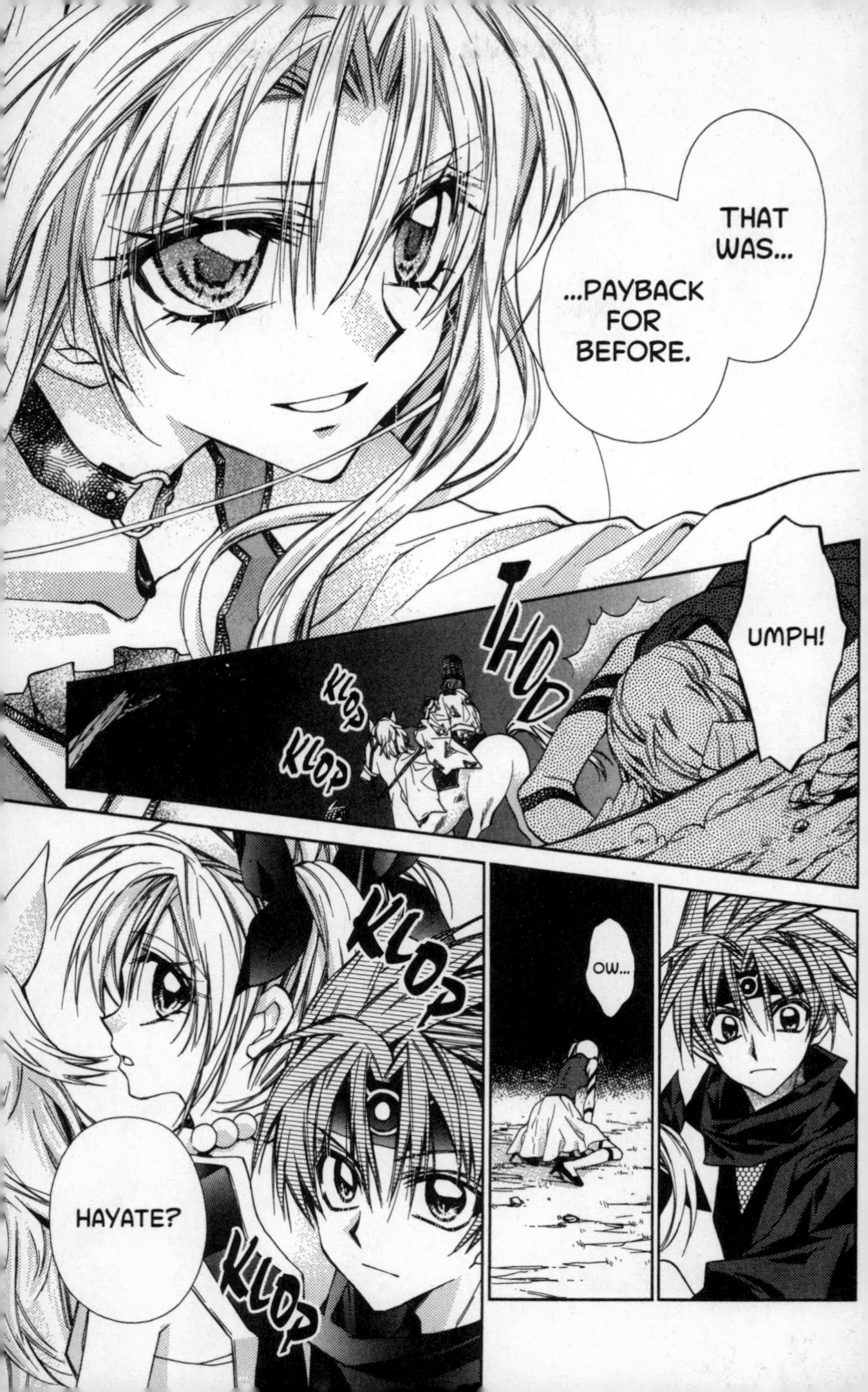
THAT WAS...
...PAYBACK FOR BEFORE.
UMPH!
THUD
KLOP
KLOP
OW...
KLOP KLOP
HAYATE?
KLOP

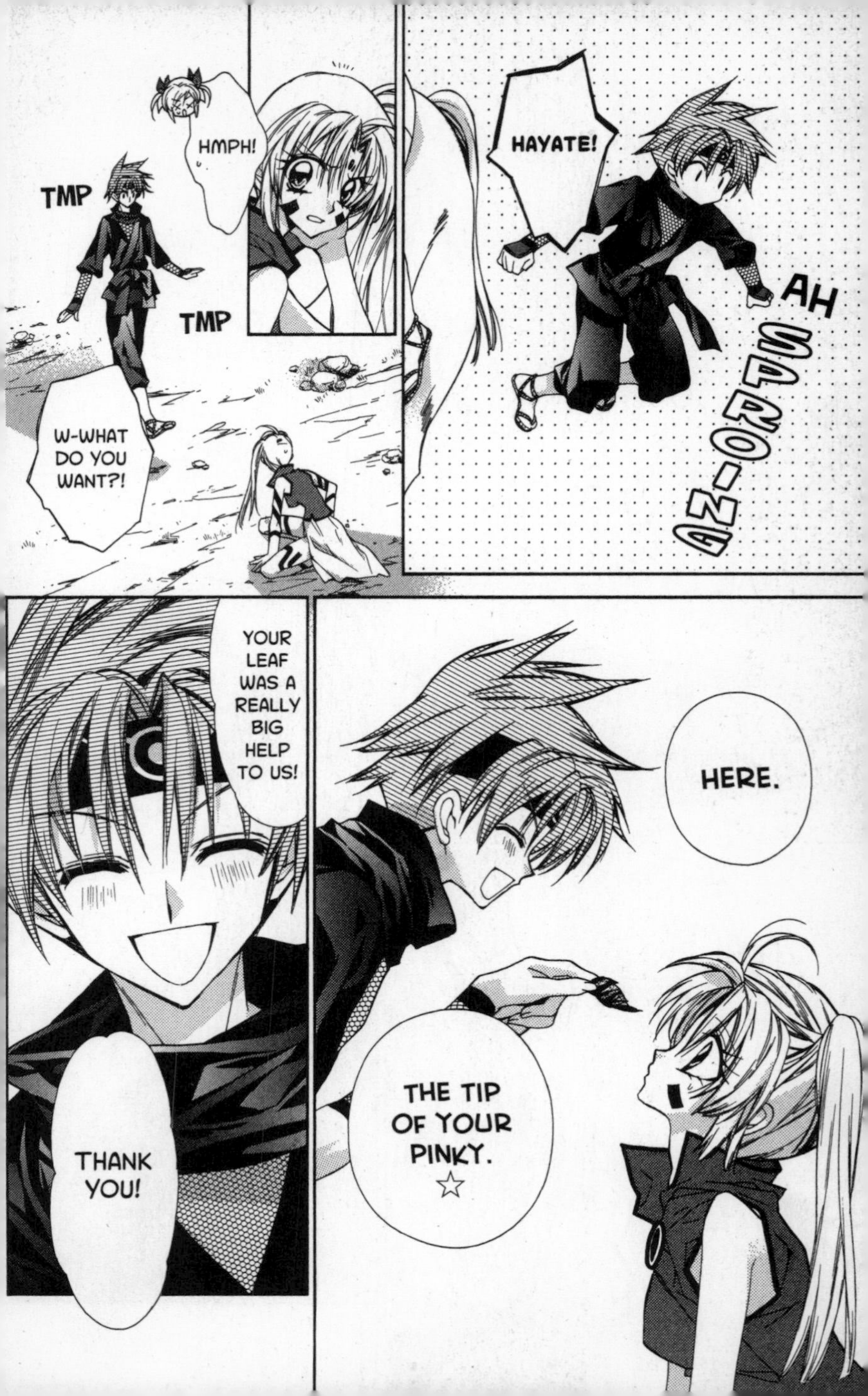
HAYATE!
AH
SPROING
HMPH!
TMP
TMP
W-WHAT DO YOU WANT?!
HERE.
THE TIP OF YOUR PINKY. ☆
YOUR LEAF WAS A REALLY BIG HELP TO US!
THANK YOU!

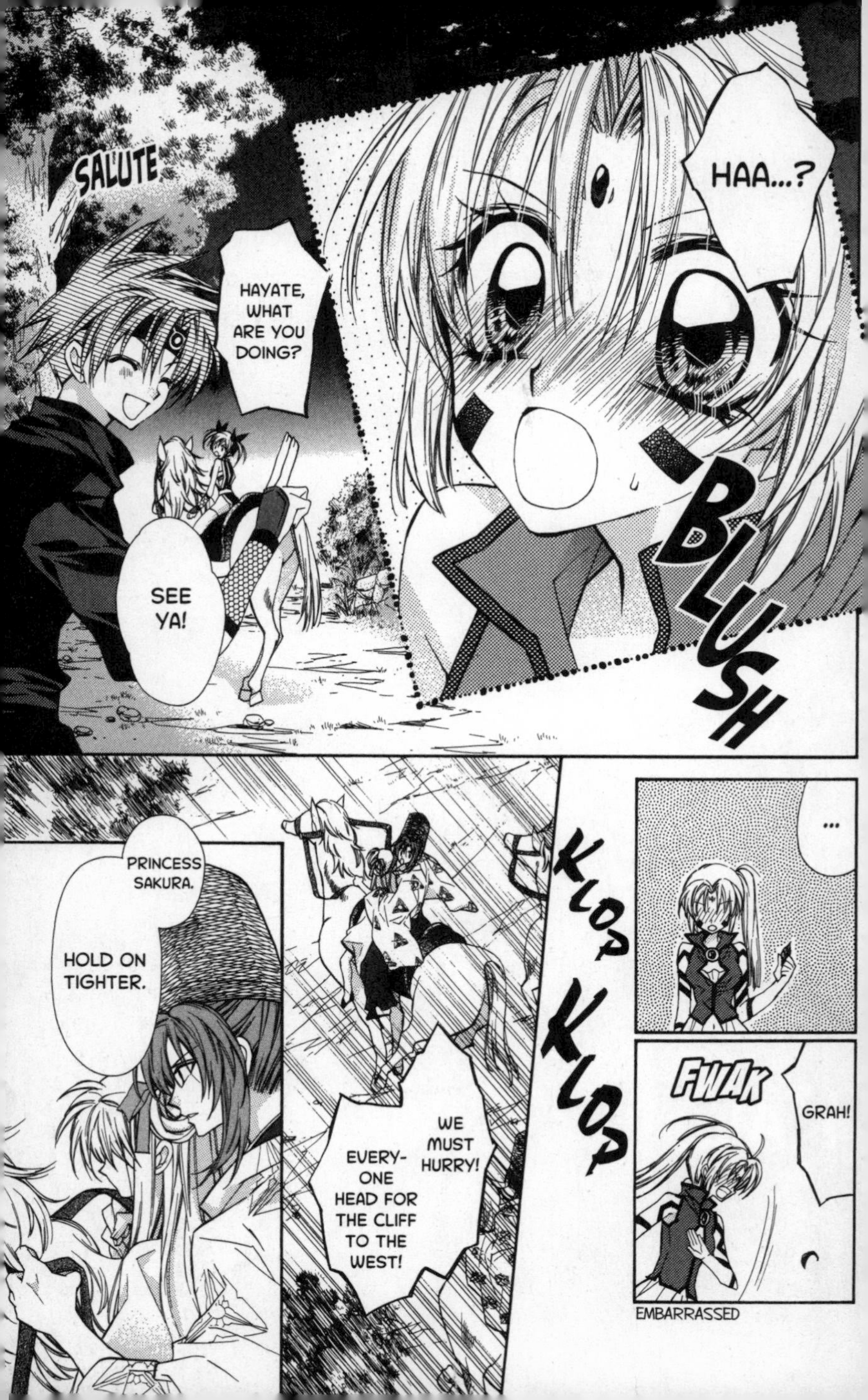
HAA...?
BLUSH
SALUTE
HAYATE, WHAT ARE YOU DOING?
SEE YA!
...
FWAK
GRAH!
EMBARRASSED
KLOP KLOP
WE MUST HURRY!
EVERY-ONE HEAD FOR THE CLIFF TO THE WEST!
PRINCESS SAKURA.
HOLD ON TIGHTER.

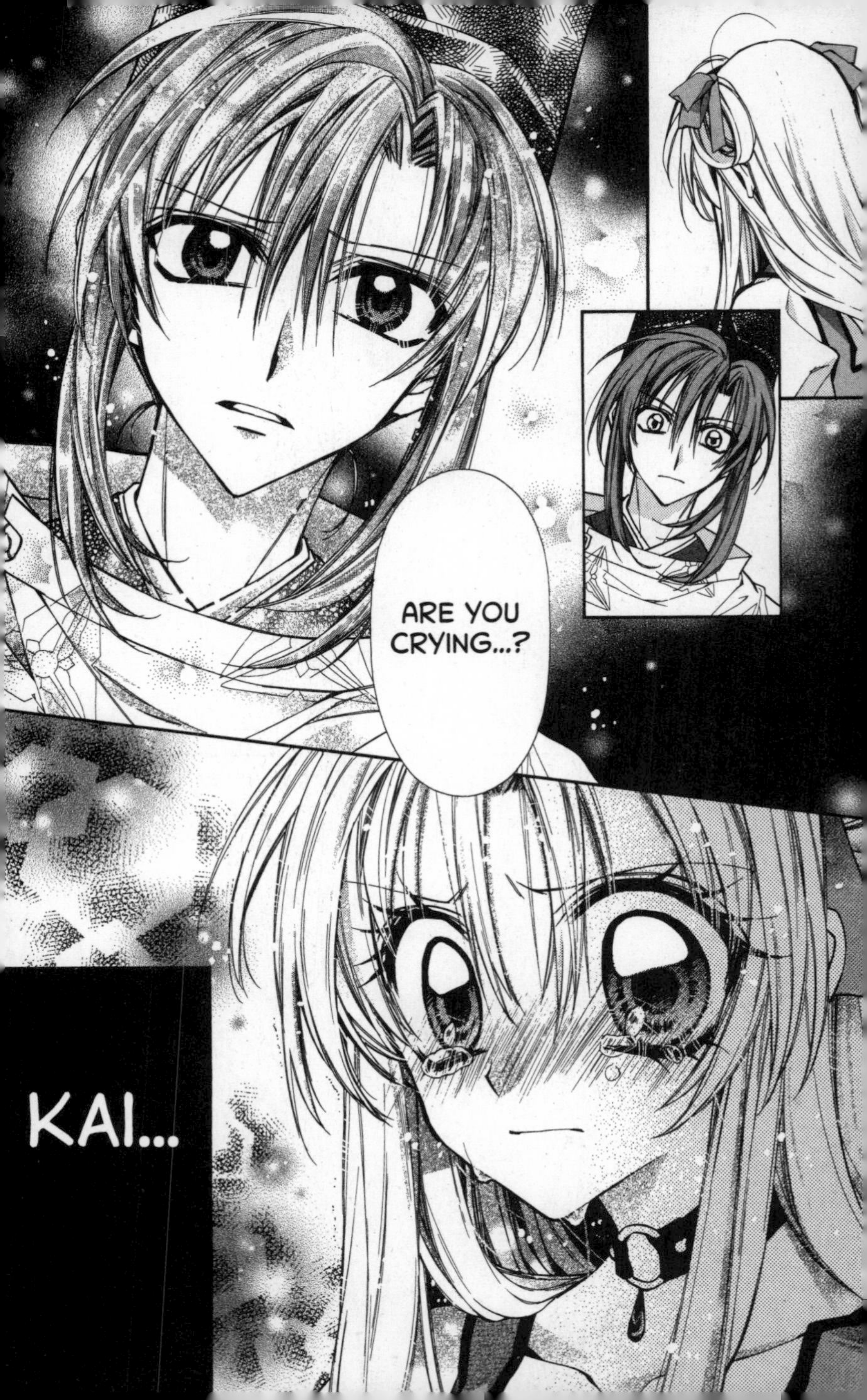
ARE YOU CRYING...?
KAI...

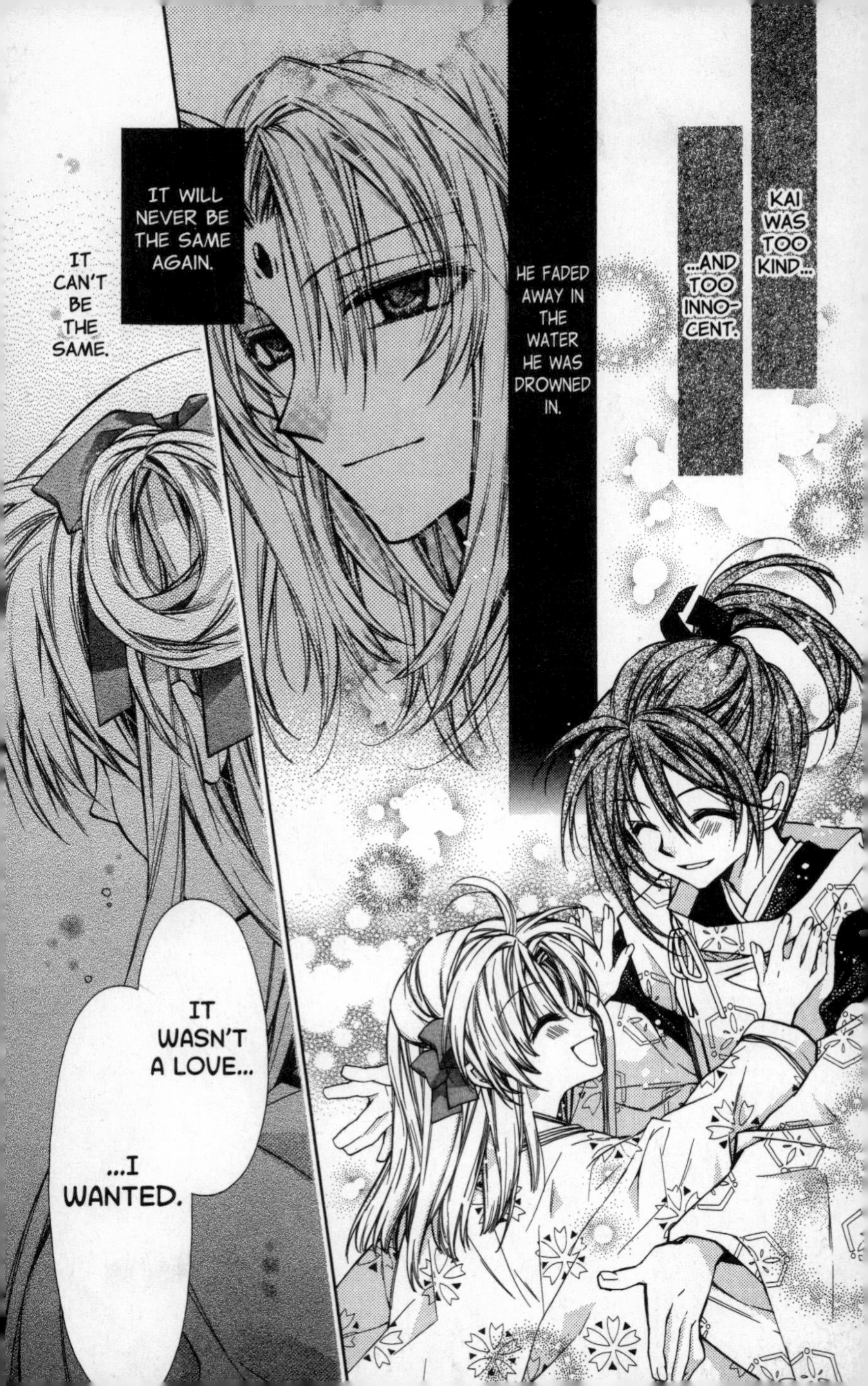
KAI WAS TOO KIND...
...AND TOO INNO-CENT.
HE FADED AWAY IN THE WATER HE WAS DROWNED IN.
IT WILL NEVER BE THE SAME AGAIN.
IT CAN'T BE THE SAME.
IT WASN'T A LOVE...
...I WANTED.

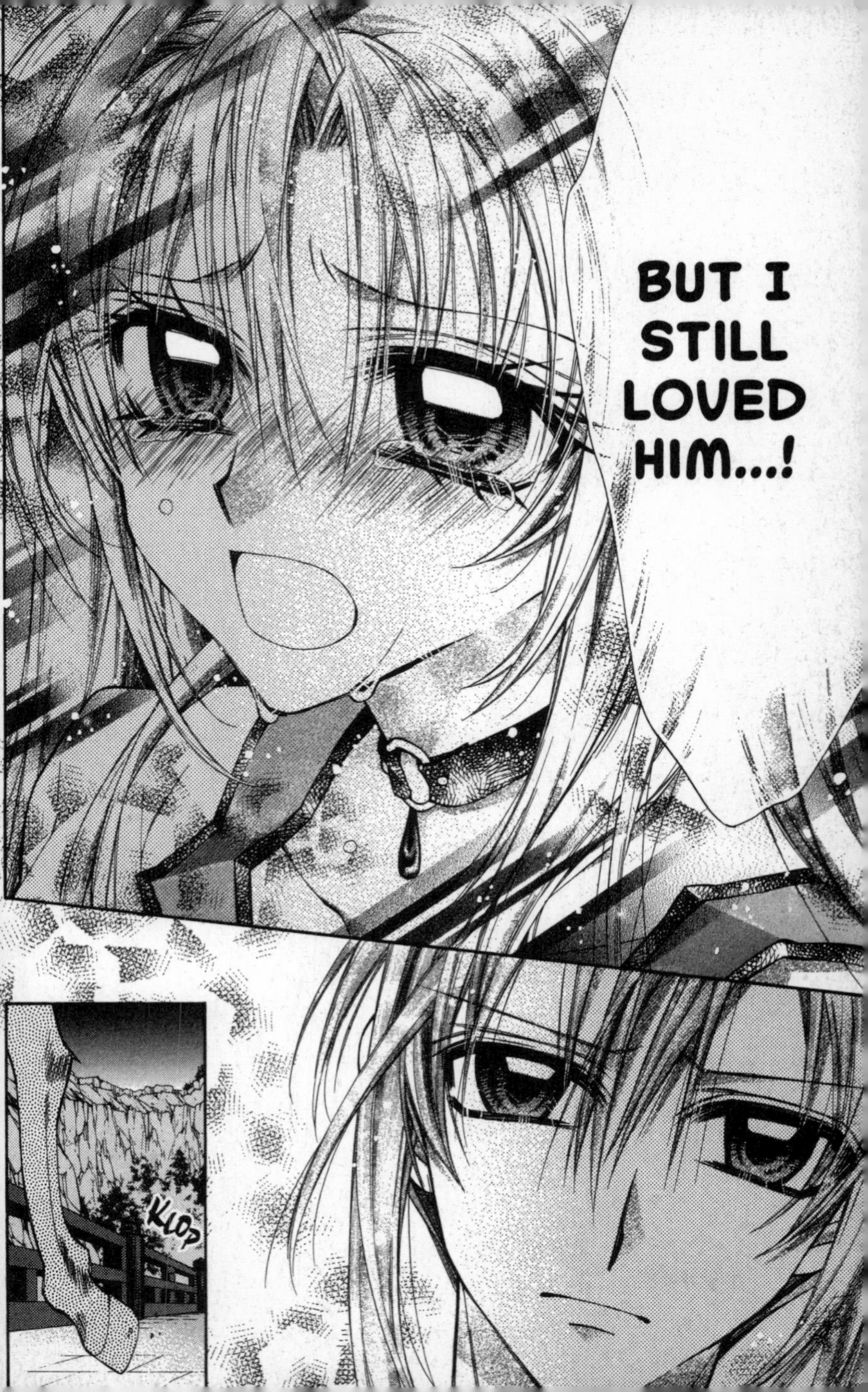
BUT I STILL LOVED HIM...!
KLOP

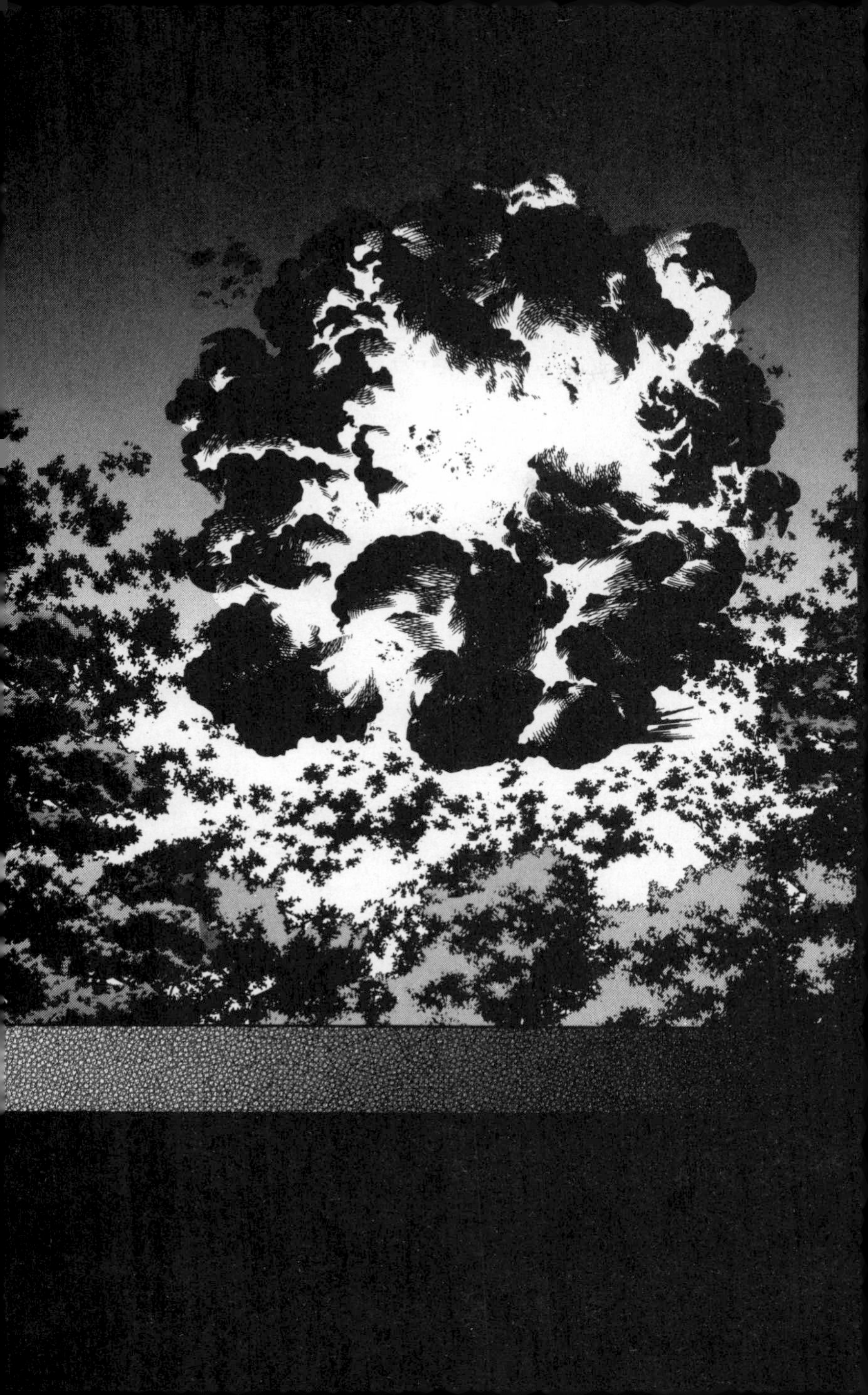

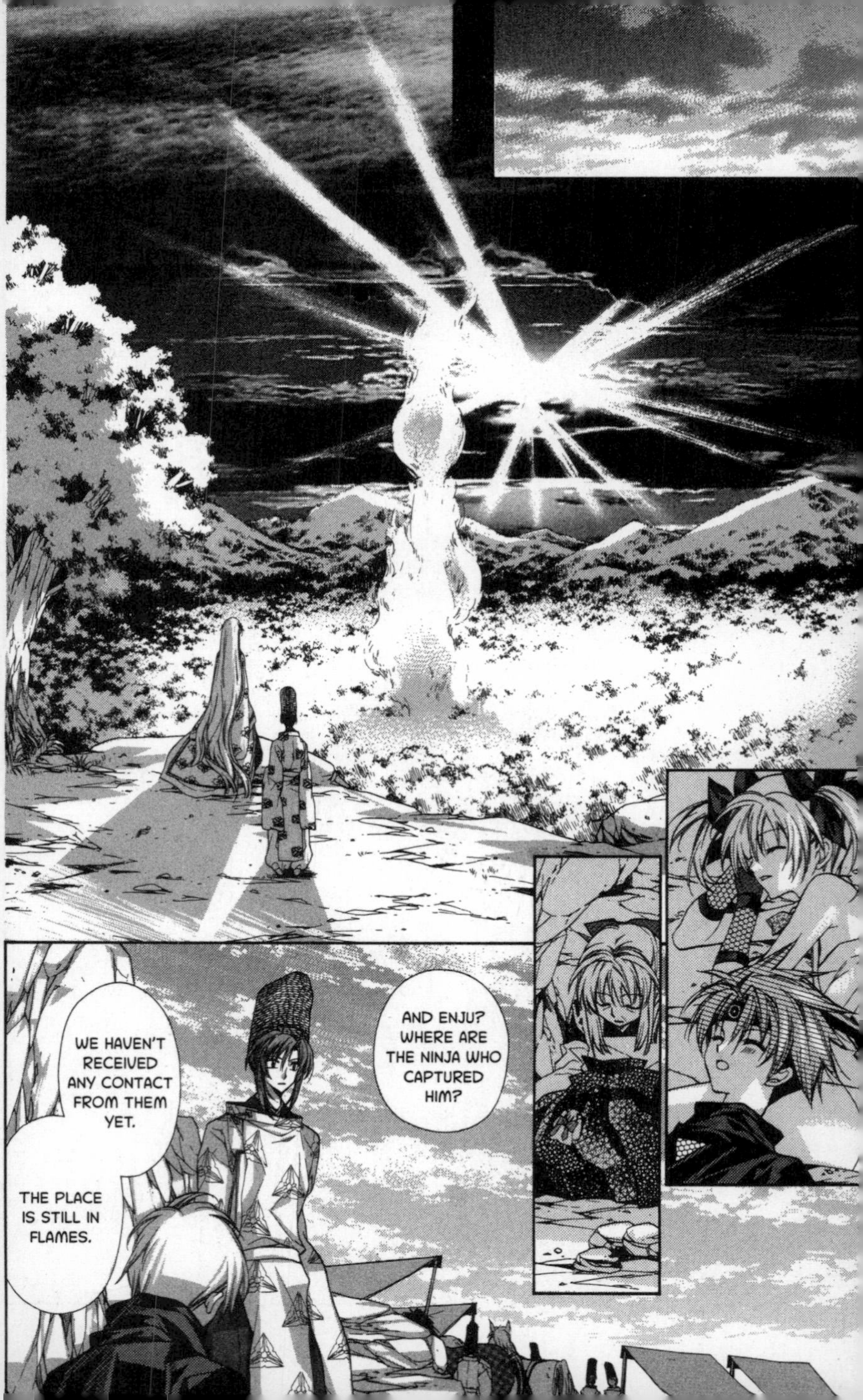
AND ENJU? WHERE ARE THE NINJA WHO CAPTURED HIM?
WE HAVEN'T RECEIVED ANY CONTACT FROM THEM YET.
THE PLACE IS STILL IN FLAMES.

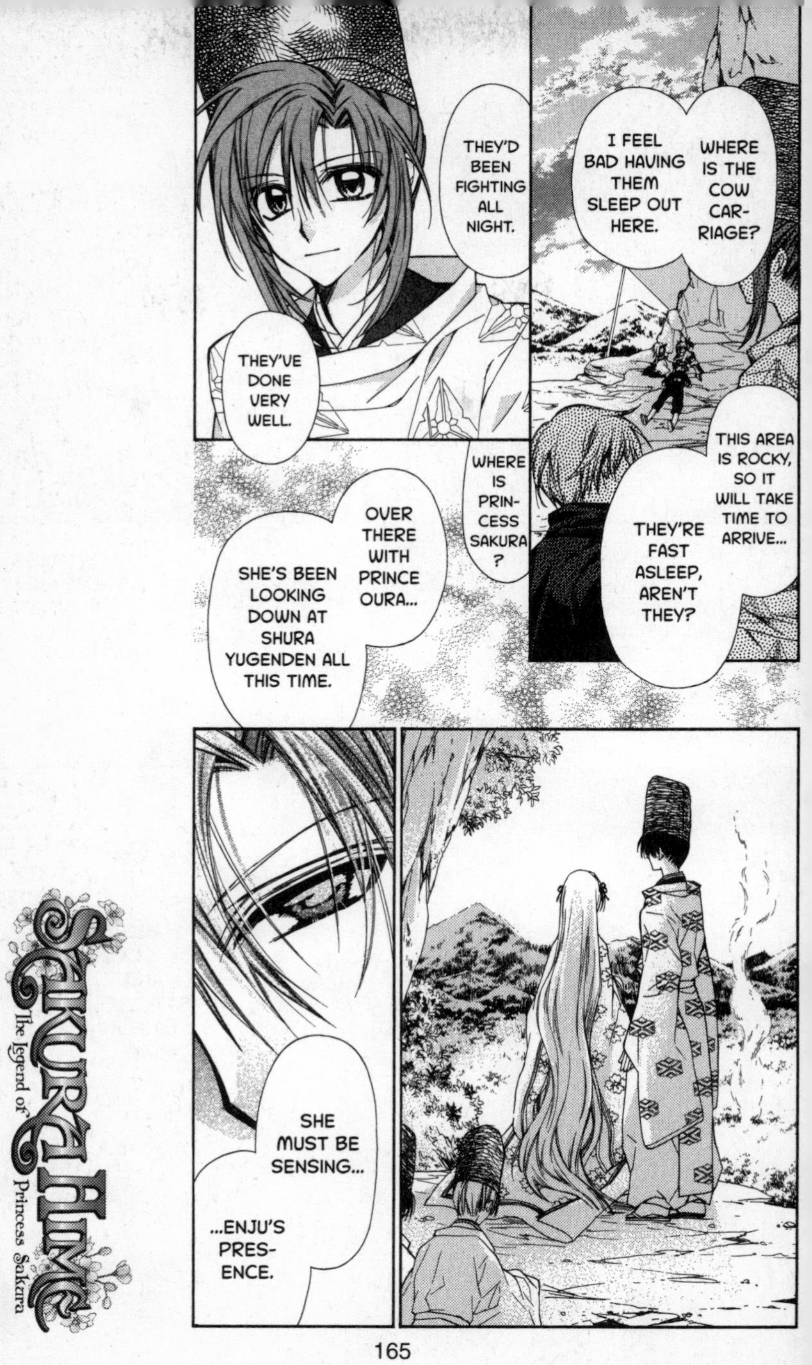
WHERE IS THE COW CARRIAGE?
I FEEL BAD HAVING THEM SLEEP OUT HERE.
THIS AREA IS ROCKY, SO IT WILL TAKE TIME TO ARRIVE...
THEY'RE FAST ASLEEP, AREN'T THEY?
THEY'D BEEN FIGHTING ALL NIGHT.
THEY'VE DONE VERY WELL.
WHERE IS PRINCESS SAKURA?
OVER THERE WITH PRINCE OURA...
SHE'S BEEN LOOKING DOWN AT SHURA YUGENDEN ALL THIS TIME.
SHE MUST BE SENSING...
...ENJU'S PRESENCE.

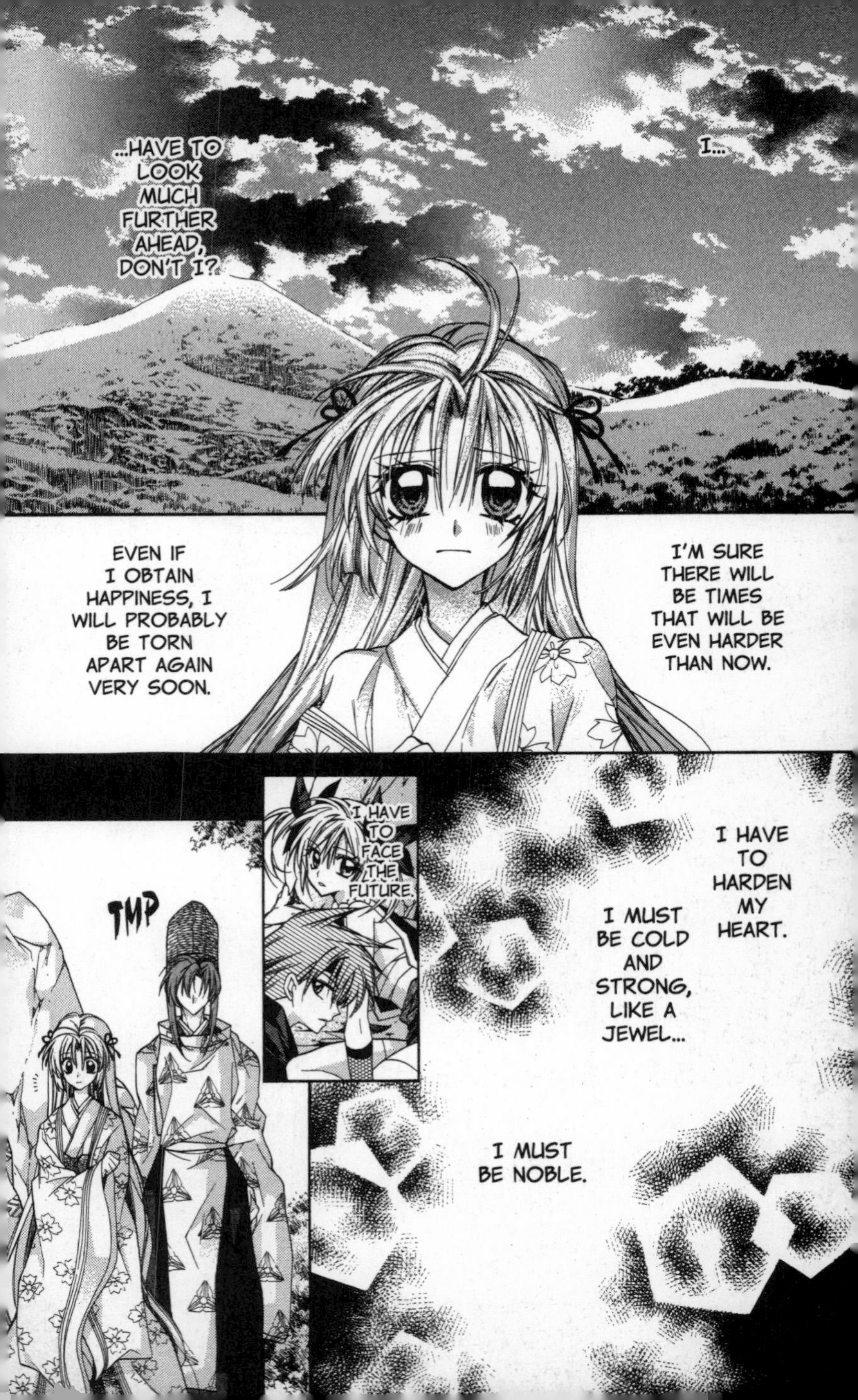
I...
...HAVE TO LOOK MUCH FURTHER AHEAD, DON'T I?
I'M SURE THERE WILL BE TIMES THAT WILL BE EVEN HARDER THAN NOW.
EVEN IF I OBTAIN HAPPINESS, I WILL PROBABLY BE TORN APART AGAIN VERY SOON.
I HAVE TO HARDEN MY HEART.
I MUST BE COLD AND STRONG, LIKE A JEWEL...
I MUST BE NOBLE.
I HAVE TO FACE THE FUTURE.
TMP

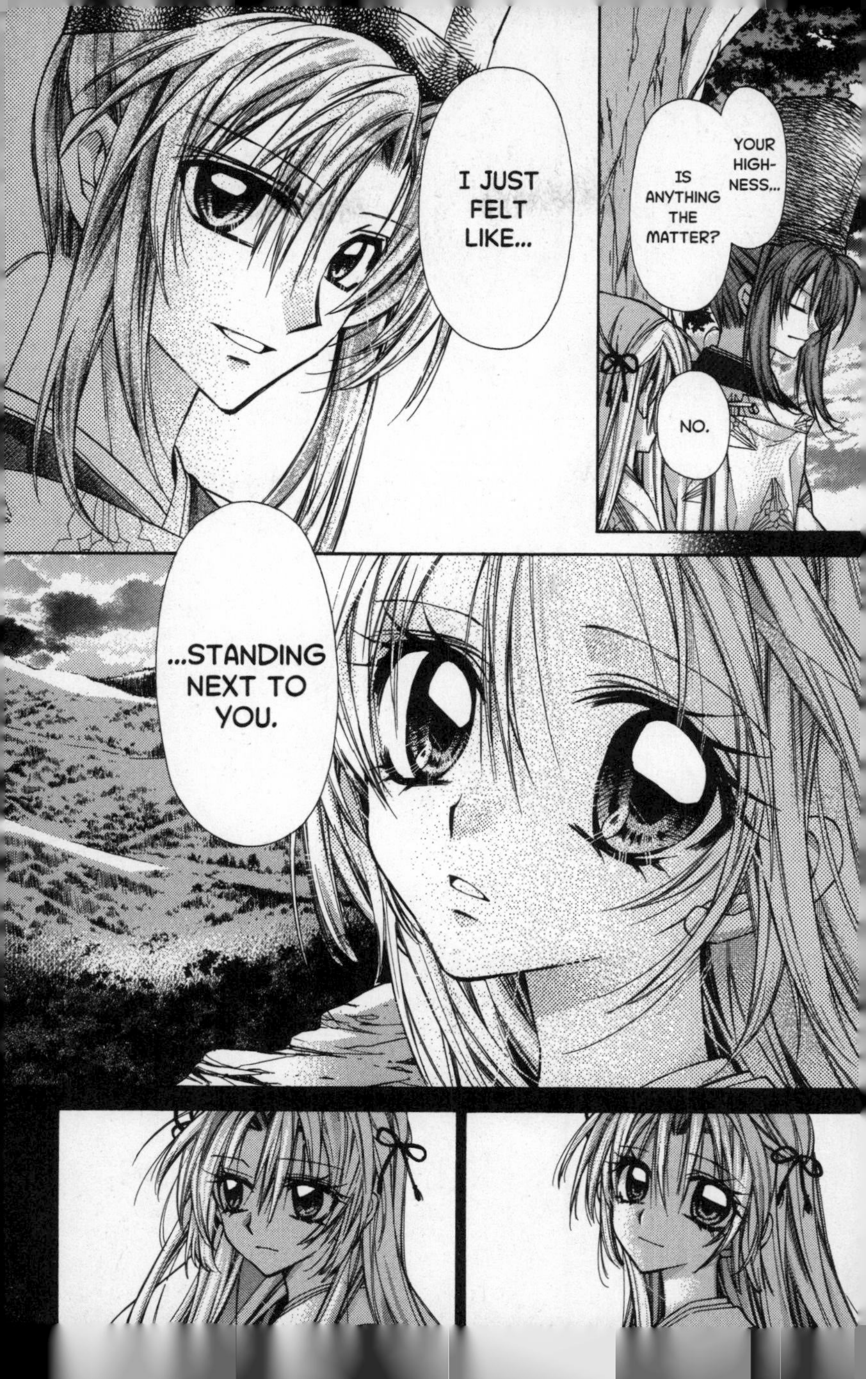
YOUR HIGHNESS...
IS ANYTHING THE MATTER?
NO.
I JUST FELT LIKE...
...STANDING NEXT TO YOU.

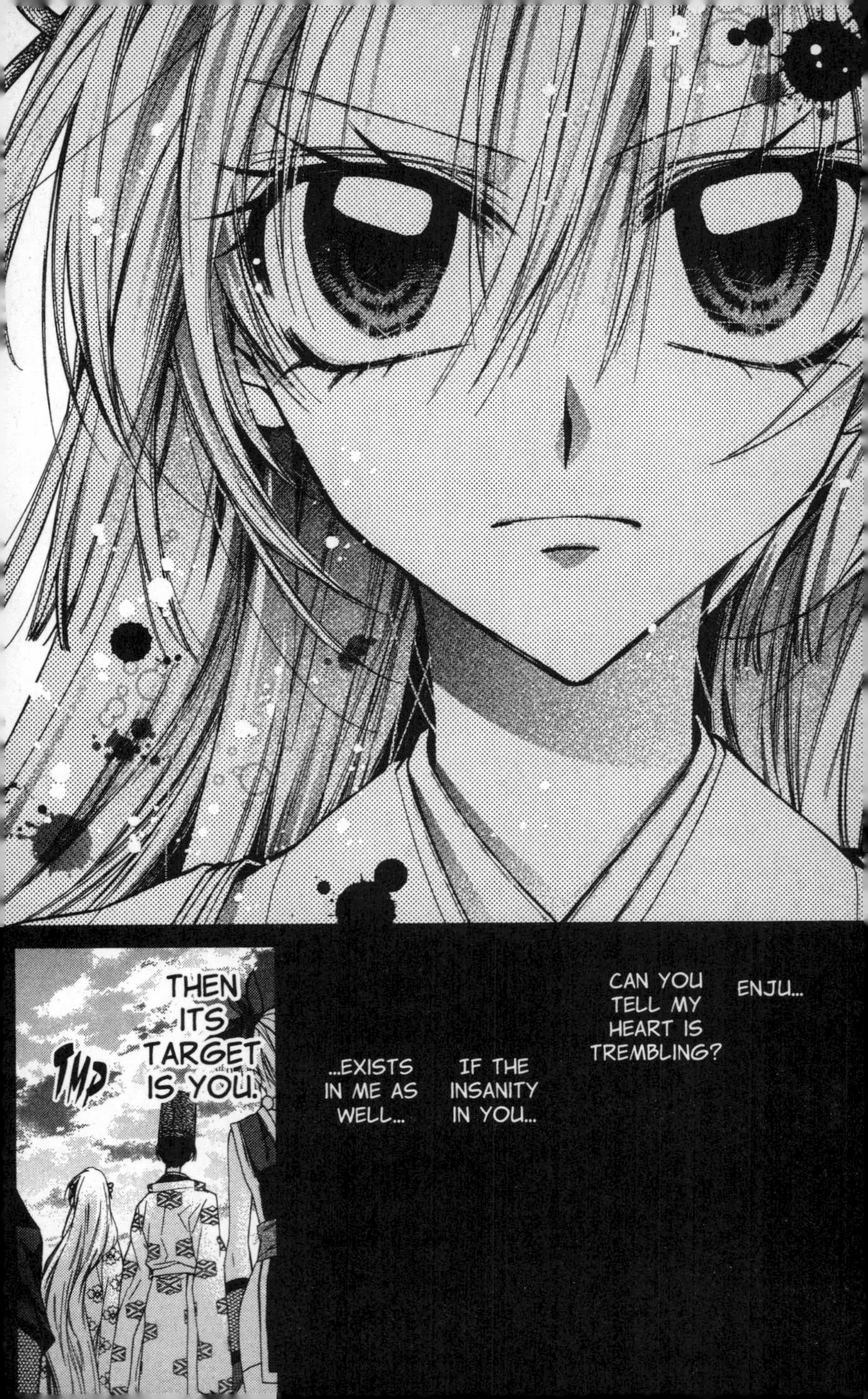
ENJU...
CAN YOU TELL MY HEART IS TREMBLING?
IF THE INSANITY IN YOU...
...EXISTS IN ME AS WELL...
THEN ITS TARGET IS YOU.
TMP

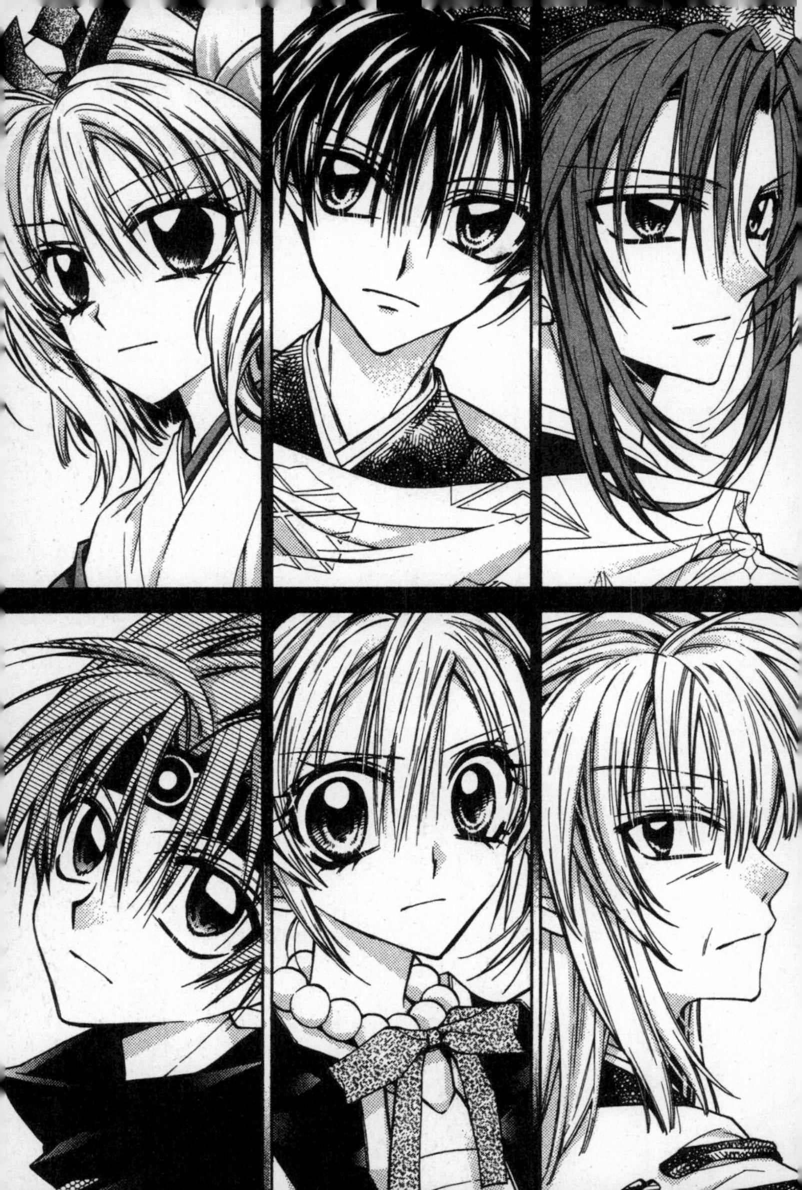

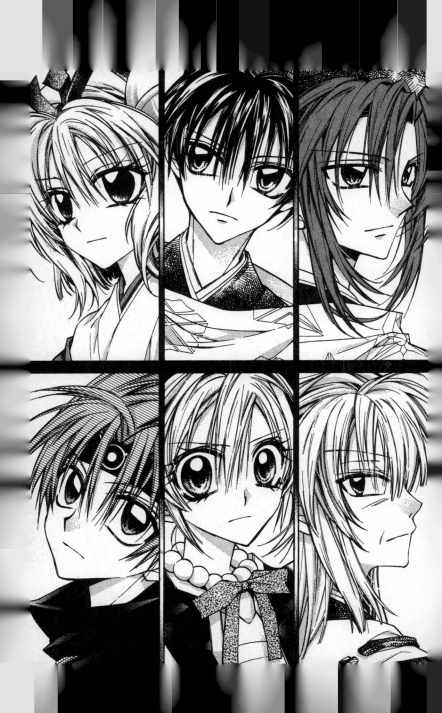

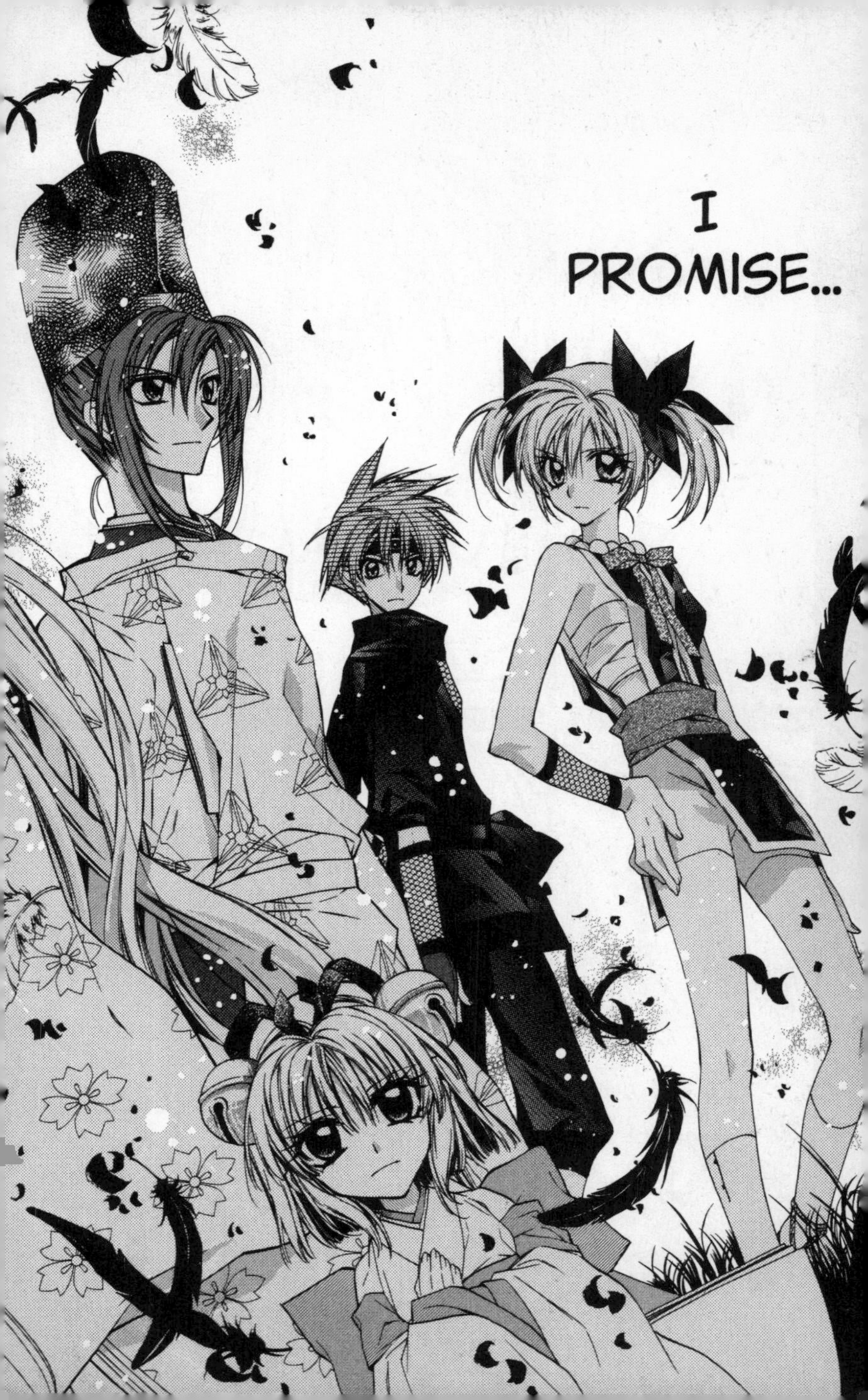
I PROMISE...

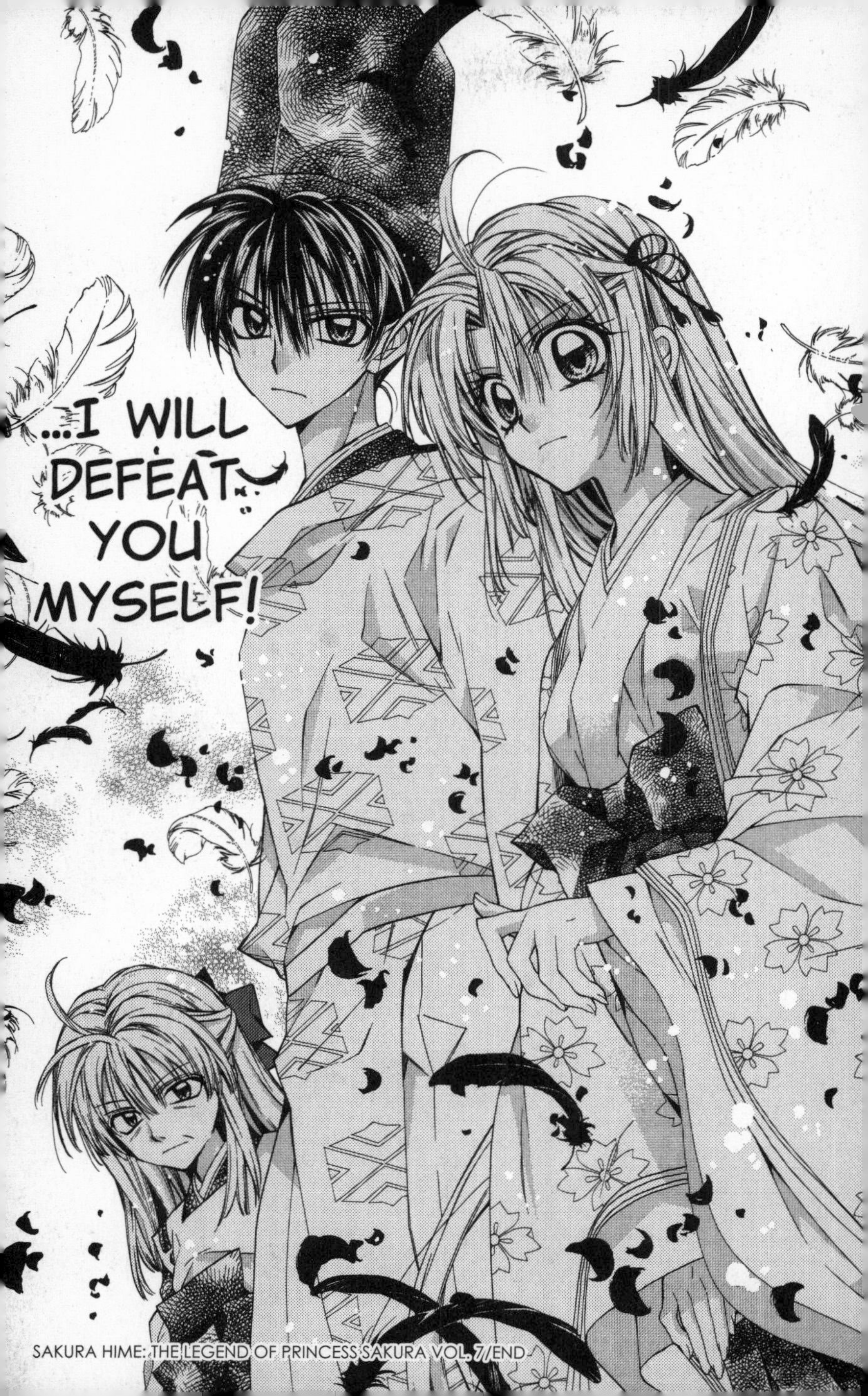
...I WILL DEFEAT YOU MYSELF!
SAKURA HIME: THE LEGEND OF PRINCESS SAKURA VOL. 7/END

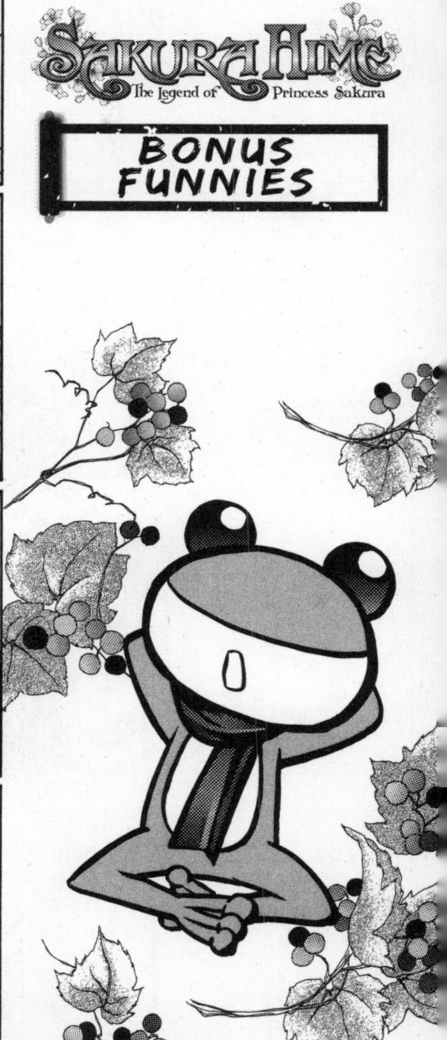
SAKURA HIME
The Legend of Princess Sakura
BONUS FUNNIES

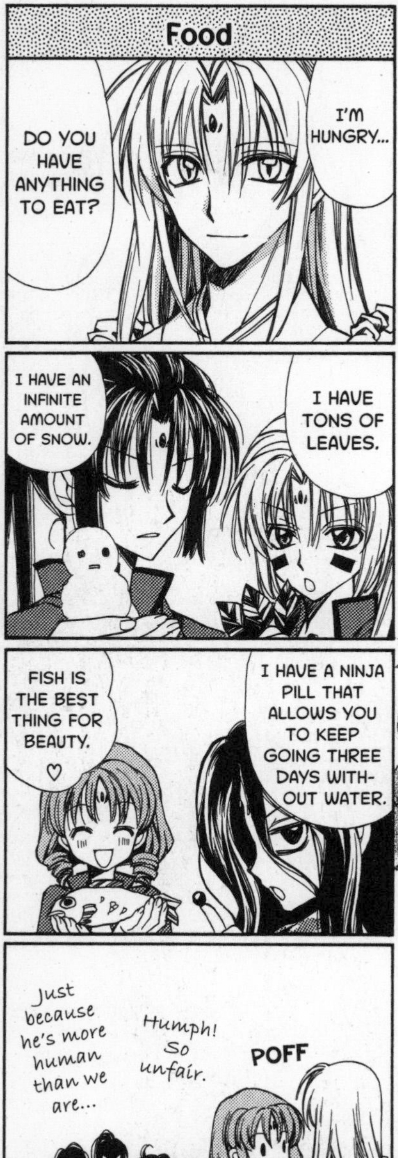
Food
I'M HUNGRY...
DO YOU HAVE ANYTHING TO EAT?
I HAVE TONS OF LEAVES.
I HAVE AN INFINITE AMOUNT OF SNOW.
I HAVE A NINJA PILL THAT ALLOWS YOU TO KEEP GOING THREE DAYS WITH-OUT WATER.
FISH IS THE BEST THING FOR BEAUTY. ♡
POFF
Humph! So unfair.
Just because he's more human than we are...

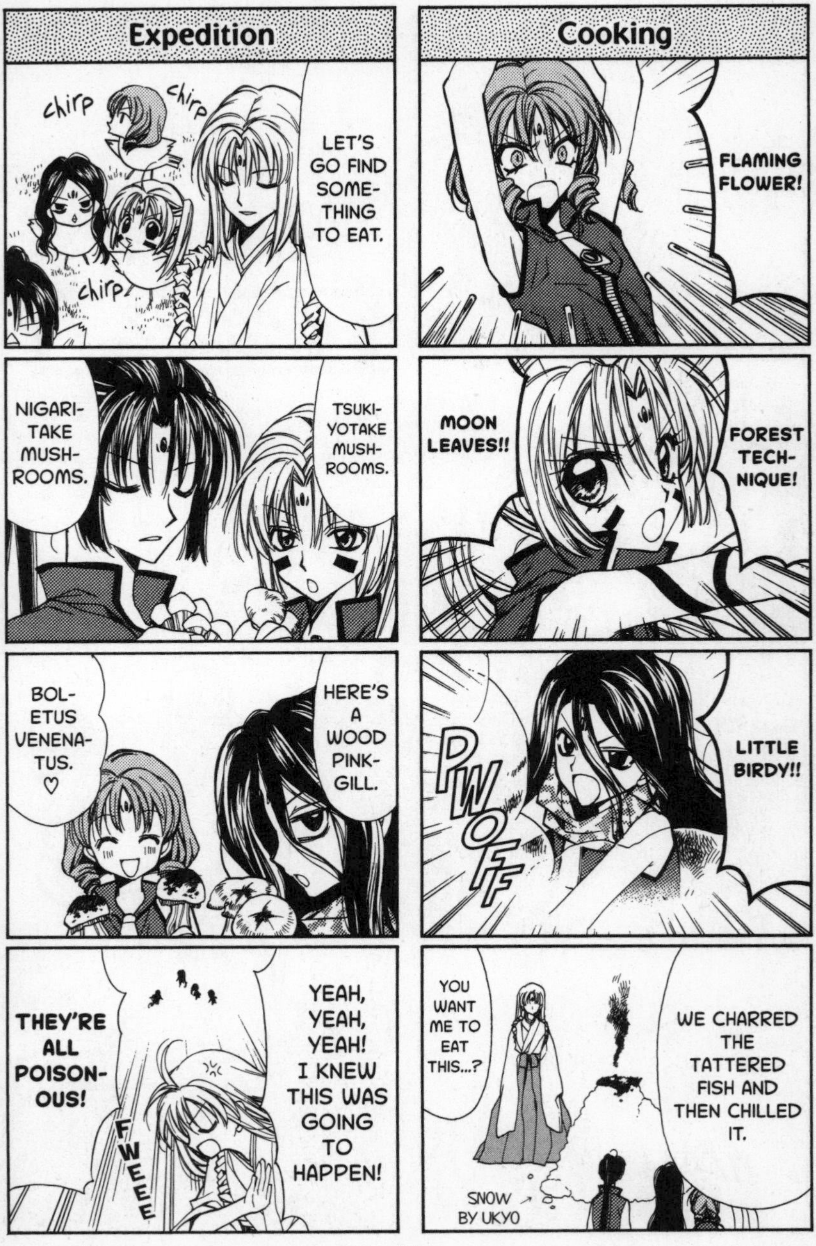
Cooking
FLAMING FLOWER!
FOREST TECHNIQUE!
MOON LEAVES!!
LITTLE BIRDY!!
PWOFF
WE CHARRED THE TATTERED FISH AND THEN CHILLED IT.
YOU WANT ME TO EAT THIS...?
SNOW → BY UKYO
Expedition
chirp
chirp
chirp
LET'S GO FIND SOMETHING TO EAT.
TSUKIYOTAKE MUSHROOMS.
NIGARITAKE MUSHROOMS.
HERE'S A WOOD PINK-GILL.
BOLETUS VENENATUS. ♡
YEAH, YEAH, YEAH! I KNEW THIS WAS GOING TO HAPPEN!
THEY'RE ALL POISONOUS!
FWEEE

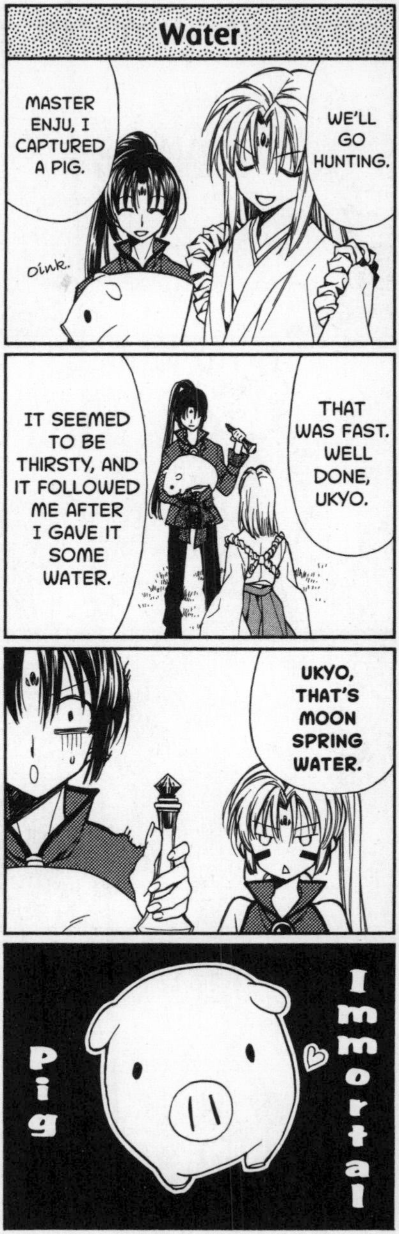
Water
WE'LL GO HUNTING.
MASTER ENJU, I CAPTURED A PIG.
oink.
THAT WAS FAST. WELL DONE, UKYO.
IT SEEMED TO BE THIRSTY, AND IT FOLLOWED ME AFTER I GAVE IT SOME WATER.
UKYO, THAT'S MOON SPRING WATER.
Immortal Pig ♡

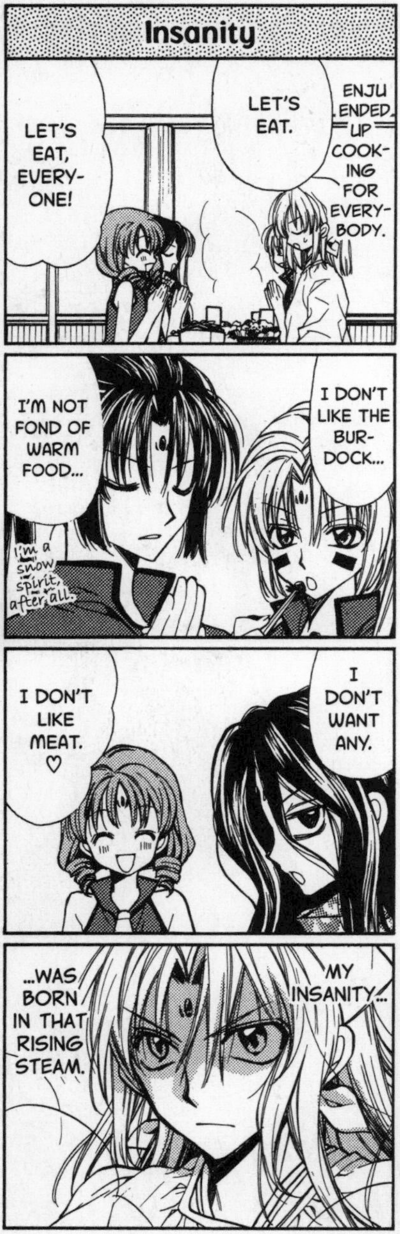
Insanity
ENJU ENDED UP COOKING FOR EVERYBODY.
LET'S EAT.
LET'S EAT, EVERYONE!
I DON'T LIKE THE BURDOCK...
I'M NOT FOND OF WARM FOOD...
I'm a snow spirit, after all.
I DON'T WANT ANY.
I DON'T LIKE MEAT. ♡
MY INSANITY...
...WAS BORN IN THAT RISING STEAM.

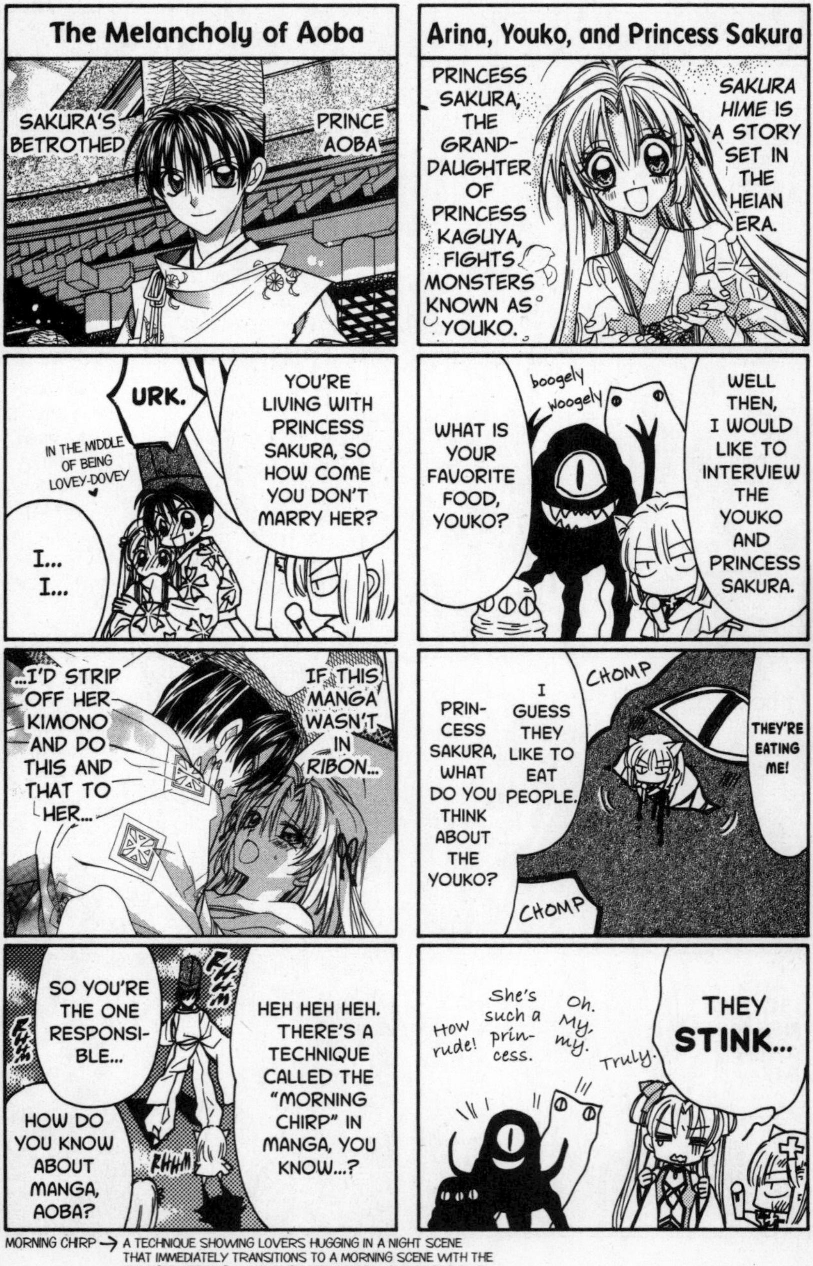

Arina, Youko, and Princess Sakura
SAKURA HIME IS A STORY SET IN THE HEIAN ERA.
PRINCESS SAKURA, THE GRAND-DAUGHTER OF PRINCESS KAGUYA, FIGHTS MONSTERS KNOWN AS YOUKO.
WELL THEN, I WOULD LIKE TO INTERVIEW THE YOUKO AND PRINCESS SAKURA.
boogely woogely
WHAT IS YOUR FAVORITE FOOD, YOUKO?
THEY'RE EATING ME!
CHOMP
I GUESS THEY LIKE TO EAT PEOPLE.
PRIN-CESS SAKURA, WHAT DO YOU THINK ABOUT THE YOUKO?
CHOMP
THEY STINK...
Truly.
Oh. My, my.
She's such a prin-cess.
How rude!
The Melancholy of Aoba
PRINCE AOBA
SAKURA'S BETROTHED
YOU'RE LIVING WITH PRINCESS SAKURA, SO HOW COME YOU DON'T MARRY HER?
URK.
IN THE MIDDLE OF BEING LOVEY-DOVEY
I... I...
IF THIS MANGA WASN'T IN RIBON...
...I'D STRIP OFF HER KIMONO AND DO THIS AND THAT TO HER...
HEH HEH HEH. THERE'S A TECHNIQUE CALLED THE "MORNING CHIRP" IN MANGA, YOU KNOW...?
RHHM
SO YOU'RE THE ONE RESPONSI-BLE...
HOW DO YOU KNOW ABOUT MANGA, AOBA?

MORNING CHIRP → A TECHNIQUE SHOWING LOVERS HUGGING IN A NIGHT SCENE THAT IMMEDIATELY TRANSITIONS TO A MORNING SCENE WITH THE SUNLIGHT SEEPING IN THROUGH THE WINDOW AND SPARROWS CHIRPING OUTSIDE. IT HINTS TO READERS THAT SOMETHING MUST HAVE HAPPENED BETWEEN THE TWO DURING THE NIGHT.

Fortune Telling

KOHAKU THE NINJA...
...AND HAYATE, WHO LOVES HER.
※ HE'S HUMAN, BUT HE WAS TURNED INTO A FROG BY HER JUTSU.
KOHAKU, YOU NEED TO BECOME MY GIRL-FRIEND...
Love you!
NO. DON'T WANT TO.
TMP TMP
FORGET IT. I'LL FIGURE IT OUT THIS WAY.
PHOO
HE'S DOING "LOVES ME, LOVES ME NOT" WITH THAT FLOWER.
THERE ARE SIX PETALS, SO HE'LL END UP WITH "LOVES ME NOT." I CAN'T DO ANYTHING ABOUT IT.
LOVES ME.
LOVES ME.
LOVES ME.
KISSES ME.
KISSES ME.
PLUK
PLUK
HEY! WAIT A MINUTE!!

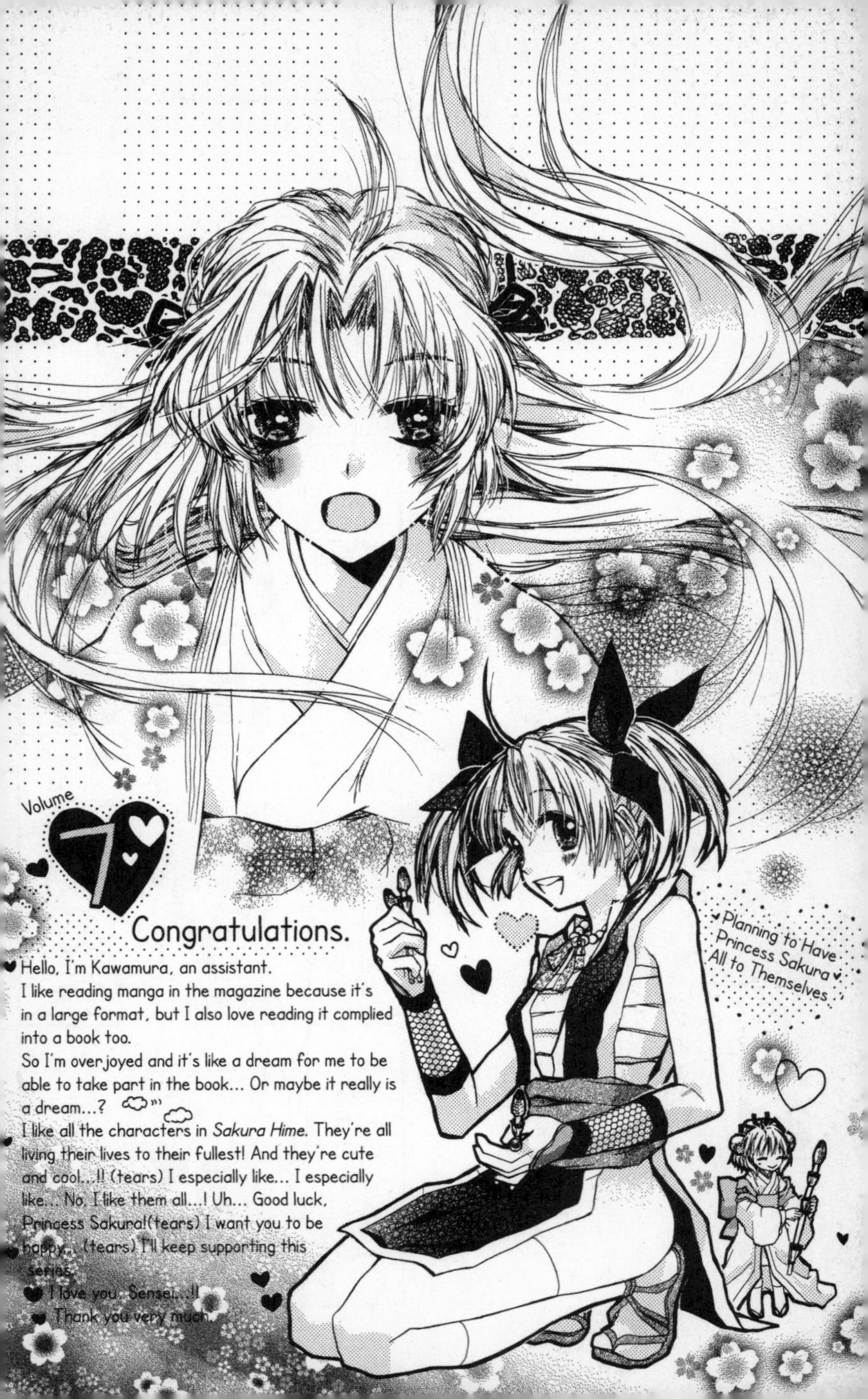
Volume 7
Congratulations.
Hello, I'm Kawamura, an assistant.
I like reading manga in the magazine because it's in a large format, but I also love reading it complied into a book too.
So I'm overjoyed and it's like a dream for me to be able to take part in the book... Or maybe it really is a dream...?
I like all the characters in Sakura Hime. They're all living their lives to their fullest! And they're cute and cool...!! (tears) I especially like... I especially like... No, I like them all...! Uh... Good luck, Princess Sakura!(tears) I want you to be happy... (tears) I'll keep supporting this series.
I love you, Sensei...!!
Thank you very much.
Planning to Have Princess Sakura All to Themselves

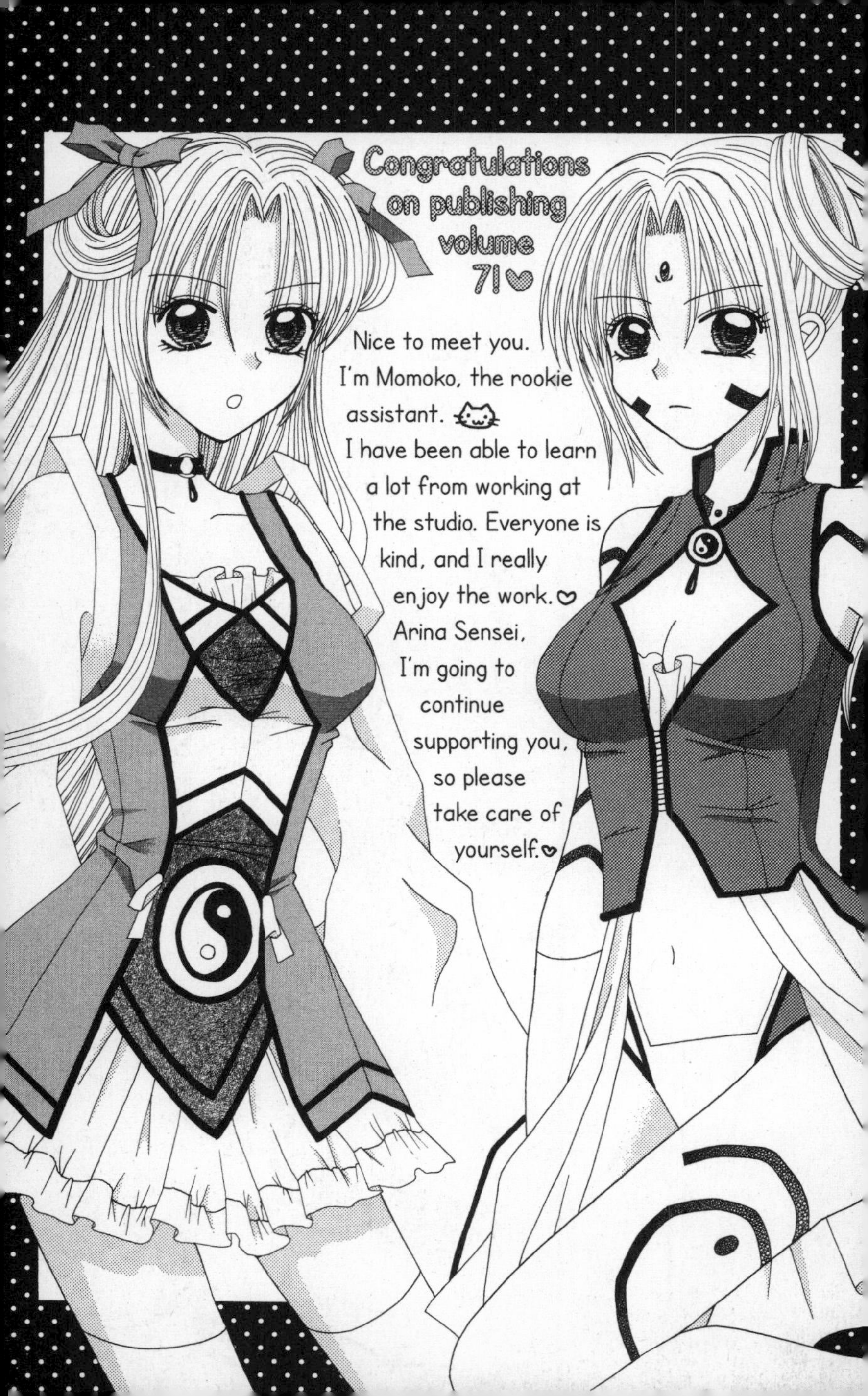
Congratulations on publishing volume 7!
Nice to meet you. I'm Momoko, the rookie assistant. I have been able to learn a lot from working at the studio. Everyone is kind, and I really enjoy the work. Arina Sensei, I'm going to continue supporting you, so please take care of yourself.

ARINA TANEMURA

The Shura Yugenden arc is finally at its climax. It's sad to see that Sakura's and Enju's feelings never come across to each other. Maybe Enju does see Sakura as a woman, but he has deified his image of his sister, so he's probably disgusted with himself for being in love with her. Rurijo is probably the outlet for that love. I hope you continue to watch over how this sad love triangle turns out.

Arina Tanemura began her manga career in 1996 when her short stories debuted in *Ribon* magazine. She gained fame with the 1997 publication of *I•O•N*, and ever since her debut Tanemura has been a major force in shojo manga with popular series *Kamikaze Kaito Jeanne*, *Time Stranger Kyoko*, *Full Moon*, and *The Gentlemen's Alliance †*. Both *Kamikaze Kaito Jeanne* and *Full Moon* have been adapted into animated TV series.

SAKURA HIME

The Legend of Princess Sakura

Sakura Hime: The Legend of Princess Sakura
Volume 7
Shojo Beat Edition

STORY AND ART BY
Arina Tanemura

Translation & Adaptation/Tetsuichiro Miyaki
Touch-up Art & Lettering/Inori Fukuda Trant
Design/Sam Elzway
Editor/Nancy Thistlethwaite

SAKURA-HIME KADEN © 2008 by Arina Tanemura
All rights reserved.
First published in Japan in 2008 by SHUEISHA Inc., Tokyo.
English translation rights arranged by SHUEISHA Inc.

Printed in the U.S.A.

Published by VIZ Media, LLC
P.O. Box 77010
San Francisco, CA 94107

10 9 8 7 6 5 4 3 2 1
First printing, April 2012

www.shojobeat.com

www.viz.com

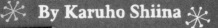